OLD TESTAMENT FORM CRITICISM

OLD TESTAMENT
FORM CRITICISM

edited by

JOHN H. HAYES

Trinity University Press   San Antonio

50905

TABLE OF CONTENTS

CONTRIBUTORS

MARTIN J. BUSS (Ph.D., Yale University, 1958) is Associate Professor of Religion at Emory University. In 1964/65, he held a fellowship from the American Council of Learned Societies to study the theory and practice of literary criticism. His previous publications include "The Meaning of 'Cult' and the Interpretation of the Old Testament," *Journal of Bible and Religion* XXXII (1964) 317-325 and *The Prophetic Word of Hosea: A Morphological Study* (BZAW 111, Berlin: A. Töpelmann, 1969). He is currently Old Testament book review editor for the *Journal of Biblical Literature*.

W. MALCOLM CLARK (Ph.D., Yale University, 1964) is Assistant Professor of Religion at Butler University. He has done postdoctoral study at Hebrew University, Jerusalem (1964/65) and taught at Princeton Theological Seminary (1965-71). Several of his articles on Genesis have been published in *VT*, *JBL*, and *ZAW*, and he has written two chapters on Old Testament interpretation to be published in *Commitment Without Ideology* (Philadelphia: Pilgrim Press, 1973).

JAMES L. CRENSHAW (Ph.D., Vanderbilt University, 1964) is Associate Professor of Old Testament in The Divinity School of Vanderbilt University. He has previously taught at Atlantic Christian College and Mercer University. In addition to numerous articles on various Old Testament subjects, he has published *Prophetic Conflict: Its Effect upon Israelite Religion* (BZAW 124, Berlin: Walter de Gruyter, 1971). He is presently doing research in Germany on Germanic and Icelandic folk literature on a grant from the Society for Religion in Higher Education.

ERHARD GERSTENBERGER (Ph.D., Bonn University, 1961) studied at Marburg, Tübingen, Bonn, and Wuppertal. From 1959 until 1964, he studied and taught at Yale Divinity School. Among his numerous writings are *Wesen und Herkunft des "apodiktischen Rechts" im Alten Testament und im Alten Orient* (WMANT 20, Neukirchen: Neukirchener Verlag, 1965) and *Der bittende Mensch. Bittritual und Klagelied des Einzelnen* (Habilitationsschrift, Heidelberg University, 1971). He is currently *Privatdozent* at Heidelberg and a pastor in Essen.

W. EUGENE MARCH (Th.D., Union Theological Seminary, New York, 1966) is currently Associate Professor of Old Testament at Austin Presbyterian Theological Seminary. His doctoral dissertation was *A Study of Two Prophetic Compositions in Isaiah 24:1-27:1*. He has published numerous reviews and articles on Old Testament subjects including "Jeremiah 1: Commission and Assurance," *Austin Seminary Bulletin* LXXXVI (1970) 5-38.

JAY A. WILCOXEN (Ph.D., University of Chicago, 1967) is Associate Professor of Old Testament in the Divinity School of the University of Chicago. His dissertation on the Hebrew Passover was awarded the Susan Colver-Rosenberger prize at the University of Chicago. Among his publications are "Some Anthropocentric Aspects of Israel's Sacred History," *The Journal of Religion* XL (1968) 333-350 and "Narrative Structure and Cult Legend: A Study of Joshua 1-6," in *Transitions in Biblical Scholarship* (Chicago: University of Chicago Press, 1968) 43-70.

ABBREVIATIONS

AA	American Anthropologist
AASOR	Annual of the American Schools of Oriental Research
AB	Anchor Bible
ABAW	Abhandlungen Bayerische Akademie der Wissenschaften
AfR	Archiv für Religionswissenschaft
AJA	American Journal of Archaeology
AJSL	American Journal of Semitic Languages and Literatures
AKG	Archiv für Kulturgeschichte
AnBib	Analecta Biblica
ANET	Ancient Near Eastern Texts Relating to the Old Testament
ANVAO	Avhandlinger utgitt av Det Norske Videnskaps-Akademi i Oslo
AO	Acta Orientalia
AOS	The American Oriental Series

ARMT	Archives Royales de Mari: Transcription et Traduction
AS	Assyriological Studies
ASTI	Annual of the Swedish Theological Institute in Jerusalem
AT	Arbeiten zur Theologie
ATA	Alttestamentliche Abhandlungen
ATANT	Abhandlungen zur Theologie des Alten und Neuen Testaments
ATD	Das Alte Testament Deutsch
AThD	Acta Theologica Danica
BA	The Biblical Archaeologist
BAfO	Beiheft Archiv für Orientforschung
BBB	Bonner Biblische Beiträge
BEvTh	Beiträge zur Evangelischen Theologie
BH	Bibliotheca Hungarica
BHHW	Biblisch-Historisches Handwörterbuch
BHT	Beiträge zur historischen Theologie
Bib	Biblica
BibOr	Biblica et Orientalia
BJRL	Bulletin of the John Rylands Library
BK	Biblischer Kommentar
BS	Biblische Studien
BSKGO	Beiträge zur Sprach- und Kulturgeschichte des Orients
BST	Basel Studies of Theology
BWANT	Beiträge zur Wissenschaft vom Alten und Neuen Testament
BZ	Biblische Zeitschrift
BZAW	Beihefte zur Zeitschrift für die alttestamentliche Wissenschaft
CBQ	The Catholic Biblical Quarterly
CBQMS	The Catholic Biblical Quarterly Monograph Series
CJT	Canadian Journal of Theology
CQ	The Church Quarterly
CR	Corpus Reformatorum
CRB	Cahiers de la Revue Biblique
CSEL	Corpus Scriptorum Ecclesiasticorum Latinorum
CW	Die Christliche Welt
DBS	Supplément au Dictionnaire de la Bible
EI	Eretz Israel
ELH	ELH, A Journal of English Literary History
EstBíb	Estudios Bíblicos

ET	Expository Times
EvTh	Evangelische Theologie
FFC	Folklore Fellowship Communications
FRLANT	Forschungen zur Religion und Literatur des Alten und Neuen Testaments
HAT	Handbuch zum Alten Testament
HBO	Handbuch der Orientalistik
HKAT	Handkommentar zum Alten Testament
HUCA	Hebrew Union College Annual
IB	The Interpreter's Bible
IDB	The Interpreter's Dictionary of the Bible
Inter	Interpretation
JANES	Journal of the Ancient Near Eastern Society of Columbia University
JAOS	Journal of the American Oriental Society
JBL	Journal of Biblical Literature
JBR	Journal of Bible and Religion
JCS	Journal of Cuneiform Studies
JE	The Jewish Encyclopedia
JEGP	The Journal of English and Germanic Philology
JEOL	Jaarbericht van het Vooraziatisch-Egyptisch Geselschap (Genootschap) Ex Oriente Lux
JJP	Journal of Juristic Papyrology
JLSM	Janua Linguarum, Series Maior
JNES	Journal of Near Eastern Studies
JR	Journal of Religion
JTS	Journal of Theological Studies
KA	Kunst und Altertum
KD	Kerygma und Dogma
KdG	Kultur der Gegenwart
KHCAT	Kurzer Hand-Commentar zum Alten Testament
LUA	Lunds Universitets Arsskrift
MGWJ	Monatsschrift für Geschichte und Wissenschaft des Judentum
MIO	Mitteilungen des Instituts für Orientforschung
MPG	Migne, Patrologia Graeca
MPL	Migne, Patrologia Latina
NEB	New English Bible
NLH	New Literary History
NumenS	Numen Supplements
Or	Orientalia
OLZ	Orientalistische Literaturzeitung
OTS	Old Testament Studies

OTWSA	Die Ou Testamentiese Werkgemenskap in Suid-Afrika
PEQ	Palestine Exploration Quarterly
PJ	Preussische Jahrbücher
POS	Pretoria Oriental Series
RA	Revue d'Assyriologie et d'Archéologie Orientale
RAC	Reallexikon für Antike und Christentum
RAL	Recueil de l'Académie de Legislation
RB	Revue Biblique
RGG	Die Religion in Geschichte und Gegenwart
RIDA	Revue Internationale des Droits de l'Antiquité
RŠ	Ras Shamra
SANT	Studien zum Alten und Neuen Testament
SAT	Die Schriften des Alten Testaments
SAV	Schwizerisches Archiv für Volkskunde
SB	Sources Bibliques
SBS	Stuttgarter Bibelstudien
SBT	Studies in Biblical Theology
Sem	Semitics
SJT	Scottish Journal of Theology
SNVOA	Skrifter utgitt av Det Norske Videnskaps-Akademi i Oslo
SSCR	Stockholm Studies in Comparative Religion
SR	Sociological Review
STU	Schweizerische Theologische Umschau
TA	Theologische Arbeiten
TB	Theologische Bücherei
TGUOS	Transactions of the Glasgow University Oriental Society
TICP	Travaux de l'Institut Catholique de Paris
TLZ	Theologische Literaturzeitung
TOA	Theologische und orientalistische Arbeiten
TTR	Tübingen Theologische Reihe
TV	Theologia Viatorum
TyndB	Tyndale Bulletin
TZ	Theologische Zeitschrift
UF	Ugarit-Forschung
UUA	Uppsala Universitets Arsskrift
VKS	Videnskapsselkapets Skrifter
VT	Vetus Testamentum
VTS	Supplements to Vetus Testamentum
VuF	Verkündigung und Forschung
WA	Martin Luthers Werke: Weimarer Ausgabe

WMANT	Wissenschaftliche Monographien zum Alten und Neuen Testament
WZKM	Wiener Zeitschrift für die Kunde des Morgenlandes
WZKMUL	Wissenschaftliche Zeitschrift des Karl-Marx Universitäts, Leipzig
WZMLU	Wissenschaftliche Zeitschrift der Martin-Luther Universität
WZLU	Wissenschaftliche Zeitschrift Leipzig Universität
ZA	Zeitschrift für Assyriologie
ZÄS	Zeitschrift für Ägyptische Sprache und Altertumskunde
ZAW	Zeitschrift für die alttestamentliche Wissenschaft
ZDMG	Zeitschrift der deutschen Morgenländischen Gesellschaft
ZMR	Zeitschrift für Missionskunde und Religionswissenschaft
ZNW	Zeitschrift für die neutestamentliche Wissenschaft
ZSSR	Zeitschrift der Savigny-Stiftung für Rechtsgeschichte
ZTK	Zeitschrift für Theologie und Kirche

PREFACE

The modern discipline of OT form criticism is now several decades old. During its history, it has made major achievements and lasting contributions to the general field of OT studies.

At the present time, OT form criticism has reached something of a plateau or perhaps what might be called a temporary impasse. On the one hand, past achievements and contributions are being reassessed and reevaluated. On the other hand, efforts are being made to relate form critical investigations to new research in linguistics, literary criticism, and social theory.

The primary purposes of the present volume are to examine the results of past form critical research and to sketch the basic issues which characterize contemporary OT form critical studies. The direction which form critical research will take in future investigations is impossible to determine, although some predictions and suggestions for development have been offered in the following essays.

Form criticism is only one of several exegetical tools with which biblical interpreters can work. It should be considered an indispensable tool, but it is no panacea for every exegetical hope and problem.

Many scholars define form criticism in categories so broad as to include what has customarily been classified as history of tradition and literary criticism. For others, form criticism is narrowly conceived as "formula criticism." Both of these extremes should be avoided.

In the past, form criticism has worked under a number of misconceptions and misapplications. Its studies have frequently been associated far too closely with only the oral stage of traditions. Written works also have their forms and structures and may be classified according to genres. The clearest structures and shortest forms have been customarily accepted as reflections of the oldest and purest stage of a genre. This assumption has persisted in OT study since Gunkel but needs serious reconsideration. The use of form critical considerations in dating materials and traditions has been a widespread practice but may reflect serious methodological shortcomings. The overly enthusiastic re-creation of all-encompassing life situations or cultic events to which numerous genres have been related has certainly on occasion been overdone. The identification of genre elements with complete genres has sometimes led to fanciful conclusions. These and other problems in form critical research will be referred to in the individual chapters which follow.

This volume has profited from, although it is not directly related to, the Old Testament Form Criticism Seminar of the Society of Biblical Literature.

Quotations in English from German works for which no English versions exist are translations which have been made either by the author of the chapter in which they appear or by the editor.

Candler School of Theology
Emory University

J. H. H.

OLD TESTAMENT FORM CRITICISM

Chapter One

THE STUDY OF FORMS

I. INTRODUCTION

D. Ben-Amos, "Analytic Categories and Ethnic Genres," *Genre* II (1969) 275-301; E. Lenneberg, *New Directions in the Study of Language* (Cambridge: M.I.T. Press, 1964); L. Wittgenstein, *Philosophical Investigations* (Oxford: Basil Blackwell, 1953).

Form criticism may be characterized as the study of patterns of speech in relation to their roles in human life. More specifically it deals with types of complete units of expression, although one should recognize that the limits of a unit are to some extent ambiguous. According to Hermann Gunkel's characterization, genres are constituted by their 1) thoughts and moods, 2) linguistic form, including largely vocabulary and grammar, and 3) connection with life (see below, pp. 49-52). Recently, Ben-Amos, in dealing with primitive literature, described these three aspects as "the cognitive, expressive, and behavioral levels of genres" (297). The interplay between these three aspects is the central concern of form criticism.

The term "form" has presented some difficulty in literary discussions, since it sometimes designates the audible features of an expression (the "signifier"), in contrast to the objects, concepts, or emotions (the "signified") to which the expression refers. While the existence of this narrow usage must be recognized, it is clearer not to use the word in that specific sense without a qualifying adjective (e.g., "expressive," "syntactic," "prosodic"). Rather, "form" is better employed in the broader sense of a pattern of relationships, such as (with Aristotle) a dynamic pattern including normal cause and effect.

An elemental point of logic states that form is not bound to an individual state, even though it may happen that a particular form has only a single exemplification. On the other hand, forms need some specificity, some outer limit of generality for operation. In common usage, the term form criticism is not applied to the theory of language as a whole (assigned to general hermeneutics) nor to the description of those features of a language that are relatively invariant for different operations within a given culture (largely phenomena below the level of a sentence). The logic of form criticism is that noticed by Wittgenstein, whose philosophical investigations led him to recognize the existence of different "language games," each an aspect of a particular "form of life."

An analogy with games is useful, since language forms, like games, have rules governing their successful operation. A language form cannot be purely individual, for a sound or sign whose meaning is not shared does not communicate and thus is not a part of language, just as it is impossible to play a game without a shared structure. Form criticism is comparable to telling someone the rules of chess or baseball. These rules can change over a period of time, but even without change they are not identical with what can be observed on any single occasion, since a particular instance of a game exhibits specific moves, scores, etc., that are variable.

Rules of languages and games are conventional in the sense that they are to a degree arbitrary or accidental. The study of "form," however, deals with reasons for the various aspects of a structure in relation to the dynamics of the whole of which they are a part. In other words, it examines the degree to which the elements are not completely irrational. For instance, one can ask, just what is it that makes baseball or chess exciting games which have continued over many years? It is apparent that such an analysis can help not only to defend a traditional form but also to provide suggestions for improving a convention or changing it in the light of new circumstances.

The ability to state the rules of language is not required for

I

2

their use. According to recent research, a child learns globally; that is, it largely learns patterns of language and general concepts rather than a sum of individual items (see, e.g., Lenneberg, 66). Nevertheless, the principles are not learned in full awareness, so that in order for them to be conscious the rules have to be taught in school even when the child already knows how to operate with them and respond to them. The notion of the "subconscious" can be used to describe such implicit knowledge. It may be distinguished from the "preconscious," which designates everything that is not in mind at the moment but is easily brought to awareness, and from the "unconscious," which represents nonmeaningful patterns as well as experiences that have been repressed as too uncomfortable to face.

A subconscious structure is one of which a speaker or hearer is sufficiently aware to act appropriately in relation to it. Such action shows itself in correct usage (such as of words or syntax) or in an appropriate response (laughing at a joke, obeying a command, accepting an implicit offer of friendship). A special form of such minimal awareness is the process of meaningful classification. All languages include terms for classes of speech-events, such as prayers, sacred narratives, or various types of greetings. These are a rudimentary stage of form critical analysis. A culture, however, can in practice make distinctions without express labels; and terms are not always used as precisely or invariably as an observer might wish.

A large part of language study, as indeed of the humanities and social sciences, consists in the bringing into awareness considerations which are known subconsciously. Such a process may be called "elucidation." A major part of form criticism is then the elucidation of genres and thus the clarification of different aspects of human life. The primary aim of form criticism, as we shall see more fully below, is not to provide data external to oneself but rather to provide insight into human existence. Some kinds of analysis raise from the unconscious an uncomfortable truth, destroying a delusion or unmasking a self-serving ideology; such insight can be incorporated into form criticism. In addition, fortuitous data are noted commonly in historical study of individuals.

A further step toward awareness is taken when analysis becomes conscious of itself and of its own bases. The present essay is an attempt to push form criticism to that level. Perhaps some general and specific human operations will become apparent.

Fortunately it is possible to avail oneself of the help of a number of histories of exegesis. Most of these, however, do not ask the kind of questions which the present study has posed for itself. They are oriented largely toward the development of so-called historical criticism and rarely relate methodologies to the social context within which they operate. One may hope that further studies will extend the present exploration of form criticism and its cultural situation.

II. CLASSICAL THEORIES OF PUBLIC SPEECH AND POETRY

W. Ahlwardt, *Über Poesie und Poetik der Araber* (Gotha: F. A. Perthes, 1856); E. Albert, " 'Rhetoric,' 'Logic,' and 'Poetics' in Burundi: Culture Patterning of Speech Behavior," *AA* LXVI (1964) 6/2, 35-54; F. Blass, *Die attische Bered-samkeit*, 3 vols. (Leipzig: B. G. Teubner, 1887²-1898²) ; *idem*, "Hermeneutik und Kritik," in *Handbuch der klassischen Altertumswissenschaft*, ed. by I. von Müller (Munich: C. H. Beck, 1892) 147-295; J. Donohue, *The Theory of Lit-erary Kinds* (Dubuque: Loras College Press, 1943) ; G. Field, *The Philosophy of Plato* (London: Oxford University Press, 1969²) ; G. Grube, *The Greek and Roman Critics* (Toronto: University of Toronto Press, 1965) ; D. Hymes, "In-troduction: Toward Ethnographies of Communication," *AA* LXVI (1964) 6/2, 1-34; R. Jebb, *The Attic Orators from Antiphon to Isaeus*, 2 vols. (London: Macmillan, 1893²) ; M. Joos, *The Five Clocks* (Bloomington: Indiana Univer-sity Research Center in Anthropology, Folklore and Linguistics, 1962); G. Ken-nedy, *The Art of Persuasion in Greece* (Princeton: Princeton University Press, 1963) ; *idem*, *Quintilian* (New York: Twayne Publishers, 1969) ; H. Lausberg, *Handbuch der literarischen Rhetorik* (Munich: Max Hueber, 160) ; H. Rahn, *Morphologie der antiken Literatur* (Darmstadt: Wissenschaftliche Buchgesell-schaft, 1969) ; D. Russell, *'Longinus' On the Sublime* (London: Oxford Uni-versity Press, 1964) ; M. Sullivan, *Apuleian Logic* (Amsterdam: North Holland Publishing Company, 1967) ; H. Volkmann, *Die Rhetorik der Griechen und Römer* (Hildesheim: G. Olms, 1885 = 1963) .

Intensive investigation has shown that Israelite speech habits reflect complexes that may properly be called genres. For some of these, the Hebrew language had names, such as *qînâ*, "dirge." Israelites, however, did not possess the same degree of theoretical interest in speech patterns as did the Greeks; for it is not to be assumed that a given culture develops all of its aspects equally.

The primary emphasis of Israel lay in practical self-criticism, in the facing of uncomfortable reality, in a judgment directed against social inequalities. The enemy of such an attitude is ide-ology defending privileges rather than innocent ignorance. The revelation often uncovers data which one prefers to repress into the unconscious. For scholarly analysis and elucidation of sub-conscious realities, biblical form criticism draws heavily from the Greeks. As we shall see, it has drawn from that source in the past and can still learn from the early works on rhetoric and poetry.

While there may be differences in emphases, the contrast between Athens and Jerusalem is by no means an absolute one. Just as the Greeks were not devoid of faith and morals, so the Israelites were not innocent of reasoned analysis. "Wisdom" is in many ways comparable to what flowered in Greece. For instance, a major concern of wisdom was with speech. The terms *peh* (mouth), *lāšôn* (tongue), *sāpāh* (lip), *dābār* (word) appear especially in the books of Proverbs, Qoheleth, Job, and in Psalms. (In other books of the OT these words occur largely in figurative senses, applied to God, swords, fire, and the like.) Israelite interest in speech, like its wisdom in general, involved a combination of self-interest with concern for the welfare of others. A few examples from Proverbs will indicate its range. "Giving answer before one hears is folly and shame" (18:13). "A lying tongue acts as an enemy to its object and a flattering mouth ruins" (26:28). "The lips of the righteous feed many" (10:21). "A man has joy in his answer; how good is a word spoken at an appropriate time!" 15:23). The naming of animals in Gen 2:20, probably a wisdom motif, classifies and comprehends a portion of reality.

There is in the OT a possible, but doubtful, reference to the knowledge of genres as a part of good speech. Prov 25:11 can be translated: "Like apples of gold in a setting of silver is speech according to its (proper) kind." The meaning of the last word, however, is obscure; it may refer to an artistic formation or to use in an appropriate setting or with good timing. A related sentence close to classical rhetoric can be found in Qoh 12:10: "The assembly speaker [i.e., the author] sought to find pleasurable words." It is difficult to tell whether the linguistic formulation or the content is considered pleasing; however, such an alternative may not have existed in the writer's mind (cf. Rahn, 148, for a frequent similar lack of contrast in Roman theory).

Greek philosophy (literally translated, the "love of wisdom") developed in close analogy to, and indeed in some contact with, the Near Eastern educational tradition. The word *sophia* even has a range of meaning virtually identical with that of the Hebrew *ḥokmâ* ("wisdom"), in that it denotes any skill, but especially skills taught and acquired in education, and finally insight of the deepest sort available to men. The Sophists were in many ways the Greek counterpart of the Hebrew "wise men," namely educators, thinkers, speakers, advisers. The knowledge of proper speech became especially important in the fifth century, when populist forms of government arose in Sicilian Syracuse (headquarters of rhetorical development) and in Athens. With this development, lawsuits had to be addressed to large juries, and political speeches needed to sway the assembly. The Sophistic teaching which then arose was virtually identical with education in speaking, which included thinking.

It was natural that some technical terms would evolve. Recurring elements of thought became known as *topoi* (literally, "places"), in the singular, *topos*, from which the English "topic" is derived; the equivalent Latin *loci communes* and English "commonplaces" later gained currency for standard themes in logic, theology, and other concerns. The process of recognizing appropriate topics is called discovery (*inventio*). Elements of expression included arrangement (*taxis*, in Latin, *dispositio* or *collocatio*) and style (*lexis* or *phrasis*, in Latin, *elocutio*). Different kinds of styles were developed and recognized as appropriate for particular contents and for different "times" or occasions (*kairoi*); the fitness of a style was known as *prepon*, in Latin *aptum*.

In the fourth century, Aristotle provided a brilliant systematization of rhetoric. Building upon, and sharpening, earlier traditions of classification, he recognized three major rhetorical genres, related, as he says, to three kinds of purposes or audiences and exhibiting at the same time three different kinds of content. Forensic or legal speech is addressed to evaluators of past events and deals with justice; epideictic speech (praising or lampooning someone) addresses observers of a person in the present and deals with honor; deliberative oratory (advice) speaks to persons about to make decisions regarding the future and concerns itself with what is useful or expedient.

Each of the three genres is divided by Aristotle in accordance with its mood, whether positive or negative: forensic speech includes accusation and defense; epideictic, praise and blame; advice, persuasion and dissuasion. It may be noted that somewhat similar classifications are implied in Arabic systems of genre terms, which are heavily based on mood and reference point: self-praise, praise of others, praise of women, blame of others, confession of sin, admonition, lament over the dead, thanksgiving, etc. (see, e.g., Ahlwart, 31).

Aristotle carefully thought through the nature of topics as types (not individual instances) of content. He saw that certain topics are general in the sense that they can be used for various purposes, that some are particularly relevant for a certain genre without being ruled out for others, and that certain thematic aspects of one genre can be closely related to corresponding themes of another one. For example, the uses of maxims and comparisons are widely applicable; a praise and a counsel may be very similar except for a difference in phrasing (*Rhetoric*, 1367b). He is thus able to avoid rigid compartmentalization while noting specialization.

Since rhetoric deals with speech to be used by anyone (Aristotle, *Rhetoric*, 1354a), it was an object of intensive training in general education; it is otherwise with the theory of poetry. Some handbooks of advice for would-be poets, or of standards by which to judge poetry, came to be written; but they were of somewhat limited appeal. More relevantly, the study of poetry was involved in "grammar"; for, on the one hand, grammar was concerned largely with the recognition of the meaning of literary works, and, on the other hand, poetic works were used for determining appropriate linguistic usage. The origin of poetry was largely attributed to inspiration.

Greek interpretation of texts generally did not attempt to be of the so-called "objective" variety, of which we will speak later. Otherwise stated, it did not divorce theory from practice or expression from content. Interpretation usually focused either on a simple explanation of individual words and sentences or on a broader interpretation called "exegesis." The latter term meant literally "a leading out" and designated the elaboration of the practical meaning of a passage, particularly of a sacred one; professional "exegetes," for instance, were those whose primary task it was to interpret holy laws. Interpretation could be moral or natural; for example, figures in the epics could be seen as good (or evil) examples or as representations of physical, social, and metaphysical dimensions.

The content, emotional effect, and meanings of poetry were of deep interest to Plato. Like others before him, he distinguished various genres: drama, epic, lyric, political speeches, laws, prayer, etc. Most relevant for theology is his use of myths as an expressive form for content that deals with ultimates, in temporal terms, origin and end. A central category for the ultimate dimension in his view was the soul, so that its immortality in both temporal directions was an important theme. (See especially *Timaeus* for creation, *Politicus* for world cycles, the world's dependence, and paradise, *Meno* for the soul's preexistence, *Gorgias* for future immortality, *Phaedrus* for love and the soul's journeys through the heavens.) The argument of *The Republic* that myths, not literally true, should be taught to citizens to account for their various roles embraces the function of foundation myths in societies.

Plato's observations were extended in Aristotle's slender and incomplete *Poetics*. The overall character of poetry is described as "imitation" (*mimesis*), more accurately, "representation," namely, an imaginative version of a somewhat typical human reality. It is not poetry's literal truth in regard to an individual event that is important, but its representative character. While Plato, especially in his early years, had feared the dramatization of harmful emotions as potentially strengthening them, Aristotle regarded portrayal as allowing one to deal with them; thus the most impressive poetry (drama) is rated highest.

Aristotle divided genres in the *Poetics* according to three considerations: medium or means (whether they use language, rhythm, or a combination of these), matter or object (primarily the social role of persons represented), and manner of presentation (direct in dramatic speech and action, indirect in narration, and mixed). It is good to note that these variables are not in principle hierarchical but cut across each other. The order in which the differentiations are applied (which has been varied) does not affect the end result in determining the most specific genres.

While the theory of poetic genres was not as intensively cultivated in the ancient world as was rhetoric, some systems of classification (usefully summarized by J. Donohue) have survived. The Coislinian Treatise, of uncertain date, lists both "nonimitative" and "imitative" genres. The first group includes history and instruction, and the latter divides into didactic and theoretical poetry. The imitative falls into narrative and drama, which includes comedy, tragedy, mimes, and satyr-plays.

Prose and poetry were often not separated. Different degrees of the use of poetic or artificial features in rhetorical speech led to theory of levels of style, or "genres of speaking" (*genera dicendi*). Typologies of literature and expression by stylistic criteria, it may be noted, are not unusual. The Chinese Ssukung Tu distinguished twenty-four modes of poetry on the basis of such criteria (Hymes, 29). Very recently, M. Joos has distinguished between the frozen (often written), formal (informational), consultative (informational with interaction), casual, and intimate styles; his discussion reveals close connections with different kinds of content and relations to the audience. Officially differentiated styles are characteristic of stratified societies (cf. Albert).

Style values expressed by Greek theorists related closely to politics. In the early period of Greek democracy, orators like Gorgias attempted to apply to public speaking the poetic style of the earlier aristocratic (Homeric) period. In the fourth century B. C., an effective but "humble" prose style was developed by Lysias, major philosophers, and others. Demosthenes varied his style, and Aristotle related levels of expression to the degree of weightiness of the subject matter (*Rhetoric*, 1408a). Politically, these two men stood between aristocracy and democracy. During the time of the Hellenistic empire, an elaborate oratory flourished. A third-century work attributed to Demetrius describes four levels of style: magnificent, charmful, simple, and energetic. These are to be varied in a given work according to the importance (in part, social) of the matter. For example, the depiction of great battles, heaven, or earth is appropriately presented in magnificent form, but the description of a cottage calls for simple style (*On Style,* 75, 190).

In Rome, a similar development took place. A poetic-prose style preceded the classic, sometimes fairly simple, oratory reaching its high point in the final years of the Republic. Cicero, dominating this period, emphasized content and morality. He recognized the need for adjustment of style to both occasion and person, as well as to weightiness of topic. But he related the styles especially to purpose: the simple style is appropriate for intellectual proof, the middle style for pleasure, the vigorous for persuasion (*Orator,* 69, and similarly in earlier works). A more ornate style tradition became widespread under the emperors. A faction that continued to argue for a simple style included the major writer Quintilian, who came from a nonaristocratic family. Even he, however, is quite frank about the need to consider—in addition to other factors—the social ranks of the speaker and the addressee (XI, 1, 43-45) in one's choice of style.

Theory of style centered heavily on so-called "schemes" (or "figures") and "tropes," the poetic features employed in "artistic" prose (*Kunstprosa*). According to Quintilian's systematization, a "trope" means an alteration of a word or phrase from its usual meaning (i.e., metaphor); a "figure of words" is a special verbal arrangement (such as odd syntax or rhythm); and a "figure of thought" includes such forms as question, irony, and apostrophe (change in address). Allegory was classified sometimes as an extended metaphor, sometimes as a figure of thought. Allocation of schemes to levels of speech can be illustrated by examples from

Demetrius. He assigns allegory to magnificent style; metaphor, to both magnificent and charmful manner; employment of proverbs and fables, primarily to the charmful style. Parallelism (especially antithetic or structural, less often synonymous) was virtually the only poetic form admitted, since Lysias, to simple rhetorical style.

During the Roman period, Jewish influence made itself felt. Especially important, though with only minor impact in its own time, is a work of uncertain date and authorship entitled *On the Sublime*. It is devoted to impressive or moving style, without limiting itself to traditionally high literature; among its examples stands the love poetry of the Greek poetess Sappho. For proof that the source of profundity and impressiveness lies in mental power rather than in ornateness the author cites, as one of two examples, Gen 1:3: "God said: 'Let there be light' and there was light." This passage and some other parts of the work have affinities with Philo and Josephus; the fact that Moses is described as "no ordinary man" suggests that the author belonged to the same faith. The relatively egalitarian outlook of the work is appropriate especially, though not only, for a Jewish author. Also typically Jewish, though again not exclusively so, is the thoroughgoing acceptance of moral responsibility. The origin of current poor style the author locates in a "craze for novelty" (ch. 5) and in love of wealth, honor, and extravagant pleasure, showing itself in acceptance of bribes and in greed for the neighbor's possessions (chs. 7, 44). Outstanding emphases of the work, though not new, include the emotional source of poetry and imagination as part of mental vigor.

Classification and characterization of speech occurred also in logical treatises. Apuleius' *Peri Hermeneias* ("Concerning Interpretation"), which was to influence medieval writers, can serve as an example. According to this work, argumenting or disputing speech is only one of several varieties; others include, for instance, commanding, wishing, admiring, and lamenting (Sullivan, 22).

III. GENRE CONSIDERATIONS IN EARLY AND MEDIEVAL BIBLICAL STUDIES

E. Auerbach, *Mimesis* (Bern: A. Francke, 1946) = *Mimesis*, tr. by W. Trask (Princeton: Princeton University Press, 1953); *idem, Literary Language and Its Public* (New York: Pantheon Books, 1965); I. Baroway, "The Hebrew Hexameter," *ELH* II (1935) 66-91; E. de Bruyne, *Études d'esthétique mediévale*, 3 vols. (Brugge: De Tempel, 1946); K. Burke, *The Rhetoric of Religion: Studies in Logology* (Boston: Beacon Press, 1961); W. Capelle and H. Marrou,

"Diatribe," *RAC III* (1957) 990-1008; H. Caplan, *Of Eloquence* (Ithaca: Cornell University Press, 1970) ; 1. Christiansen, *Die Technik der allegorischen Auslegungswissenschaft bei Philon von Alexandrien* (Tübingen: J. C. B. Mohr, 1969) ; J. Daniélou, "Les genres littéraires d'après les Pères de l'Église," in *Congreso de Ciencias Eclesiásticas, Los generos literarios de la Sagrada Escritura* (Barcelona: J. Flors, 1957) 275-283; D. Daube, "Rabbinic Methods of Interpretation and Hellenistic Rhetoric," *HUCA* XXII (1949) 239-264; R. Gögler, *Zur Theologie des biblischen Wortes bei Origenes* (Düsseldorf: Patmos-Verlag, 1963) ; G. B. Gray, *The Forms of Hebrew Poetry* (London: Hodder and Stoughton, 1915) ; A. Heschel, *The Prophets* (New York: Harper and Row, 1962) ; A. Kerrigan, *St. Cyril of Alexandria, Interpreter of the Old Testament* (Rome: Pontifical Biblical Institute, 1952); S. Lieberman, *Hellenism in Jewish Palestine* (New York: Jewish Theological Seminary, 1962[2]) ; R. McKeon, "Rhetoric in the Middle Ages," *Speculum* XVII (1942) 1-32; E. Norden, *Die antike Kunstprosa* (Darmstadt: Wissenschaftliche Buchgesellschaft, 1958[5]); P. Spicq, *Esquisse d'une histoire de l'exégèse latine au Moyen Age* (Paris: J. Vrin, 1944) ; G. Strauss, *Schriftgebrauch, Schriftauslegung und Schriftbeweis bei Augustin* (Tübingen: J. C. B. Mohr, 1959) ; W. Tatarkiewicz, *History of Aesthetics*, II (The Hague: Mouton, 1970) ; H. Wolfson, *Philo*, I (Cambridge: Harvard University Press, 1947) .

Jewish and Christian exegetes learned extensively from established rhetorical and poetic theory. They rarely did so slavishly, however; attempts were made to create special categories for biblical material when that seemed necessary or appropriate. Neither the borrowing nor the originating of concepts appears always successful in hindsight, but is it otherwise in modern scholarship? In any case, it is clear that many of the ancients understood the need for recognizing forms of speech and that they saw both similarities and differences in comparison with other traditions. Only the highlights of the development can be presented here, to set forth the issues.

Jewish exegetical rules reflected basic genre recognitions. It was clear that large portions of the Pentateuch are laws; the application of these laws had natural affinities with the work of the Greek "exegetes" (see above, p. 7). As D. Daube has shown, rabbinic rules of legal (*halakhic*) exegesis are similar to those employed in the forensic branch of classical rhetoric; for instance, it was a fundamental principle that laws are formulated on a minimal illustrative basis and that cases not explicitly covered are to be interpreted by analogy. The rules gradually devised for nonlegal (*haggadic*) exegesis include a few that are mysterious, especially: *gematria*, based on the numerical value of letters or on a supposedly secret alphabet, and *notarikon*, treating parts of words as abbreviations. Such principles were used widely for the interpretation of dreams and oracles (Lieberman, 70-75) and imply an oracular view of certain portions of scripture.

Philo Judaeus divided narratives into "genealogies" (stories about human beings) and accounts of Creation. In view of similarities with Greek myths and traditional narrations, he recognized that certain details were "of the nature of myth"; these include the formation of woman from man's rib and the tempting serpent (*Leg. Alleg.* II, 19, etc.; see Wolfson). In various narratives he saw an allegorical meaning in addition to, or sometimes instead of, a literal sense. I. Christiansen has indicated that Philonic allegory is thoroughly logical in approach and represents a special form of analogy; indeed, some form of analogy is necessary for the application of a text.

Allegorical interpretation, practiced widely by both Jewish and Christian exegetes, reflected a very common Hellenistic approach to poetic texts, especially to those held in high esteem. Demetrius, it may be remembered, regarded allegory as a feature of magnificent style. Since the exegesis of Greek poets and the ornate rhetorical tradition were both cultivated especially in Alexandria, long the cultural center of the imperial world, it is not an accident that the most intensive and extensive interest in allegories was expressed by Alexandrians, including Philo and Origen.

Origen pointed to the existence of "various tropes of eloquence and different species of speech" and urged attention to "the general form of the words." As genres whose meaning is partially nonliteral, he lists parables, riddles, and "stories" (*mythoi*). He can, of course, point to explicit statements in the bible in which figurative speech is employed, such as Ps 78:2; Is 29:11. (See Gögler, 358, 363, 365, 367.) The Song of Songs is viewed as profoundly poetic literature. It has the character of an "epithalamium" (marriage song) and of a drama, with change in speakers. The spiritual meaning, representing the church's desire for Christ, is not secondary, but rather archetypal; "it is from this book that the heathen appropriated the epithalamium" (*The Song of Songs*, tr. by R. Lawson [Westminster: Newman Press, 1957] 268).

Rhythm, another aspect of poetry, was brought out by Josephus, with genre implications. He held that the Psalms were written in meter, especially trimeters and pentameters, and the Song of Moses in hexameter. This analysis reverberated widely and was extended in Patristic and later literature. Since it was known that hexameter verse represented the standard meter of didactic poetry, such form was identified especially in wisdom and wisdom-

I

12

oriented literature by Jerome and others. (For details, see Gray and Baroway.)

The psalms almost cry out for form critical treatment, with attention to their basic processes and to types. Several fourth-century exegetes gave attention to such an analysis. Eusebius (MPG, XXIII, 66) held, somewhat tentatively, that the terms *psalmos* (Hebrew *mizmôr*) and *ode* (Hebrew *šîr*) referred to differences both in musical performance and in content. The *psalmos* is recited with musical background, while the *ode* is sung; "if an allegorical view may be taken," he judged, the former is oriented toward the believer's works, while the latter is spiritual with meditation on divine reality. This distinction was accepted by St. Basil (MPG, XXIX, 305) and Jerome (MPL, XXVI, 1219; etc.). Hilary elaborated the typology, including attention to the combination of these terms (CSEL, XXII, 15-17). Less formal, but more appropriate, is Athanasius' categorization; a synopsis at the head of the exegesis of each psalm generally describes what happens in the psalm: requesting, exhorting, praising, etc. (MPG, XXVII, 60-545).

At the end of the fourth century a number of grammatically and rhetorically trained writers contributed significantly to biblical interpretation. Several, including John Chrysostom, learned from Neo-Platonic exegesis to pay attention to the main point or "aim" (*skopos*) of a writing (Kerrigan, 92-93; Daniélou). The typification of such aims, of course, leads to form critical analysis. Thus Chrysostom's *Synopsis of the Sacred Scriptures* speaks of denunciations, entreaties, exhortations, and predictions by the prophets (MPG, LVI, 376-377), as well as of their visions and of such categories as proverbs. Similar to this is the literal aspect of the exegesis of Cyril of Alexandria (early fifth century). Cyril paid attention to prophetic style, with change in speaker and addressee, to the operations of reproof, exhortation, and encouragement, and to tropes and figures (Kerrigan).

Both Chrysostom and Theodore of Mopsueste, the most prominent member of the school of Antioch, were students of Libanius, a major rhetorician devoted to pure "Attic" (relatively simple) style, as well as of the theologian Diodore, Bishop of Tarsus. For members of their circle, as for most rhetoricians, allegory was merely one among many tropes. (Allegory belonged primarily to poetry or to magnificent prose.)

Various members of the school of Antioch followed, in part, a traditional Jewish view of differences in sacredness or revelatory character among portions of scripture. A comment attributed to Theodore states that Solomon composed his books "from his own person," since he received the "grace of prudence" rather than of prophecy, with an allusion to I Cor 12:8-10 (MPG, LXVI, 697). Hadrian, reflecting this school, divides scriptural language into "historical" (or "inquiring") and prophetic patterns; historical is what is available to the senses, perhaps best rendered "worldly" (cf. Kerrigan, 39-50). These two major types are each subdivided according to time dimensions, in line with the temporal orientations of rhetorical genres. Unfortunately, Hadrian does not furnish descriptions of the dimensions of "history" (do aspects of wisdom form an inquiry of the future?). The prophetic past is illustrated by creation, the prophetic present by Elijah's knowledge of Gehasi's sin, and the prophetic future by predictions, including fulfillment in Christ. The Antioch school placed the Psalter under the heading of prophecy, in a partial deviation from Jewish tradition.

According to Hadrian, the psalms are shaped in meter for singing purposes, other prophets in "prose-poetry" (two words are drawn into one), and wisdom literature in recitational "stichoi" (extended rows). Prophetic forms include ordinary speech, visions, and symbolic actions.

The first systematic treatise of the language of faith was furnished in the handbook on *Christian Teaching* by St. Augustine, an almost precise contemporary of Theodore. He had taught rhetoric for thirteen years prior to his conversion. Originally repelled by the lowliness of the Latin bible, he accepted its form of expression for two reasons. On the one hand, the spiritual-allegorical approach he heard expounded in Ambrose's sermons implied profundity, to be understood by the mindful. On the other hand, he saw the "humble genre of speaking" as a "holy humility" of scripture, by which it reaches the lowly multitudes (*Confessions*, VI, 8; see also Strauss, p. 33).

For several centuries, the church fathers—emphatically already Origen—had stressed a need for lowly style in biblical literature and in sermons (Norden, 521-530). In this point they resemble and sharpen the theory implied in the "diatribe," a form of popular exhortation by ethical philosophers who sought to lead hearers to an ultimate goal, an "end (*telos*) of God" (Capelle, 991-993). It is widely true that faith in a supreme deity includes a concern for the weak and the poor. The fact that the humbleness of the speech of faith resides not only in expression but specifically in content has been shown by E. Auerbach: Israelite and Christian sacred stories, dealing with world history from origin to end, depict events as happening to simple people; relatively secular or narrow-scoped polytheistic narrations present only members of the aristocracy with significance or seriousness, such as in tragedy.

Aware of the role of "holy humbleness," Augustine expresses ambivalence toward the employment of rhetorical training. In the prologue to *Christian Teaching*, he defends such a use partly on the ground that men have in general received the basics of language from secular sources; he argues that what can be learned from men should be "learned without pride" (5). In outline, the work proceeds from "discovery" (content) to style, according to a traditional sequence; in fact, Aristotle, Cicero, and Augustine added their discussions of elocution to their rhetorical writings only after a considerable lapse of time. Biblical material is included in Augustine's work as an integral, indeed normative, part of Christian teaching. Thus his outlook is similar to that of the Greek exegetes, for whom exposition is equivalent to application of a sacred text.

Augustine relates the content of the speech of faith to that of standard rhetoric. For the latter, a central concept is "the useful," for deliberative speech in particular and for all branches in general; Augustine understands "the useful" (*utilis*) as the means to an end. In contrast stand things to be "enjoyed," loved for their own sake (I, 3-4), thus, ends in themselves. What is inherently enjoyable is the Trinity, the foundation of all things (I,5). A central *topos* of faith is love for all men (I, 22-29). Other topics include the church, the scriptures, eternity, and incarnation. (Kenneth Burke, a modern theorist of rhetoric, has discussed the role and significance of the topics of beginning, end, evil, sacrifice, word, etc., in Augustine's system of speech.)

Augustine's formal observations include an extended discussion of narration and description, both traditional aspects of rhetoric. He points out an overlap of these categories, since the point of some narratives is to describe presently observable locations or objects (II,45). Only very reluctantly does Augustine enter into questions of elocution. Examples from Paul and Amos 6:1-6 demonstrate the use and acceptability of verbal schemes, such as a climactic sequence of phrases or sentences (IV, 11-20). However, eloquence is also shown to be independent of elaborate tropes and figures. He cites Jer 5:30-31, about false prophecy, as an example of an eloquent passage all the more powerful since it is "pure" (IV, 30).

The various streams that had developed somewhat independently during the fourth and fifth centuries flowed together in the commentary of Cassiodorus (sixth century) on the Psalter, which came to be widely used in the Middle Ages. Its introduction (MPL, LXX, 9-26) delineates the character of sacred literature as a whole (with reference to Augustine), the characteristics of prophecy as a subdivision, and the "particular eloquence" of the psalms and their groupings (similar to Hilary). It deals with content, style, and the psalms' role in the church's praise. The exegesis of individual psalms makes use of "figures" and applies rhetorical categories relating to disposition or arrangement (opening, close, and sequence of themes).

The rhetoric of the Middle Ages was deeply occupied with the relations between faith and culture. An adequate treatment of medieval interpretation would need to deal with exegetical literature and various kinds of theoretical treatises in interaction (see McKeon and Tatarkiewicz). A number of writers dealt with various "modes of speaking" (St. Thomas) and with the purposes of different parts of scripture (see Spicq, 146, 245-247; MPL CLXXVIII, 783, for Abelard).

A major development lay in the formulation of the "art of preaching." Handbooks for this genre placed major emphasis on discovery (topics), including attention to the needs of various kinds of people or circumstances; they did not neglect elocution and rules of exegesis. The themes were of course heavily oriented to biblical content, but they could also be drawn from non-Christian material. Alain de Lille's *Sum of the Art of Preaching* (MPL, CCX, 109-198), late twelfth century, has affinities with the ancient diatribe in moral emphases; it employs illustrations from Greco-Roman philosophers and myths in addition to numerous references to biblical literature.

The poetic and expressive characteristics of the bible were appreciated by both Christian and Jewish commentators and philologists, with no sharp line between sacred and other writings. Isidore of Seville (MPL, LXXXII, 108; ca. 600 A. D.), for instance, quotes Deut 33:6 as an example of the traditional category of amplified expression. A century later, the Venerable Bede, theological writer and poet, devoted a work to the schemes and tropes of the scriptures. Jonah Ibn Janah, of the eleventh century, "drew upon rhetoric and upon analogies in Arabic, seeking to explain biblical expressions as metaphors and other tropes familiar to him from Arabic literature" (Heschel, 369). Other aesthetic observations included the recognition of parallelism (Heschel, 375).

The richness of genres in biblical writing is perhaps most impressively described in Ulrich's *Of the Highest Good* (thirteenth century; de Bruyne, II, 314, 316). The bible is "historical," since it recounts events with general significance, and "poetic," with images; it is didactic, juridical, thoughtful, emotional, prophetic (revealing past, present, and future), and musical (metrical). The bible combines certainty with uncertainty, clarity with mystery, delight with horror; it is simple but sometimes ornate to show that the simple is not due to lack of ability. Its many themes reveal the divine, display beauty, and announce various kinds of good.

IV. POST-MEDIEVAL BIBLICAL FORM CRITICISM

W. Barner, *Barockrhetorik* (Tübingen: Max Niemeyer, 1970); I. Baroway, "The Bible as Poetry in the English Renaissance," *JEGP* XXXII (1933) 447-480; *idem*, "The Imagery of Spenser and the *Song of Songs*," *JEGP* XXXIII (1934) 23-45; J. Brody, *Boileau and Longinus* (Geneva: E. Droz, 1958); M. Croll, *Style, Rhetoric, and Rhythm* (Princeton: Princeton University Press, 1966); E. Curtius, *Europäische Literatur und Lateinisches Mittelalter* (Bern: A. Francke, 1948); G. Ebeling, *Evangelische Evangelienauslegung* (Darmstadt: Wissenschaftliche Buchgesellschaft, 1962); N. Frye, *Anatomy of Criticism* (Princeton: Princeton University Press, 1957); O. Hardison, Jr., *The Enduring Moment* (Chapel Hill: University of North Carolina, 1962); W. Howell, *Logic and Rhetoric in England, 1500-1700* (Princeton: Princeton University Press, 1956); E. Kraeling, *The Old Testament Since the Reformation* (New York: Harper & Bros., 1955); G. Krause, *Studien zu Luthers Auslegung der Kleinen Propheten* (Tübingen: J. C. B. Mohr, 1962); W. Krauss, *Grundprobleme der Literaturwissenschaft* (Reinbek/Hamburg: Rowohlt, 1968); W. Maurer, *Der junge Melanchthon*, I (Göttingen: Vandenhoeck & Ruprecht, 1967); S. Monk, *The Sublime: A Study of Critical Theories of XVIII-Century England* (New York: Modern Language Association, 1935); B. Nelson, *The Idea of Usury* (Chicago: University of Chicago Press, 1969²); C. Roth, *The Jews in the Renaissance* (New York: Harper & Row, 1965); H. Schöffler, *Abendland und Altes Testament* (Frankfurt: Klostermann, 1941²); B. Stierle, "Schriftauslegung der Reformationszeit," *VuF* XVI (1971) 1:55-88; B. Weinberg, *A History of Literary Criticism in the Italian Renaissance* (Chicago: University of Chicago Press, 1961); H. Wolf, *Die Einheit des Bundes* (Neukirchen: Verlag des Erziehungsvereins, 1958).

The Renaissance was marked by interest in Greco-Roman literature and theory, while the Reformation pointed toward the scriptures. The contrast of these directions sometimes led to a relative dissociation of faith and culture, but often connections were close. In biblical studies, interaction almost invariably showed itself in form critical treatments.

Martin Luther made some use of poetic concepts, with primary interest in metaphors (Krause, 191-202). However, he was more restrained in the use of figures and focused strongly on a literal meaning, in harmony with an emphasis on the clarity of the bible for all readers and with an innerworldly asceticism (WA, VIII, 236, 587; XVIII, 484, 487; XXXII, 223). "Enthusiasm," he once declared, "is the origin, power, and strength of all heresies," both on the right and on the left (WA, L, 246; Ebeling, 313). He was more inclined to historical criticism, including a recognition of the diversity of points of view within the bible. In this area his work, as somewhat similarly Calvin's, led to perspectives which required centuries to develop (see Kraeling, 10-25).

In line with their antecedents, Luther and Calvin employed in their exegesis a number of basic descriptive terms for the character of a passage, though in a nonsystematic and minimal fashion. Thus, for Luther, Ps 37 is a moral psalm; Ps 94, an imploration for deliverance; and Ps 118, a general thanksgiving (WA, III, 204; IV, 88; XXXI/I, 68). Calvin denied that Ps 11:1-3 is a complaint, recognized Ps 79 as a collective lament, and saw that Ps 119 largely exhorts, while psalms like 147 incite to praise. The book of Jonah he viewed as partly historical and partly didactic. In Calvin's view, more than in Luther's, Christ is present in the OT in "figures, pictures, signs, types, and shadows" (Wolf, 69-73).

More heavily form critical is the work of P. Melanchthon, Lutheran theologian, professor of classics, and theorist of rhetoric. (For studies of his work see Stierle.) He organized theology around *loci communes* or topics. In his exegesis, Melanchthon made extensive use of rhetoric and logical concepts. Individual psalms are classified according to genres: "demonstrative," "parenetic," "legal," "persuasion," "request," etc. (CR, XIII, 1005-1472). Their "disposition" or arrangement is analyzed, as had been done already by others. The Lamentations are called, not surprisingly, "mourning poems' (CR, XIII, 817-822). His commentaries on Romans carefully apply rhetorical and logical categories, a procedure anticipated by Faber Stapulensis shortly before him and adopted also by H. Bullinger. OT narration received attention as a genre, with notice given to fables and ethical topics (Maurer, 213).

Melanchthon's student Matthias Flacius, a Hebrew specialist, formulated a "Guide to the Holy Scriptures" (*Clavis Scripturae Sacrae*, 1567). This extensive and often excellent work includes an exegetical and theological lexicon, an outline of sacred hermeneutics, a grammar, a detailed discussion of tropes and schemes and close analysis of several biblical styles. The discussion of hermeneutics drew together and elaborated various themes that had gradually come to be recognized during the Middle Ages (Krause, 241-243).

General requirements for an understanding of the scriptures, according to Flacius, are faith and moral commitment—the bible is not a dead book (precept 3)—and willingness to employ dialectic and rhetoric. Specific procedure centers on the relatedness of the parts of a passage or book to its dominating concern, so that it is seen as an organic whole. "Scope" (aim) is defined as that which gives unity to a work. Determination of the scope and parts of a work can be aided by attention to genres. Each type of speech has a typical or customary relation to the "life of men," to content, and to social actions (precept 20).

In addition to mentioning several of the standard rhetorical forms as examples, Flacius devotes close attention to the genres of biblical literature. Sacred history differs from secular history by dealing with "primary" (ultimate) causes and events. The prophets point out penalties, correct their audience, and provide hope through promises. The psalms are either directed from man to God, in requests or thanks, or from God to man—teaching, promising, admonishing, or consoling. Wisdom is related to philosophical disputations. The book of Proverbs is partly religious and partly civil, drawing largely from experience.

In England, Thomas Wilson's influential handbook on rhetoric (*Arte of Rhetorique*, 1553) analyzed the story of David and Goliath as an example of "demonstrative" speech. As is appropriate for a narrative, the account answers the following questions in relation to the action: "who," "what," "where," "with what help," "wherefore," "how," "at what time."

During the sixteenth and seventeeth centuries, Puritans attempted to relate daily life to the OT, though not as strongly as did members of still poorer groups (Schöffler; Nelson, 133). The Puritan circle produced unusually great poets, who related themselves closely to biblical literature. Spenser, sometimes considered the greatest English lyricist, produced renditions of Canticles, Psalms, and Qoheleth in addition to his more original productions. Philip Sidney's "Defense of Poetry" (1595) cited the parables of Nathan and Jesus in support of imaginative literature ("the application most divinely true, but the discourse itself fained," E3); poetry praising "the excellencies of God" represented to him the highest type (C2). Like Spenser and George Wither, Sidney wrote both paraphrases of the psalms and stylistically simple pastoral poetry. Wither's *Preparation to the Psalter*, 1619, provided a somewhat traditional form critical introduction with attention to style, content, and genres. In another work, *The Hymns and Songs of the Church*, 1623, he recommended the "funeral elegy" of II Sam 1:19-27 as "a pattern for our funeral poems." John Milton valued the biblical Song of Songs as a "divine pastoral drama" (Baroway, 1934, 23). He presented Christ as praising the prophets' "majestic unaffected style" in opposition to the "swelling epithets" of the rhetorical eloquence valued by Satan *(Paradise Regained,* 1671, IV, 343-359).

Connections between the bible and poetry were recognized and fostered rather widely. In the sixteenth century, the Italian Jew Leone de' Sommi attributed the origin of the theater, in which he excelled, to Moses and prepared rhymed versions of forty-five psalms (Roth, 261-262). Biblical poetry continued to be praised by various Italian authors (Weinberg, 336-491, 567), although the identification of poetry with revelation by some notable fourteenth-century writers was toned down in response to criticism against such an equation (Hardison, 6-7). The important German poet M. Opitz rendered the Psalms, Lamentations, and Song of Songs in fresh form. For him, "poetry was originally nothing other than hidden theology" *(Das Buch von der deutschen Poeterey*, 1624, B1). Poetry as a divine gift to man, and as characteristic of the bible, was the main theme also of the anonymous Spanish work *Panegyrico por la poesia*, 1627 (Curtius, 532-542).

Schemes and tropes are probably best regarded as poetic features which are also employed in relatively high prose style. One strain of medieval and, even more, of subsequent theory limited rhetoric largely to a study of these while assigning content to logic. Several works of the sixteenth and seventeeth centuries devoted specifically to schemes and tropes draw many of their illustrations from the bible. Among these, R. Sherry's *Treatise of Schemes and Tropes*, 1550, gave as the reason for its discussion a better understanding of literature; he compared ignorance of their varieties to entering a garden without knowing the names and properties of herbs and flowers. Sherry, Susenbrotus

(1540), and Peacham (*The Garden of Eloquence,* 1577) drew from both biblical and other literature for illustrations. D. Fenner (1584) substituted biblical examples for the classical ones in Ramus' work on which he largely relied (Howell, 219). In all cases, it is clear that a fundamental continuity between sacred and secular literature is assumed.

With gradual decline of aristocratic rule, traditional high-style rhetoric was attacked or avoided by both religious and secular writers. Specifically, at the end of the sixteenth century, verbal schemes were downgraded in favor of figures of "wit and thought" (Croll, 54, 204; Barner, 247). Since it is obvious that biblical literature contains many figures, the only open question is whether their literary character is strictly poetic or that of high prose. This question was left unsettled during the seventeenth century. Lists of schemes and tropes appeared under the heading of "sacred rhetoric," such as in S. Glass' *Philologia Sacra* (1623) and in Thomas Hall's *Centuria Sacra* (1654, with "about one hundred rules" for scriptural interpretation). The notion of a special biblical hermeneutic became attractive during this century. Bishop John Prideaux's *Sacred Eloquence,* 1659, even derived its own organization from a holy number; it had seven parts, each again divided sevenfold: tropes, figures, schemes, pathetics (passions), characters, antitheses, and parallels.

The decline of the social level of literature is noticeable not only in style but also in content. Northrop Frye (34-65) has observed a general drift from high to low literature in western culture. He sees tragedy, as in the work of Shakespeare and Racine (seventeenth century) and near the beginning of democracy in Greece, as characteristic of periods in which aristocracy is sharply losing ground. Indeed, during this time, the view was expressed that tragedy is designed to warn aristocrats (G. Puttenham, *The Arte of English Poesie,* 1589, I, ch. 15; Krauss, 59). A middle class, soon to become dominant, was emerging, partly as a result of the development of print making both bibles and other writings widely available.

The new stylistic tendencies led to a rediscovery of the study *On the Sublime* (described above, p. 10). This work had been copied often enough to survive but was sufficiently contrary to the attitudes of an imperial or feudal society to be given little attention. Rising interest can be seen in the appearance of several editions of the original writing, as well as of translations, since 1554. Widespread attention came to it when Boileau presented in 1674 both a free translation of *On the Sublime* and his own theory in *L'Art Poétique.* Boileau insisted that "sublimity" meant not high but good style, specifically a style which is both relatively simple and moving; the style thus embodies a union of what had often been considered opposite characteristics (Brody, 91).

Boileau's treatment marked, and aided, the virtual collapse of theories concerning social levels of style. Sublimity, instead, became the supreme word of eighteenth-century criticism. Meanings of the word ranged widely (Monk), involving varying degrees of dignity and simplicity, but an overpowering emotion was almost always implied. The concept naturally fit biblical literature, which had furnished an illustration for it from the start. It was applied in F. Fénélon's *Dialogues*, 1718, to Moses, psalms, and the prophets; in C. Vitringa's *Commentary on Isaiah*, 1724; in A. Blackwell's *The Sacred Classics*, 1727, dealing primarily with the NT; and by J. Turretin's lectures on method (published, without his authorization, 1728; *Opera*, II, 1775, 105). Sublimity played a considerable role in Robert Lowth's *De sacra poesi Hebraeorum*, 1758, which influenced subsequent works. At the end of the eighteenth century the theme shaded over into romanticism. A late use is that by S. Pratt, *The Sublime and the Beautiful of Scripture*, 1828, with strong emphasis on the touching simplicity of narratives.

Lowth's "Lectures on the Sacred Poetry of the Hebrews," delivered originally at his inauguration as professor of poetry at Oxford, represent a high point in OT form criticism. They were grounded in both classical and biblical studies and in touch with newer developments of his day. Lowth delineated the methodological basis of his work succinctly and with sophistication. He distinguished between an unnecessarily prescriptive approach, stating rules for a prospective composer of poetry, and a critical approach, which recognizes the principles of literature. The producing "genius" need not know or be concerned about the rules of the art; but the purpose of criticism is "to perceive and comprehend clearly the reasons, principles, and relations of things." All sciences, including that of poetry, are based on "observation," noting what is "conducive to the attainment of certain ends" (II).

The fact that classical categories and regulations are not always reflected in the organization of biblical literature was viewed by Lowth not as a defect, but as an advantage. Lack of adherence to arbitrary rules shows that biblical poetry is truly good

I

22

literature, deeply emotional and universal in character. Since poetry "appears to be an art derived from nature alone, peculiar to no age or nation, and only at an advanced period conformed to rule and method, it must be wholly attributed to the more violent affections of the heart, the nature of which is to express themselves in an animated and lofty tone" (I). The Greek view of poetry as a divine gift fits very well the sacred writings, "the only specimens of primeval and genuine poetry" (II).

A major portion of Lowth's work is devoted to poetic style. The main observable features of Hebrew poetry are the "sententious" arrangement in lines, the "figurative" use of images drawn from various spheres, and the "sublime" expression of high mind and vehement passion. Together these form the "parabolic" character denoted by the Hebrew word *māšāl* (IV-XVII). Lowth was well aware of the fact that style involves not only "diction," but "sentiment" and "mode of thinking" (IV). The first topic, or "common place," of sacred history is the contrast between chaos and creation; it also acts as a recurring motif for "any remarkable change in the public affairs" (IX).

Purpose is so closely connected with content and expression that "nature and design" (XX) fuse into a single concept. In general, the purpose of sacred poetry is to lead men to virtue and piety, exciting "the more ardent affections of the soul . . . to their proper end" (II). More specifically, its "office" is "to commend to the Almighty the prayer and thanksgiving of his creatures and to celebrate his praises"—human expression toward God—and, in a reverse direction of speech, "to display to mankind the mysteries of the divine will, and the predictions of future events" (II).

Lowth divided Hebrew poetry into prophetic, elegiac, didactic, lyric, idyllic (hymnic), and dramatic forms. He recognized schools of prophecy and the connection of their activity with music. Parallelism in prophetic speech is appropriately called poetic. Lowth discussed the basic patterns of funeral recitation (*qînâ*), the inequality of its lines, and Amos' application of the genre. The Song of Songs (interpreted allegorically) is described as semidramatic; for while it contains alternation of speech and a chorus, it lacks a connected story or "fable." Similarly, according to Lowth, Job lacks a plot and "contains merely a representation of those manners, passions, and sentiments, which may actually be expected in such a situation" (XXXIII).

Genre analysis could also appear to a limited extent in works by biblical scholars. J. Carpzov's *Introduction to the Canonical Books of the Old Testament*, 1721, a Latin work published in Germany, divided OT literature into histories, poetry, and prophecy. The psalms can be didactic, prophetic, petitionary, penitential, thankful, and consoling; they can be mixed in type. Turretin (*Opera*, II, 95-96) declared that the sacred books contain four genres, "or better" four types of matter: historical, prophetic, moral, and dogmatic. He noted that the aim of Gen 1 is to commend the observation of the sabbath (96), in other words, that it functions as a foundation story.

In the meantime a somewhat different outlook had gathered momentum. Its force was to dominate the period from about 1775 to 1875 and temporarily overshadow, though not completely eliminate, form critical concerns.

V. A TEMPORARY ECLIPSE OF GENRE STUDIES

L. Alonso-Schökel, *Estudios de poética Hebrea* (Barcelona: J. Flors, 1963) ; E. Auerbach, *Scenes from the Drama of European Literature* (New York: Meridian Books, 1959) ; F. Barnard, *Herder's Social and Political Thought* (London: Oxford University Press, 1965) ; E. Bickermann, *Four Strange Books of the Bible* (New York: Schocken Books, 1967) ; G. Ebeling, "Hermeneutik," *RGG*3 III (1959) 242-262; H. Gunkel, "Die israelitische Literatur," in *Die orientalischen Literaturen*, ed. by P. Hinneberg (KdG I/7, Leipzig: B. G. Teubner, 1906, 1925²) 53-112 = *Die israelitische Literatur* (Darmstadt: Wissenschaftliche Buchgesellschaft, 1963) ; W. Hasbach, *Untersuchungen über Adam Smith und die Entwicklung der politischen Okönomie* (Leipzig: Duncker & Humbolt, 1891) ; J. Herder, *Sämmtliche Werke*, ed. by B. Suphan (Berlin: Weidmann, 1879–) ; D. Hume, *Writings on Economics*, ed. by E. Rotwein (Madison: University of Wisconsin Press, 1955) ; A. Kathan, *Herders Literaturkritik* (Göttingen: A. Kümmerle, 1970) ; H. Knuth, *Zur Auslegungsgeschichte von Psalm 6* (Tübingen: J. C. B. Mohr, 1971) ; H. Kraus, *Geschichte der historisch-kritischen Erforschung des Alten Testaments* (Neukirchen: Neukirchener Verlag 1969²) ; idem, *Die Biblische Theologie* (Neukirchen: Neukirchener Verlag, 1970) ; K. Mannheim, *Ideology and Utopia* (London: Routledge & K. Paul, 1936) ; J. Miller, *The Disappearance of God* (New York: Schocken Books, 1965) ; idem, *The Form of Victorian Fiction* (Notre Dame: University of Notre Dame Press, 1968; B. Nelson, *The Idea of Usury*; A. Richardson, *The Bible in the Age of Science* (London: SCM Press, 1961) ; F. Ruch and P. Zimbardo, *Psychology and Life* (Glenville: Scott, Foresman, 1971) ; K. Scherpe, *Gattungspoetik im 18. Jahrhundert* (Stuttgart: Metzler, 1968) ; J. Schmidt, "Karl Friedrich Stäudlin—ein Wegbereiter der formgeschichtlichen Erforschung des Alten Testaments," *EvTh* 27 (1967) 200-218; B. Schwarzbach, *Voltaire's Old Testament Criticism* (Geneva: E. Droz, 1971) ; E. Sehmsdorf, *Die Prophetenauslegung bei J. G. Eichhorn* (Göttingen: Vandenhoeck & Ruprecht, 1971); W. Stanton, *The Leopard's Spots* (Chicago: University of Chicago Press, 1960) ; J. Wach, *Das Verstehen*, 3 vols. (Hildesheim: G. Olms, 1966 = 1926-33) ; R. Wellek, *A History of Modern Criticism: 1750-1950*, 4 vols. (New Haven: Yale University Press, 1955-1965) ; A. Wheeler, *Society History in*

Eighteenth-Century Scotland (Diss., Emory University, 1966); T. Willi, *Herder's Beitrag zum Verstehen des Alten Testaments* (Tübingen: J. C. B. Mohr, 1971); H. Wölfflin, *Principles of Art History* (New York: Henry Holt, 1932?).

The eighteenth century witnessed the victory of emphases on individuality, including personal freedom and the recognition of characteristic differences between men and nations. Such emphases had begun to play a significant role at the end of the Middle Ages, in the Renaissance and Reformation, and now flowered more fully. An important aspect of individuality was the denial of authority, either of an empire over a "nation" with its own language and cultural identity, or of an aristocracy within a society. Nationalism played a major role already during the Reformation; the growth of anti-aristocratic notions extended through the following centuries. The anti-authoritarian spirit led to a gradual turning from an orientation toward the past as norm to a future-oriented perspective, with a belief in progress.

In literary studies, such as of the bible, "historical criticism" came to be the key term. Different in many ways from other kinds of historical study, the newer approach had the following characteristics. It emphasized difference (even uniqueness), change, distance in time and character (Ebeling, 253; Knuth, 342). It aimed to be "objective," untrammeled by an authoritarian tradition. Sometimes its call for objectivity included the theme of self-denial by the investigator, an intellectual form of inner-worldly asceticism (Wach, I, 140, 161; II, 251, 328; III, 126-127). Interest in history and individuality was revealed also by creative literature and the visual arts (Wölfflin, 19, 233; Richardson, 45).

From a dominantly individualistic perspective, the study of genres was called into question or sharply revised. Traditional criticism had viewed genres as realistic "essences" and as "species," or subdivisions, of the whole of literature. Now it became normal to focus on individual items and to employ genres, if at all, in terms of convenient groupings of them (as formulated by John Locke, *Essay Concerning Human Understanding*, III, ch. 3, §20).

Genre discussions lost some of their traditional concerns. A major element of poetic theory had been classification according to subject matter in the light of the social status of the protagonists. The "aptness" of an expression—i.e., its appropriate relation to content—had been largely, though not entirely, discussed in such terms. These considerations became suspect or irrelevant. Of Aristotle's threefold classification of art, only two distinctions remained significant, namely, that based on "means" (language, rhythm, etc.) and the difference in "manner of representation" involved in epic (narration), drama, and lyric.

Those types that remained were not viewed as exclusive structures, to be applied precisely. Even ancient theory had not insisted on pure genres, although the ideal of purity had been discussed from time to time. Now combinations of different features could be frankly accepted or positively valued (Scherpe, 121-128, 161-169; cf. Wellek, I, 213-215, 251). Overall, critics and authors stood in rebellion against all rules for a work of art. As a result, genre theory become increasingly vague; after 1815, its usefulness was often rejected, and every work could be declared individual in character (Wellek, II).

An expressed key interest in some circles was "novelty," earlier decried by the author of *On the Sublime*. The important critic and promoter of industry, Lord Kames (*Elements of Criticism*, 1762, ch. 6), held novelty to be "the most powerful influence" for raising emotions; he noted approvingly that surprise awakens self-love. Recently, it has been recognized experimentally, as has long been known informally, that variety is necessary to stimulate an individual in a goal-oriented frame of mind, while for someone in a receptive mood even unchanging or continuing sensations stay alive (Ruch and Zimbardo, 410). It thus appears that interest in novelty is related to the emerging achievement orientation.

Lord Kames' point of view can serve as a symbol for an important complex, whose various facets were closely related. He was a member of a group of Scottish thinkers, including A. Smith, D. Hume, A. Ferguson, and W. Robertson, who furthered historiography in general and developmental theory in particular between 1750 and 1780, in partial contact with similiar movements elsewhere. Kames, in 1774, even attacked the idea of the unity of mankind and relegated some primitives (such as American Indians) to a different species, opening a discussion concerning racial distinctions that was to play a major role in the nineteenth century (Stanton). Adam Smith, influenced by Hume's skeptical psychology (Hasbach, 95), developed a model for a new economy. In general, the group held that conflict engendered by self-love leads to progress (Wheeler, 127; a picture of so-called bourgeois characteristics of egotism and continual

I

involvement in change was sharply drawn by K. Marx, who knew the work of this group).

Hume brought about a philosophical revolution on the basis of skepticism, one involving not merely procedure (Descartes) but, more specifically, beliefs concerning realities and their fundamental relationships. Such relativism of knowledge is contrary both to traditional feudal designs and to eschatological or egalitarian visions favoring the poor (cf. Mannheim). Hume placed his faith in the "middling rank of men" to secure property and liberty (1955, cii); Kames relied on the same group for the standards of good taste (*Criticism*, ch. 25). In Germany, Herder expressed a similar outlook (Barnard, 76) and advocated the new historiography as useful for an age dominated by commerce and education (IV, 483). Together with competitive self-assertion, there spread widely a sense of the disappearance of God from the world and of the absence of an ultimate order for society (Miller).

The authority of the bible, then, fared no better than did genre theory. Especially the OT with its legal structure was under a cloud of suspicion; this had been deepened through a rejection of Hebrew and Greek prohibitions of usury or interest (Nelson), partly under the leadership of pioneers in historical criticism. For instance, Voltaire had criticized religion for inhibiting commerce, industry, and the luxurious arts (Schwarzbach, 233). The role of the OT was seen largely in terms of a negative to be overcome or of an anticipation of subsequent events; its continued value for Christians was seriously questioned (see Bickermann, Kraus, and studies cited by them).

As Auerbach (59) has correctly pointed out, an older "figural" understanding of events lost ground. Individuals were now rarely seen as a reflection or impress of a more fundamental religious event or meaning. Some of the advances of biblical studies in the "historical" age are constituted by a reduction of the multiplicity of meanings sought. Thus Herder (in a view published 1778) interpreted the Song of Songs simply as love poetry, without application to a divine attitude.

Herder's work was still fairly strongly form critical, although in his writings genre terms are often quite fluid (cf. Kathan, 2, 93). His specific interpretation of the Song of Solomon was influenced by Opitz, who had divided the song into a series of poems. Like Opitz, Herder composed paraphrases of biblical materials (1771-73), including Ps 23 and parts of Habakkuk and Job. Indeed, his great work on the *Spirit of Hebrew Poetry* (1782-83) clearly bears the mark of a poet and literarily sensitive person. An interest in Asian and other cultures (cf. Willi) provided Herder with the comparative perspective which is almost a necessity for genre criticism.

In describing Hebrew poetry, Herder employs a considerable number of formal terms, not so much for differentiation into sharply separable classes as for characterization; genres can interpenetrate or move from one to another. He found picture speech, poetry about persons, fables, riddles, word play, joyful song, praise, victory songs, blessings, royal psalms, and national songs. Psalms are classed according to their complexity. In his preface to another work (1787) he grouped elegies according to concern about a general state of affairs, for particular problems, or for one's country (XII, 331-334).

Herder's analysis gives a fairly secular impression and makes little allowance for the basic religious dimensions that were outlined in earlier studies. An unpublished sketch from the year 1769 did furnish an extensive treatment of Gen 1:1-2:3, an "old oriental poem explaining the arrangement of the week from the creation of the world" (VI, 70). But it denied that this is a divine oracle about creation (VI, 74), giving credit instead to human insight. Later, in the *Spirit of Hebrew Poetry*, the tendency of Israel and of other ancient nations to derive everything from God is declared childish, contrary to the will and inquiry of man (XI, 361).

At the end of the eighteenth century, the concept of "myth" came to play a prominent role in OT studies, in part as a result of theories for Greek literature put forward by C. Heyne, professor of eloquence and classical philologist. Biblical scholars were aware that the term applied especially to accounts of the origin of the world or of mankind (notably W. Teller, in his edition of Turretin's lectures, 1776, 689). For Heyne, however, it meant an original form of literature, so that the term received a strongly historical flavor in writings by J. Eichhorn (since 1779), J. Gabler, and others.

Eichhorn spoke sometimes of genres, but in an extremely vague fashion. He tended to view expressive form as external, calling it a clothing, *Einkleidung*, of the word (Sehmsdorf, 63, 191). He was more interested in the questions of time and circumstance

I

of a writing; his student Gabler formulated in a famous work of 1787 the shift toward an historical perspective, in which biblical theology becomes independent of dogmatics. Herder and Eichhorn were followed rather closely by K. Stäudlin (1783, etc.; see Schmidt). For him also, form was a largely external matter.

An approximation, though not actualization, of genre criticism appeared thereafter in W. de Wette's writings, which were grounded in a broad acquaintance with the history of religion. His outlook was basically individualistic. "Every writing requires its own hermeneutic; it can be known and understood only in its own form" (*Kritik der israelitischen Geschichte*, 1807, 25). De Wette felt constrained to reject a formal-aesthetic division of the psalms by Augusti, since Hebrew poetry is "formless and special"; he declared that similarities are due to "imitation" and thus not truly poetic (*Commentar über die Psalmen*, 1829, 4, 16-18). Instead he listed psalms by groups, not considered as genres, according to "contents": hymns honoring God, national psalms, Zion and temple songs, supplicating and plaintive psalms, religious odes (Pss 23, 91, etc.), and didactic poems.

A different classification of psalms according to their "subjects" was outlined by T. Horne, *An Introduction to the Critical Study and Knowledge of the Holy Scriptures*, 1818–. It involves "prayers," psalms of "thanksgiving," "praise and adoration," those which are "instructive," "more eminently and directly prophetical," and "historical" psalms. E. Hengstenberg (*Commentar über die Psalmen*, 1842–.) furnished a grouping according to mood: joyful, sad, and calm (or contemplative, i.e., didactic). In this, he was followed by K. Keil (*Lehrbuch*, 1859²) and S. Davidson (editor of Horne's tenth edition, 1856). Another classification, according to content and usage, was presented by I. Taylor, *The Spirit of Hebrew Poetry*, 1861. All of these authors were fairly conservative in their outlook.

For aesthetic treatments of biblical literature during the middle of the nineteeth century one must look largely to presentations outside the main stream of historico-critical scholarship. They include J. Wenrich, *De poeseos Hebraicae atque Arabicae*, 1842, applying classical categories (Alonso-Schökel, 25-26), and G. Gilfillan, *The Bards of the Bible*, 1851 (published also under the title *The Poets and Poetry of the Bible*, 1853). Gilfillan, author of many studies of English literature, declared that "the proof of great thoughts is, will they translate into

I

figured and sensuous expression?" (1851, 42). As he saw it, to the Hebrew poet "the poetical and the religious were almost the same" (56). He divided Hebrew poetry into two main classes (65): the Song, subdivided according to mood, and the Poetical Statement, ordered by content. Closer to current OT scholarship stood various works by the orientalist H. Ewald, who had an interest in coherence and literary characteristics.

Discontent about the scholarly state of affairs was expressed in 1856 by E. Meier, a professor of Near Eastern languages and literatures. While valuing the new freedom of thought and the recognition of differences, he deplored a lack of attention to the complete nature of man, including aesthetic and social aspects. With the partial exception of de Wette's work, OT introductions contain "an inorganic, arbitrary collection of learned memoranda" (*Geschichte der poetischen National-Literatur der Hebräer*, iii, v, xv-xvi). Therefore he sought to combine two facets in his study: a historical side, with relations to concrete conditions and to laws of development, and an aesthetic side, continuing the work of Lowth and Herder (viii). Meier did not furnish genre analyses as such, but discussed poetic forms at appropriate points in his history. He observed, for instance, that prophetic literature, like didactic poetry in general, includes a mixture of lyric, satiric, narrative, and instructional forms (248).

In 1865, a *Gymnasium* teacher, C. Ehrt, presented as part of the graduation program of his school (the average age of the graduates being about 22) an analysis of Hebrew poetry according to its "matter" or type of concern (*Versuch einer Darstellung der hebräischen Poesie nach Beschaffenheit ihrer Stoffe*). Its genres include secular and religious types; nature poetry combines secular and sacred aspects. The author left for another occasion an analysis of the poetry according to its "forms"; what that may have meant for him is unclear. H. Gunkel later mentioned the work of both Meier and Ehrt as partial anticipations of his own approach (1906, 101).

The achievements of the "century of history" were considerable, both in historiography and in developmental theory. Even genre criticism did not die out, although several of the more significant studies (by Hegel, Uhland [see below, p. 51], and others) were published posthumously. The significance of this period should not be denied; one needs to incorporate its contributions while going beyond them.

VI. RENEWAL OF INTEREST IN FORM

A. The General Situation

A. Aarne, *Verzeichnis der Märchentypen* (Helsinki: Soumalaisen tiedeaka-temian toimituksia, 1910) ; R. Arnheim, *Entropy and Art* (Berkeley: University of California Press, 1971) ; A. Bastian, *Ethnologische Forschungen*, I (Jena: H. Costenoble, 1871) ; E. Bernheim, *Lehrbuch der historischen Methode* (Leipzig: Duncker & Humblot, 1908[5]) ; R. Boggs, "Types and Classification of Folklore," *Funk & Wagnalls Standard Dictionary of Folklore, Mythology and Legend*, II (New York: Funk & Wagnalls, 1950) ; K. Bücher, *Arbeit und Rhythmus* (Leipzig: Hirzel, 1896) ; J. Buckley, *The Triumph of Time* (Cambridge: Harvard University Press, 1966) ; M. Bunge, *Causality* (Cambridge: Harvard University Press, 1959) ; E. Cassirer, *The Logic of the Humanities* (New Haven: Yale University Press, 1961) ; L. Coser, *Georg Simmel* (Englewood Cliffs: Prentice-Hall, 1965) ; D. Daube, *Forms of Roman Legislation* (London: Oxford University Press, 1956) ; A. Daur, *Das alte deutsche Volkslied* (Berlin: E. Felber, 1902: Leipzig: Quelle & Meyer, 1909) ; W. Dilthey, *Gesammelte Schriften*, V (Stuttgart: B. G. Teubner, 1957) ; I. Ehrenpreis, *The "Types Approach" to Literature* (New York: King's Crown Press, 1945) ; J. Firth, "Personality and Language in Society," *SR* XLII (1950) 37-52; H. Friedmann, *Die Welt der Formen* (Munich: C. H. Beck, 1930[2]) ; N. Frye, *Anatomy of Criticism*; R. Funk, "Saying and Seeing: Phenomenology of Language and the New Testament," *JBR* XXXIV (1966) 197-213; G. Gomme, ed., *The Handbook of Folklore* (London: D. Nutt, for the Folklore Society, 1890) ; M. Hamburger, *Das Form-Problem in der neueren deutschen Asthetik und Kunsttheorie* (Heidelberg: C. Winter, 1915) ; J. Harrison, *Ancient Art and Ritual* (New York: Henry Holt, 1913) ; K. Hartmann, *Sartres Sozialphilosophie* (Berlin: Walter de Gruyter, 1966) ; D. Hymes, ed., "The Ethnography of Communication," *AA* LXVI (1964) 6/2; B. Jarcho, "Organi-sche Struktur des russischen Schnaderhüpfels (Castuska)", *Germano-Slavica* III (1937) 31-64: A. Jolles, *Einfache Formen* (Halle: Max Niemeyer, 1930) ; W. Kayser, *Das sprachliche Kunstwerk* (Bern: A. Francke, 1948) ; G. Kubler, *The Shape of Time* (New Haven: Yale University Press, 1962) ; B. Küppers, *Die Theorie vom Typischen in der Literatur* (Munich: Sagner, 1966) ; B. Malinowski, *Myth in Primitive Psychology* (New York: Norton & Co., 1926) ; M. McLuhan, *The Gutenberg Galaxy* (Toronto: University of Toronto Press, 1962) ; K. Menger, *Die Irrtümer des Historismus in der deutschen National-ökonomie* (Vienna: A. Hölder, 1884) ; F. Nietzsche, *Philologica*, II (*Werke*, XVIII; Leipzig: A. Kröner, 1912) ; J. Piaget, *Le Structuralisme* (Paris: Presses Universitaires de France, 1968) ; *idem, Structuralism*, tr. and ed. by C. Masch-ler, 1970 (New York: Basic Books, 1970) ; K. Pike, *Language in Relation to a Unified Theory of the Structure of Human Behavior* (JLSM 24, The Hague: Mouton & Co., 1967[2]) ; E. Rose, *A History of German Literature* (New York: New York University Press, 1960) ; G. Rousseau, ed., *Organic Form: The Life of an Idea* (London: Routledge & Kegan Paul, 1972) ; J. Royce, *Studies of Good and Evil* (New York: D. Appleton, 1898) ; W. Ruttkow-ski, *Die literarischen Gattungen* (Munich: Francke, 1968) ; F. de Saussure, *Cours de linguistique général* (Paris: Payot, 1916) = *Course in General Linguistics*, tr. by W. Baskin (New York: Philosophical Library, 1959) ; M. Scheler, *The Nature of Sympathy*, tr. by P. Heath (London: Routledge & Kegan Paul, 1954 [first German ed., 1913]) ; F. Schevill, *Six Historians* (Chicago: University of Chicago Press, 1956) ; P. Selz, *et al., Art Nouveau* (New York: Doubleday, 1960) ; G. Simmel, *Die Probleme der Geschichtsphilosophie* (Leipzig: Duncker & Humblot, 1892, 1922[4]); *idem, Lebensanschauung* (Leipzig: Duncker & Humblot, 1918) ; *idem, Sociology of Religion*, tr. by C. Rosenthal

(New York: Philosophical Library, 1959); S. Thompson, *The Types of the Folk-Tale* (Helsinki: Suomalainen tiedeakatemian toimituksia, 1928); A. Weber, *Der dritte oder der vierte Mensch* (Munich: R. Piper, 1953); R. Weimann, "Past Significance and Present Meaning in Literary History," NLH I (1969/70) 91-109; R. Wellek, *A History of Modern Criticism IV: The Later Nineteenth Century* (New Haven: Yale University Press, 1965); A. Whitehead, "Mathematics and the Good," in P. Schilpp, ed., *The Philosophy of Alfred North Whitehead* (Evanston: Northwestern University, 1941) 666-681; L. Whyte, ed., *Aspects of Form* (Bloomington: Indiana University Press, 1951); W. Worringer, *Abstraction and Empathy*, tr. by M. Bullock (London: Routledge & Kegan Paul, 1953).

During the last two decades of the nineteenth century and thereafter, a profound change in outlook took place, embracing virtually all fields of endeavor and extending throughout most of Europe and America. It involved deep dissatisfaction with the kind of historical orientation that had become dominant about a century earlier. Some of the reaction was elitist in spirit, while other movements sought a more popular form of culture; both sides were critical of the "bourgeoisie." In general, the criticism of prior attitudes was moderate enough to seek supplementation rather than rejection of the work of the preceding years. Under certain conditions during the twentieth century, however, aversion became so strong as to lead to denial of earlier achievements. The newly popular key terms were "form," "structure," and "function" (cf. Piaget).

Probably the most important factor was the increasing human interdependence made necessary and possible by technology (Weber, 214; McLuhan, 253). Together with this went a disenchantment with overemphasis on individuality. The wisdom of the old adage *individuum est ineffabile*, the purely individual cannot be meaningfully expressed, was again respected. Early in the nineteeth century, F. Schleiermacher had called on "divination" to establish contact with another person; now it was recognized that society and language are prior to the individual and that in some ways knowledge of another precedes knowledge of oneself (Royce, 1898, 201; Scheler). For an understanding it is necessary to have general categories; thus in the study of literature, and also of art and music, there began (about 1890) a turn to "science" or *Wissenschaft*, i.e., the construction of principles and the recognition of human processes, including those that are not fully conscious. The notion of separate substances, implying clearly delimited units, was widely dropped in favor of a vision of patterns.

The optimistic notion of gradual progress came under attack.

The phenomenon of evolutionary change—generally from simplicity to complexity—was now fairly well established, but one could ask whether change is equivalent to improvement. The new tensions within society and the effects of a division of labor on individuals did not favor a simple optimism (Buckley, 54-58). Darwin's theory of natural selection (1859) supported an evolutionary perspective as such but undermined its moral character. Self-criticism led to renewed questioning of an attitude which regards other cultures or groups as below one's own in value and subject to colonization. Such reflections extended also to the field of religion, especially after recognition, in the latter portion of the nineteeth century, of the role of primitive high gods.

The change in outlook involved literary and visual arts, on the one hand, and natural sciences and mathematics, on the other. In fact, these two extremes stood in close relationship—not surprisingly, since mathematics (as has increasingly been recognized) is the study of formal structures or the science of patterns (cf. Whitehead). The Second Law of Thermodynamics led to the widely held conclusion that the universe would ultimately run down; this contributed, together with other considerations already mentioned, to an ahistorical mood during the 1890's in the arts and other fields (Arnheim, 9; Scheville, 157-177). Both technology and primitive art were valued by many artists; by some, a distinction between "fine art" and usefulness was considered a bourgeois aberration (Selz, 12-14; Kubler, 14). At the same time, reactions against mechanistic versions of science and technology rallied under the banner of "form" (Cassirer, 71). Thus "form," as earlier in Goethe's "morphology," became the theme which united science and art (cf. Whyte; Rousseau; Friedmann, 405).

A key aspect of form involves relationship, particularly the interrelationship between the parts of a whole. The totality is commonly called a "structure"; the word "form" is best used to designate the emergent characteristics of the whole, which are dependent on the features of the parts but can be quite different from them. As was realized at the end of the century (e.g., by A. Hildebrand in aesthetics, in pragmatic and other philosophies) and even more later, form and structure are not purely "objective," but relate to an observer; the latter must select the whole and determine the significant parts, while features themselves are expressions of perceptions. Within the field of history, considerable attention came to be given to history writing as a literary form. At the same time, it became clear that human consciousness and subjectivity are never independent of the world and of the body (including sexuality). Thus the ascetic subject-object split, a problem for two centuries, was largely overcome.

The grasping of dynamic form came to be known as "understanding." It centers on the coherence of a pattern related to a goal (Dilthey, 201, 207, 318, 332; similarly, M. Weber and T. Parsons). Some have argued that such understanding is different from the operation of the natural sciences; but it can be pointed out that notions of causality within the latter were being reconceived (cf. Bunge, 333; Weimann, 95-96). Especially if one acknowledges human participation in mathematics, differences between the sciences may well be a matter of degree, related to the level of consciousness of the realities examined. A contrasting of the humanities and arts to other aspects of life was often connected with elitist or conservative attitudes, in part derived from Nietzsche; the lack of such contrast was associated, in actuality and in the image of opponents, with socialism (Wellek, IV, 319, 410, 435, 443, 458; Rose, 284-289; Bernheim, preface). In the humanities and especially in the sciences, the word "function" could designate the dynamic aspect of patterns.

Understanding in a broad sense, namely, the explication of patterns both static and dynamic, became the central interest of philosophy, in both the "phenomenological" and the "analytic" movements. The former has had a considerable association with Catholicism and certainly transcends individualism. While Husserl dealt strictly with the content of consciousness, other phenomenologists have turned to the "pre-conceptual, pre-reflexive substructures of consciousness " (Funk, 200). A strength of phenomenology, with its search for "essences" or fundamental characteristics, has been its application to a number of fields and problems. The phenomenology of religion, however, is only indirectly related to the philosophical movement and dates back to 1887 (introduced by Chantepie de la Saussaye). Heidegger dealt with "fundamental ontology," the basic structure of reality. The "analytical" movement (which includes Wittgenstein quoted above, p. 2) grew out of philosophical approaches deeply concerned with structure and relations (e.g., in B. Russell's work), formalized and thus made clear by symbolic logic.

A crucial phase of the reorientation at the end of the nineteeth century lay in the rise of the social and behavioral sciences, bridging the traditional division between nature and spirit. They deserve special attention.

As is well known, the foundations of scientific psychology were laid by W. Wundt and W. James during the decades after 1860. Vienna proved to be a center for advance in this area. Here F. Brentano (teacher of Husserl, who also learned from James) sought to develop a "descriptive psychology" relating man's consciousness to its world, and E. Mach began a revolution in scientific philosophy by drawing together the seemingly disparate areas of physics and psychology. In the same city a few years later, Freud and his circle (almost entirely Jewish) faced and accepted both the natural and the repressed unconscious of man. Subsequently, under other circumstances, the phenomena of "fields" and "structures" that appeared in physics led to the formulation of *Gestalt* and dynamic field psychologies. (More recent develoments cannot be recounted here.)

Sociology developed in close conjunction with religious and reformist political factors. Jews, including the founders E. Durkheim and G. Simmel, played a particularly prominent role. Those operating in an academic setting were rarely radical but favored moderate reforms; e.g., Durkheim was the fountainhead of the so-called "solidarist" school of political philosophy in France. Simmel, despite an officially humble role because of discrimination, had an electrifying impact in Berlin and beyond (Coser, 3-5, 38; Worringer, ix) ; thus Gunkel, who developed his form critical principles while teaching at the same university, must at least have heard of him. Simmel questioned the objectivity of historiography (since 1892) and held that for different "forms of life" there are different "truths" according to the form's "function" (1918, 55) . In opposition to the notion of art for art's sake, he saw form as arising from "life" and returning to shape life. A major theme in his "formal" sociological analysis was reciprocity, though not necessarily of a harmonious sort. (This theme has become important for Sartre's ethics; cf. Hartmann, 78.) Religion, in his view, is based on equality, rather than on differentiation or competition (1959, 61) .

The study of so-called primitives in anthropology was then being put on a more scientific basis in data collection and theory. Probably the most important pioneer for the new anthropology was A. Bastian, professor of ethnology at Berlin and an avid traveler. His program, in partial opposition to a search for the historical diffusion of ideas, called for a comparative mythology, in which variations of content are related to their circumstances. He credited primitives with greater "ethical strength" than that possessed by moderns, because the attainment of harmony is easier in a simple society (1871, c). A more popular and better-known study of simple culture—one of Gunkel's favorites—was that by K. Bücher on work songs (*Arbeit und Rhythmus,* 1896, and later editions). The author, professor of economics, came to that topic through his observation that modern men and women do not enjoy their work, especially in factories. He opposed the view that slavery has been a useful institution in educating men to engage in the unpleasant jobs necessary for civilization and hoped that art and technology may yet find a way to unite with each other.

The use of the word "historicism," as a derogatory term for a one-sided concern with the accumulation of descriptive data, apparently originated with the economist K. Menger (in Vienna), who wished to formulate general laws (1884). Already before then, Léon Walras in Switzerland developed an economic "equilibrium" theory, distinguished by the concept of the mutual influence of factors, as in physical equilibria. Similar types of economic theory were developed in England by S. Jevons and A. Marshall during the same period. The economic theorists mentioned, like many others of their day, urged varying degrees of limitation of private capitalism.

The two axes of historical sequence and mutual interaction were labeled "diachronic" and "synchronic" by the great linguist F. de Saussure, whose lectures were published posthumously in 1916. (The final formulation, at least, was aware of the developments in economic theory.) The work is widely known because of its clear terminology and sharp formulations. A linguistic sign is described as a relation between an arbitrary (i.e., conventional) signifier to the signified; the combination of sound and thought produces a form, not a substance (1959, 113). Relations are crucial for all aspects: "language is a system of interdependent terms in which the value of each term results solely from the simultaneous presence of the others" (114). Generalizations applying to any language he labeled "panchronic."

While some linguists, such as Saussure, abstracted language from its concrete role in human life, other investigators pointed to the interaction of speech with its cultural and sociological situation. P. Wegener had furnished in 1885 a systematic formulation of a situational approach to language, with attention primarily to individual occasions. Several decades later, B. Malinowski (who had studied under Wundt and Bücher) and J. Firth extended the theory to deal both with individual contexts and with types of situation. Firth suggested, for instance, that one ask about a sentence: "What is the minimum number of participants?," "Where might it happen?," "What are the relevant objects?," or "What is the effect of the sentence?" (1950, 43). In systematic fashion, K. Pike's theory of language (1967[2]) — which grew out of an involvement in bible translation for small tribes—includes formal attention to "behavioremes," typical units of behavior, with integral regard to their societal and physical situation. A recent movement in the "ethnography of communication" (Hymes) is bridging the gap between linguistics and folklore in a manner reminiscent of, and useful for, biblical form criticism.

The study of folklore advanced rapidly at the end of the nineteenth century. Not surprisingly, such literature was treated largely by genres, especially since individual authors were not known, although extensive study earlier in the century had overthrown the notion of a spontaneous group production. G. Gomme prepared a cross-cultural classification for the use of the Folk-Lore Society; more elaborate classifications followed in later years, with attention to both manner and content (e.g., Boggs). Very narrow "types" of folktales, according to content, were listed by A. Aarne, 1910 (used by Gunkel), and, in revised form, by S. Thompson, 1928. Analyzing a single culture, A. Daur showed (in 1902 and 1909) that popular German songs, including love poems, were heavily stylized in themes and expressions, in contradiction to theories valuing uniqueness. Clear relations between content and situation were dramatically presented by B. Malinowski when he showed that myth, legend (or historical account), and fairy tale occur in a single primitive community, with differences in occasion and function (1926). Using statistical procedures, B. Jarcho in Moscow (1937) has demonstrated a correlation between theme and syntax. Ben-Amos' full definition of a genre, including content, expression, and context (1969, cf. above, p. 1), may have been stimulated by OT scholarship, with which he shows some familiarity.

In the field of general literature, genre concepts regained some popularity. In the United States, literary types were widely seen in a nonevolutionary framework and were a favorite teaching device for some decades after 1895 (Ehrenpreis, 55). A number of German critics have dealt with genres, especially since 1923 (cf. Kayser, Ruttkowski). A leading role in the analysis of form and genres was played (since 1914) by O. Walzel, who edited the series to which J. Hempel contributed his form critical survey of Israelite literature in 1930. A number of discussions have centered around the human character of lyric, epic, dramatic, and (with variations) didactic forms. Probably more useful are descriptions of specific genres (fable, legend, hymn, etc.), such as by A. Jolles (1930), whose work has enjoyed a major impact on OT studies. Marxist theory has emphasized "types" of characters and situations; thus genres could be viewed as "typical life-facts," namely repeated relations between man and society (Küppers, 328). A rich system, with several dimensions, has been developed by N. Frye (1957); it includes discussions of heroic levels, archetypes of mood and content, and presentational types.

The relevance of genre analysis for classical literature has, of course, long been recognized. Interest in classical rhetoric and in the forms of Greco-Roman literature was quite strong in the decades before and after the turn of the century. One stimulus for such study came from Nietzsche (although his lectures on classical genres were not published until 1912). His friend E. Rohde, for instance, played an early role in the new wave of interest (1876); yet, since similar studies emanated from other circles, the general movement cannot be attributed to a single source. Considerable interest was raised by Jane Harrison's studies (e.g., 1913) relating Greek genres and other aspects of art to religious rituals. D. Daube's study of Roman law forms (1956) was probably triggered by biblical studies, to which he has actively contributed.

It would be an error to draw an altogether sharp contrast between the moods of different periods. Perhaps especially the greatest figures are fairly well balanced in their perspectives. The more sober spirits of the twentieth century incorporated individual and evolutionary considerations into their work, just as earlier historiographers and philosophers of history had made interactional and even universal observations. Yet the emphases differed. Appreciation for the concerns both of the OT and of Greece rose again, although accompanied by a sense that the world has changed since the ancient period. In the light of this reorientation one can understand the new movement of biblical form criticism.

B. The Rise of Modern Form Criticism

L. Abbott, *The Life and Literature of the Ancient Hebrews* (Boston: Houghton, Mifflin, & Co., 1901) ; L. Alonso-Schökel, "Die stilistische Analyse bei den Propheten," *VTS* VII (1960) 154-164; M. Arnold, *Literature and Dogma* (New York: Macmillan, 1883) ; *idem, God and the Bible* (New York: Macmillan, 1901); C. Beyer, *Deutsche Poetik*, II (Berlin: Behr, 1914⁴ = 1886²); F. Bowen, *A Layman's Study of the English Bible* (New York: C. Scribner's Sons, 1885) ; F. Brown, "Introduction," in *Old Testament and Semitic Studies in Memory of William Rainey Harper*, I (Chicago: University of Chicago Press, 1908) xiii-xxxiv; J. Burtchaell, *Catholic Theories of Biblical Inspiration Since 1810* (London: Cambridge University Press, 1969) ; D. Cassel, *Geschichte der Jüdischen Literatur* I (Berlin: L. Gerschel, 1872) ; *idem, Die Armenverwaltung im alten Israel* (Berlin: C. Müller, 1887) ; H. Cohen, *Jüdische Schriften*, I (Berlin: Schwetschke, 1924) ; S. Curry, *Vocal and Literary Interpretation of the Bible* (New York: Hodder & Stoughton, 1903) ; A. Dieterich, *Eine Mithrasliturgie* (Leipzig: B. G. Teubner, 1903) ; D. Dinsmore, *The English Bible as Literature* (Boston: Houghton, Mifflin, & Co., 1931) ; C. Eberhardt, *The Bible in the Making of Ministers* (New York: Association Press, 1949) ; J. Genung, *The Epic of the Inner Life, Being the Book of Job* (Boston: Houghton, Mifflin, & Co., 1891) ; *idem, Ecclesiastes, Words of Koheleth* (Boston: Houghton, Mifflin, & Co., 1904) ; *idem, A Guidebook to the Biblical Literature* (Boston: Ginn & Co., 1919) ; A. Gercke and E. Norden, eds., *Einleitung in die Altertumswissenschaft*, I (Leipzig: B. G. Teubner, 1910) ; R. Girdlestone, *The Grammar of Prophecy* (London: Eyre & Spottiswoode, 1901) ; H. Graetz, *Kritischer Commentar zu den Psalmen*, I (Breslau: S. Schottlaender, 1882) ; H. Gressmann, *Albert Eichhorn und die religionsgeschichtliche Schule* (Göttingen: Vandenhoeck & Ruprecht, 1914) ; H. Gunkel, *Die Wirkungen des Heiligen Geistes: Eine biblisch-theologische Studie* (Göttingen: Vandenhoeck & Ruprecht, 1888) ; *idem, Schöpfung und Chaos in Urzeit und Endzeit* (Göttingen: Vandenhoeck & Ruprecht, 1895) ; *idem, Genesis* (*HKAT* I/1, Göttingen: Vandenhoeck & Ruprecht, 1901); *idem,* "Die israelitische Literatur" (1906, 1925²); *idem, Die Religionsgeschichte und die alttestamentliche Wissenschaft* (Berlin: Protestantischer Schriftenvertrieb, 1910) ; *idem, Ausgewählte Psalmen* (Göttingen: Vandenhoeck & Ruprecht, 1911³) ; *idem, Reden und Aufsätze* (Göttingen: Vandenhoeck & Ruprecht, 1913) ; *idem, Die Propheten* (Göttingen: Vandenhoeck & Ruprecht, 1917) ; *idem, Die Psalmen* (Göttingen: Vandenhoeck & Ruprecht, 1926) ; *idem, What Remains of the Old Testament and Other Essays*, tr. by A. K. Dallas (New York: Macmillan, 1928) ; *idem, Einleitung in die Psalmen*, completed by J. Begrich (Göttingen: Vandenhoeck & Ruprecht, 1933) ; M. Hamburger, *Das Form-Problem*; F. von Hummelauer, *Exegetisches zur Inspirationsfrage* (Freiburg: Herder, 1904) ; M. Kähler, *Der sogenannte historische Jesus und der geschichtliche, biblische Christus* (Leipzig: A. Deichert, 1892) = *The So-Called Historical Jesus and the Historic, Biblical Christ*, tr. by C. Braaten (Philadelphia: Fortress Press, 1964) ; *idem, Zur Bibelfrage* (Gütersloh: Bertelsmann, 1937) ; C. Kent, *The Wise Men of Ancient Israel and Their Proverbs* (New York: Silver, Burdett & Co., 1895); *idem, The Messages of Israel's Lawgivers* (New York: Charles Scribner's Sons, 1902); *idem, The Student's Old Testament*, 6 vols. (New York: Charles Scribner's Sons, 1904-1927) , I: *Narratives of the Beginnings of Hebrew History* (1904) ; *idem, The Origin and Permanent Value of the Old Testament* (Boston: Pilgrim Press, 1906); *idem, The Social Teachings of the Prophets and Jesus* (New York: Charles Scribner's Sons, 1917) ; *idem, The Growth and Contents of the Old Testament* (New York: Charles Scribner's Sons, 1925) ; W. Klatt, *Hermann Gunkel* (FRLANT 100, Göttingen: Vandenhoeck & Ruprecht, 1969); T. Kuhn, *The Structure of Scientific Revolutions* (Chicago: University of Chicago Press,

1970²) ; H. Kuist, *These Words Upon Thy Heart* (Richmond, Va.: John Knox Press, 1947) ; S. Leathes, *The Structure of the Old Testament* (Philadelphia: Smith, English, & Co., 1873) ; R. Moulton, *Shakespeare as a Dramatic Artist* (Oxford: Clarendon Press, 1885, 1897³) ; *idem, The Literary Study of the Bible* (Boston: D. C. Heath, 1895, 1899²) ; *idem, The Modern Reader's Bible* (New York: Macmillan, 1895) ; *idem, A Short Introduction to the Literature of the Bible* (Boston: D. C. Heath, 1901) ; *idem, World Literature and Its Place in General Culture* (New York: Macmillan, 1911) ; W. Moulton, *Richard Green Moulton* (New York: Macmillan, 1926) ; S. Muños-Iglesias, *Los Generos literanos y la interpretacion de la Biblia* (Madrid: Casa de la Biblia, 1968) ; J. Orr, *Revelation and Inspiration* (New York: Charles Scribner's Sons, 1910) ; K. von Rabenau, "Hermann Gunkel auf rauhen Pfaden nach Halle," *EvTh* 30 (1970) 433-444; B. Ramm, *Special Revelation and the Word of God* (Grand Rapids: Wm. B. Eerdmans, 1961) ; L. Sweet, *The Study of the English Bible* (New York: Association Press, 1914) ; M. Tetz, "Über die Formengeschichte in der Kirchengeschichte," *TZ* XVII (1961) 413-431; R. Traina, *Methodical Bible Study: A New Approach to Hermeneutics* (New York: Ganis & Harris, 1952) ; L. Uhland, *Alte hoch- und niederdeutsche Volkslieder*, III: *Abhandlung über die deutschen Volkslieder* (Stuttgart: J. Cotta, n.d.) ; W. Wundt, *Völkerpsychologie*, II: *Mythus und Religion*, I (Leipzig: W. Engelmann, 1905) .

The general reorientation at the end of the nineteeth century had an especially striking manifestation in OT studies. A number of similar movements sprang up simultaneously in different contexts, involving a variety of religious traditions in several countries. The similarities between the various groups are often remarkable.

In 1872, D. Cassel presented an aesthetically sensitive history of Israelite literature as the first part of a comprehensive survey of Jewish literature. (Gunkel acknowledged it as a partial precursor of his approach; 1906, 49.) While not advancing the field substantially in a technical sense, the work would be useful even today as a meaningful introduction. Cassel's social involvement can be seen in a short, but incisive study of the care for the poor in ancient Israel (1887) with implications for political issues of his own day; his thesis stresses enablement—for instance through interest-free loans, not merely alms. Another Jewish scholar, H. Graetz, used the term "genres" (*Gattungen*) for groups of psalms (1882) . He recognized three major genres: laments, hymns, and didactic psalms. Four further genres (bringing the total to seven) act as subdivisions of the three major ones: request and penitence, thanksgiving, and reprimand (*Rüge*) . He noted that laments and prayers occur also in hymns (13) and that the reprimands resemble prophetic speech. Cutting across the divisions are distinctions between a focus on individuals, the nation, or the king (14-15) .

I

The notable Jewish philosopher H. Cohen held that *Gestalt* (pattern) is the "unity of body and soul," in which form and content are identical (cf. Hamburger, 93). In an essay on the style of the prophets (written 1901) he treated the content and style of this "literary type" (263) in a completely inseparable manner. "Their style designates the relation between religion and ethics" (264) ; love is a basic element of their style, although anger—sometimes in jarring proximity—also plays a major role (272-274). "The end of days," he explains, "is the end of those days which are not the days of God" (272) ; the prophetic style, he concludes, has created the ideal of world history.

The Neo-Thomist, generally Aristotelian, outlook dominant in the Catholic church after the Council of Trent aided the formulation of a genre theory by P. Lagrange in relation to the question of inspiration (*RB* V [1896] 496-518; etc.). He drew on St. Thomas' view, which located direct revelation only in prophetic literature, while other biblical writers employed reason "inspired" by God, and found an antecedent in Cajetan's acceptance of certain nonliteral interpretations (early in the sixteenth century). Lagrange, with a personal aesthetic bent, distinguished between edifying fiction, imaginatively embellished historical accounts, and origin stories. His program was carried out in greater detail by F. von Hummelauer (1904), with primary attention to narrative forms. Hummelauer made use of E. Meyer's observation that classical historiography included consciously imaginative elements, such as the construction of speeches; he defended a comparison of such a style with that of Hebrew narration on the basis of ancient writers' having already pointed to the similarity in type (14-18).

The critical study of literary forms was ended under a new pope in 1905 (cf. Burtchaell, 146) but was revived by the encyclical *Divino Afflante Spiritu* in 1943. Since then, Catholic scholarship in the area of genre criticism, as well as of other aspects of literary criticism, has been quite extensive. An important stimulus has come from the Spanish literary figure L. Alonso-Schökel, who adopted OT study as an additional interest. (For a survey, see Muños-Iglesias.)

In a predominantly Protestant tradition, Matthew Arnold, professor of poetry at Oxford, attempted a literary approach to the bible in 1883 (and again in 1901). His primary emphasis was on content, more specifically on the thrust or kind of content to be found in literature; he characterized literature as "a criticism of life." His analysis finds that "the word and thought of righteousness" fills the OT (1883, 23). The word "God" receives a functional definition in the light of the literature within which it appears; it designates "the not ourselves which makes for righteousness" (46).

Following Arnold, R. G. Moulton held that literature deals with "Life" in an unspecialized sense; therefore, he believed, all forms of literature—including the frivolous—require attention (W. Moulton, 35). He played an important role in a major movement which extended university education throughout England and the United States, in a democratizing effort to include "poorer" persons (20) and women. The study of literature had for him a scientific character in that it is "inductive"; but unlike other sciences, which deal with only one aspect of life, it is integrative. To accomplish integration, literary study must have a universal perspective. Moulton covered a number of literatures, almost always for the benefit of a general audience; his most extensive writing, however, was devoted to the genres of biblical literature (1895, etc.).

Moulton characterized his procedure of "literary morphology" as "the inquiry into the foundation forms of literature"; he held that it is particularly applicable to the scriptures since a long oral transmission and the prevalence of floating literature make a reconstruction of its individual sources virtually impossible (1899, v, 98). The method's "underlying principle is that a clear grasp of outer literary form is an essential guide to the inner matter and spirit" (1899, vi). While accepting the major results of historical criticism, Moulton argued that the value of writings is independent of their date and that dating is often quite uncertain. The literary study of the bible appeared to be "a common meeting ground" of the conservatively devout, the liberal, and the skeptic (1899, iv). His primary interest lay in a firsthand reading and appreciation of the texts.

It is impossible to summarize briefly the wealth of Moulton's observations. The combination of styles characteristic of prophecy he termed "rhapsody"; very short oracular sayings which lie side by side in some prophetic books are characterized as "sentences" which can be united in "cycles." Deuteronomy contains "spoken rhetoric" and the epistles, "written rhetoric." The word "idyl" applies to Ruth and other works because of their "homely" subject matter. Wisdom literature is considered a form of "philosophy."

I

At about the same time (1901), a genre analysis, or "grammar," of prophecy was presented by a conservative scholar in England, R. Girdlestone. His comprehensive survey of styles, recurrent formulas, and patterns of speech includes the observation that "the future is expressed in terms of the past" (Creation, Sodom and Gomorrah, Exodus, David, etc.; 66-73). A little earlier, the American S. Leathes had discussed the "structure of the OT" (1873), namely the different roles played by the historic, prophetic, poetic, and legal elements. Such an analysis is fundamentally in line with traditional approaches to the bible. More advanced in its historical sense, though standing basically in the same tradition, was the insight of the Scottish professor J. Orr that biblical literature appears in many genres, including even that of legend (1910). More recently, similar insights have emerged in conservative American circles (especially, Ramm, 1961).

Writings somewhat similar to Moulton's appeared in the United States. Francis Bowen, author of a considerable number of volumes in philosophy and history, published in 1885 a sensitive treatment of biblical literature under the headings of narratives, parables, philosophy, poetry, history, and institutions. The union of content and expression can be seen, for instance, in the following statement: "This sympathy with all living things, but especially with the weak, the needy, and the unfortunate, is the source of what is tender and pathetic in Hebrew poetry" (101). J. Genung, author of handbooks on rhetoric, discussed in 1891 "the epic of the inner life," namely Job. Later he wrote on other aspects of wisdom and produced a general survey of biblical genres (1919). He called his spirit "constructive, as distinguished from the purely critical" (1904, vii).

Influenced by Moulton, Genung, and biblical scholars like G. A. Smith, L. Abbott presented a moving account of the religion of Israel according to literary types (1901). His theology was strongly incarnational (seeing "God as dwelling in matter," 11); literary analysis he founded on "the theological assumption that God's revelation is in and through a human experience" (17). He proceeded largely by types but also emphasized the evolutionary side. Since "literature is an interpretation of life" (201), he treated content (including concern for the poor and oppressed) as an integral and central part of the literature. Literary genres played a considerable role in S. Curry's guide to the vocal and literary interpretation of the bible (1903). The reason is that, for effective rendering of a text, the reader "must link his soul in unity with the aspirations, the sorrows, and joys of his kind. He must appreciate the universal forms, which in every age and clime have been the necessary expression of human feeling. He must relive the truth" (57). Vocal interpretation, such as the public reading during a church service, Curry regarded as the "climax of true literary study," in agreement with the principle, stated by A. von Humboldt, that "the real word is spoken" (56).

In 1894, Moulton was brought to the University of Chicago by W. R. Harper, notable OT critic and first president of that university. At least since 1887, Harper had authored or edited "inductive bible studies" (in the periodical *Old Testament Student*), with considerable attention to the outlining of contents. Following Harper, but more conservative theologically, W. W. White attempted to stimulate firsthand study of the bible; for this purpose he founded in 1900 a school which was eventually known as "The Biblical Seminary in New York." White and his followers declared as their main aim the study of the scriptures themselves. They called their method "inductive" in order to characterize at once a scientific and an independent spirit (cf. Eberhardt, 120). The essential feature of that method lay in a "compositive" approach, studying both internal and external connections of a text (145-152). The main stress lay on close observation, namely, of the relationships between parts on various levels, including that of the bible as a complex of literary structures (Sweet, 78) and of genres, and on "correlation" with "life-as-a-whole" (Traina, 226). H. Kuist followed a theory of "re-creative criticism," going beyond "historical reconstruction" (56-60).

Harper has been described as one who "grasped the relations of things" (Brown, xxii). For a general audience, he prepared guides to OT literature arranged by major genres and, within these, according to historical development. Although these do not contain a rigorously detailed analysis comparable to Gunkel's "Introduction" to the psalms, they include various observations regarding styles, roles, content, and minor genres. These were offered to the public between 1900 and 1905 but may well reflect earlier teaching (see Brown, xxvii, for bibliographical details). His student C. F. Kent wrote extensively along such lines, beginning in 1895. Kent believed that, if the book of Proverbs "is to fulfill its mission to the present age, order must be evolved

out of chaos" (1895, 4). He executed his aim through classification, with primary emphasis on theme, and provided in effect
a survey of the "topics" of Israelite wisdom. Eventually, he
covered the entire OT according to a principle stated as follows:
"For practical purposes a logical arrangement is more important
than a chronological. The canons of scientific literary classification, in which community of theme, point of view, authorship,
and literary style are the guide, must first be applied. . . . When
kindred narratives, laws, prophetic address, and proverbs have
been grouped together, it is then possible and practical to arrange
the material within each group and subdivision in its chronological order" (1904, vii; cf. R. Moulton, 1897[3], 32: "inductive
criticism is mainly occupied in distinguishing literary species").

Kent's program corresponded closely to Gunkel's aim of coherent order, see below, p. 48), to his description of genres, and
to his call for a two-dimensional "history of literature" (with both
synchronic and diachronic aspects). Gunkel's formulations, however, appeared either simultaneously or slightly later. Kent did
spend two years in Germany, but too early (1891/92 and 1896/97)
and too far removed from Gunkel's circle to make a direct connection plausible. In all likelihood, the resemblance with Gunkel
must be regarded as resting on a common intellectual situation.

Kent never examined the forms and history of the literature in
painstaking detail. Thus his studies remain useful more as an
arrangement of data than as a finished product of scholarship.
He had a strong practical interest, particularly in meeting the
needs of students at colleges and universities. Kent described his
own time as a period of the "rediscovery of the OT" (1906, 3).
Appreciation was expressed for Israelite ethics; humanitarian
laws represent "the high-water mark of Hebrew thought and
teaching" (1902, 208). Kent spoke of Moses' assertion of the
rights of the industrially oppressed and expected that the
prophets' social principles would form a common ground on
which conservatives, radicals, and persons from different religious traditions can unite (1917, vi, 3).

The literary structures of the bible in general, or of the OT
in particular, became the concern of a large number of studies
appearing in England, Canada, and the United States (too many
to list even their titles). Some of them were written by professors
of English: J. Gardiner (1906), E. Baldwin (1910, 1927, 1929),
J. Penniman (1919), W. Phelps (1919, 1923), W. Sypherd
(1938), and M. Reid (1959, an anthology); others, by an his-

torian (A. Fiske, 1896, 1897, 1911), a scholar of Islamic culture
(D. Macdonald, 1933), and an author of novels and other literature (M. Chase, 1944, 1952, 1955, 1961, 1963). Several were
produced by churchmen (E. Howse, 1956) and biblical specialists, including A. R. Gordon (1907, 1912, 1919), G. A. Smith
(1912), H. Fowler (1912), I. Wood and E. Grant (1914), A.
Culler (1930), L. Longacre (1945), E. Goodspeed (1946), T.
Robinson (1947), and others. (This listing is not exhaustive.)
J. Muilenburg (1923, 1961) taught English prior to receiving
a graduate degree in biblical literature. The works mentioned
were almost uniformly directed to general audiences. A number
of popular presentations, such as by E. Leslie (1945, 1949, etc.),
followed Gunkel closely.

The outlook of the movement is stated by C. Dinsmore, author
also of works on other literatures: "The Bible in recent times has
passed through two distinct phases and is entering upon a third.
There was a period when it was regarded as an infallible authority, the divine element was emphasized and the human
overlooked; then came the age of the critic with his eager search
for authors, dates, and documents; his main contentions having
been established, his battle is losing its heat and absorbing
interest. Now we are entering upon the era of appreciation.
Educators are beginning to realize that Hebrew literature is
not inferior to Greek and Roman in cultural value" (1931, v). It
should be carefully noted that members of the movement did not
as a rule see the literature from an externally aesthetic point of
view but saw statement and content in an integral unity. Ethics
was a major, though by no means the only, interest.

A significant shift is reflected in the treatment of Amos (as
of other prophets). Prior to 1900, it was common to describe
Amos in rather general terms as favoring righteousness and, in
particular, as opposing the luxury of the rich. (So already,
Herder, *Werke*, XII, 114, contrasted luxury with work-oriented
moderation.) Now more sympathy came to be expressed with
Amos' denunciation of oppression, i.e., of actions resulting in
suffering by the poor and weak. The shift involved a turn from a
middle-class revolt against the aristocracy to a concern for those
injured by the new society. We have already seen that the shift
in focus is integrally connected with the rise in genre studies,
since these express less interest in differentiation or discreteness
than did so-called "historical criticism."

In Germany, a call for focus on biblical literature was made

I

by M. Kähler, in an attempt to mediate between warring conservative and liberal groups. He argued for a "transhistorical" (not unhistorical) perspective, in which the general is seen in connection with the particular, so that history is not viewed in terms of isolated entities (1892 [1964, 47]). This broader perspective does not reject, but supplements, an approach which deals with the relation of literature to the various times in which it was produced (1896 [1937, 168]). Kähler denied that the purpose of the gospels was to present documents for an objective biography of Jesus; they should be read for their dynamics pointing toward meaning. Similarly, the significance of the OT lies in its complete form rather than in individual reconstructions by historical criticism (1896 [1937, 140, 175]). A number of genres are characterized briefly; they include stories of creation (which lies beyond history) and sagas combining historical realities with poetry (1896, 1904 [1937, 158, 244-245]).

Near the occasion in which Kähler pointed beyond a historiography dealing with separate moments in time (*Zeitgeschichte*), H. Gunkel, in parallel fashion, presented a sustained attack on the sufficiency of such an approach (also using the term *Zeitgeschichte* for it), by showing the connection of the book of Revelation with Israelite, Jewish, and Babylonian creation stories (1895). His analysis highlights "traditions," that is, themes and expressions continuing over a long period of time, specifically the fundamental religious categories of creation and chaos, origin and end. Like Kähler and representatives of the Anglo-American "bible as literature" movement, Gunkel regarded his approach as going beyond "historical criticism" (1901, preface; 1910, 4, 10; *CW* XXXV [1921] 828). Unlike Kähler, however, Gunkel was ready to go far afield for comparison, believing in the fundamental unity of mankind. Both Kähler and Gunkel were interested in "biblical theology" (cf. the subtitle of Gunkel's work on the activity of the Holy Spirit, 1888). For Gunkel, however, a properly executed biblical theology is identical with the "history of religion" (*Religionsgeschichte*), that is, a presentation elucidating religious realities (*RGG²*, I, 1089-1091). He stated as a fundamental conviction that history is an overarching unity, moving toward a goal recognizable only by faith, and that within its connectedness everything is both special and comparable (1910, 10).

Gunkel's conception of history allowed him to refer, for purposes of comparison, not only to earlier but also to later poems and to literature geographically far removed, such as that of East Asia. His interest, like Bastian's (above, p. 35), lay less in tracing the diffusion of themes by direct contact than in shedding light on a literary structure through analogy (1926, viii, and often). Such a broad view, of course, conflicted with that of the pan-Babylonian school which exaggerated the role of Mesopotamia as a source for religious themes. Already in 1891, B. Weiss was struck by "the mutual illustration of kindred phenomena" in Gunkel's lectures (Rabenau, 438). Gunkel accepted the academic tradition of laborious historical analysis but stressed—like other form critics of his day, already mentioned—that its results are often "hypothetical" (1901, preface) and warned against excessive text-critical speculation (1911, x). In fact, the frequent impossibility of precise dating is given as a negative reason or justification for genre criticism (1906, 53-54).

Gunkel's central interest lay in recognizing an order or pattern in the material. He noted with dismay that traditional commentaries contained primarily separate bits of information and regarded these as no more than a step toward an understanding of the "meaning of the OT," his primary aim (1901, preface). In opposition to procedures interpreting the psalms in isolation from each other, his task was to "bring light and order into the multifarious data and to show their inner structure" (1933, 8, 168). Two-dimensional "history of literature" is to provide coherence and "scientific"—i.e., systematic—knowledge (1913, 32; RGG[2], III, 1677). A semiautobiographical passage described his empathetic process and inner vision as follows: "At first, the individual poem flows together in the soul of the re-creator, out of individual observations. Then the individual pictures of psalmists fall into religious types, and all these fuse finally into an over-all picture of religious poetry" (1926, vii).

In addition to the imagery of seeing implied in such words as "light" and "picture," Gunkel employed the symbol of listening for a relation to the present. For him, an essential aspect of study lay in a resonance of the ancient sounds within his soul. Since such resonance (unlike the light of understanding reached by observation) does not come by effort, his writing was sometimes delayed until the inner hearing could take place (1926, vii). Gunkel indeed believed, as a presupposition of his effort, that the psalms contain "bells of eternity," whose sound carries to "our own day," and that one can "learn to pray" from the

I

Hebrew psalmists (*CW* XXXVI [1922] 109 [1928, 114]) . He published a few religious poems anonymously (*CW* XX [1906] 409, 433, 601, 649, 913) and directed a considerable portion of his energy toward reaching the larger public. To join both aesthetic and theological concerns intimately with precise scholarship was his aim. The pedant lacking sensitivity, the "philistine" who divorces form from content, and the purely emotional esthete—are all viewed as one-sided (1904, 1906 [1913, 23, 24, 32]) . The interplay of subject and object, of reason and feeling, of activity and receptivity, is considered necessary for understanding (e.g., 1913, 33) .

Gunkel's political interest can be deduced from some direct as well as indirect indications. He greatly admired the socially concerned F. Naumann (Klatt, 265) . To the encyclopedia *RGG*, of which he was co-editor, he contributed an article on the Hebrew concern for the poor (I, 1909, 693-695) and one on "individualism and socialism in the OT" (III, 1912, 493-501) , with mention of the prohibition of interest, a topic rarely discussed by Protestant scholars. In laws, psalms, and prophecy he saw attempts to counteract oppression by the rich and powerful (1906, 79; *CW* XXXVI [1922] 83; cf. 1917, 79-83) . One can argue, of course, that in biblical exposition he is merely reporting the content; but a personal interest is evident at least in the *RGG* articles, which appear to have been especially created for him. And it is to his credit that he did not avoid the content through attention to external form. That the awakening social sense constituted the very basis for the "religio-historical" school, in which Gunkel played a central role, was recognized already by H. Gressmann (39) .

Content and mood were always ranked by Gunkel ahead of linguistic form, just as the discussion of "topics" preceded that of elocution in rhetoric (1913, 32 [1906]; 1917, 109; *ZAW* XLII [1924] 177-208; 1925, 109; 1928, 115; 1933, 22) . When such a relative emphasis is not preserved, the result becomes known as "formalism," i.e., a one-sided emphasis on external form or abstract patterns. To a considerable extent, academic form criticism after Gunkel has probably fallen prey to such a temptation, just as has the so-called "new criticism" dominant until a few years ago. A problem with formalism is that it avoids some of the critical and practical issues of the day. A major remaining task of OT form criticism is to examine closely the relation of content, as well as of style, to the various aspects of life, with the hope of providing analogies for the present. This will require attention to social psychology and related concerns.

A large part of the strength of Gunkel's work lay in the breadth of his vision and his contact with various disciplines. Precise connections are sometimes difficult to establish, however, especially since Gunkel, seeking to reach a wide audience, sought moderation in references to secondary literature (1901, preface).

The friendship circle to which Gunkel belonged, led by A. Eichhorn, included a classicist, a philosophically oriented student of W. Wundt, and a German specialist, as well as several concerned with Christian literature and history. Eichhorn urged breadth of perspective and concern for the present (Gressmann, 8, 21, 39). Another important impact may have come from Gunkel's close friend and advisor A. Lasson, who according to P. Wendland (*RGG*², III, 1496), was particularly influenced by Aristotle, Paul, and Hegel; one can speculate to what extent Gunkel's affinity to Aristotelian method and Hegelian perspective (cf. Klatt, 35, 264) is derived from this contact. Gunkel's shift toward a primary concern with the OT (he was denied opportunity for a NT or broadly biblical position, largely because of a reputation for radicalness) facilitated the interaction of perspectives which often leads to important advances by relatively new entries into a field (Kuhn, 89). In fact, especially his wide vision of religion was unpopular in the theological faculties (see Klatt, 41; Rabenau).

Gunkel came in contact with classical scholarship in part because P. Wendland and E. Norden, both focusing on literary forms and genres, included Christian literature in their range of concerns. The connection was undoubtedly strengthened by the fact that Norden had been taught by H. Usener, whose circle stood in a close working relationship with the "religio-historical" school with which Eichhorn and Gunkel identified themselves (Gressmann, 29). Usener called for a recognition of the forms (*Formenlehre*) of mythology, with an interest in images, and was followed by A. Dieterich; the latter encouraged the study of the history of styles, motifs, and aims of prayer, begun by classicists (1903; *AfR* VIII [1905] ii, 484). Quite widely known in these circles was the 1882 statement by F. Overbeck, a friend of Nietzsche's, in regard to Christian literature: "A history of a literature lies in its forms; thus every real history of literature

I
_____
50

will be a history of forms" (cf. Tetz). P. Wendland, who published a genre analysis of the diatribe in 1895, spoke of "firm topics and stereotyped linguistic-form *(Formensprache)* " on the pages of the German NT journal *ZNW* (V [1904] 344) ; the term *Formensprache* was used thereafter by Gunkel for characterizing one aspect of genres *(CW* XXI [1907] 850-851, and later). The details of how much Gunkel absorbed from previously published studies (see Gercke-Norden, 426-450, 585, for a considerable number of relevant volumes and essays) and from oral contacts will, of course, always remain to a degree uncertain and may shed less light on his work than does the larger cultural context presented earlier.

Gunkel's approach had a number of parallels in the field of Germanics; it is impossible to say, however, to what extent similarities were due to direct or indirect dependence or to common stimuli. For instance, the term *Sitz im Leben* (literally, "seat, or place, in life"), coined by Gunkel, had antecedents. In 1740, during a time when genres still stood at the center of critical interest, J. Breitinger's study of parables (including at least one from the OT) spoke of the *Sitz* (or *Platz*) of parables within didactic or judgmental poems *(Critische Abhandlung,* 110, 117). In a similar manner, Gunkel referred in 1895 to the *Sitz* of storm theophanies in old poems regarding Sinai (104). One may hesitate to suggest that Gunkel knew Breitinger's work; but the reference shows the age of the notion of a "place in literature," recently discussed by L. Alonso-Schökel (1960, 162).

In 1906, Gunkel began to speak of *Stelle, Sitz im Leben,* or *Sitz im Volksleben,* "place in the life of a people." Both the term and its usage reveal close affinity to a widely respected analysis of popular poetry by L. Uhland, written about 1840; left incomplete—perhaps because it did not fit the spirit of that time— the analysis was issued in its fragmentary form soon after Uhland's death (1866) and was available in the 1890's and thereafter in an inexpensive edition. Uhland classified the poetry according to genres and related at least several of these to their "home *(Heimatstätte)* where they grow and from which they stem" (236, similarly 129; cf., e.g., Gunkel, *ZAW* XLII [1924] 183) ; the "occasions" on which they are used he called *Anlässe im Volksleben* (13). Like Gunkel (1933, 10), he based categorizations on content rather than on external aspects and found that the groupings emerged "almost spontaneously" in the light of their occasions (15). Uhland described his genre analysis as entering into "the inner life" of the people (13; similarly Gunkel, *CW* XXXVI [1922] 3 [1928, 72]).

Did Gunkel know Uhland directly or indirectly? He could have read the following in a handbook on German poetics: "Scholarship divides popular songs according to spheres of life (*Lebenskreisen*), materials, content, and mood, etc." (Beyer, 87). Typical occasions were also discussed by K. Bücher (above, p. 36), and W. Wundt (1905, 310: "*bestimmte Gelegenheiten*"; cf., e.g., Gunkel, 1913, 33 [from 1906]), as well as by classicists (Nietzsche, Reitzenstein, Wendland, Bethe; Gercke-Norden, 330, 427, 430, etc.).

It is clear that Gunkel did not stand as an isolated figure. His work was in tune with the spirit of his time, as shown by developments in secular and, to some extent, in biblical scholarship. A. Wünsche, K. Budde, E. Kautzsch, P. Haupt (W. F. Albright's teacher), and E. König produced at least similar work in German. For Israelite law, basic typologies were being discussed, especially by B. Baentsch and H. Holzinger; for psalms, by E. Riehm and others. Gunkel met perhaps an especially warm response in the English-speaking world; T. K. Cheyne dedicated to him his 1904 commentary on the psalms (although it shows hardly any traces of form critical procedure, which Gunkel had not yet fully developed). Perhaps Gunkel's remark in 1911 (viii), that "in Germany" no sustained effort to describe the aesthetic-literary character has been made, indicates his acquaintance with R. Moulton's work, but he does not cite it.

C. The Relation of Form Criticism to the Dynamics of Existence

J. Ackermann, *On Teaching the Bible as Literature* (Bloomington: Indiana University Press, 1967); I. Baldermann, *Biblische Didaktik* (Hamburg: Furche Verlag, 1964[2]); P. Böckmann, *Formgeschichte der deutschen Dichtung*, I (Hamburg: Hoffman & Campe, 1965[2]); K. Bücher, *Arbeit und Rhythmus* (1902[3]); H. Gunkel, "Die israelitische Literatur" (1906); *idem, Reden und Aufsätze* (1913); *idem, What Remains of the Old Testament* (1928); *idem, Einleitung in die Psalmen* (1933); F. Heiler, *Das Gebet* (Munich: E. Reinhardt, 1923[5]); B. Inhelder and J. Piaget, *The Growth of Logical Thinking from Childhood to Adolescence*, tr. by A. Parsons and S. Milgram (New York: Basic Books, 1958); H. Jordan, *Geschichte der altchristlichen Literatur* (Leipzig: Quelle & Meyer, 1911); T. Munro, *Form and Style in the Arts: An Introduction to Aesthetic Morphology* (Cleveland: Press of Case Western Reserve University, 1970); E. Norden, *Agnostos Theos: Untersuchungen zur Formengeschichte religiöser Rede* (Leipzig: B. G. Teubner, 1913); H. Prang, *Formgeschichte der Dichtkunst* (Stuttgart: W. Kohlhammer, 1968); P. Sands, *The Literary Genius of the Old Testament* (London: Oxford University Press,

1926) ; W. Scherer, *Poetik* (Berlin: Weidmann, 1888) ; L. Uhland, *Abhandlung über die deutschen Volkslieder*; P. Wendland, *Die urchristlichen Literaturformen* (Tübingen: J. C. B. Mohr, 1912) ; W. Wimsatt, Jr., and C. Brooks, *Literary Criticism* (New York: A. Knopf, 1964); W. Wundt, *Mythus und Religion*, I.

The greatness of Gunkel lay not in an isolated creativity, but in an unusual ability to draw together aspects which were often treated separately: content, linguistic form, life-situation, history, world-wide analogies, present involvement, etc. In fact, many prominent biblical form critics in ancient and more modern times have been well trained in secular culture; often they were not primarily biblical specialists. In Germany after Gunkel, an authoritarian and triumphalist theology (competing with a political outlook similar in character) reduced the vision. It may be noted, however, that significant advances in the field continued to be carried out in association with other disciplines. As is well known, S. Mowinckel and others were deeply influenced by the history of religions. Not so well known is the circumstance that C. Westermann had ample and easy opportunity to be familiar with anthropology and linguistics—and thus with the basic spirit of structural analysis—through his father, a notable specialist on Africa.

One of the more questionable elements of Gunkel's system is one which he held somewhat in isolation, namely the assertion—for which he cites no support—that popular genres were "always completely pure" (1913, 36 [original, 1906], and 1933, 28 [sharpened from an earlier "almost always completely pure," 1906, 56]) . The source of this notion is difficult to find (was it W. Scherer, 18, in a work he used?) . Virtually all studies of primitive literature, including works Gunkel knew, stated or implied at least partially otherwise (Uhland, 13, 15, 19, 235; Bücher, 1902[3], 169, 356-373; Wundt, 1905, 310; Heiler, 1923[5], 40, 50; and others) . In actual practice Gunkel recognized mixtures, viewing them either as creative borrowings of style or as the decline of a form. OT form critics have often not seen, as others have, that genres are abstractions ("ideal forms") and that virtually all human experiences involve a combination of categories applied simultaneously and that partly for this reason no more than statistical correlations between phenomena can be expected.

The concept of a matrix, or field, involving several dimensions has proved fruitful in many areas recently (e.g., Munro) and can be applied meaningfully to the OT. If, for instance, one sees the psalms in terms of at least two dimensions, such as mood (positive, negative, or complex) and subject of concern (ordinary individual, king, Zion, etc., or a mixture of these), one will reach a relatively simple classification system for the handling of complex data. Gunkel came very close to this in a lecture directed to the public. On that occasion, he divided the psalms according to "spheres," particularly those of the king, the nation, and the individual; one category, that of the hymns, transcends these spheres and deals with "fundamental thoughts and moods" (*CW* XXXVI [1922] 4 [1928, 72]). Here is a move toward a systematic order, which was never fully carried out and remains a task for the future.

A multidimensional and flexible approach permits a meaningful assessment of individuality. A very simple object which involves only a few dimensions is not likely to be distinct from many other instances of a similar combination of characteristics. A more complex entity which draws together many different features, however, can have a relatively unique status. (Gunkel saw the role of such a rich complexity in prophetic literature but assigned it too strongly to a secondary process associated largely with writing [1906, 88; 1913, 36 = 1928, 65].) In other words, individuality is not opposed to comparability. It may be noted that this observation applies also to the field of religion; the meaningful individuality of biblical faith is enhanced, not denied, through a wide range of contacts. If forms are understood not as exclusive genres, but as potentially interacting structures, the study of forms becomes of increasing, rather than of decreasing, importance for highly important phenomena.

A difficulty for twentieth-century form criticism has been the relation of form to history, as reflected in terminological problems. Form criticism has sometimes been described, especially in NT scholarship, as a study of the oral stage of the history of a literary text. However, there is no reason to limit form criticism to oral expressions; moreover, it is questionable whether an oral prehistory can be reconstructed in any detail on the basis of literary forms. (In fact, form criticism is best taken as dealing primarily with fairly general aspects, rather than with irrational particularities.) While terminology is necessarily arbitrary—differences can be permitted—Gunkel's usage had the advantage of clarity and simplicity. He viewed the tracing of oral history as part of the study of "tradition" (e.g., 1928, 156); for that task he involved a number of considerations in addition to those of forms. The one term "tradition criticism" adequately

I

covers the study of both oral and written aspects of transmission, especially since these are frequently intertwined (as I. Engnell and others have stressed).

The most natural meaning of the word *Formgeschichte* is the "history of form," rather than "history reconstructed on the basis of literary forms." The term *Formengeschichte* was introduced in classical scholarship for the study of forms with their history, applying to both oral and written material, such as that of the NT (Norden, 1913; cf. Jordan, 1911, and Wendland, 1912). In later secular work, the shortened version *Formgeschichte* continued basically this same sense (e.g., Prang). The aim of such study, according to P. Böckmann (13), is to elucidate forms of human existence, including man's reaction to himself, to others, to the outer world, and to the transcendent. This usage justifies the use of "form criticism" (or, according to some, "morphology") for the clarification of meaningful structures.

Gunkel's historical perspective was largely an evolutionary one (not to be confused with a belief in "progress"). In this basic attitude he may have been correct, although many of his specific beliefs in this regard were undoubtedly erroneous. Insofar as history itself has a structure, as an integral part of human dynamics, form criticism can and must include a temporal dimension and become involved in a philosophy of history.

The "Bible as Literature" movement in the U.S. was strongly, although not exclusively, oriented to college teaching. P. Sands' *The Literary Genius of the Old Testament*, 1926, published in England, was designed for use in "schools." With the recent opening of the possibility of teaching biblical literature in public high schools (ages 14 to 18) in the United States, a guide *On Teaching the Bible as Literature* (1967) has been prepared by J. Ackermann, with at least some attention to genres. The appropriateness of form criticism for the instruction of younger children has been discussed in Germany, at least since 1928 (see Baldermann). Experience has shown that this question is related to the intellectual development of children. At an early age, children do not clearly distinguish between "is" and "ought" but are "traditional" in their outlook; thereafter, children enter a period of "critical realism." At neither of these stages are they ready for a conscious understanding of the various dynamics of speech, the potentiality for which does not awaken until early or late adolescence (14, 143).

Roughly at adolescence there emerges a complex which Inhelder and Piaget (1953) call "formal thought": it involves a "combinatorial structure," acting as an integrated whole through the notion of reciprocity. This pattern of thought is able to handle multifactor situations through a consideration of several variables and an assessment of probability, correlation, and proportionality. At this level of sophistication, but not earlier, it is possible to understand the different functions of language and to handle analogies. As Baldermann points out, the adolescent is able to learn that the scope of a text may not lie simply in an intellectual "kerygmatic assertion" or in a purely factual statement about "salvation history"; positively, he is now ready to become involved in the relational movement of the text, for instance, of praise or warning (49-50).

Form criticism, by its recognition of different genres, indicates that life is multifaceted and that not all problems are solved in the same manner. By showing how certain paths relate to certain aspects of life, it can help lead the way. Many aspects continue, despite considerable changes. According to W. F. Albright, "it is precisely the generic quality found in the Psalms which makes them so universally valid for men of all subsequent times" (*HUCA* XXIII/1 [1950/51] 2). Modern man, after the industrial revolution, can no longer identify himself completely with the ancient world; but analogies often apply. In fact, interest in Israelite law has revived in the current "century of the common man" (Wimsatt and Brooks, 734).

Thus form criticism transcends a contrast between historical study, faith, and science. As experience has shown, it cannot be successfully executed in isolation. For instance, Israelite wisdom is related to education and philosophy, Hebrew law to social questions, prophecy to transcendence of the present, psalms to emotional reactions, and presentations of history to the question of divine presence and action in existence. Form criticism includes an irrational aspect in that it deals with conventions, which have only arbitrary values, and with local variations of form, without ultimate significance. But the aim is to discover the meaning of the conventions and their relational significance in such a way as to permit insight and challenge.

MARTIN J. BUSS

I

Chapter Two

NARRATIVE

While Hermann Gunkel was the pioneer of the form critical method in most types of OT literature, his work on OT narrative types holds a special place. It was while working on the narratives of Genesis that Gunkel first developed his method of *Gattungsforschung* (study of literary types) , and the results achieved then and in the next few years have persisted to a remarkable degree in subsequent scholarship. What one reads in current handbooks about the narrative literary types has a clear origin in the work of Gunkel and, in close cooperation with Gunkel, of Hugo Gressmann. There are differences of detail, a few problems of terminology, and, more importantly, a certain loss of historical perspective that was crucial to Gunkel's practice of the method, but the basic outline and conceptualization remain the same. That does not mean, of course, that form criticism of narratives à la Gunkel is uniformly and universally practiced by OT scholars; the method is at times rejected, neglected, or misunderstood. But when form criticism of OT narratives is undertaken, the Gunkel approach is almost always evident.

Especially with narratives, therefore, it is appropriate to take a history of research approach to OT form criticism. Present issues are best seen against the background of where Gunkel started, how his views changed, how those views became codified in general surveys, and what current problems and ambiguities they present the OT student. Accordingly, the present chapter will trace the emergence of the systematic application of form criticism to narratives by Gunkel and Gressmann, the consolidation of the results by Gunkel's pupils and others in the subsequent generation, and conclude with a consideration of critiques, developments, and reformulations of the form criticism of narratives in recent scholarship. In this survey the different groups of OT narratives cannot be equally taken into account. It is the development of method that is the primary question. Unavoidably, there are a number of treatments of form critical issues in studies of particular parts of the OT that will have to be passed over here without mention.

I. THE FOUNDATIONS: GUNKEL AND GRESSMANN

A. The Sagas of Genesis

W. F. Albright, "Verse and Prose in Early Israelite Tradition," in his *Yahweh and the Gods of Canaan* (Garden City: Doubleday & Co., 1968) 1-52; B. W. Anderson, *Creation Versus Chaos* (New York: Association Press, 1967); H. Gunkel, *Genesis* (HKAT I/1, Göttingen: Vandenhoeck & Ruprecht, 1901, 1902[2], 1910[3]); idem, *The Legends of Genesis*, tr. by W. H. Carruth (Chicago: The Open Court Publishing Co., 1901), a translation of the introduction to *Genesis*, reissued with an introduction by W. F. Albright (New York: Schocken Books, 1964); idem, "Die israelitische Literatur," *Die orientalischen Literaturen*, ed. by P. Hinneberg (KdG I/7, Leipzig: B. G. Teubner, 1906, 1925[2]) 53-112 = *Die israelitische Literatur* (Darmstadt: Wissenschaftliche Buchgesellschaft, 1963); idem, *Schöpfung und Chaos in Urzeit und Endzeit* (Göttingen: Vandenhoeck & Ruprecht, 1895); H. Holzinger, *Genesis* (KHCAT, Tübingen: J. C. B. Mohr, 1898); G. S. Kirk, *Homer and the Epic* (Cambridge: Cambridge University Press, 1965); W. Klatt, *Hermann Gunkel: Zu seiner Theologie der Religionsgeschichte und zur Entstehung der formgeschichtlichen Methode* (FRLANT 100, Göttingen: Vandenhoeck & Ruprecht, 1969); K. Koch, *Was ist Formgeschichte?* (Neukirchen: Neukirchener Verlag, 1964, 1967[2]) = *The Growth of the Biblical Tradition*, tr. by S. M. Cupitt (New York: Charles Scribner's Sons, 1969); A. B. Lord, *The Singer of Tales* (Cambridge: Harvard University Press, 1960); R. Scholes and R. Kellogg, *The Nature of Narrative* (London: Oxford University Press, 1966).

Gunkel did not develop a theory for the study of literary types and then seek a way to apply it; rather, the theory gradually evolved from his practice. Thus, in his first major work on narrative forms, his Genesis commentary of 1901, little of the systematic terminology and classification of later discussions of narratives appears. The basic approach is already developed,

II

however, in response to the issues Gunkel faced in interpreting Genesis. Six years earlier, Gunkel had published *Schöpfung und Chaos*, an epoch-making work in the religio-historical study of the bible. That work was devoted to tracing the persistence of a particular mythic drama—the creator god slaying the chaos monster and fashioning the world from its body—from its old Babylonian form through variations in Israelite poetic allusions, through Genesis 1, and finally to Revelation 12. (For a recent discussion strongly informed by Gunkel's work, though updated, see Anderson.) In that earlier study the emphasis had been on the mythic subject matter, which had migrated through several different literary forms. In his Genesis commentary, the interest has shifted more to the literary forms through which such traditional subject matters (*Stoffe* is the term usually used in the Genesis commentary) have passed. Thus, in a way, the shift in emphasis was from content (*Inhalt*) to form (*Form*), and Gunkel occasionally used these terms in describing the task of form criticism of narratives (see 1925, 109). *Gattungsforschung* appears, therefore, as the study of different literary types in which a traditional subject matter might be given expression. ("One can trace how the same narrative materials in Israel recur, according to the spirit of the time, as myths, sagas, *Märchen*, legends, novellas, or novels," 1925, 56.) As such, *Gattungsforschung* is part of a more comprehensive study, *Literaturgeschichte*, history of literature, which includes the study of the traditional subject matters and the history of their transmission. (Gunkel's programmatic outline for the work of the history of Israelite literature was first published in 1906 in "Die israelitische Literatur.")

By the time Gunkel was preparing his Genesis commentary, critical OT scholarship had concluded that Genesis could not be read in the same fashion as sober historical writing. The preceding generation of scholars had concentrated upon the separation of the different documents that went into Genesis, and upon possible historical evidence underlying the materials of those documents. As Klatt observes (110-111, n.28), the commentary of H. Holzinger, published in 1898, is representative of the approach prevailing before Gunkel's work. In a way previous scholars had not, Gunkel raised the question of how Genesis should be read if not as history. As evidenced by numerous citations in his commentary, Gunkel seems to have taken his clue for this approach from E. Reuss. At the head of section one of his commentary introduction (*Genesis*[2], IX,) he cites only two works of Reuss (see also XXXII, n.1 and Klatt's persuasive quote from Reuss, 110, n.28). Given an established view that disparaged the historicity of Genesis, how should Genesis be appreciated? Gunkel's introduction seems intended to answer that question. The long and spirited section on the "Kunstform der Sagen der Genesis" (which has been somewhat weakly translated as "The Literary Form of the Legends") embodies clearly Gunkel's particular interest in an esthetic appreciation of the sagas of Genesis. (See also Klatt, 116-25, where this esthetic interest is discussed.)

If Genesis is not historical writing, what kind of literature is it? That question Gunkel answers in the first section of his introduction. Genesis is a collection of sagas, he concludes, devoting the remainder of the section to a systematic distinction between saga and history. ("Saga" has made its way into English, as recent translations of German works indicate. Older translations rendered the Germanic *Sage* by "legend," which has a broader meaning in English. "Legend" is best reserved, however, for a more specialized use, as is indicated below.) First, the distinction is not simply one between true and false; sagas contain kernels of historical truth. If one's concern is to extract those kernels of truth, one is taking a historical-critical approach. If one's concern is to appreciate the process by which historical kernels have been elaborated imaginatively, one is taking a literary-historical and esthetic approach. That established, sagas as a literary type can be distinguished from historical writing as a literary type by five polarities. 1) They differ in mode of transmission: saga by oral tradition, history by writing. 2) They differ in subject matter: saga deals with things in the private worlds of men, particularly family relations; history deals with public and particularly political events. 3) They differ in the sources upon which they depend: saga draws on tradition and imagination; history on witnesses and records. 4) They differ in part, at least, in the probability of the action they relate: saga tends to be credulous, incorporating the miraculous and the improbable; history, to be credible, confining itself to the possible and the probable. Finally, 5) they differ in their ends or purposes: saga is poetic in tone, aiming to entertain and inspire; history is prosaic, aiming to inform. (For all of this, see *Genesis*[2], XI-XVI and *Legends*, 1-12.)

By these criteria saga can be distinguished from historical

writing. A great deal remains, however, on the saga side of this cut. The next task is to distinguish different kinds of sagas, or of narratives that do not meet the criteria of historical writing. Gunkel turns to this task in the second section of his introduction. In Genesis there is one great division between sagas: mythical sagas found in the primeval history of Gen 1-11 and patriarchal sagas found in Gen 12-50. These two types may also be distinguished from each other by means of some polarities: 1) They differ in subject matter: mythical sagas deal with the origins of the world and of men; patriarchal, with the ancestors and the origin of Israel. 2) They differ in their spatio-temporal setting: mythical sagas are remote in time and space; patriarchal sagas treat events of Canaan and its neighbors. 3) Particularly do they differ in their main actors: the first have God or the gods as actors; the latter, men, though occasional divine appearances may be included. Under this same point might fall another important criterion: 4) the mythical sagas are polytheistic in their religious orientation: the patriarchal sagas are monotheistic. Finally, 5) some differences in origin can be distinguished: mythical sagas originate as answers to universal questions, that is, questions about natural phenomena throughout the world and about man qua man; patriarchal sagas originate in questions about tribal history and natural phenomena local to Canaan and its environs (*Legends*, 13-23; *Genesis*², XVI-XXII). There is a steady decrease in the emphasis upon tribal history reflected in the patriarchal stories in the successive discussions of Genesis by Gunkel. This emphasis is strong, however, in the first edition, upon which the English translation, *Legends*, is based. For Genesis, these two groups of sagas are sufficient. Within a few years, however, Gunkel put alongside them a large third group, the *Volksheldensagen*, sagas of folk heroes (1925, 71-73). These, as will be seen below, form the transition from saga to history writing.

Viewed simply quantitatively, Genesis is made up much more of patriarchal sagas than of mythical sagas, and Gunkel's discussion reflects this proportion. Within the large group of patriarchal narratives he distinguishes further subdivisions. There are "historical," "ethnographic," and "etiological" sagas. The historical ones are those that reflect some historical occurrence. Ethnographic sagas portray life circumstances that actually existed for some people or between some peoples. Abraham's treaty with Abimelech at Beersheba (Gen 21:22-34) is in the historical category, since the existence of some actual treaty between Israelites and the city state of Gerar is reflected in the narrative (*Legends*, 24; *Genesis²*, XXIII and 269-270). The sagas of Jacob and Esau, on the other hand, are ethnographic, since they reflect primarily tribal relations between Israelites and Edomites. In addition to historical and ethnographic sagas, there are etiological ones. These are intended to explain something and can be subdivided according to what they seek to explain. There are "ethnological" etiological sagas, which explain how certain circumstances in the life of one or more people came into being; there are "etymological" etiological sagas or saga motifs, which explain the origin of some word; there are "cult" etiological sagas, which explain how some religious custom or sacred place came to be established; and there are "geological" etiological sagas, which explain peculiarities of the landscape. (*Legends*, 25-34; *Genesis²*, XXIII-XXVII. As elsewhere, the above terminology is drawn from the German, not from the English translation.)

Having developed this classification of patriarchal sagas, Gunkel has to add an extremely important qualification:

> Very often different saga motifs are found united in the sagas. The saga of Hagar's flight (Gen 16) is ethnographic in so far as it portrays the existence of Ishmael; ethnological in so far as it explains (the origin of) these circumstances. With respect to one motif it belongs to the cult sagas, for it establishes the sacredness of Lahai-roi. At the same time it has etymological motifs, for it explains the names Ishmael and Lahai-roi. . . . The etymological motifs in particular never appear in Genesis independently, but regularly in conjunction with other saga motifs (*Genesis²*, XXVII).

What this passage makes clear is that the classification Gunkel has just developed is not, in fact, a classification of *sagas*, but of *saga motifs*. Few, if any, of the actual narratives, the "individual sagas" (*Einzelerzählungen*), can be placed in only one of Gunkel's categories. Gunkel's mode of presentation here invites confusion, and, as will be noted later, the confusion is amplified in subsequent discussions of narrative literary types.

Having distinguished saga from history and classified the typical (motifs of) sagas, Gunkel comes to the heart of his subject: the nature of these sagas as folk literature. Broadly speaking, he covers three topics in this connection: the sagas in their early life situation (the technical term *Sitz im Leben* was used in 1906, in

"Die israelitische Literatur" [56], contrary to Koch's statement that it did not appear until 1917 [37, n. 23]), their literary, artistic features, and the development of larger, more elaborated literary units. Only the first and third are of particular significance here. Three questions are pertinent to sagas in their original life setting. The first is whether they are poetry or prose (*Legends*, 37-39; somewhat revised already in *Genesis*², XXIX-XXX). The sagas are basically prose, though with some features of poetry. In 1902 Gunkel was impressed by Sievers' argument for meter in the prose of Genesis (*Genesis*², XXIX), but in his 1906 outline, which distinguishes "sung poetry," "recited poetry," and "prose," the sagas come out prose (1925, 54-55). There are ambiguities in the term "poetry" in this connection. Gunkel insists at certain points that they are not simply historical narratives but imaginative elaborations upon (possible) historical data. (See *Genesis*², XXVIII, where the patriarchal narratives in their present form are characterized as "pure poetic creations.") On the other hand, Gunkel is of the opinion that the present sagas derive, in many cases, from earlier poetic compositions that were recited or sung. That would have been the case particularly with cult sagas, which, from the analogy of Babylonian texts, are a popular distillation of subject matters originally recited by priests in verse. (*Legends*, 41-42; *Genesis*², XXXI. W. F. Albright has elaborated this point in his studies of early Israelite poetry, most recently in "Verse and Prose in Early Israelite Tradition.")

The second question about the sagas in their life setting is whether they are folk traditions or the original creations of individual poets. Gunkel recognized, of course, that in the very first instance every narrative must originate with a single storyteller, but he argued that in the case of Genesis that stage was so far in the past that it is only correct to view these narratives as, for the most part, the common property of the people. That conclusion must be qualified to some extent in that the conspicuous, if simple, artistry of these individual narratives points to practiced narrators as their source. In Israel, as among the Arabs, there must have been the professional storyteller who, in pursuing his occupation ("Stand der Geschichtenerzähler"), circulated among the tribes and appeared at festival occasions to recite the traditional lore of the people according to his particular skill (*Legends*, 41; *Genesis*², XXXI). Thus, the sagas of Genesis are primarily folk traditions, presented now as skillful popular narrators have shaped them (with the qualification, of course, that subsequent collectors and redactors have sometimes significantly altered the individual narratives for their own purposes).

A third question concerns the proper unit the interpreter should deal with in the Genesis narratives. According to the principles informing Gunkel's whole approach, the answer must be that the basic unit of Genesis is the individual folk saga. "By its very nature, popular saga exists in the form of the individual saga" (*Genesis*², XXXII). Accordingly, two criteria establish the originality and antiquity of individual popular sagas, in Gunkel's view: the self-sufficiency of the narrative, and its brevity. "The more self-sufficient the narrative, the surer it is that it is preserved in an older form"; "the shorter a saga, the more probable it is that it has been preserved in an older form" (*Genesis*², XXXIII, XXXIV). The crucial criterion here is brevity, since a relatively long narrative, such as the Joseph story, can be self-sufficient. The criterion of brevity for the original unit seems to be based on Gunkel's conception of the original life situation in which the sagas thrived.

> They (the old sagas) deal with very simple occurrences which can be adequately described in a few words. And this compass accords also with the artistic ability of the narrator and the comprehension (*Auffassungskraft*, in this context, perhaps, "attention span") of the hearer. The earliest storytellers were not capable of constructing artistic works of any considerable extent. . . . Primitive times were satisfied with quite brief productions which required not much over half an hour ("ein viertel Stündchen"!, translation from *Legends*, 47; cp. *Genesis*², XXXIV).

These assumptions about the attention span of audiences and the artistic capacity of the narrators may be subject to question. More recent studies of poetic rendering of traditional topics by oral composition make it clear that preliterary stages of culture are not confined to brief compositions. (See Albert Lord, *The Singer of Tales*, and a number of recent studies of Homer, such as G. S. Kirk's *Homer and the Epic*. Also, for a broader perspective, "The Oral Heritage of Written Narrative," ch. 2 of Scholes and Kellogg's *The Nature of Narrative*.) In these cases, of course, there are many special techniques involved and the works are in verse, but it is clear that the attention span of the audience is not determined by the availability or nonavailability of writing. As a psychological phenomenon, it does not seem likely that the attention span of people would have increased greatly during three or four hundred years of early Israelite history. What is more likely is that changing life situations may have cultivated new interests and made new literary forms possible, but it is not obvious that steppe-dwelling herdsmen would be less capable of sustained interest in a two- or three-hour narrative, in verse or in prose, than tradesmen or courtiers in cities. There were, of course, *short* literary forms in the ancient world (such as Aesop's fables and the stories in the Persian-Arabian *Thousand and One Nights*), but it is the nature of the literary compositions in question that makes them short, not the stage of cultural development.

Another possibility may be mentioned in passing, though it does not seem to have played any role in the study of OT narratives to date. That is that the episodes now presented in Genesis are only succinct summaries of stories that skilled narrators could elaborate at any appropriate length on different occasions. Most of the episodes of Genesis, if each is told as a separate story, invite or demand filling in of detail and imaginative elaboration. It is hard to believe that any ancient narrator who succeeded in grasping the imagination of his hearers would have missed the opportunities these succinct plots offer. That is to say that Gunkel may have missed the point of the brevity of the present texts. The individual stories are not brief because ancient narrations were brief, but because these texts only present basic plots which in any actual narration would be expanded and elaborated according to the skill of the storyteller and the occasion of his performance. (Alexander Rofé has recently made this point about the prophetic legends: "The Israelite storyteller was not a primitive who could not even master his language, and the Israelite public was not so backwards as not to be able to sustain a story which lasted more than one minute. The oral stage must have been longer, much longer, than the version we have now in scripture. The conciseness of the present stories rather reveals the opposite: the man who reduced these narratives to writing took the pains, and had the skill, to condense them. He gave to the reader the kernel of the story only . . . ," "The Classification of the Prophetical Stories," *JBL* LXXXIX [1970] 432-433.) A collection of such concise stories would be essential to men who were renowned as tellers of good stories, and out of such a collection of brief stories, eventually written down perhaps, other men could form larger and quite different literary compositions in which the dramatic power depended upon a long chain of brief episodes rather than the elaboration of a single one. Gunkel himself recognized that a short saga could be elaborated into a long, relatively complex narrative (the Joseph story is his model), but the possibility raised here is that his assumptions about the essential and original brevity of the sagas confuse the narrator's resources, a group of terse basic plots, with the narrations that occurred in ancient Israelite life situations.

After establishing that the sagas of Genesis were more or less prose, were popular tradition rendered by skilled narrators, and were self-sufficient and brief, Gunkel discusses their artistic character. The original sagas were marked by simplicity in that they always involved few characters, the action took priority over any complexity of character in the actors, and the diction was clear and repetitious to a degree not acceptable to modern taste (*Legends*, 47-49; *Genesis*[2], XXXIV-L). At the same time, sagas show a lack of *Tendenz*, biased viewpoint, which distinguishes them from the later narrative literature influenced by the prophets, the legend and historical writing.

Larger literary forms developed from the saga, for the most part still in the oral transmission stage. These larger units are of two kinds: "saga chains" and "novellas." A saga chain is a series of individual sagas concerning the same persons arranged to tell a larger story. Common examples are the saga chains of Abraham and Lot and of Jacob and Esau. The Abraham-Lot cycle originally related the characters' departure from Mesopotamia, their separation in Canaan, the two parallel visitations by divine beings—one promising Abraham an heir (Gen 18:1-15) and the other delivering Lot from the destruction of Sodom (Gen 19:1-26) —and concluded with the births of Lot's two sons, Moab and Ammon, and of Abraham's son Isaac. This saga chain was formed and given a unity of its own in the oral stage. Subsequently, other sagas about Abraham were incorporated into it, amplifying it and to some extent interrupting the unity of the Abraham-Lot chain. Such amplifications were Abraham's visit to Egypt (Gen 12:10-20), the Yahwist's account of the covenant between God and Abraham (Gen 15), and the flight of Hagar (Gen 16). These sagas show no connections with each other, except that they all deal with Abraham, and thus did not form a saga chain of their own. Finally, the Yahwist document includes with these sagas other kinds of materials, such as lists of sons of the patriarchs and more elaborate speeches, like Abraham's speech pleading for the city of Sodom (Gen 18:16-33). Thus, in the J materials of the Abraham

II

cycle four stages can be recognized: 1) the individual sagas, 2) the saga chain of Lot and Abraham, 3) addition of further sagas, and 4) additions of other kinds, not strictly sagas at all. (*Genesis*[2], 140-143. This discussion, along with the commentary on the flight of Hagar episode, exemplifies Gunkel's method particularly well.) The chain, therefore, represents an intermediate unit between the individual saga and written collections of sagas.

Larger units were built up also by expanding a single saga internally, multiplying episodes within one basic story, developing lengthy speeches for the actors, and so on. The prime example is the Joseph story. That story may have begun as a chain (Gunkel begins by calling it such), but in its length, the interest in the character of its actors, and in its expansive narrative style, it must now be characterized as a novella. The expansive style in particular indicates that a new or different level of taste has developed, one appealing to a more sophisticated audience with a longer attention span. Since this style otherwise appears fairly well developed in early historical writing (a different *Gattung*), it must be dated no later than the early monarchic period. The brief style of the sagas, accordingly, would have flourished in earlier times. (*Genesis*[2], 350-353, on Joseph; *Legends*, 79-87 and *Genesis*[2], LI-LIII on the expansive style, translated "epic discursiveness")

The preceding discussion was the *Gattungsforschung* side of Gunkel's method. There remained the more historical side of *Literaturgeschichte*. While his discussion is filled with many examples and details, the main argument is quite simple. The different motifs found in the sagas show a wide variance in their religious, moral, and esthetic levels of sophistication. By starting with the simplest, not to say crudest, motifs and progressively adding more sophisticated ones that have been incorporated into a saga, it is possible to trace the main stages of oral transmission. For the most part this process shows a progressive "Israelitizing" of the sagas. For most of them prove not to be Israelite in origin: there are Babylonian parallels to some of the mythological ones, Egyptian parallels to Joseph episodes, Greek parallels, and, in some cases, especially the sanctuary sagas, Canaanite antecedents can be reliably inferred. From the present sagas it is possible to identify the kinds of changes that derived from Israelite influence: mythology has been suppressed, but not all traces of it totally removed; God as an actor has been withdrawn from familiar converse with men (thus, the visitation to Abraham in Hebron, Gen 18, is an exceedingly old, originally non-Israelite, feature); divine purposes tend to be worked out through human events, as in the case of Abraham's servant securing Isaac's wife (Gen 24) ; and divine favor toward men has come to be expressed in relation to their righteousness, not simply in relation to their power or success (thus Jacob's devious ways reflect an early stage in the history of the sagas) . In some sagas these Israelite influences have come to full expression; in others they have just begun and are somewhat rudimentary. The individual literary units thus reveal an early pre-literate or extra-literate stage of Israelite life and culture. (*Legends,* 88-120; *Genesis*[2], LIII-LXXI. The force of Gunkel's argument should be assessed by his exegetical treatments of the relevant passages in addition to, or prior to, the generalizations of the introduction.)

Two points about this first form critical treatment should be emphasized. First, the term "saga" is used in two senses, generically, in applying to all prose traditional narratives that do not qualify as historical writing, and specifically, in the capacity for distinction, for example, from novella. The Genesis introduction is primarily interested in saga in the generic sense, and no particular attention is given to distinguishing it from other narrative forms such as legend, *Märchen* (tale) , or fable. The *Gattung* "novella" is introduced only because the Joseph story exceeds by too much the characteristics of the saga as Gunkel had already described them. Classification of narrative literary types had not yet become the center of attraction. Another point is the strong historical aspect of Gunkel's approach. By the use of his criterion of progressive sophistication, or "Israelitizing," he could reconstruct three or four stages in the formation of a single saga. In addition, he could reconstruct the process by which original ones developed into different forms, particularly novellas (a process not confined to the Joseph story, but found, e.g., in Gen 24; see *Genesis*[2], 220-221) . In the case of the mythological sagas, he thought it possible to trace the outline of original myths from which the sagas developed (*Genesis*[2], 67-68, a myth behind the Noah story, and XVII-XIX; *Legends,* 14-18) . While there are no longer actual myths in Genesis, the subject matter and motifs of myths are present in the form of sagas, and Gunkel makes some attempt to interpret the original myths that can be identified behind the sagas. (*Genesis*[2], 24-27 contains an etiological interpretation of the paradise myth, and 67-68, the Noah myth.) For this reason, the characteristics of myth as a literary type are indirectly revelant to form criticism of the sagas. Given this strong

II

historical perspective, the saga is not a static entity in Gunkel's conception; rather, it is a stage in the history of literature, succeeding myth making and leading to the novella and historical writing.

B. The *Märchen*

W. Baumgartner, "Israelitisch-Griechische Sagenbeziehungen," *SAV* XLI (1944) 1-29 = his *Zum Alten Testament und seiner Umwelt* (Leiden: E. J. Brill, 1959) 147-178; *idem*, "Bibel und Volkskunde," in his *Zum Alten Testament*, 358–370; *idem*, "Amerikanische Volkskunde," in his *Zum Alten Testament*, 379-384; E. Bethe, *Mythus, Sage, Märchen* (Leipzig: Quelle & Meyer, 1922); O. Eissfeldt, "Die Bedeutung der Märchenforschung für die Religionswissenschaft, besonders für die Wissenschaft vom Alten Testament," *ZMR* XXXIII (1918) 65-71, 81-85 = his *Kleine Schriften*, vol. I, ed. by R. Sellheim and F. Maass (Tübingen: J. C. B. Mohr, 1962) 23-32; *idem*, "Stammessage und Novelle in den Geschichten von Jakob und von seinen Söhnen," *Eucharisterion: Studien zur Religon und Literatur des Alten und Neuen Testaments* (FRLANT 36/I, Göttingen: Vandenhoeck & Ruprecht, 1923) 56-77 = his *Kleine Schriften*, vol. 1, 84-104; H. Gressmann, *Mose und seine Zeit* (FRLANT, NF1, Göttingen: Vandenhoeck & Ruprecht, 1913); *idem*, "Sage und Geschichte in den Patriarchenerzählungen," *ZAW* XXX (1910) 1-34; *idem*, "Ursprung und Entwicklung der Joseph-Sage," *Eucharisterion*, 1-55; H. Gunkel, "Jakob," *PJ* CLXXVI (1919) 339-362; *idem*, "Die Komposition der Joseph-Geschichten," *ZDMG* LXXVI (1922) 55-71; *idem*, *Das Märchen im Alten Testament* (Tübingen: J. C. B. Mohr, 1917).

The two literary forms that were of primary importance for Gunkel's Genesis commentary were the saga and the novella. Myth as a literary type might be relevant if one undertook to reconstruct the older form of materials now given as mythological sagas. Legend as a literary type Gunkel identified only in the story of Abraham's rescue of Lot (Gen 14) taking "legend" in the strict sense of a marvelous story about a man of faith (*Genesis*[2], 255). (On the later, broader use of "legend," see p. 78 below.) Another literary type that was soon to receive extensive attention—the *Märchen*—rarely appears in the first two editions of the Genesis commentary. (In the commentary, the present writer has noted the use of the term only in connection with the Joseph novella, where the motif of the bad brothers seeking to dispose of the good brother is identified, by North African parallels, as a *Märchen* motif, *Genesis*[2], 353. The German term *Märchen* will continue to be used here. In OT discussions it is usually best translated "folk tale," though the connotations of "fairy tale" should not be forgotten.) When Gunkel did the first two editions of the commentary he adhered to the view of the relation between saga and myth that had been advanced by

Wilhelm Grimm, namely, that sagas and *Märchen* developed out of much older myths (Klatt, 110; Eissfeldt, 1962, 24). By the time of the third edition of the commentary, however, he had shifted to the more recent view that the oldest literary form was the *Märchen,* from which both sagas and myths had developed. (Klatt lists the passages that were changed from the first to the third editions of the Genesis commentary in accordance with this shift in viewpoint, 133, n. 24. For the shift in viewpoint that gave the priority to *Märchen* rather than myth in the evolution of literary forms, see Gressmann [1910] 1, where Wilhelm Wundt's *Völkerpsychologie* is cited as influencing Gressmann; Bethe, 6-15; and Eissfeldt, 1962, 24-25.)

While this change in orientation began in the third edition of the Genesis commentary, it was advanced more programmatically by Hugo Gressmann in his 1910 article entitled "Saga and History in the Patriarchal Narratives." Gunkel called this article "epoch-making" ("Jacob," 154 and cp. "Die israelitische Literatur," 111). Werner Klatt has pointed out that the relative priority of influence between Gunkel and Gressmann on this matter cannot be determined because of the constant oral and written correspondence between the two during the years from 1904 to 1910 (Klatt, 136). Gressmann focused on the question of the origin of the figures of the patriarchs. In recent treatments, the patriarchs had been viewed as demythologized gods (i.e., the names of the patriarchs were originally the names of deities) or as personifications of tribal groups. Gressmann argued, on the contrary, that the core of the Abraham, Jacob, and Joseph stories were *Märchen,* folk tales not attached to any particular locale or persons but subsequently localized to Israel by having the main characters identified with traditional figures of Israelite ancestral history. Thus, the *Märchen,* the folk stories, had become attached to certain specific personal names (not divine or tribal ones) among the Israelites and had thereby become sagas, rather than simply *Märchen.* From there, further elaborations were made by later Israelite narrators and writers. Once again, as in the case of myths and the mythological sagas of the primeval history, this was an argument for different literary forms that had eventually become sagas or, in some cases, novellas.

Both Gressmann and Gunkel applied this view to the Jacob and Joseph stories more than once. (Gunkel, later than the Genesis commentary, in "Jakob" [1919] and "Die Komposition der Joseph-Geschichten" [1922]; and Gressmann, in "Sage und

II

70

Geschichte in den Patriarchenerzählungen" [1910] and "Ursprung und Entwicklung der Joseph-Sage" [1923].) In Gunkel's last treatment of the Jacob cycle, this approach led to the following results. The original core of the Jacob-Esau story was a *Märchen* about competing occupations: the sly shepherd (Jacob) outsmarted the dumb hunter (Esau), thereby winning a superior heritage. The names of the characters in this *Märchen* were entirely variable. In time, however, the old personal name Jacob came to be applied to the shepherd and the name Esau applied to the hunter. A different *Märchen* about shepherds, in which a clever young one gained wives and wealth by outsmarting an older one, also came to be associated with the name Jacob. This became the Jacob-Laban cycle, which was eventually combined with the first Jacob-Esau story. The second Jacob-Esau story, the reconciliation after twenty years, was the product simply of narrators' impulses to round out the larger composition. It was only at a time when this basic three-part narrative outline already existed that the main characters began to be identified with peoples or tribal groups; Jacob with Israel, Esau with Edom, and Laban with the Arameans. (Tribal personifications were thus quite secondary in the process.) Meanwhile, other stories about the tribes and sanctuaries of Israel had come to be associated with the name Jacob and to have places in the larger Jacob composition. Examples of these were the separate stories of Jacob's children (e.g., Simeon and Levi in Gen 34, Judah in Gen 38) and the founding of sanctuaries such as Bethel (Gen 28:10-22), Peniel (Gen 32:22-32), Mahanaim (Gen 32:1-2), and Shechem (Gen 33:18-20). This last stage was mostly a matter of inserting otherwise separate traditions into the older self-contained narrative complex.

The primary distinction between a *Märchen* and a saga is that the first is a free-floating story not connected to any particular person, place, or time, while the saga is attached to actual persons, places, or situations. The mode of the *Märchen* is, "Once upon a time, there were two brothers, one a shepherd and the other a hunter." The mode of the saga is, "And there was a famine in the land, and Abraham went down to the land of Egypt." It can be seen, however, that many OT narratives that now classify as sagas might have the specific local references removed from them and still remain coherent stories. By such a process older *Märchen* might be inferred from many sagas. In fact, without following this process, there is scarcely anything to be found in the OT that will qualify as a *Märchen.* (Gunkel does take the present form of Jonah to be a *Märchen,* 1925, 75.) Just as the process of "Israelitizing" had virtually eliminated mythological narratives from surviving Israelite literature, so the tendencies of Israelite taste, morals, and religion worked against the spirits and magic of the *Märchen* world. Therefore, when Gunkel turned to a book-length treatment of the *Märchen* in the OT he was confined to discussion of *Märchen* motifs or traces that appear in other kinds of narratives (e.g., Balaam's talking ass or Elijah's magic mantle) or that were adapted in prophetic, psalm, or apocalyptic writings (e.g., the world tree in Ez 31 and Dan 4, the world mountain in Ps 48 and Is 2:1-4, or the story of the ungrateful foundling girl used by Ezekiel as an allegory of Jerusalem, Ez 16). By scouring the OT, intertestamental literature, and the NT, Gunkel found a large number of such motifs. In his concluding chapter, he discusses the identifying characteristics of the *Märchen* in those writings. Of first importance is the element of fantasy, of make believe and dream worlds. In fact, Gunkel assembles in his book almost all the improbable or supernatural phenomena of the Old Testament under the heading *Märchen* motifs. Also characteristic of *Märchen* is that they tend to endow all kinds of objects, animals, and spirits with human features— speech, self-interest, family relationships, etc.—and they prefer their heroes without names.

Strictly speaking, the *Märchen* is only indirectly relevant to OT form criticism. The extant narratives are not *Märchen,* even if they contain such motifs, and the prophetic allegories and eschatological visions are at least drastic alterations of hypothetical *Märchen.* The one respect in which the study of *Märchen* as a literary type may be important is in reconstructing the earlier stages of extant narrative complexes, as Gunkel and Gressmann did with the Jacob and Joseph cycles. Even there, however, their assumption about the priority of the *Märchen* elements did not gain a strong following. Otto Eissfeldt not only made strictures against Gunkel's subjective method in his book but offered his own alternative analysis of the Jacob and Joseph cycles which argued for the priority of the tribal sagas to the *Märchen* hypothesized by Gunkel and Gressmann.

Märchen study could also be important, however, in so far as it played a role in the historical criticism of sagas. This appears more readily in Gressmann's comprehensive analysis of the Moses traditions than in the Genesis narratives. In facing the question of the historical value of sagas, Gressmann distinguished between "individual motifs" and "typical motifs." The individual ones are those that reflect specific local or temporal realities. In sagas, they are always mixed with typical motifs, that is to say, with *Märchen* motifs. These are such that they "are narrated at all times and by many peoples in the same manner" (*Mose*, 364). Therefore, in the analysis of sagas, if a motif is encountered (e.g., the mode of Moses' deliverance at his birth, Ex 2:1-10) that also appears in the literature of other peoples (e.g., the Legend of Sargon, *ANET*, 119), it must be taken as typical and assigned no historical value. This method requires, therefore, some way of determining which motifs appear in other folk literatures and which do not. That is to say, comparison of folk literatures is required, and the extensive materials of modern folklore study become relevant to the criticism of OT sagas. As Eissfeldt pointed out in criticism of Gunkel, comparison of stories or story elements from widely diverse times and cultural contexts raises complex methodological difficulties and dangers (Eissfeldt, 1918). In many cases it will be doubtful whether a motif has been narrated "by many peoples in the same manner." These issues of comparative method lead, however, to large problems of the history of religion and culture in the ancient Near East and cannot be pursued in a discussion of form criticism of narratives. Lines along which the study of folklore and the OT may be conducted in a careful and disciplined way were developed by Walter Baumgartner, one of Gunkel's pupils mentioned in the acknowledgments of the book on *Märchen* in the OT.

C. Historical Sagas and Historical Writing

H. Gressmann, *Die älteste Geschichtsschreibung und Prophetie Israels* (SAT II/1; Göttingen: Vandenhoeck & Ruprecht, 1921[2]) ; H. Gunkel, "Geschichtsschreibung im A. T.," *RGG*[1] II 1348-1354; *idem*, "Sagen und Legenden: II. In Israel," *RGG*[2] V 49-60; H. Rosenfeld, *Legende* (Stuttgart: J. B. Metzler, 1964[2]) ; H. Schmidt, *Die Geschichtsschreibung im Alten Testament* (Tübingen: J. C. B. Mohr, 1911) .

As indicated earlier, Gunkel recognized three groups of sagas, distinguished by subject matter: mythological or primeval, patriarchal, and heroic or historical sagas. In "Die israelitische Literatur[2]" (71) he designates the subject of the third group *Volkshelden*, folk heroes. However, the marginal reference at his discussion of that group is "Historische Sagen" (73), and in his much later discussion of sagas in the second edition of *RGG*

(1931) he also labels the third group "historische Sagen" (*RGG²* V 53). Since he treats these narratives in terms of the great figures they refer to, the difference does not seem significant. In detail, however, the categorization "hero saga" often misses the mark, as Gressmann's work with the Moses traditions frequently indicates. There are too many cases in which the sagas of Moses are not really "heroic" in any usual sense. The "historical" sagas are by far the most conglomerate of the three groups and were also the group least investigated by Gunkel himself. When he briefly summarized their character, he emphasized that they dealt with figures prominent in and important for the community, which he took to mean that they expressed a particular "political" interest on the part of the early Israelites. ("These saga figures [Moses, Joshua, Gideon, David, etc.] are therefore, for the most part, public persons, corresponding to the strong political interests of the ancient people," 1925, 73. See also *RGG²* V 53.) By labeling the sagas treating figures from Moses to Elisha "historical," Gunkel meant that they have a close and evident relation to actual persons, places, and events. Nevertheless, they remain sagas to the extent that the heroes are drawn larger than life and the magnitude of their deeds or sufferings is exaggerated. The miraculous and the improbable still play a role in enhancing the heroes: Moses' upraised arms bring military victory (Ex 17:8-15), Solomon's surpassing wisdom renders a decisive judgment (I Kings 3:16-28), Elijah crosses the river dryshod (II Kings 2). The presence of such *Märchen*-like elements marks off historical sagas from actual historical narratives, though no sharp division between the two is possible. There is no question that the stories of Moses' birth and David's slaying of Goliath are sagas, but about the narrative of Saul's victory over the Ammonites (I Sam 11) one may remain in doubt. (Gressmann, *Geschichtsschreibung*, XIV. On Moses and David, *ibid.*, 71-72, and *Mose*, 1-16.)

Gunkel and his followers emphasized that there is considerable difference between historical writing and historical documents. (Gunkel's "Geschichtsschreibung im AT," Schmidt's *Geschichtsschreibung*, and the introduction to Gressmann's *Geschichtsschreibung* cover essentially the same ground. The following points are drawn mainly from Gressmann's discussion.) Historical documents such as king lists, royal annals, inscriptions, and chronicles were common in older Near Eastern cultures. These, however, pointed only in a halting fashion toward historical narration for its own sake. Genuine historical writing flourished only in Israel and, later, Greece. Unlike the other narrative literary types, there is some possibility here of tracing the beginning of the *Gattung* itself. One point that Gunkel and his followers thought was clear about historical writing is that it did not evolve from historical documents. It was not through a refinement and elaboration of the narrative element in inscriptions, annals, or chronicles that historical writing emerged. Historical writing evolved from the narrative art of the sagas. It evolved when that art was employed without drawing upon the "typical" motifs of *Märchen,* when the sequence of important (=political) events was seen to contain a "story." (German *Geschichte* means both "history" and "story." See especially Gunkel, 1925, 75.)

Gressmann compared saga with historical writing in the following way. The latter learned its *technique* from saga narration, that is, from the narration of the more sophisticated and elaborate sagas Gunkel had described. Both follow the narrative law of putting the less important before the more important; both increase the suspense by "retarding" moments, by inserting extra incidents prior to the anticipated ending; both love to pair up their heroes, whether in friendship or enmity; both extend the action slowly to a high point, then move rapidly to the conclusion; both often leave certain things unclear for the hearer at first in order to later relieve the aroused curiosity; and both often use repetitions of an action, only slightly altered, in order to fully exploit the kind of situation involved (Gressmann, 1921, XIII). Unfortunately, Gressmann does not give illustrations of these techniques in this discussion. But if history writing and saga narration agree in technique, they differ in choice of subject matters and manner of treating them. History chooses its subject from the present or recent past. Its heroes are kings, crown princes, prophets—in short, the leading persons of the nation. Saga, on the other hand, portrays events from the more distant past. Its heroes are patriarchs, their wives and children, or the mighty men of old time, Moses, Joshua, and the judges. In treating its subjects, history portrays what actually happened, the unique and individual. Saga, on the other hand, is fond of the marvelous and the typical. This does not mean, however, that history writing has no religious character. It simply presents its piety differently, by discerning the hand of God working behind human deeds instead of in *Märchen*-like interventions. It also shows a remarkable objectivity toward its subjects; that is, judgments about the moral character of persons or deeds are always implicit, not explicit (1921, XIII-XIV).

These criteria make it clear that historical writing is not defined by the length of the narrative. A relatively short account such as the episode of Abimelech in Judg 9 may be history. A distinction should be made, however, between historical writing and historical narration. At least Gressmann recognizes that there probably were historical narrations before the time of David not yet written down (1921, XIV-XV). By that time, however, history became "novelistic"; that is, historical accounts were narrated in the "expansive style" of the Joseph story and similar "novellas." The flowering of this type of history writing (particularly exemplified in II Sam) in the time of David and Solomon is no accident, for with the founding of an extensive kingdom, sensitivity to political events and their meaning was greatly enhanced, and history writing always derives from an awakened political consciousness.

Just as historical sagas and historical writing must be distinguished, so must historical writing and historical "works." Historical writing refers to single unified historical accounts. Not many of these have survived intact in the OT. Some fairly complete examples may be the account of David becoming king of Israel (II Sam 2-5), the account of Absalom's rebellion (II Sam 15-20), and the account of Jehu's revolution (II Kings 9-10). These as well as other pieces of historical writing have survived, however, only as they have been incorporated into more comprehensive and complex "historical works." These works are made up of a variety of literary types in addition to historical writing. Thus, cult sagas appear alongside historical writing (I Sam 4:1-7:1 + II Sam 6; II Sam 24), as do "place sagas" (II Sam 5:17-21; II Kings 2:19-22), "anecdotes" (II Sam 21:15-22; 23: 8-23), and especially hero sagas (stories of the judges, of David in the wilderness, etc.). In some cases whole "saga chains" have been included in these historical works, i.e., the Elijah and Elisha story groups (1921, XVI-XVII). Tracing the component materials and stages of formation of these historical works is, of course, a very complex process that requires, but also greatly exceeds, the specific tasks of form criticism. It is a task to which the generation after Gunkel and Gressmann especially contributed, building on the work of those men.

One type of narrative falls somewhere between historical writing and historical document. That is the memoir or biography.

(For what follows, see primarily Schmidt, 1921, 44-47.) Writings in the first person singular were common in royal inscriptions in the ancient Near East, but such documents are entirely unknown for Israel. Quasi-autobiographical writing seems to appear in Israel in service of the prophetic vocation. Hosea (3:1-3) and Isaiah (8:1-4) report actions of their own as revealing Yahweh's will, and this kind of first person report of prophetic actions becomes even more common with Jeremiah (e.g., 13:1-11; 18:1-12) and Ezekiel (e.g., 12:1-16; 24:15-24). But others also understood the experiences of the prophets to be of revelatory significance, with the result that these experiences came to be narrated in the third person, in biographic form (Hos 1; Am 7:10-17; Is 7:1-17). In time, of course, this biographic rendering of the prophet's activity could lead to simply edifying stories portraying the prophets as religious heroes. This seems to happen with the stories of Isaiah's activity at the siege of Jerusalem (Is 36-39). This type of tendentious narrative of prophets is perhaps better labeled "legend" than the prophetic biography (see below, p. 174). The best candidate for genuine prophetic biography in the OT is the story of Jeremiah, presumably written by Baruch the scribe (especially Jer 36-45).

What distinguishes the prophetic narratives from strict autobiography or biography is that they are not related simply out of interest in the personal life of these men; they are told for the sake of portraying God's work through the characters. By the same token, the "memoirs" of Ezra and Nehemiah from the post-exilic period have their own particular religious interests. The first person account of Nehemiah in particular (Neh 1:1-7:5; 11:1-2; 12:27-13:31) shows such an interest in that it is intended to preserve a memory of his faithful deeds before God and not simply before men ("Remember for my good, O God, all that I have done for this people," Neh 5:19). While such works are not strictly historical writing, they were important sources for the complex historical "works," in this case that of the chronicler.

No fully consistent catalogue of literary types, or at least of the terms employed to refer to literary types, seems to have been drawn up by Gunkel, Gressmann, or their fellow workers. Certain major distinctions are regularly observed and assumed, but the different writings of these scholars vary considerably in their terminology for more specific units. Gunkel vacillates in his terminology for the third type of saga, "hero" or "historical" (see above, p. 73). Gressmann tends at times toward overly specialized subdivisions, such as "giant sagas" and "wisdom sagas" (e.g., 1921, XV). This terminological ambiguity is in addition to a more basic one by which the same narrative can be classified as "place saga," "hero saga," etc., because such terms really apply to saga motifs rather than narratives (see above p. 62).

The preceding discussion has aimed at clarifying the basic distinctions and categories shared by most scholars who followed Gunkel's lead. Accordingly, sagas occupy the center of attention. Myths and *Märchen* are finally only tangentially related to the sagas and become important only as efforts are made to reconstruct earlier stages of the literary culture of ancient Israel. By the same token, history writing, which does not, indeed, have to be reconstructed hypothetically, is seen and accounted for against the broad and rich background that the saga is understood to have supplied. Consequently, more or less peripheral literary types such as "anecdote" and "idyll" have been passed over in this discussion. (For "idyll," see Gressmann, 1921, 1-11 and Gunkel, *RGG*² V 54.) Some of these terms will require attention in the next section of this chapter.

There is one term that cannot go entirely without discussion, however. That is "legend." The generation of Gunkel and Gressmann tended to use this term in something close to its original sense—an account of the saints for edifying reading at services and meals in monasteries (Rosenfeld, 1-2). As such, the legend tended always to have a strong religious bias; it was demonstrating the power of its particular deity or religious figure. Gunkel applied the term to the basic story of Gen 14, Abraham's marvelous victory over the four Mesopotamian kings. The cogency of this interpretation seems discussable. Gressmann termed legends such narratives as Samuel's cultic victory over the Philistines (I Sam 7), the narrative of David's anointing (I Sam 16:1-13), and the story of the prophet from Judah and the prophet from Bethel (I Kings 13) (1921, XVI). In the view of both scholars the legend was a late development within Israelite literary history. It was another offspring of saga narration alongside history writing. The impulse toward reality in saga narration was distilled into history writing; the impulse toward fantasy was channeled into legend (Gressmann, 1921, XVI). Like sagas, though even more so, legends mix actual persons and events with imaginative and marvelous motifs. Unlike sagas, legends have a strong religious bias. They are intended to be edifying and to inculcate their religious viewpoint. They emerged primarily

II

78

through the influence of the great prophets and flowered especial-
ly in the post-exilic period in such stories as Jonah, Ruth, and
Judith, as well as in the narratives of Chronicles and Daniel
(Gunkel, 1925, 99 and *RGG²* V 58; Schmidt, 48-52) .

II. CONSOLIDATION

A. Alt, "Joshua," *Werden und Wesen des Alten Testaments*, ed. by F. Stum-
mer and J. Hempel (BZAW 66, Berlin: A. Töpelmann, 1936) 13-29 = his
Kleine Schriften zur Geschichte des Volkes Israel, vol. I (Munich: C. H. Beck,
1953) 176-192; A. Bentzen, *Introduction to the Old Testament*, 2 vols. (Copenhagen: G. E. C. Gad, 1957³) ; J. A. Bewer, *The Literature of the Old Testament* (New York: Columbia University Press, 1922) ; O. Eissfeldt, *Einleitung
in das Alte Testament* (Tübingen: J. C. B. Mohr, 1934, 1964³) = *The Old
Testament: An Introduction*, tr. P. R. Ackroyd (New York: Harper and Row,
1965) ; S. Herrmann, "Die Königsnovelle in Aegypten und in Israel. Ein Beitrag zur Gattungsgeschichte in den Geschichtsbüchern des AT," *WZLU* III
(1953) 51-62; E. Jacob, "Sagen und Legenden II. Im AT," *RGG³* V 1302-1308;
M. Lüthi, L. Röhrich und G. Fohrer, *Sagen und ihre Deutung* (Göttingen:
Vandenhoeck & Ruprecht, 1965) ; M. Noth, *Überlieferungsgeschichtliche Studien* (Tübingen: Max Niemeyer, 1948) ; G. von Rad, *Das formgeschichtliche
Problem des Hexateuch* (BWANT IV/26, Stuttgart: W. Kohlhammer, 1938)
= his *Gesammelte Studien* (TB 8, Munich: Chr. Kaiser, 1958) 9-86 = "The
Form-Critical Problem of the Hexateuch," in *The Problem of the Hexateuch
and Other Essays*, tr. by E. W. T. Dicken (New York: McGraw-Hill, 1966)
1-78; *idem*, "Der Anfang der Geschichtsschreibung im Alten Israel," *AKG*
XXXII (1944) 1-42 = *Gesammelte Studien*, 148-188 = "The Beginnings of
Historical Writing in Ancient Israel," *The Problem of the Hexateuch*, 166-
204; L. Rost, *Die Überlieferung von der Thronnachfolge Davids*, (BWANT
III/6, Stuttgart: W. Kohlhammer, 1926) = *Das kleine Credo und andere
Studien zum Alten Testament* (Heidelberg: Quelle & Meyer, 1965) 119-253;
E. Sellin-G. Fohrer, *Einleitung in das Alte Testament* (Heidelberg: Quelle &
Meyer, 1965¹⁰) = *Introduction to the Old Testament*, tr. by D. E. Green
(Nashville: Abingdon Press, 1968) ; E. Sellin-L. Rost, *Einleitung in das Alte
Testament* (Heidelberg: Quelle & Meyer, 1950⁸) .

By 1925 Gunkel and Gressmann had done their work on the
form criticism of OT narratives. Their last years were occupied
with their work on eschatology and form criticism of the psalms.
The following decades saw more of the incorporation of their
foundations into OT study in general than of significant advances or changes in their basic approach. On one side, the
main lines of the form criticism of narratives came to be presupposed in investigations of the composition of the larger "historical works." (A very few examples: Rost, "Thronnachfolge";
Alt, "Josua"; von Rad, "Problem"; Noth, *Überlieferungsgeschichtliche Studien*; Herrmann, "Königsnovelle.") On the other
side, a discussion of the narrative literary types came to be
regularly included in introductions to the OT. It is this latter
development that is to be considered in the present section. The

purpose is to note, though without undue repetition, the considerable extent to which Gunkel's work is simply repeated, but also to identify problems and complications that appeared as other men appropriated his work. Only a few of the introductions that took account of form criticism in this period can be considered.

In Gunkel's conception of *Literaturgeschichte* the historical dimension is very important. Different literary types predominated in different periods of Israelite history, and a single subject matter might evolve through more than one literary type. Accordingly, he divided his programmatic sketch of Israelite literary history into chronological periods: popular literature until the advent of the great writers (about 750), the great writer personalities (about 750-540), and the epigoni (exilic and after). (See "Die israelitische Literatur.²") Within each of these periods Gunkel discusses the literary forms particularly pertinent to it. He thus sought to combine a diachronic with a synchronic treatment of his subject. In general it can be said that subsequent scholars abandoned the attempt to hold these two together within one presentation. On one side, narrative histories of Israelite literature came to be written which moved from a discussion of all the earliest literary types to a discussion of all the latest ones. (Bewer's *Literature of the Old Testament*, cited with approval by Gunkel, *ibid.*, 108, was one of the earliest.) On the other hand, the literary types were arranged systematically as poetry and prose, law and narrative, etc., regardless of their chronological appearance in Israelite history. This latter method was adopted particularly in the comprehensive discussion of Otto Eissfeldt, first published in 1934. Emphasizing the constancy of literary types in the ancient world, Eissfeldt held it proper to make a systematic arrangement of the *Gattungen* with only occasional reference to historical perspective (*Einleitung*, 10-11; *Introduction*, 11).

The first distinction Eissfeldt makes among literary types is between prose and poetry. In practice, however, an intermediate category must be recognized, namely, the "sayings," which he holds to be prose in content and poetic in form. This grouping seems clearly to be based on Gunkel's distinction between "sung poetry," "recited poetry," and prose. ("Die israelitische Literatur,²" 54-55. Gunkel does not speak of a form and content distinction here.) Narratives come into consideration only under the heading of prose. (It should be noted that this is an accident of history. The Israelites simply did not have or did not preserve poetic narratives like the Mesopotamian or Greek epics; see Bentzen, I, 233, n. 3.) Prose literary types, however, are divided into speeches, records, and narratives. Of these, speeches are said to be closest to real life, that is, closest to the practical activities for the description of which men employ verbal structures (see *Introduction*, 9). Narratives, on the other hand, stand farthest from real life; they are the least practical of prose forms. In the continued subdivision of prose literary forms, narratives are either "poetic" or "historical," the difference here being that poetic narratives are those "which are shaped with an imaginative or a purposeful attitude to the world and to life" while historical narratives "set out to tell how things actually took place" (*Introduction*, 32). With this distinction, Eissfeldt arrives at Gunkel's beginning point in his Genesis introduction, the distinction between saga (generic sense) and history (see above, p. 60). Eissfeldt's subsequent discussion differs from Gunkel's, however, in its much greater interest in a systematic *classification* of types of poetic narrative.

Eissfeldt discusses six types of poetic narrative: myths, *Märchen* (with fable included), sagas, legends, anecdotes, and novellas. They are distinguished as follows: The first four all deal with more or less marvelous events strange to the present and to everyday experience. Anecdotes and novellas, on the other hand, place their action in the world of familiar, ordinary experience. Myths and *Märchen* both deal with actions in the realm of the supernatural; myths with actions among the gods, *Märchen* with supernatural and magical events in the world of men. Sagas and legends differ from these last two in that they are attached to specific places, persons, and times, though they also include elements of the miraculous and marvelous. Legends differ from sagas only in that the specific places, persons, or times they deal with are of religious importance. With the partial exception of "legends," it will be seen that these definitions do not differ from Gunkel's. Since anecdotes and novellas take the ordinary world of experience as their setting, they stand closest to historical narratives. They differ from history, however, in that their purpose is to please and entertain, not to preserve a memory of things that have happened. (Cp. *Einleitung*[1], 35, with *Introduction*, 34.) Anecdotes differ from novellas not in subject matter but in type of action portrayed. In novellas the hero is relatively passive before reacting to the circumstances that come upon him

(Joseph); in the anecdote the hero acts aggressively in his situation, mastering it (David's warriors, II Sam 23:8-23). This last distinction between anecdote and novella does not seem to have been clearly developed by Gunkel.

When Eissfeldt comes to apply these types to the OT materials (*Einleitung*[1], 35-51; *Introduction*, 35-47), the results differ little from those of Gunkel and Gressmann. For both myths and *Märchen* the OT offers virtually no true examples. What are found are many motifs of myths and *Märchen* that appear in other literary types, both prose and poetic. (By the third edition, of course, Eissfeldt is able to refer to far more comparative material in his notes than Gunkel and Gressmann had.) The fable appears in only two true cases, and anecdotes are so few that no separate discussion of them is given. There are indeed a number of novellas to be recognized, but their discussion requires less than half a page (in translation) compared to almost ten pages for sagas and legends. Even legends would merit relatively little space (two pages) if Eissfeldt employed the same definition of the term as Gunkel and Gressmann. The latter tended to confine "legend" to stories of religious heroes (priests and prophets), while Eissfeldt extends it to include stories about sacred places, objects, and times. What Gunkel called cult sagas, Eissfeldt calls cult legends (Eissfeldt, *Einleitung*[1], 45). With this kind of sorting, it becomes clear that the overridingly important literary type of poetic narrative for the extant OT is the saga or, in the expanded sense of legend, the saga and the legend. It is somewhat misleading to list a series of literary types as if all were on the same plane when it turns out that myths and *Märchen* are present only as motifs in sagas, that novellas are mostly sagas cast in the expansive narrative style, and that legends are simply sagas about religious matters.

Given this importance of sagas, it is natural that different kinds are to be distinguished. Eissfeldt gives two broad classes, those dealing with places and natural phenomena and those dealing with tribes and leaders. Correspondingly, there are two groups of legends, ones dealing with sacred places, objects, and times, and ones dealing with sacred persons. Eissfeldt emphasizes that both broad groups of sagas may be etiological, may explain the existence of something familiar to the hearers. This etiological element often takes the form of explaining the name of something so that "a whole series of sagas are simply etymological . . . they have arisen out of the desire to explain a name and have no aim beyond this" (*Einleitung*[1], 39; *Introduction*, 38-39). This last point is in most, if not all, cases very difficult to sustain. Eissfeldt gives as an example the name of the town Zoar, "small," which Lot asks to have spared from the cataclysm that struck Sodom and Gomorrah because it is only a small thing (Gen 19:20-22). There are two difficulties with calling this an etymological saga: first, it is not a saga, but only a minor incident within a much larger story, the Lot-Sodom-Gomorrah story; and second, by Eissfeldt's own interpretation the Zoar incident is intended to explain the peculiar existence of a town within this otherwise desolate area (*Introduction*, 39); that is to say, this is as much a place saga as an etymological one. The problem is with calling it an etymological *saga*, rather than something like an etymological motif within a saga. (Gunkel had, of course, recognized this, see above, p. 62). It is quite misleading to speak as if there were a class of sagas that can be distinctly labeled "etymological." This difficulty points, however, to a yet larger problem, which will be returned to below. That is, how is it to be determined exactly what is a saga (narrative) and what is not?

In his classification of historical narratives Eissfeldt does not make a strong distinction between historical documents and historical writing. He lists five literary types: reports, popular history, autobiography, accounts of dreams and visions, and prophetic autobiography (*Introduction*, 49-56). Reports are more or less official accounts, such as annals and chronicles. They are distinguished from "records," which are not narratives. Autobiography, as Eissfeldt treats it, does not appear in Israel until the Persian period, with the memoirs of Ezra and Nehemiah, though this *Gattung* is widespread elsewhere in the ancient Near East. The accounts of dreams and visions and prophetic autobiography are indeed narrative in form, but what qualifies them as historical writing, rather than historical documents or sources, is not explained.

Under the heading "popular history" Eissfeldt includes those briefer historical accounts that may have persisted for some time in oral form before being written down. Such are the accounts of Gideon's pursuit of the Midianites (Judg 8:4-21), Abimelech's episode (Judg 9), and the several events of David's rise to power (II Sam 1-5). The question of larger, unified instances of historical writing is complicated in Eissfeldt's study by the fact that he separates his treatment of preliterary *Gattungen* from that of "the literary prehistory" of the OT books.

The character of the "throne succession of David" (II Sam 9-20 + I Kings 1-2) comes up, therefore, in the context of analysis of sources in larger historical "works," and not in a form critical discussion (*Introduction*, 137-139). Yet, if the character of historical writing as a distinct literary type is to be esablished, this prime example of the type must be taken into account, as von Rad did so well in a study subsequent to Eissfeldt's first edition (von Rad, "The Beginnings of Historical Writing"). Thus, if anything, Eissfeldt's treatment of "historical narratives" is more ambiguous than those of Gunkel and Gressmann.

Subsequent introductions to the OT were in large measure in dialogue with Eissfeldt as well as Gunkel in their treatment of narrative literary types. Since for the most part they simply follow their predecessors, only important differences of classification or definition will be noted here. In 1949 Leonard Rost did the eighth edition of Ernst Sellin's introduction. For that edition he supplied a discussion of literary types. Like Eissfeldt, he distinguished between poetry and sayings in addition to prose. The prose group, however, he divided into nonnarrative prose, narrative prose, and historical writing. Under narrative prose he gave myths, *Märchen*, fables, sagas, and legends. He treated each of these on the same lines as Eissfeldt. In one respect, however, Rost made an interesting departure from Eissfeldt. Myth, *Märchen*, fable, saga, and legend he says are defined by content, while anecdote and novella are defined by form. An anecdote presents only one feature of its hero in a single, brief action. A novella, on the other hand, presents several aspects of a hero acting in a series of situations. The narrative of the conquest of Bethel in Judg 1:22-26 is an anecdote, while the long narrative of the conquest of Jericho in Josh 1-6 is a novella. The tale of Elisha and the inexhaustible flask of oil (II Kings 4:1-7) is an anecdote, while that of the series of incidents between Elisha and the Shunamite woman (II Kings 4:8-37; 8:1-7) is a novella, as is the presentation of Elijah in I Kings 17-19 (Rost, *Einleitung*, 15, 19-20). Anecdote and novella are not, therefore, literary types alongside myth, *Märchen*, etc. Rather, it would seem, a saga might be an anecdote or a novella in form, and the same would be true for legends. Under the heading historical writing Rost distinguishes documents from historical writing proper. As documents he gives lists, contracts, letters, and collections of laws. These are nonnarrative prose types. Under historical writing proper, Rost discusses annals, historical narratives, and autobiography (*Ichbericht*). In the last category he includes reports of dreams and the use of first person narrative by prophets, which Eissfeldt had distinguished from autobiography.

The Danish OT scholar Aage Bentzen had produced an introduction in his native language in 1941. In 1948 it appeared in a revised two-volume edition in English. The first volume contained an extensive discussion of OT literary types, drawing on not only Gunkel and Eissfeldt, but the work of Scandinavian scholars, especially the Swedish scholar Gunnar Hylmö. In discussing literary types in general, Bentzen emphasized that the types should be defined by stylistic and formal criteria rather than by content, and that the history or evolution of the literary types cannot often be reliably traced. The last point was in contrast to the historical side of Gunkel's treatment of literary types and was related to the "anti-evolutionistic" view of Israelite religion taken by some other Scandinavian scholars (Bentzen, I, 109-111).

Bentzen divided the literary types simply into poetry or prose without an intermediate group. Under the heading "narratives," he discusses sagas (his term is "aetiological legends," he being unwilling to impose the term "saga" upon English usage), *Märchen* ("fairy tales"), myths, and history writing (I, 232-251). He rejects the criterion of "credibility," which is required to make Gunkel's and Eissfeldt's distinction between "poetic" and "historical" narratives, and says that narratives must be classified by "purely formal points of view." A distinction is then introduced between sagas that are short and single-episodic and sagas that are long and multi-episodic. The latter are called hero sagas. (These two forms of sagas seem to correspond to Rost's "anecdote" and "novella," though Bentzen wrote before Rost's work appeared.) Both kinds of saga serve the dual purpose of entertaining and instructing and have a historical nucleus, an event or person to be remembered or explained (I, 233-234). *Märchen* are also long and multi-episodic but are intended only to entertain (I, 234). Myths are said to have no independent literary form but to be sagas that deal with divine persons in a "supranatural environment." No pure *Märchen* or myths are found in the OT, only motifs. Bentzen uses "legend" (his phrase is "devotional legend") in the same sense as Gunkel and Gressmann, that is, for stories with religious tendency and edifying form, usually dealing with holy persons. Therefore, narratives about the founding of sanctuaries and the origin of other cultic phenomena are cultic sagas, not legends as in Eissfeldt's usage.

Bentzen's discussion of historical narratives runs along much the same lines as Gunkel's and Gressmann's. History writing developed from saga narration, following the same "epic laws" as saga, and dispensed with miraculous elements, though it might still have a religious character. Annals, autobiographical novels, and the complex historical "works" can be distinguished.

It may be questioned whether Bentzen really succeeds in using only formal criteria to establish the literary types. The divine persons and supernatural environment of myths would seem to be features of content rather than form, and it is not clear how a purpose simply of entertaining (*Märchen*, "fairy tale") or the presence of a religious *Tendenz* (legend) can be determined apart from content. It must be said, however, that Bentzen comes much closer than other scholars to representing the actual situation of narrative types in the OT in that he assigns great priority to the sagas and relates the other types to them somewhat secondarily.

The contributions Gunkel and his associates made to the encyclopedia *Die Religion in Geschichte und Gegenwart* were revised for the third edition of that work. The important article on "Sagen und Legenden" was done, in its OT part, by the French scholar Edmond Jacob. His treatment is in essential agreement with Gunkel's work, but he adds some distinctions apparently intended to clear up ambiguities in the classification of sagas. First, he rejects the distinction between sagas and legends altogether, observing that etymologically the two terms are synonyms. Then he discusses sagas from the viewpoint of types of content: those with mythical content, those with *Märchen*-like features, and those with historical content. Next Jacob observes that most sagas have an etiological purpose, and he lists the types of etiologies found: natural phenomena; personal and place names; cultic objects, practices, and places; and ethnological relations. After a discussion of the artistic character of the sagas and the non-Israelite origin of some of them (following the third and fourth chapters of Gunkel's introduction to Genesis), Jacob lists the major "themes" with which specifically Israelite saga narration dealt: the theme of the patriarchs, the theme of the heroes, and the theme of the prophets. Within the last theme, martyr sagas and priest sagas are included.

It is obvious that these three classifications are not mutually exclusive. A single saga might have historical content, contain an etiology, and treat the theme of the heroes (e.g., David's pursuit of the Amalekites, I Sam 30). Even further, however, a single saga might contain a *Märchen*-like feature and have historical content, and it might contain more than one kind of etiology. Thus, if anything, ambiguities of classification have been increased. What Jacob's reformulation of the categories does make particularly clear, however, is the need to separate the etiological elements of sagas from other elements considered in their classification. He does not use the term, as Gunkel did, but it would be clearer to speak of etiological *motifs* than of etiological sagas.

A slightly different tack to the classification of OT literary types has recently been taken by Georg Fohrer in the tenth edition of Sellin's introduction. Rather than treating all literary types in one section of the introduction, as Rost had done in earlier editions, Fohrer dealt separately with all aspects of the historical and legal books, all aspects of the poetic books, all aspects of the wisdom books, and all aspects of the prophetic books. Each of these parts, accordingly, contains its form critical discussion. For the different literary types of the historical and legal books Fohrer introduced a new terminology, one based on the functions each type served. Thus, he treats "directive literary types" (laws, etc.), "requesting and wishing literary types" (blessings, etc.), "proclaiming and instructing literary types" (oracles, etc.), "communicating literary types" (speeches, letters, etc.), "narrative literary types," and "reportorial literary types" (lists, history, etc.) (*Introduction*, 9-10).

Within the "narrative"and "reportorial" groups very much the same subdivisions appear as in previous treatments. Under narratives he discusses myth, *Märchen*, novella, anecdote, saga, and legend. He defines novella and anecdote in the way Eissfeldt had (above, p. 81) rather than the way Rost did (above, p. 84). Fohrer also uses the term "legend" as Eissfeldt had, namely, to refer to any saga dealing with religious matters. His discussion of kinds of sagas and legends and of the extensive etiological element in them is proportionately quite large, reflecting the actual situation in the OT, but departs in no important respects from previous ones. Fohrer does add a section to the discussion of sagas that seeks to identify the tendencies that worked within the history of saga narration in Israel. In the course of their long history of transmission, the sagas were gradually "personalized," "nationalized," "Yahweh-ized" (*jahwisiert*), and "theologized." These criteria make it possible to follow the history of some sagas through the process that Gunkel called "Israelitization" (see above, p. 67). Fohrer drew together his interpretation of saga in Israel in his lecture in Lüthi's *Sagen und ihre Deutung*, 59-80.) Fohrer's discussion of "reportorial" literary types follows almost entirely previous discussions of "historical writing," making it particularly clear that from Eissfeldt to Fohrer a "consolidation" had indeed taken place.

Within the broad, common framework of this consolidation some divergences and disagreements have been noted. These may be simply enumerated here before turning to the current situation. Perhaps the most basic, though also the most difficult, issue is Bentzen's insistence that literary types be defined only by formal criteria. While it seems unlikely that Bentzen himself was able to adhere to this principle, the form-content problem is sure to persist in the discipline of "form" criticism. It may be suggested that in the case of narrative, the question of "form" has not been properly shaped. (See below on the problem of defining narrative qua narrative.) A separate but related issue is the different ways of defining anecdote and novella. Rost's combination of form and content criteria seems more cogent than Eissfeldt's passive-active criterion for defining the two, but the first approach seems not to have been pursued in more recent work. A third issue within the consolidation is the treatment of etiology and the persisting tendency to classify some narratives as etiological rather than as containing etiological motifs. As will be noted below, more recent studies have probably worked this problem through. A fourth problem is the treatment of myth and *Märchen* as classes of narratives alongside saga and legend. In Gunkel's approach, with its strong historical emphasis, there was some pertinence to this, but in Eissfeldt's more nonhistorical classification, the parallel listing of apparently distinct narrative types is misleading, and it is Eissfeldt's tendency that has persisted in the consolidation. Finally, the two different definitions of "legend" may be noted. The Eissfeldt and Fohrer definition of this term seems rather artificial, and more recent study appears to favor the usage of Gunkel and Bentzen in which legends are mainly about persons and have a clear religious *Tendenz*. (See the article by A. Rofé in the following bibliography.)

III. CURRENT ISSUES

L. Alonso-Schökel, "Erzählkunst im Buche der Richter," *Bib* XLII (1961) 143-172; J. Bright, *Early Israel in Recent History Writing* (SBT 19, London: SCM Press, 1956); B. S. Childs, "A Study of the Formula 'Until This Day'," *JBL* LXXXII (1963) 279-292; G. W. Coats, *Rebellion in the Wilderness*

(Nashville: Abingdon Press, 1968) ; W. Dommershausen, *Die Estherrolle, Stil und Ziel einer alttestamentliche Schrift* (Stuttgart: Katholisches Bibelwerk, 1968) ; J. Fichtner, "Die etymologische etiologie in der Namengebung der geschichtlichen Bücher des Alten Testaments," *VT* VI (1956) 372-396; D. Greenwood, "Rhetorical Criticism and Formgeschichte: Some Methodological Considerations," *JBL* LXXXIX (1970) 418-426; C. A. Keller, " 'Die Gefährdung der Ahnfrau.' Ein Beitrag zur gattungs -und motivgeschichtlichen Erforschung alttestamentlicher Erzählungen," *ZAW* LXVI (1954) 181-191; M. Kessler, "Narrative Technique in I Sm 16, 1-13"; *CBQ* XXXII (1970) 543-554; K. Koch, *The Growth of the Biblical Tradition*; E. Leach, *Genesis as Myth and Other Essays* (London: Jonathan Cape, 1969) ; Norbert Lohfink, "Die Bundesurkunde des Königs Josias. Eine Frage an die Deuteronomiumsforschung," *Bib* XLIV (1963) 261-288; *idem*, "Darstellungskunst und Theologie in Dtn 1, 6-3, 29," *Bib* XLI (1960) 105-134; B. O. Long, *The Problem of Etiological Narrative in the Old Testament* (BZAW 108, Berlin: A. Töpelmann, 1968) ; D. J. McCarthy, "An Installation Genre?," *JBL* XC (1971) 31-41; *idem*, "Moses' Dealings with Pharaoh: Exodus 7:8-10:27," *CBQ* XXVII (1965) 336-347; *idem*, "Plagues and Sea of Reeds: Exodus 5-14," *JBL* LXXXV (1966) 137-158; J. Muilenburg, "Form Criticism and Beyond," *JBL* LXXXVIII (1969) 1-18; *idem*, "A Study in Hebrew Rhetoric: Repetition and Style," *VTS* I (1953) 97-111; B. Nathhorst, *Formal or Structural Studies of Traditional Tales* (SSCR 9, Bromma: P. A. Norstedt & Söner, 1969) ; Martin Noth, *Das Buch Josua* (HAT I/7, Tübingen: J. C. B. Mohr, 1953²) ; *idem*, "Der Beitrag der Archäologie zur Geschichte Israels," *VTS* VII (1960) 262-282; D. B. Redford, *A Study of the Biblical Story of Joseph* (VTS 20, Leiden: E. J. Brill, 1970) ; H. Ringgren, "Literarkritik, Formgeschichte, Überlieferungsgeschichte. Erwägungen zur Methodenfrage der alttestamentlichen Exegese," *TLZ* XCI (1966) 641-650; A. Rofé, "The Classification of the Prophetical Stories," *JBL* LXXXIX (1970) 427-440; I. L. Seeligmann, "Hebräische Erzählung und biblische Geschichtsschreibung," *TZ* XVIII (1962) 305-325; *idem*, "Aetiological Elements in Biblical Historiography," *Zion* XXVI (1961) 141-169 (Hebrew with Eng. summary) ; H. J. Stoebe, "Gedanken zur Heldensage in den Samuelbüchern," *Das ferne und nahe Wort* (BZAW 105, Berlin: A. Töpelmann, 1967) 108-118; M. Weiss, "Einiges über die Bauformen des Erzählens in der Bibel," *VT* XIII (1963) 456-475; C. Westermann, "Arten der Erzählung in der Genesis," in his *Forschung am Alten Testament* (TB 24, Munich: Chr. Kaiser, 1964) 9-91.

If recent introductions and encyclopedias give the impression that OT form criticism is firmly established and ordered, current specialized literature does not seem to confirm that impression. Methodological discussions are prominent, and among them a leading concern seems to be to establish the limits of form criticism. What is not form criticism? What other methods must be recognized alongside form criticism? Within his own time Gunkel had quite self-consciously distinguished his approach from "literary criticism," meaning by the latter the analysis of component documents in the Pentateuch and elsewhere. He understood the methods of *Literaturgeschichte* to be complementary to literary criticism. His "literary history" was a broad approach, however, and encompassed several subdisciplines. One can view some recent

II

89

developments of OT research as the breaking up into separate disciplines of the different components of Gunkel's *Literatur-geschichte*. Alongside form criticism in the narrow sense (*Gattungsforschung*), tradition history and redaction criticism have emerged to deal more systematically with the historical aspects of *Literaturgeschichte*. The strong esthetic interest Gunkel took in OT literary forms may be seen to anticipate somewhat more recent "aesthetic criticism." (Muilenburg's phrase, 1969, 7.) The recent methodological discussions, however, tend to identify Gunkel's main contributions with *Gattungsforschung* (*ibid.*, 1; Ringgren, 643-644), and such a view is justified considering the great advances the generation after Gunkel made in tradition history and related research.

When scholars have turned to identifying and employing other methods of research, they criticize or set limits upon form criticism. Thus, James Muilenburg, in his presidential address to the Society of Biblical Literature entitled "Form Criticism and Beyond," holds Gunkel's *Gattungsforschung* to be limited by the necessary generality of its approach. It lays such stress on

> the typical and representative that the individual, personal, and unique features of the particular pericope are all but lost to view. . . . Form criticism by its very nature is bound to generalize because it is concerned with what is common to all the representatives of a genre, and therefore applies an external measure to the individual pericopes (Muilenburg, 1969, 5).

The same point, though not viewed as a problem, is made by Alonso-Schökel (1961, 171-172). What is needed to compensate for this limitation of form criticism is another discipline that can do justice to the concreteness and specificity of an individual text. Muilenburg proposes to call this second discipline "rhetorical criticism" and sees it as complementary to form criticism. Others designate such an approach "esthetic criticism," "structural criticism," and "literary criticism" in a restricted sense (*ibid.*, 7; Greenwood, 421-422). In exhibiting his "rhetorical criticism," Muilenburg unfortunately discusses mostly poetic texts rather than narratives. In general, however, the rhetorical critic must first define the limits or scope of the literary unit. For this purpose he will use not only the devices of form critics but rhetorical techniques like climax points and patterns of verbal repetition. He will also be sensitive to instances when the true literary unit

II

90

consists of smaller components, such as strophes, and not mistake the latter for separate literary units.

A second concern of the rhetorical critic is with the function of rhetorical devices in the structure of the composition. "It is our contention that the narrators and poets of ancient Israel and her Near Eastern neighbors were dominated not only by the formal and traditional modes of speech of the literary genres or types, but also by the techniques of narrative and poetic composition" (Muilenburg, "Form Criticism and Beyond," 10). The rhetorical critic does not seem to differ from the form critic, therefore, with regard to the size of the unit with which the two work. Both, it would seem, work on the same units, but the form critic is comparing many units in terms of their common and general features, while the rhetorical critic will discern how the general form has been rendered specific by artistic and rhetorical techniques. Both start by defining the limits of the unit, which is clear on the part of form critics from Gunkel to Koch.

In narrative literature, an earlier study by I. L. Seeligmann seems to fit rather well Muilenburg's rhetorical criticism. Seeligmann intends to demonstrate that literary-critical, form-critical, and tradition-historical methods can be fruitfully combined in dealing with OT narrative literature. Affirming the use of the customary form critical terminology for narratives, he observes that the main type is the saga. Then he identifies customary forms of introduction and conclusion for the individual saga units. The conclusions of such stories regularly consist of a twofold statement of departure: "When the Lord had finished talking with Abraham, he left him, and Abraham returned home" (Gen 18:33, NEB). "And Saul went back to his home, while David and his men went up to their fastness" (I Sam 24:22, NEB). Such a statement seems to be a device employed in oral narration. When, then, this twofold departure formula is found followed by other kinds of material, it can be presumed that the latter were not part of the original oral narration. (E.g., I Sam 15:34-35, "Saul went to his own house at Gibeah, and Samuel went to Ramah; and he never saw Saul again to his dying day. . . .") A rhetorical device thus serves to establish the limits of an original narrative unit. Seeligmann observes a similar device employed for composition technique as well. When an originally autonomous unit is to be inserted into a previously continuous narrative composition, the last statement before the insertion is repeated in some form immediately following the insertion (examples are Gen 37:36 and

39:1; II Chron 12:2-9 compared with I Kings 14:25-26). Seeligmann considers this an instance in narrative of the "literary principle" of repetition, which Muilenburg would call a "rhetorical"
principle (Muilenburg, "A Study in Hebrew Rhetoric").

Many studies of narratives from a style critical or rhetorical
critical approach have been made in the last decade, usually with
little or no explicit relationship to previous form critical treatment of narratives. (Alonso-Schökel's "Erzählkunst im Buche der
Richter" is both one of the earliest and most important. Other
random examples are the studies of Weiss, Lohfink, McCarthy,
and Kessler.) A recent study of Esther by Werner Dommershausen, however, attempts a systematic treatment of literary types in
that book from a style critical approach. Dommershausen describes his method as consisting of four steps. First, the individual
literary unit must be defined on grounds of style. Then the syntactical, linguistic, and poetic forms of the individual unit are
studied, especially to observe usages that depart from ordinary
speech or from the usual features of the literary type in question.
(The criterion of departure from common usage for artistic or
rhetorical purposes belongs to the classical discipline of "style" or
"diction," Aristotle's *lexis, Poetics,* 22; *Rhetoric,* III. 2.) The
third step is a complex one. It is the "co-ordinating intuition" by
means of which the scholar recognizes how the different features
of syntax, of poetic turns, and the like complement each other
to form a unified sense of the unit ("Hauptsinn der Einheit,"
Estherrolle, 15). At the fourth step the literary unit will be classified as belonging to one or another literary type on the basis of
its syntactical-stylistic features, and the coalescence of style and
content of the literary unit will become apparent. Here Dommershausen reiterates a common motif of earlier style criticism, namely, that the high points or climactic points stylistically will coincide with the high points or climaxes of theme or content (16).

Dommershausen applies his method with a certain rigor, proceeding through the book of Esther unit by unit. At the conclusion, he is able to define several different *Gattungen* primarily by
style criteria. The literary types that appear in Esther are narrative, report, description (*Schilderung*), decree, notice, and speech.
In accordance with his approach, Dommershausen defines narrative primarily by stylistic features. A narrative begins quietly with
a general statement in the form of a verbal clause in perfect tense
or a noun clause. It builds tension through imperfect consecutive
clauses and reaches some kind of stylistic climax at the high point.

II

92

Here stands always a speech or a dialogue. Tension is maintained through an alternation of verbal and noun clauses, and inversion of word order in verbal clauses produces special emphasis. The denouement is always given in an imperfect consecutive clause, and a formula stands at the conclusion (154). Narrative is distinguished from report and description in that the latter two do not have a buildup and release of tension and the stylistic features accompanying it. They present their subject matters in simply a neutral, level way.

Two aspects of Dommershausen's treatment of narrative are significant. One is the use of syntactic and stylistic criteria to define the literary type. How successful this combination of style criticism and form criticism may be in materials other than Esther remains to be seen. The second aspect is his definition of narrative in terms of the buildup and release of tension. Most earlier form critical discussions of narratives gave much more attention to distinguishing different kinds of narrative than to making clear what constitutes a narrative. (Still, see Gressmann's discussion of historical writing, above, pp. 74-76, and Bentzen's appreciation of the "epic laws" sketched by the Danish folklorist Axel Olrik; Bentzen, I, 234, 244.) That a narrative must have a "plot"—that beginning, middle, and end which contribute to the buildup and release of dramatic tension—may at times have been assumed by form critics, but it has rarely played any important part in discussions of OT narratives.

An important exception to this neglect of plot in narrative is Claus Westermann's discussion of the types of narrative in Genesis. ("Arten der Erzählung in der Genesis." Westermann is also doing the commentary on Genesis in the comprehensive *Biblischer Kommentar: Altes Testament* series.) Westermann begins with the question whether it is appropriate to speak of a literary type called "promise narrative." The question, which arises because of the prominence of the promise theme in the patriarchal narratives, requires a definition of narrative, and Westermann is at pains to give one: "In a narrative an event is related in which a tension (*Spannung*) leads to a resolution (*Lösung*)" (Westermann, 33). The question about a promise narrative *Gattung* then becomes whether there are narratives in which the development of the tension and resolution consist in the promise itself. If the promise is peripheral to the buildup of tension, it is not strictly speaking a promise narrative. When these points are applied to the patriarchal materials of Genesis it becomes clear that there is a long tradition history behind the promise theme. Westermann distinguishes four relationships of promise to narrative forms. The first and earliest is a promise narrative proper, seen in the assurance of a son to be born (Gen 16 and 18:1-15) . Here the tension is resolved by the giving of the promise. In a second type, the tension is similarly resolved, but the structure was originally that of a lament with salvation oracle (seen in Gen 15:1-6 and 7-21) rather than a narrative. A third type is a narrative, with the vow only a single scene incorporated into it in some way, the buildup of tension and resolution not requiring a promise scene. This is seen in the pledge at the end of the sacrifice of Isaac (Gen 22:15-18) and in that after the separation from Lot (Gen 13:14-17) . Finally, a promise may appear as simply a notice and not a narrative at all, that is, without tension and resolution. Such is Gen 12:7, which does not even constitute a scene in another narrative.

By taking this view of the nature of narrative, Westermann is also able to set the old difficulties about etiologies in sagas or narratives in a new light. A narrative should be called etiological only if the question and narrated answer themselves form the tension and resolution of the story. By this criterion, however, scarcely any etiological narratives can be found. Westermann refers to Gunkel's discussion of etiology in the sagas of Genesis and points out that Gunkel's classification into "ethnological," "etymological," "cultic," and "geological" etiologies is not a classification of narratives but of motifs. Even when this is recognized, however, etiological motifs should not be grouped according to the content Gunkel's terms indicate but to the realm in which the question the etiology answers arises. Etiologies in the primeval history address quite different questions; they are distinct from those that address questions arising from the family world of the patriarchs or from the political world of historical writing (39-43) .

The problem of etiology and the historicity of narratives containing etiologies had occupied much attention prior to Westermann's study and may be mentioned here in passing. Albrecht Alt and Martin Noth had emphasized the untrustworthiness of etiological narratives as bearers of sound historical tradition. W. F. Albright and John Bright, on the other hand, minimized the extent to which an etiological element could generate complete narratives and that actual historical tradition might take etiological form. (Westermann summarizes the contributions to this discussion by Noth, Bright, J. Fichtner, B. S. Childs, and I. L. Seeligmann [43-47]. See also the work of Long, 1-3.) Westermann's con-

clusion about the rarity of true etiological narrative is complemented by other recent studies of etiological formulas employed
in narratives. Brevard Childs studied the formula "until this
day," and Burke O. Long studied the formulas by which names
are given in etiologies, by which something is called a "sign," and
by which the meaning of a thing is explained. Both concluded
that in most cases the formula has been secondarily added as a
redactional commentary on existing traditions.

The recognition that etiological elements are mostly motifs included in narratives rather than a class of narratives points toward a larger problem, namely, how the relations of a narrative
as a whole to its component parts, motifs, should be understood.
One of the virtues of Klaus Koch's recent introduction to form
criticism, *The Growth of the Biblical Tradition* [the German title
(translated) is "What Is Formhistory?"], is the serious attention
it gives to this problem. First there is the distinction between
(literary) form and formula.

> A literary type is indicated by the typical characteristics of
> an individual linguistic unit, whereas a formula is a set of
> connecting words, which, though they can indeed convey a
> meaning in themselves, usually consist of only one sentence
> and are used in association with a greater literary type. The
> transition from one to another, from formula to literary type,
> is of course scarcely noticeable (Koch, *Growth*, 5).

It has been noticed above that etiological motifs usually consist
of or contain formulas, whereas the whole saga or narrative
would be the literary type. Narratives also often include nonnarrative literary types such as blessings (Gen 26:3-5; Koch,
120-121) or apodictic commands (Gen 26:11; Koch, 121). This
phenomenon calls for a distinction between *component* literary
types and *complex* literary types (Koch, 23-25), a distinction that
Koch observes has been previously neglected in form critical
study. It should be evident that narratives most of all would be
likely to contain other literary types, since in narratives speeches
are made, letters are written, laws quoted, prophetic messages
delivered, and the like. When Koch comes to discuss examples
of form critical studies of narratives, he fails, as did his predecessors, to raise the question of the definition of narrative itself and
of the role of plot in narrative. If he had raised that question he
might have distinguished between components of narratives that
are required for the buildup and resolution of dramatic tension
and those components not required for that plot structure. He

treats the blessing of Isaac in Gen 26:3-5 as a part of the narrative of the "endangering" of the matriarch Rebekah (120-121). That blessing makes no contribution at all, however, to the buildup and resolution of the tension of that narrative. Thus, one may conclude that a more fruitful form critical treatment of narratives could be achieved by combining the key points of Westermann's and Koch's contributions.

The problem of defining the essential structure of narrative also appears in C. A. Keller's critique of Gunkel's method. Keller observes that confusion persists in classification of narrative literary types and argues further that Gunkel's whole approach was misguided because almost all narratives can be classified under more than one of the usual headings. The problem is that narratives are composed of several "building elements" (*Bauelemente*) or motifs, and different building elements may fall under different headings, even though they appear in the same narrative. In a way, therefore, Keller generalizes the point about etiological motifs and applies it to all motifs of a narrative. Thus, the old classifications should be disposed of and narratives should be approached by means of "motif analysis." Keller exemplifies this approach on the three stories of the "endangering of the matriarch." He distinguishes each motif that appears in these narratives, dividing them into two groups: a "basic motif" (*Grundmotiv*), which is the only thing common to all three versions of the story, and "composition motifs," which are the complementary ones varying in each narrative. It is possible to assign each motif to a particular life setting (*Sitz im Leben*), but not the extant narratives. A systematic analysis and classification of narrative motifs is very much needed, Keller thinks. Each narrative that results from the combination of motifs manifests a unique, historically and artistically specific creation of the Israelite soul. The finished narratives should be viewed in this light instead of as parallel versions of the same story.

Unfortunately, Keller gives much more attention to the analysis of separate motifs than he does to composition, and he does not make clear whether the "basic motif," the one common to all three narratives, is itself a narrative. That is, does the "basic motif" have a plot, so that it constitutes a narrative? If so, is it only a "motif"? Once again, Keller's critique, if more fully developed, would seem to point in the direction of Westermann's and Koch's labors to improve the older approach of Gunkel.

The question of the relation between motif and narrative

II

arises also in George W. Coats's recent study of the wilderness narratives, which includes a form critical analysis (29-43). The "murmuring motif," the accusatory speech the Israelites direct against Moses and Aaron when they encounter distress in the wilderness (e.g., Ex 16:2-3; Num 11:4-6), gradually came to be included in several wilderness narratives that originally related simply how Yahweh graciously met the needs of the Israelites. While the murmuring motif is not quite a formula, it does tend to have stereotyped language and a constancy of content (such as calling into question the goodness of the exodus). This would seem to be a particularly striking instance, however, in which Westermann's approach to the promise narratives in Genesis might be applied. Even if Coats is right about the murmuring always being secondary to older narratives (the Dathan-Abiram rebellion, Num 16, may be a qualified exception), it seems quite clear that the murmuring speeches establish a high level of dramatic tension at the beginning of these narratives and that the function of the mighty deeds of Yahweh is to resolve the tension created by those murmuring speeches. It would seem quite appropriate, therefore, to speak of "murmuring narratives," and not simply of a "murmuring motif." Given this common dramatic structure of the narratives, the designation "murmuring narrative" would seem to be much more adequate to the character of the narratives than such designations as "place saga," "hero saga," and the like used in Gressmann's study of the Mosaic traditions (Gressmann, *Mose und seine Zeit*). One might discern, then, the same stages in the development of murmuring narratives that Westermann discerned in the development of promise narratives in Genesis.

When Koch undertook to give examples of form criticism on several different kinds of narrative, he quite naturally leaned toward examples that are in some sense parallel to each other or may be thought to be alternative versions of each other. Thus, he dealt with the three narratives of the endangering of the matriarch and then, as instances of the hero saga, with the two about David declining opportunities to kill Saul in the wilderness (I Sam 24 and 26). In the case of the matriarchal stories he had the precedent of Gunkel as well as more recent studies, like Keller's, to follow. He found, however, that form critical studies of narratives like those of David and Saul and the prophetic legends of Elijah (he treated II Kings 1) are not abundant (132, 186). It would seem that Gunkel's method, even though subject to several limitations pointed to in recent times, still has much to contribute to the study of OT narratives. Alongside the newer tendencies toward style criticism and redaction criticism, valuable form critical work continues to be done and may be expected to continue in the future.

To mention only three recent instances of continuation on past lines: one should note the article by Stoebe, which complements Koch's work on the David-Saul narratives; Rofé's study, which goes a long way toward overcoming the ambiguities of the old rubric "legend"; and McCarthy (1971), who does a penetrating analysis of an "installation genre" in various OT narrative books. In an impressive study of the Joseph story, Redford has continued the lines of Gunkel's work (see especially, 66-105). Quite a different approach to OT narratives is represented by Edmund Leach's *Genesis as Myth and Other Essays*, which applies Levi-Strauss's structural analysis of "myth" to narratives in Genesis and Samuel, as well as in the NT. "Myth" here has an entirely different meaning from that in earlier form critical discussions, but the issues involved considerably exceed a discussion of form criticism. The methodologies of both Levi-Strauss and Leach have been sharply criticized by Bertel Nathhorst (37-70).

JAY A. WILCOXEN

II

Chapter Three

LAW

I. OLD TESTAMENT AND ANCIENT NEAR
EASTERN SOURCES

G. Boyer, *Archives Royales de Mari: Textes juridiques* (ARMT 8, Paris: Imprimerie Nationale, 1958) ; *idem*, "Les tablettes juridiques de Mari," *Melanges d'Histoire du droit Orient* (RAL 92, Paris: Sirey, 1965) 29-43; G. Cardascia, *Les lois assyriennes* (Paris: Éditions du Cerf, 1969) ; H. Cazelles *et al.*, *Populus Dei I* (Communio 10, Rome: L. A. S., 1969), including: A. Barucq, "La notion d'alliance dans l'AT et les débuts de judaïsme," 5-110, H. Cazelles, "Le sens religieus de la loi," 177-200, G. Ercole, "The Juridicial Structure of Israel from the Time of Her Origin to the Period of Hadrian," 389-461, J. P. M. van der Ploeg, "Les juges en Israël," 463-507; M. Civil, "New Sumerian Law Fragments," in *Studies in Honor of Benno Landsberger*, ed. by H. G. Güterbock and T. Jacobsen (AS 16, Chicago: University of Chicago Press, 1965) 1-12; G. R. Driver and J. C. Miles, *The Assyrian Laws* (London: Oxford University Press, 1935) ; *idem*, *The Babylonian Laws*, 2 vols. (London: Oxford University Press, 1952) ; Z. Falk, *Hebrew Law in Biblical Times* (Jerusalem: Wahrmann, 1964) ; *idem*, *Current Bibliography of Hebrew Law* (Tel Aviv: Tel Aviv University, 1965-) ; A. Falkenstein, "Das Gesetzbuch Lipit-Ištar von Isin. I. Philologisches zum Gesetzbuch," *Or* XIX (1950) 103-111; *idem*, *Die neusumerischen Gerichtsurkunden*, 3 vols. (ABAW 39-40, 44, Munich: C. H. Beck, 1956-57); J. J. Finkelstein, "The Laws of Ur-Nammu," *JCS* XXII (1968-69) 66-82; J. Friedrich, *Die hethitischen Gesetze* (Leiden: E. J. Brill, 1959, 1971²) ; J. Gilissen, ed., *Introduction bibliographique à l'histoire du droit et à l'ethnologie juridique* (Brussels: Université libre de Bruxelles, 1965-) ; A. Goetze, *The Laws of Eshnunna* (AASOR 31, New Haven: American Schools of Oriental Research, 1956); O. R.

Gurney and S. N. Kramer, "Two Fragments of Sumerian Laws," in *Studies in Honor of Benno Landsberger*, 13-19; R. Haase, *Einführung in das Studium keilschriftlicher Rechtsquellen* (Wiesbaden: Otto Harrassowitz, 1965); S. N. Kramer and A. Falkenstein, "Ur-Nammu Law Code," *Or* XXIII (1954) 40-51; E. Neufeld, *The Hittite Laws* (London: Luzac & Co., 1951); J. Sedláková, "Bibliographisches zum hebräischen Recht," *JJP* XI-XII (1957-58) 263-292, XIV (1962) 89-107; E. Seidel *et al., Orientalisches Recht* (HdO, Erste Abteilung, Ergänzungsband III, Leiden: E. J. Brill, 1964); F. R. Steele, "The Code of Lipit Ishtar," *AJA* LII (1948) 425-450; É. Szlechter, "Le code de Lipit-Ištar," *RA* LI (1957) 57-82, 177-196, LII (1958) 74-90; R. Thompson, *Moses and the Law in a Century of Criticism since Graf* (VTS 19, Leiden: E. J. Brill, 1970); R. de Vaux, *Les institutions de l'Ancien Testament*, 2 vols. (Paris: Éditions du Cerf, 1956, 1960) = *Ancient Israel: Its Life and Institutions*, tr. by J. McHugh (New York: McGraw-Hill, 1961); J. A. Wilson, *et al., Authority and Law in the Ancient Orient* (AOS 17, New Haven: American Oriental Society, 1954); R. Yaron, *The Laws of Eshnunna* (London: Oxford University Press, 1969).

A large percentage of the OT consists of legal stipulations, traditions, and explanations. The vast bulk of this material is found in four major collections: the Covenant Code (Ex 20:22-23:33), the Deuteronomic Code (Deut 12-26), the Holiness Code (Lev 17-26), and the Priestly Code (Ex 25-31; 34:29-Lev 16 and parts of Num). A smaller but far better known collection is the so-called Decalogue, which appears twice with slight differences (Ex 20:2-17 and Deut 5:6-21). These major collections of Hebrew law, however, do not exhaust the legal traditions of the OT. Individual stipulations (such as Gen 9:6) and short series (as in Ex 34:11-26) are also found or presupposed. Many texts reflect legal processes, such as trials, contracts, and treaties. In the boundary area between legal and nonlegal materials are texts relating to political administration, including investitures, lists, and edicts.

Before the advent of form criticism, literary criticism had concerned itself primarily with such issues as the relationship between these major collections of law and the various literary strands or histories in which they appeared within the Pentateuch; the cultural, sociological, and religious content of the laws as reflections of stages in the historical development of the ancient Hebrews; and the dates to be assigned to these collections. Most literary critics, in terms of the supplementary hypothesis concerning the origin of the Pentateuch, regarded the major collections as supplements added in block to the various literary strands. Frequently, the lack of unity within large collections was recognized, and many scholars sought to elucidate the literary growth of these collections out of literary fragments of varying origins, in

III

100

terms similar to those utilized in the so-called fragmentary hypothesis concerning the origin of the Pentateuch. (For a discussion and bibliography on the literary treatment of the OT legal traditions, see R. Thompson, 53-105.) Within literary criticism, the generally assumed and approximate chronological sequence of the final redacted codes was thought to be the following: the Covenant Code, the Decalogue, the Deuteronomic Code, the Holiness Code, and the Priestly Code. Form criticism has now enabled scholars to go behind the immediate literary context and process and reconstruct something of the prior history of particular texts and collections, as well as the life setting and development of the different legal genres and formulas.

Fortunately, for OT scholars in general and form critics in particular, we now possess a number of ancient Near Eastern law codes and documents on related matters and subjects. The principal ancient Near Eastern law codes are the Sumerian Ur-Nammu (c. 2050 B.C.; *ANET*, 523-525) and Lipit-Ishtar codes (c. 1875; *ANET*, 159-161); the Akkadian Eshnunna (*ANET*, 161-163) and Hammurabi codes (*ANET*, 163-180, the most widely known, used, and influential), both c. 1700, and the Middle Assyrian Laws (c. 1450-1000; *ANET*, 180-188); the Hittite Laws (c. 1500; *ANET* 188-197), and the fragmentary Neo-Babylonian Laws (*ANET*, 197-198), c. 600 B.C. No codes are preserved from Egypt. The collections show recensional activity and complex origin but leave many legal areas unmentioned. Their function is disputed: Were they books of decisions to guide judges, royal law, or scholarly collections? Also preserved are a vast number of contracts (family, property, loans, work, rent, lease; *ANET*, 217-223, 548-549); administrative documents (wage lists, distribution lists, grants, instructions, price tariffs, royal edicts; *ANET*, 207-211, 526-528); lawsuits (*ANET*, 216-217, 542-547); and international treaties (*ANET*, 199-206, 529-541).

When making genre and form critical comparisons between these Near Eastern codes and OT legal traditions, it should be noted: 1) There are many chronological and geographical gaps. 2) While there may be general similarity in the ancient Near East as to basic elements of a genre, form critical analysis shows great variation in detail. 3) To avoid inappropriate conclusions based on isolated similarities of form or content alone, as far as possible independent form critical analyses must be made prior to comparison with similar genres in related cultures.

II. ANTHROPOLOGY OF LAW

R. Bach, *Die Aufforderungen zur Flucht und zum Kampf im alttestamentlichen Prophetenspruch* (WMANT 9, Neukirchen: Neukirchener Verlag, 1962); M. Barkun, *Law without Sanctions* (New Haven: Yale University Press, 1968); P. Bohannan, ed., *Law and Warfare* (Garden City: Doubleday & Co., 1967), including: P. Bohannan, "The Differing Realms of the Law," 43-56, L. Pospisil, "The Attributes of Law," 25-41, and R. Redfield, "Primitive Law," 3-24; F. C. Fensham, "The Battle between the Men of Joab and Abner as Possible Ordeal by Battle?" *VT* XX (1970) 356-357; C. Friedrich, *The Philosophy of Law in Historical Perspective* (Chicago: University of Chicago Press, 1963); E. Gräf, *Das Rechtswesen der heutigen Beduinen* (BSKGO 5, Walldorf-Hessen: Verlag für Orientkunde, 1952); E. Hoebel, *The Law of Primitive Man* (Cambridge: Harvard University Press, 1954); H. Maine, *Ancient Law* (London: J. Murray, 1861); G. von Rad, *Der Heilige Krieg im alten Israel* (Göttingen: Vandenhoeck & Ruprecht, 1951); J. Schacht, *An Introduction to Islamic Law* (London: Oxford University Press, 1964); R. Smend, *Yahwekrieg und Stämmebund* (FRLANT 84, Göttingen: Vandenhoeck & Ruprecht, 1963) = *Yahweh War and Tribal Confederation*, tr. by M. G. Rogers (Nashville: Abingdon Press, 1970).

In examining the anthropology of law, three questions stand out. The basic is what is law? Redfield defines law as "the systematic and formal application of force by the state in support of explicit rules of conduct" ("Primitive Law," 4). Law then consists of two essential elements: the concepts ("explicit rules" = substantative law) and the structure (process and courts = procedural law). The process and courts need be neither formalized nor public nor dependent on a central state power (Hoebel, 25, 285; Redfield, 10, 17). A crucial matter for discussion, for example, of OT "apodictic law" is the relationship between law and custom. Posipil speaks of a law field defined by certain attributes which overlaps on either side with the fields of custom and of political decisions where certain but not all of the attributes of law are found. Bohannan states that "law may be regarded as a custom that has been restated in order to make it amenable to the activities of the legal institutions" ("The Differing Realms," 46-47). This double institutionalization, within both social custom and legal institution, accounts both for the formal nature of law and its clearly visible institutional rooting—two characteristics which make law especially receptive to form critical analysis—and for substantive links between legal and some nonlegal areas.

The second question is the relationship between law and religion. The beginnings of law are diverse (Redfield, 6). Nevertheless, there is a strong religious influence (Hoebel, 26, 259; Redfield, 8; Cazelles, "Le sens religieux de la loi"). The third question concerns the development of law. Many accept Maine's thesis of a movement "from status to contract" (Hoebel, 327-329). Covenant in Israel involved both the contractual and communal elements, while the sense of oneness correlated with the strong religious coloring of the law. Functionally, the purpose of law is to handle conflict. There must be a means of 1) disengagement of difficulties from the institutions in which they arose, 2) a method of handling the difficulty in the legal institution, and 3) a means by which the results are "re-engaged within the processes of the non-legal institutions from which they emerged" (Bohannan, 46). The other major conflict-resolving mechanism is war. Several studies have emphasized the juridical nature of warfare in the ancient Near East (e.g. Fensham, and cf. Harvey, VI. B. below). There are form critically oriented studies of warfare in Israel (von Rad, Smend). Bach has outlined two prophetic genres, "call to fight" (Jer 46:3-6) and "call to flee" (Jer 48:6-8), which he claims had their original setting in holy war procedures.

III. SUBSTANTIVE LAW

A. Genres of Legal Stipulations

A. Alt, *Die Ursprünge des israelitischen Rechts* (Leipzig: S. Hirzel, 1934) = his *Kleine Schriften zur Geschichte des Volkes Israel I* (Munich: C. H. Beck, 1953) 278-332 = *Essays in Old Testament History and Religion*, tr. by R. A. Wilson (Garden City: Doubleday & Co., 1966) 81-132; *idem*, "Zur Talionsformel," *ZAW* LII (1934) 303-305 = *Kleine Schriften* I, 341-344; H. J. Boecker, *Redeformen des Rechtslebens im Alten Testament* (WMANT 14, Neukirchen: Neukirchener Verlag, 1964, 1970²); H. Cazelles: Letouzey et Ané, 1946); *idem*, "Loi israélite," DBS V (1952) 497-530; K. Elliger, "Das Gesetz Leviticus 18," *ZAW* LXVII (1955) 1-25 = his *Kleine Schriften zum Alten Testament* (TB 32, Munich: Chr. Kaiser, 1966) 232-259; A. Erman, *Die Literatur der Ägypter* (Leipzig: J. C. Hinrich, 1923) = *The Literature of the Ancient Egyptians*, tr. by A. M. Blackman (London: Methuen & Co., 1927; re-issued as *The Ancient Egyptians* with an introduction by W. K. Simpson, New York: Harper Torchbooks, 1966); F. C. Fensham, "The Possibility of the Presence of Casuistic Legal Material at the Making of the Covenant at Sinai," *PEQ* XCIII (1961) 143-146; C. Feucht, *Untersuchungen zum Heiligkeitsgesetz* (TA 20, Berlin: Evangelische Verlagsanstalt, 1964); J. J. Finkelstein, "Some New *Misharum* Material and Its Implications," in *Studies in Honor of Benno Landsberger* (Chicago: University of Chicago Press, 1965) 233-246; G. Fohrer, "Das sogenannte apodiktisch formulierte Recht und der Dekalog," *KD* XI (1965) 49-74 = his *Studien zur alttestamentlichen Theologie und Geschichte (1949-1966)* (BZAW 115, Berlin: Walter de Gruyter & Co., 1969) 120-148; A. Gardiner, "A New Moralizing Text," *WZKM* LIV (1956) 43-45; B. Gemser, "The Importance of the Motive Clause in Old Testament Law," *VTS* I (1953) 50-66 = his *Adhuc Loquitur* (POS 7, Leiden: E. J. Brill, 1958) 96-115; H. Gese, "Beobachtungen zum Stil alttestamentliche Rechtssätze," *TLZ* LXXXV (1960) 147-150; E. Gerstenberger, "Covenant and Commandment," *JBL* LXXXIV (1965) 38-51; *idem*, *Wesen und Herkunft des* "*apodiktischen Rechts*" (WMANT 20, Neukirchen: Neukirchener Verlag, 1965); S. Gevirtz, "West-Semitic Curses and the Problem of the Origins of Hebrew Law," *VT* XI (1961) 137-158; H. Gilmer, *The If-You Form in Israelite Law* (dissertation, Emory University, 1969; cf. DA XXXI, 1969/70, 821A); H. Gressmann, *Die älteste Geschichtsschreibung und Prophetie Israels* (SAT II/1, Göttingen: Vandenhoeck & Ruprecht, 1910) 223-241; H. Gunkel, *Die israelitische Literatur* (Darmstadt: Wissenschaftliche Buchgesellschaft, 1963 = *Kultur der Gegenwart* I/7, 1906, 1925²); G. Heinemann, *Untersuchungen zum apodiktischen Recht* (dissertation, Hamburg, 1958); R. Hentschke, "Erwägungen zur israelitischen Rechtsgeschichte," *TV* X (1965/66) 108-133; S. Herrmann, "Das apodiktische Recht," *MIO* XV (1969) 249-261; D. Hillers, *Treaty-Curses and the Old Testament Prophets* (BibOr 16, Rome: Pontifical Biblical Institute, 1964); A. Jepsen, *Untersuchungen zum Bundesbuch* (BWANT III/5, Stuttgart: W. Kohlhammer, 1927); A. Jirku, *Das weltliche Recht im Alten Testament* (Gütersloh: Bortelsmann, 1927); R. Kilian, *Literarkritische und formgeschichtliche Untersuchung des Heiligkeitsgesetzes* (BBB 19, Bonn: Peter Hanstein, 1963); idem, "Apodiktisches und kasuistisches Recht im Licht ägyptischer Analogien," *BZ* VII (1963) 185-202; W. Kornfeld, *Studien zum Heiligkeitsgesetz* (Vienna: Herder, 1952); F. Kraus, *Ein Edikt des Königs Ammi-saduqa von Babylon* (Leiden: E. J. Brill, 1958); B. Landsberger, "Die babylonischen Termini für Gesetz und Recht," in *Symbolae ad Jura orientis—Paulo Koschaker dedicatae* (Leiden: E. J. Brill, 1939) 219-234; M. Lehmann, "Biblical Oaths," *ZAW* LXXXI (1969) 74-92; G. Liedke, *Gestalt und Bezeichnung alttestamentlicher Rechtssätze: Eine formgeschichtlich-terminologische Studie* (WMANT 39, Neukirchen: Neukirchener Verlag, 1971); R. A. F. Mackenzie, *The Forms of Israelite Law* (dissertation, Pontifical Biblical Institute, 1949); idem, "The Formal Aspect of Ancient Near Eastern Law," in *The Seed of Wisdom*, ed. by W. S. McCullough (Toronto: University of Toronto Press, 1964) 31-44; idem, *Two Forms of Israelite Law* (privately distributed, 1961); A. Marzal, "Mari Clauses in 'Casuistic' and 'Apodictic' Styles," *CBQ* XXXIII (1971) 333-364, 492-509; D. J. McCarthy, *Treaty and Covenant* (AnBib 21, Rome: Pontifical Biblical Institute, 1963); G. E. Mendenhall, "Ancient Oriental and Biblical Law," *BA* XVII (1954) 26-46 and "Covenant Forms in Israelite Tradition," *BA* XVII (1954) 50-76 = *The Biblical Archaeologist Reader III*, ed. by E. F. Campbell and D. N. Freedman (Garden City: Doubleday & Co., 1970) 3-53; S. Mowinckel, *Le décalogue* (Paris: L. Alcan, 1927); M. Noth, *Die Gesetze im Pentateuch* (Halle: Max Niemeyer, 1940) = his *Gesammelte Studien zum Alten Testament* (TB 6, Munich: Chr. Kaiser, 1960) 9-141 = *The Laws in the Pentateuch and Other Essays* tr. by D. R. Ap-Thomas (Philadelphia: Fortress Press, 1967) 1-107; S. Paul, *Studies in the Book of the Covenant in the Light of Cuneiform and Biblical Law* (VTS 18, Leiden: E. J. Brill, 1970); idem, "Types of Formulation in Biblical and Mesopotamian Law," *Leshonenu* XXXIV (1970) 257-266; H. Petschow, "Zu den Stilformen antiker Gesetze und Rechtssammlungen,' *ZSSR*, Rom. Abt. LXXXII (1965) 24-38; A. Phillips, *Ancient Israel's Criminal Law: A New Approach to the Decalogue* (Oxford: Basil Blackwell, 1970); J. P. M. van der Ploeg, "Studies in Hebrew Law II: The Style of the Laws," *CBQ* XII (1950) 416-427; K. Rabast, *Das apodiktische Recht im Deuteronomium und im Heiligkeitsgesetz* (Berlin: Heimatdienstverlag, 1949); I. Rapaport, "The Origins of Hebrew Law," *PEQ* LXXIII (1941) 158-167; E. Reiner, *Surpu. A Collection of Sumerian and Akkadian Incantations* (BAfO 11, Graz: self published, 1958); H. G. Reventlow, *Das Heiligkeitsgesetz formgeschichtlich untersucht* (WMANT 6, Neukirchen: Neukirchener Verlag, 1961); idem, "Kultisches Recht im Alten Testament," *ZTK* LX (1963) 268-304; W. Richter, *Recht und Ethos* (SANT 15, Munich: Kösel-Verlag, 1966); K. Sauber, *Die Abstraktion im israelitischen Recht* (dissertation, published in microfilm, 1951, cf. *TLZ* LXXVII [1952] 574-

576) ; H. Schmökel, "Biblische 'Du-Sollst' Gebote und ihr historisches Ort," *ZSSR*, Kan. Abt., XXXVI (1950) 365-390; W. Schottroff, *Der altisraelitische Fluchspruch* (WMANT 30, Neukirchen: Neukirchener Verlag, 1969) ; H. Schulz, *Das Todesrecht im Alten Testament* (BZAW 114, Berlin: A. Töpelmann, 1969) ; T. and D. Thomson, "Some Legal Problems in the Book of Ruth," *VT* XVIII (1968) 79-100; V. Wagner, "Umfang und Inhalt der motjumat-Reihe," *OLZ* LXIII (1968) 325-328; J. G. Williams, "Concerning One of the Apodictic Formulas," *VT* XIV (1964) 484-489; *idem*, "Addenda to 'Concerning One of the Apodictic Formulas,' " *VT* XV (1965) 113-115; R. Yaron, "Forms in the Laws of Eshnunna," *RIDA*, 3rd series, IX (1962) 137-153; W. Zimmerli, "Ich bin Jahweh," in *Geschichte und Altes Testament* (BHT 16, Tübingen: J. C. B. Mohr, 1953) 179-209 = his *Gottes Offenbarung* (TB 19, Munich: Chr. Kaiser, 1963) 11-40.

It may help to note that there have been three stages through which form critical research on OT legal materials has passed: 1) The typological stage, with efforts to draw up an outline of all the genres. 2) The investigation of covenantal links (from 1954 on) . 3) The relationship of law genres to wisdom and the intensive analysis of specific genres (since 1965) .

One of the first efforts to comment form critically on OT law was the development of the distinction between casuistic and categorical law made by Gunkel and Gressmann. Both types were considered oral. Gressmann derived apodictic (i.e., religious) law from priestly oracular decisions and noted similarities to the entrance liturgies of the OT (Ps 15), the "sin catalogue" of Mesopotamia (cf. Reiner), and the negative confession of the Egyptian Book of the Dead (ch. 125; see *ANET*, 34-36) . Casuistic law was rooted in the administration of secular justice by the elders, and only for this type are there parallels in the ancient Near Eastern law codes.

In one of the first two detailed studies, Jepsen (1927) —a student of Alt—made three fundamental contributions to the field: 1) He distinguished four types of laws, adding the participle form to the casuistic and categorical. 2) He raised the question about the "Israelite" nature of some genres. 3) He noted the less legal character of categorical law, its relationship in content to participle law and to wisdom. Jepsen argued that "Hebrew *mishpatim*" (casuistic law) had its setting among the non-Israelite Hebrews of Shechem. The basic form of this type, according to Jepsen, was *ki* + third person verb + subject + apodosis (penalty) . Subordinate cases were introduced by *'im* ("if") . This form has now been further refined by Liedke (1971), who argues that different *'im* clauses are coordinately dependent on the same main clause. A *w'im* ("and if") clause is dependent on a preceding *'im* clause. If no *'im* clause precedes, then the *w'im* clause is coordinate with the main clause rather than dependent (31-34). Jepsen's second group, "Israelite *mishpaṭim*" (participle + object + *môṯ yûmaṯ*), was considered pre-Mosaic, Israelite, and rooted in private blood revenge of the family. The rhythmic nature indicated similarities to the curses of Deut 27:15-26. Tora (i.e., categorical: *lō'* + second imperfect, rhythmical) was also considered Israelite in origin and the source of both the participle form and wisdom exhortation. Jepsen's fourth type, cultic stipulations, had no clear genre characteristics and was a dubious catchall based on content. The composite nature of the Covenant Code was correlated by Jepsen with the composite nature of ancient Near Eastern codes.

A study by Jirku the same year epitomizes the typological concern. Jirku distinguished ten law styles but gave insufficient attention to life setting and function. Three of his presuppositions which now appear dubious were: 1) Any original code contains only one law style, and all examples of any one style go back to a single code with a separate geo-political setting. 2) Characteristics of a law style must be established on the basis of those laws which are not paralleled in content by formulations in other law styles. 3) The shorter form is the older form. The ten styles were: 1) "If-then": "If a man borrows anything from his neighbor and it is hurt . . . then he shall make full restitution" (Ex 22:14, English). 2) "Thou shalt (not)": "Thou shalt not oppress a sojourner" (Ex 23:9). 3) "He who" (*'iš* + relative clause + apodosis): "He who lies with his father's wife, both of them shall be put to death" (Lev 20:11). 4) Curse (*'ārûr* + participle or relative clause): "Cursed is the remover of the boundary mark of his neighbor" (Deut 27:17). 5) "You shall (not)" (plural): "You shall not do injustice in judgment" (Lev 19:5a). 6) "Jussive" (third person singular or plural statement): "A single witness shall not prevail against a man in any crime. . . ." (Deut 19:15). 7) "Participle": "The one murdering a man shall be put to death" (Ex 21:12). 8) "If thou": "If thou buildest a new house, thou shalt make a parapet for thy roof" (Deut 22:8). 9) "If you" (plural): "If you come into the land . . . you shall count their fruit as forbidden" (Lev 19:23). 10) "Second If" style ("a man if": *'iš* [*'iš 'iš*] + *kî*): "A man who abuses his God, he shall bear his sin" (Lev 24:15b). Jirku argued that the "if then" and the "thou" styles are the oldest, with the "thou" forms being

III

relatively older. Hence their absence in the less primitive ancient Near Eastern codes.

In his seminal study of OT law, Alt wished to account for the mixture of casuistic and apodictic (Alt's accepted term for categorical) law which is unique in the OT. The combination of a lack of any distinctively Israelite characteristics and the setting in an established community led Alt to conclude that OT casuistic law is part of a common ancient Near Eastern tradition taken over by Israel only after its settlement in Canaan. As elsewhere, the institutional setting was the local juridical process. However, Alt's contention that the elders directly applied this law is oversimplified. Nor is it likely that he was correct in arguing that a law had relevance only for a case which agreed with it totally (cf. T. and D. Thomson).

The points of departure for Alt's study of apodictic law were: 1) the correct assumption that Israel had some legal customs prior to the settlement and 2) the observation of the encounter between this older law and the newly adopted casuistic style law in Ex 21:23-25 and 21:14 + 13, which start out in casuistic style but switch to direct address at the apodosis. Under apodictic law Alt included participle (relative is a "decayed" form); curse (for acts done in secret: Deut 27:15-26); and "thou" (negative) styles. Deut 27:15-26 and 31:9-13 pointed to a life setting in which the law was proclaimed in the name of Yahweh every seven years at the feast of booths to renew the covenant. Apodictic law has the following characteristics according to Alt: 1) Longer series. 2) Metrical. 3) Categorical, general, and inclusive. 4) Similarity of formulation of different stipulations of a series. 5) Folk and Yahwisticly bound. Alt's article was epoch making and represents something of a watershed in OT legal studies. He built an impressive case, but questions remained. For example, if apodictic law has no relationship to secular justice, Alt has not solved the question of the presettlement law of Israel.

Although, naturally, reservations were expressed (e.g., Landsberger), Alt's thesis justly met with general acceptance. Rapaport far overstated his case against Alt when he pointed to isolated occurrences of "apodictic" (but third person) laws in the Hammurabi Code, denied the dominance of casuistic law in Canaan (as did Liedke) and the composite nature of ancient Near Eastern codes, and argued that a few verses of the Covenant Code show Israelite influence. More significant was Noth's rejection of the equation of case law with profane law and sacral law with apodictic law and his argument that the use of "Israel" in apodictic law showed its institutional presupposition to be the covenantal amphictyony of the settlement period. Apodictic amphictyonic law, according to Noth, formed the core of the Covenant Code.

After WW II, a number of studies expanded Alt's work. Rabast uncritically took over four of Alt's theses and applied them within a rigid developmental framework to apodictic law in the OT. Rabast contended for the following hypotheses: 1) Apodictic law occurs in ten- to twelve-member series of general nature. Later come specific series of the same length, then short ones, then single commandments. 2) Apodictic law is strictly metrical. Various reasons lead to a gradual loss of strict metricality (e.g., motivations and desire for exactitude). Other styles develop inevitably from the original styles, unrelated to changes in sociological setting. 3) A content-laden conflict takes place between profane-casuistic and religious-apodictic genres. 4) The original Israel and Yahweh bound nature of apodictic law dissolves before advancing secularization.

More important are some contributions of Kornfeld's significant study. 1) He attempts a compromise by allotting the styles of Jirku (with modification) to the two basic types of Alt. 2) The inclusion of participle under casuistic raises a question about the distinction between apodictic and case law. Following Mackenzie (1949), Kornfeld says that apodictic law is prospective in looking forward to a future situation and the positive act to be done rather than back to a committed act and its punishment. Formally, casuistic law has a protasis and apodosis. Kornfeld admits that participle law is not adapted to court usage but is perhaps linked with a liturgical response to the proclamation of the decalogue. Thus in his determination of the category to which the participle style belongs he ignores life setting so that casuistic and apodictic are no longer true form critical designations. This illustrates the contrast of typological and form critical approaches. 3) Is apodictic law (often similar to wisdom) really law?

To further illustrate the discussion at this period (1945-1953), we will mention the studies of five additional scholars. Cazelles emphasized the need to take account of sociological, geological, economic, historical, political, psychological, and religious factors in studying law but did not correlate these with genre analysis.

III

Significant parallels in content and style to Egyptian literature led him to very fanciful historical conclusions. Schmökel recognized the need to investigate separately the individual genres, but he uncritically accepted Jirku's view of rigid stylistic uniformity. The original "thou" style (negative) stipulations were traced to a fifty-member code with a life setting as a temple catechism (cf. Mowinckel). Sauber's thesis that "thou" laws originated in the demands of the prophets and are therefore abstract was also unlikely. In order that further progress be made, in-depth investigation of particular topics was necessary, such as Gemser's exploration of the motive clause in OT laws. Such clauses occur in all periods, more frequently at later times, and are linked to a preceding stipulation. Gemser distinguished four types of motive clauses: explanatory, ethical, religious-cultic, and religious-historical. Such clauses are lacking in ancient Near Eastern law, which is addressed not to the people but to "judges." The same year Zimmerli showed that one of the formulaic motivations, "I am Yahweh," functioned as a legitimation of the law proclaimer (Judg 6:10). It originally occurred at the beginning of the proclamation and later was attached to the end of individual commands or groups of commands.

The year 1954 marked the first basic modification of Alt's thesis and the beginning of the "covenantal period" of OT research, with the publication of Mendenhall's influential and programmatic thesis that the OT covenant is patterned after the form of the Hittite suzerainty treaty. OT law codes would therefore correspond to the stipulation of the treaty document. The demand for no other gods corresponds to the demand for one suzerain, while the mixture of apodictic and casuistic styles is linked with a similar combination in the treaty stipulations. Mendenhall offered no thorough examination of any of the OT law collections, and his thesis is more relevant for suggesting a secondary usage than the origin of OT stipulation genres. Heinemann argued that the treaty tradition (to be linked with apodictic laws) was mediated to Israel through Shechem (cf. Judg 8:33), while Fensham and Kilian (*Literarkritische*, 2-3) suggested the presence of casuistic law at Sinai without discussing whether the sociological conditions presupposed by casuistic law were present at Sinai.

A more basic modification of Alt's thesis was necessitated by Elliger's study of Lev 18, in which he found in 18:7-17 an old ten-member decalogue ("the nakedness of X thou shalt not uncover"). The persons named indicate that the original setting is the extended family of the presettlement period. No Yahwistic or folk-bound elements occur until a much later stage (v. 6). Published posthumously in 1964, Feucht's 1959 study anticipates many later trends. It begins with a not particularly helpful re-juggling of the typology of styles (fifteen) but shows much flexibility in tracing a variety of settings for the different genres: family, court, state administration, prophets, cultic recitation, priestly instruction, levitical law preaching. Also he allows for the possibility of the same style having more than one independent function. The setting of the participle (and related) styles is in juridical procedures and unrelated to apparent ancient Near Eastern stylistic parallels. He stresses the parallels to apodictic law in Proverbs as a function of (non-cultic) instruction. Influence of "tora" and "daat" on "you shall" and "jussive" styles is noted, and formulaic expressions common in legal stipulations are discussed.

Beginning about 1960 a series of articles examined in more detail ancient Near Eastern parallels to OT law styles and dealt with the nature of participle law. Kilian (and Hentschke) stated the features which seemed to align participle law partly with apodictic law (sacral links, metrical nature, series) and partly with casuistic law (a particular case, involves a sanction, can be changed into a relative). Already in 1960 Gese (and Gerstenberger, *Wesen*) had argued for participle law's casuistic nature. Williams reasserted the apodictic nature, challenging the "protasis-apodosis" translation (so Reventlow, 1963, and Schulz). A better translation would be: "thou shalt put to death the striker of a man." As to possible parallels to participle law, Kilian pointed to the execration texts (e.g., "die must PP"; *ANET*, 328-329), but the similarities were not compelling (cf. Schottroff, 121-122). Williams noted similar participle formulations elsewhere in the OT (e.g., Gen 4:15; 12:3; 26:11). Many involve capital crimes, as is generally true of participle law. A relationship to the edict style would not be unreasonable, especially as the relative form in ancient Near Eastern codes is apparently a secondary incorporation into legal stipulations of a style used in edicts (Hentschke). Rather than concentrate on the participle, Boecker took his departure from the death sentence (*môt yûmat*) which is the official punishment declaration pronounced after the secular court decision. (Reventlow says sacral court.) He concluded that particular decisions gave rise to legal stipulations

III

which were formulated using the court sentence for their apodosis.

As to apodictic formulations, Kilian (1963) pointed to "thou shalt not" statements in wisdom instructions of Merikare (*ANET*, 414-418) and Onkhsheshonqy (Erman-Simpson, XXI-XXII), in two ten-member series in an ostracon of the time of Ramses II (see Gardiner), and in instruction for the vizier, without claiming direct borrowing. Gevirtz's one West Semitic tomb curse example—"Whoever thou art, any man, who shall discover this sarcophagus, do not . . ."—is no apodictic sentence. Gevirtz noted four types of casuistic constructions in these grave curses and concluded that all differences in legal formulations (including apodictic) were purely stylistic. Marzal recognized the free interchange of relative, participle, and casuistic styles in Mari texts while affirming the presence of distinct genres. The line of investigation being discussed has brought forth significant new data but tends to conclude that a similarity of style proves an identity of genre or that a mixture of style invalidates the case for distinct genres. Also in looking for ancient Near Eastern parallels, problems of linguistic transformation from one language to another have rarely been faced (but cf. Richter).

A decisive refutation of Mendenhall's proposal of a primary link of OT genres with treaty stipulations was presented by McCarthy and Gerstenberger (*JBL*, 1965). McCarthy argued that the treaty pattern is not found in the oldest Sinai tradition. Formally, in the treaty stipulations there is no distinct second person genre but a mixture of styles with the "if" type dominant. Also there are no series of independent stipulations. Even OT casuistic law is not linked to treaty stipulations, as the latter look towards actions to be taken under future contingencies while casuistic law looks forward to punishments for past proscribed actions.

Partly stimulated by OT discussions, a valuable contribution was made by studies of genres in ancient Near Eastern law codes by Yaron, Petschow, and Hentschke. 1) The dominant (except in Neo-Babylonian laws) conditional ("if") genre has its setting in the law courts. As a general process, particular court decisions became precedents and in abstracted form gave rise to specific casuistic laws. The apodosis preserves the court decision, while the protasis narrates the situation giving rise to the case. This same two-part structure is reflected in Mesopotamian court records of particular cases. Liedke attempts to make more precise the grammatical form of casuistic law in arguing that the verb of the protasis is a short imperfect (*yiqtol*-x), while the verb of the apodosis is a "heischendes Präsens" ("prescriptive-present") (x-*yiqtol*) or equivalent (34-39). This outline of historical origin should not obscure the fact that the actual relationship of casuistic law and juridical process, once both are firmly established, was more reciprocal and complex. The court did not simply apply the statute, nor did the statute simply put into writing past decisions and in every case derive from an actual court case. 2) The frequent (e.g., Eshnunna Code 12, 19) relative genre dominates the Neo-Babylonian laws and the "reform edict" of King Ammisaduq (Kraus and Finkelstein). Hentschke suggests four stages of development for the relative genre: a) Originates as a style of oral proclamation; b) used for oral proclamation of a reform edict; c) incorporated into the written version of the edict; d) occasionally incorporated into legal collections from the edict. Hentschke apparently equates the relative with both OT relative and participle styles, while Marzal claims some examples of ancient Near Eastern laws in participle form (Hammurabi Code 177; Eshnunna Code 34-35; Middle Assyrian Laws 3, 40; cf. Schottroff, 97-104). 3) Fairly rare are commands, all third person, with or without penalty (Hammurabi Code, 36, 38-40, 187; Eshnunna Code, 15-16, 51-52; Middle Assyrian Laws A 40, F 2; Hittite Laws 48, 50-51, 56; Ammisaduq 12). The life setting is the command of a ruler (Yaron). 4) Prices and wages (e.g., Hittite Laws 178-186) have a life setting in the market. Thus there are several genres in law codes with distinct content and life setting whose origin lies outside the strictly legal area.

Gerstenberger's monograph on the apodictic (prohibitive) genre begins the third stage of research with attention concentrating on the relation of law and wisdom and producing in-depth studies of individual legal genres. In legal material, the content and scope of the prohibitive points to its authoritative and secular nature (Lev 18; Ex 23:1-3, 6-9; Deut 24:6-22). The basic form is *lō'* (negative) + second person imperfect + object or clause, without any motivation. Two- and three-member series are characteristic. A detailed analysis of wisdom admonitions, the other major source for prohibitives, shows a similar correlation of content, intent (authoritative instruction), form, and life setting (clan and family). Thus Gerstenberger argues that the prohibitive originated as a genre by which the father passed on to the next generation the common "clan ethos" (cf. Prov

III
―――
112

3:27-30; Jer 35:6). Later differentiation accounts for differences between wisdom and legal usage. The genre also includes positive statements. Gerstenberger's thesis has been extremely influential, but naturally some questions remain. 1) The use of *'al* in admonition in contrast to *lō'* in apodictic law. 2) The nonindependence of the positive command. 3) The secondary nature of all motivations. 4) Possible multiple origins. 5) The asserted nonlegal nature of these norms.

Richter's study basically confirms Gerstenberger's thesis but distinguishes four "related" styles: 1) The vetitive: *'al* + short imperfect + motivation. 2) The prohibitive: *lō'* + long imperfect (mostly in legal sections). Both of these styles originated, according to Richter, as everyday speech patterns used in many areas. 3) The positive correspondent to the vetitive is the imperative. 4) The positive correspondent to the prohibitive is the "heischendes Präsens": x-*yiqtol* (also *qatal*-x or infinitive absolute), an independent genre of cultic regulation. The prohibitive is not law. Rather it was employed, Richter argues, in series in a Jerusalem "school" (except Lev 18) to instruct members of the upper class oriented to public service in their class ethos. The vetitive as developed in the admonition is strongly influenced by the prohibitive, having the same setting except that it is used for the education of the children of the upper classes. While such a usage is not contrary to Gerstenberger's position, such a restriction seems unlikely. The distinctive feature of Richter's presentation is his commendable effort to relate precise syntactical analysis to form critical investigation. However, he tends to identify genre and grammatical form and assume that for each grammatical form there must be found one life setting (cf. Gerstenberger, "Zur alttestamentlichen Weisheit," *VuF* XIV/1 [1969] 28-44, especially 36-40).

Schulz says that one must combine analysis of the style of the isolated stipulation with "rechtsanalyisches" (legal analysis) and "institutionsgeschichtliches" (institutional-historical) approaches. Genres develop not in isolation but in response to changed sociological setting. Schulz distinguishes the sentence formulation (style), the legal genre (which may use various styles; cf. Marzal on the *šiptum* genre), and a legal concept. Following up Boecker on participle law, Schulz concludes that the *môt* laws are always based on prohibitives. With the change from clan to tribal organization, the nonlegal prohibitive norms were incorporated into the juridical sphere. "Todesrecht" is that law genre which links the death declaration to the deed area delimited by the prohibitive norms. Schulz's thesis is well integrated but depends at crucial points on tendentious interpretations of individual texts (Gen 26; I Kings 21; Jer 26). The juridical function of participle laws appears indisputable (Schottroff, 120-129), although it is not clear why prohibitive norms were first given juridical import at the tribal stage.

Most of Schulz's conclusions are rejected by Liedke. He criticizes Schulz's exclusive attention to texts with the *môṯ yûmaṯ* formula, saying that if texts with analogous formulas were included (e.g., the "be cut off" formula), then the content parallels to the prohibitives would not be so pervasive. This overlooks the fact that a significant, if not clearly successful, element of Schulz's approach is to try to define the area of investigation differently from the way it has traditionally been approached, i.e., by the particular type of judgment clause rather than by assuming that all participle laws form part of a unitary group. In a more positive manner, Liedke follows the lines of Richter's linguistic analysis in describing the syntax of participle law: a compound nominal sentence ("zusammengesetze Nominalsätze) in which the second part is a true verbal sentence containing a "heischendes Präsens." The frequent infinitive absolute in the apodosis functions to clarify the following verb as a "heischendes Präsens." This interpretation supports the "conditional" rather than the single clause translation of participle laws (see above, p. 110). For Liedke, it is the participle law genre (including relative formulations) which is true apodictic law because of its authoritative nature, its having instituting rather than restorational character, and its being imposed by a superior upon a subordinate in impersonal style.

Schulz has dismissed as late the *'ārûr* (curse) stipulations of Deut 27, often previously linked with participle law. In the same year that Schulz's study appeared, Schottroff presented an exhaustive descriptive analysis and study of the curse. He summarized his conclusions under five points: 1) The original form is "cursed are you" (*'ārûr 'attâ*). Its life setting is the pre-settlement clan where in a conflict situation the *'ārûr* was spoken by the clan head to a person to exclude (ban) him from the community. 2) Various expansions (conditions, working out of the curse, divine logical subject) reflect unrelated curse forms and concepts (life diminution) of the settled land. 3) The *'ārûr* is non-cultic in origin. 4) Even for Deut 27:15-26 the cultic

III

114

setting is secondary. 5) Thus there is (contra Lehmann and Hillers) no original link of OT curse to covenant or cult. Such an association is considered an unjustified overgeneralization. This significant study is open to criticism at many points. 1) The lack of any examples of original usage and few of original form suggest caution in advancing unverifiable "nomadic" explanations, especially since the "original" form is devoid of specific content. 2) The method has an intrinsic bias towards an original short simple form from which all others can be derived. 3) Schulz's distinction of style, genre, and concept needs to be extended to the treatment of curses. Hillers' study had offered a typology of four curse styles, without going into life settings and functions.

Finally, among monographs on specific genres, H. Gilmer's dissertation treats the "if you" style, often regarded as a secondary development. Gilmer outlines five "speech patterns" in two main categories (distinguished by presence or absence of an imperative) : request, directive, agreement, counsel, threat/promise. These were used in many situations.

Clearly strong cases have been made for the existence of the following genres: casuistic; prohibitive; (capital) participle; curse ('*ārûr*) ; jussive (not yet studied in depth) and possibly talions law (Gen 9:6, Alt, 1934, and Schulz) . Prohibitive, '*ārûr*, and participle law genres are without significant attestation in ancient Near Eastern law, although there are many stylistic parallels in legal and nonlegal material which may have influenced the origin of the genres. By and large the genres are related to or arise from speech patterns or genres in other areas.

Some methodological considerations deserve emphasis. 1) Institutional and legal-historical analysis must be extended to include the interrelationship of the various legal genres while keeping distinct questions of historical origin and later function. Liedke makes a useful initial effort in this area but does not separate clearly historical origin and later function. 2) Further progress is necessary in relating different levels of analysis— linguistic-syntactical, stylistic, and genre. A useful illustration is Marzal's study of Mari law where he approaches the texts a) at a morphological level (types of sentences, verb forms, sequence) , b) in terms of complex and simple sentences which he thinks correspond to and confirm Alt's casuistic-apodictic dichotomy, and c) via genres utilized, including curses, court decisions, legal contract clauses, and edicts (*šipṭum*) . 3) Covenant must not be looked to for an explanation of the origin of most

OT law genres. Liedke (59-61) thinks that the "if-thou" law style is the one most closely linked with covenant and treaty genres (but not necessarily derived from them) due to their mutual parenetic thrust. Thus it is not surprising that this style is relatively common in Deuteronomy. The ambiguity of the style which shares characteristics of both casuistic law (conditional) and prohibitives (direct address) facilitated the secondary incorporation of these originally independent genres into covenantal contexts. 4) The assumption that norms (i.e., prohibitives) are nonlegal is overhasty, pending clarification of how substantive law functioned in the juridical process. 5) The simplicity of "original" genres is a presupposition linked to their "oral" character. This may not be fully applicable to legal materials.

B. Law Collections

1. General Considerations and Short Series

E. Auerbach, "Das Zehngebot—Allgemeine Gesetzes-Form in der Bibel," *VT* XVI (1966) 255-276; C. Carmichael, "Deuteronomic Laws, Wisdom, and Historical Traditions," *JSS* XII (1967) 198-206; *idem*, "A Singular Method of Codification of Law in the *Mishpatim*," *ZAW* LXXXIV (1972) 19-25; D. Daube, "Codes and Codas," in his *Studies in Biblical Law* (London: Cambridge University Press, 1947) 74-101; K. Galling, "Das Gemeindegesetz in Deuteronomium 23," *Festschrift für Alfred Bertholet* (Tübingen: J. C. B. Mohr, 1950) 176-191; H. Gese, "Der Dekalog als Ganzheit betrachtet," *ZTK* LXIV (1967) 121-138; R. Haase, "Zur Systematik der zweiten Tafel der hethitischen Gesetze," *RIDA*, third series, VII (1960) 51-54; J. L'Hour, "Une législation criminelle dans Deutéronome," *Bib* XLIV (1963) 1-28; *idem*, "Les interdits toᶜebah dans le Deutéronome,"*RB* LXXI (1964) 481-503; J. McKay, "Exodus XXIII 1-3, 6-8: A Decalogue for the Administration of Justice in the City Gate," *VT* XXI (1971) 311-325; R. Merendino, *Das deuteronomische Gesetz* (BBB 31, Bonn: Peter Hanstein, 1969) ; H. Petschow, "Zur Systematik und Gesetzestechnik im Codex Hammurabe," *ZA* XXIII (1965) 146-172; *idem*, "Zur 'Systematik' in den Gesetzen von Eschnunna," in *Symbolae Iuridicae et historicae Martino David dedicatae*, vol. II, ed. by J. Ankum, *et al.* (Leiden: E. J. Brill, 1968) 131-143; V. Wagner, "Zur Systematik in dem Codex Ex 21: 2-22:16," *ZAW* LXXXI (1969) 177-182.

In the 30's and 40's some held that the Covenant Code consisted originally of decalogues and pentalogues or that the Covenant, the Deuteronomic, and the Holiness Codes were all based on decalogues. More restrained but still dubious is Auerbach's effort to work out a number of independent decalogues. However, Galling's study of Deut 23:1-9 exemplifies the benefits of concentrating on particular short series rather than imposing a general organization principle on the text. Larger ancient Near

III

Eastern collections did impose three kinds of structures on previously existing independent materials (Haase, Petschow) : 1)
The gathering into separate collections of cultic, moral, and civil
laws (Landsberger, "Die babylonischen Termini"; Paul, *Studies*,
8-9, 37) . In the Covenant Code, all three types are combined. 2)
The framing of the impersonal legal corpus by a first person,
nonjuridical, largely historical section (Paul) . Thus what has
been taken as the influence of the treaty pattern may be due to a
common law code construction tradition (so Paul for the Covenant Code) . Nonetheless, it is still necessary to consider the prior
history and genre characteristics of the legal code. 3) A traditional
organization of content is argued by Petschow for the Code of
Hammurabi: a) slavery; b) bodily injury; c) commerce and
wages; d) family law. Wagner has tried to demonstrate a similar
organization in the Covenant Code: a) Ex 21:2-11; b) 21:18-32;
c) 21:33-22:7; 22:9-24; d) lacking (for various reasons) .

In addition, there are techniques for linking together smaller
sections, including association of ideas, words, phrases, and motifs.
Wagner argues for a systematic ordering according to such considerations as the area of life, with subdivisions in regard to
status, worth, case and counter case, and natural or legal sequence of similar cases. Here also we might mention Daube's
discussion of a technique by which a law collection is officially
supplemented at a later date; the addition is appended to the end
of the relevant section (but not at the end of an extensive collection) rather than attached to the law to which it is directly
related. By comparing Ex 22:20-30 and Ex 23:9-19, Carmichael
(1972) has shown that when a second sequence of laws is added
to a previously existing sequence, then the arrangement of the
second follows the arrangement of the first. Concerning other
joining techniques, Gese demonstrates that pairing of commandments occurs in shorter poetic series (e.g., Lev 19:3-4, 11-12, 14) .
Carmichael (1967) thinks that there is mutual influence between
narrative accounts which illustrate certain laws and the sequence
of the laws: the sequence of Deut 18:15-19:14 as influenced by the
narrative in Deut 3:12-4:49.

It is impossible to examine all studies of particular law series.
McKay finds in Ex 23:1-3 + 6-8 an apodictic decalogue which has
its life setting in instructions or oaths given to elders and witnesses at secular juridical proceedings. Yet the assumption that
such oaths were administered is without other support, and his
extensive textual alterations are unconvincing. Two studies by

L'Hour deserve mention. 1) There are a number of casuistically formulated laws ending with a death sentence followed by the *bi'artâ* formula ("and so shall you consume the evil from your midst," e.g., Deut 21:18-21). The content is criminal legislation; the sociological setting is the local community in the period of the judges. L'Hour's further results are interesting but hardly conclusive. 2) There are a number of apodictic laws followed by the particle *kî* (because) introducing the construct phrase *tô'ebâ* Yahweh ("abomination of Yahweh," Deut 23:19). L'Hour argues that these formulations are more instruction than law but have a juridical implication because an external sanction is involved. In both cases L'Hour fails to exploit fully his observation concerning the resemblance of the final phrase to formulas used in juridical court process; nor is it certain that we do not have a law type rather than a single series as L'Hour (and Merendino, 327-345, with an arbitrarily reconstructed short original form) argues.

2. The Covenant, Deuteronomic, and Holiness Codes

K. Baltzer, *Das Bundesformular* (WMANT 4, Neukirchen: Neukirchener Verlag, 1960, 1964²) = *The Covenant Formulary*, tr. by D. E. Green (Philadelphia: Fortress Press, 1971); W. Beyerlin, "Die Paränese im Bundesbuch und ihre Herkunft," in *Gottes Wort und Gottes Land*, ed. by H. G. Reventlow (Göttingen: Vandenhoeck & Ruprecht, 1963) 9-29; A. Campbell, "An Historical Prologue in a Seventh Century Treaty," *Bib* L (1969) 534-535; G. Fohrer, "Altes Testament—'Amphiktyonie' und 'Bund,'" *TLZ* XCI (1966) 801-816, 893-904 = his *Studien zur alttestamentlichen Theologie und Geschichte (1949-1966)* (Berlin: Walter de Gruyter, 1969) 84-119; R. Frankena, "The Vassal-Treaties of Esarhaddon and the Dating of Deuteronomy," *OTS* XIV (1965) 122-154; H. Huffmon, "The Exodus, Sinai and the Credo," *CBQ* XXVII (1965) 101-113; V. Korošec, *Hethitische Staatsverträge* (Leipzig: Verlag T. Weicher, 1931); *idem*, "The Cuneiform State Treaties. The Growth of Their Substance," *RIDA*, third series, XII (1965), 503-504; S. Loersch, *Das Deuteronomium und seine Deutungen* (SBS 22, Stuttgart: Katholisches Bibelwerk, 1967); N. Lohfink, *Das Hauptgebot* (AnBib 20, Rome: Pontifical Biblical Institute, 1963); J. Morgenstern, "The Book of the Covenant: Part I," *HUCA* V (1928) 1-151, "Part II," VII (1930) 19-258, "Part III: The Huqqim," VIII-IX (1931-32)) 1-150, 741-746, "Part IV: The Miṣwot," XXXIII (1962) 59-105; E. Nicholson, *Deuteronomy and Tradition* (Philadelphia: Fortress Press, 1967); M. Noth, *Überlieferungsgeschichtliche Studien* (Tübingen: Max Niemeyer, 1934); L. Perlitt, *Bundestheologie im Alten Testament* (WMANT 36, Neukirchen: Neukirchener Verlag, 1969); G. von Rad, *Das formgeschichtliche Problem des Hexateuch* (BWANT IV/26, Stuttgart: W. Kohlhammer, 1938) = his *Gesammelte Studien zum Alten Testament* (TB 8, Munich: Chr. Kaiser, 1958) 9-86 = "The Form-Critical Problem of the Hexateuch," in *The Problem of the Hexateuch and Other Essays*, tr. by E. W. T. Dicken (New York: McGraw-Hill, 1966) 1-78; *idem*, *Deuteronomium Studien* (FRLANT 58, Göttingen: Vandenhoeck & Ruprecht, 1947) = *Studies in Deuteronomy*, tr. by D. Stalker (SBT 9, London: SCM Press, 1953); H. G. Reventlow, *Das Heilig-*

keitsgesetz formgeschichtlich untersucht (WMANT 6, Neukirchen: Neukirche-ner Verlag, 1961) ; L. Rost, "Das Bundesbuch," *ZAW* LXXVII (1965) 255-259; W. Thiel, "Erwägungen zum Alter des Heiligkeitsgesetzes," *ZAW* LXXXI (1969) 40-73; M. Weinfeld, "Deuteronomy—The Present State of Inquiry," *JBL* LXXXVI (1967) 249-262; *idem, Deuteronomy and the Deuteronomic School* (London: Oxford University Press, 1972) .

There is little to add to what has been said concerning form critical study of the Covenant Code. Beyerlin argues that the pare-nesis in the code points to its organic growth through use in the covenant cult, but Rost responds that the relevant passages are secondary (Ex 20:22-26; 22:17-24) . Unlike the Deuteronomic Code, the Covenant Code does not show the characteristic form or content of a treaty. Thus, even though it may have functioned as a covenant document, genre characteristics are not thereby ex-plained. (For extensive bibliographical references in the Covenant Code, see Paul, *Studies in the Book of the Covenant.*)

Von Rad's shift of emphasis from source critical and historical problems to form critical perspectives opened a new phase of Deuteronomic research. Taking up the observation of Klosterman about the "preaching" style of Deuteronomy, von Rad concluded that this indicated a life setting in the cult. The stylization as a Moses speech indicated a function of the interpretation of the law by the Levites (already suggested by Bentzen) . This view remains dominant despite recent arguments for a link with prophetic (Nicholson) or scribal (Weinfeld) circles.

Von Rad (1938) also observed that the structure of Deuterono-my parallels that of the Sinai pericope of Exodus. 1) Deut 1-11: Historical survey and parenesis; 2) 12:1-26:15: Law proclama-tion; 3) 26:16-19: Conclusion of the covenant; 4) c. 27-30: Bless-ing and curse. According to von Rad, the life setting of the Sinai tradition was in the covenant festival at Shechem celebrated at the feast of booths.

New insights into the understanding of OT covenant were opened by the observation of structural parallels between OT cov-enants and ancient Near Eastern suzerainty treaties decisively pre-sented by Mendenhall (1954) . The structure he outlined—follow-ing Korošec's 1931 analysis—is: 1) Preamble ("thus [saith] NN, . . ."). 2) Historical prologue. 3) Stipulations. Baltzer's study added a "basic stipulation" (e.g., loyalty) after the prologue, but this element lacks consistency as to position and formulation. 4) Provision for deposit in the temple and periodic public read-ing. Baltzer and McCarthy later showed that this is not a necessary part of the treaty genre. 5) The list of gods as witnesses. 6) The curses and blessings formulas. Mendenhall pointed out the similarities with various covenant traditions in the OT (especially Jos 24). Assertions that the treaty parallels validated the early date of the OT covenant tradition proved to be methodologically questionable and factually erroneous. McCarthy has shown that the prologue is not essential to all treaties, and isolated examples of historical prologues have turned up from periods other than the Hittite-Mosaic (Campbell; cf. Huffmon, for a different opinion). Unlike that of Mendenhall, Baltzer's work was more precise in terms of form critical methodology, and his conclusions were more restrained.

Returning to von Rad's analysis of the structure of Deuteronomy, it is in Deut 5-28 that the treaty pattern is most obvious in the OT. (Many scholars now follow Noth in assigning Deut 1-4 to the work of the Deuteronomistic historian which extends from Deut 1 to the end of Kings and was written shortly after the fall of Jerusalem in 586 B.C.) Although other texts might seem to reflect the pattern, key elements are often missing. In the case of the Sinai pericope, traditio-historical analysis shows that it originally contained neither blessings and curses nor legal stipulations (McCarthy). Lohfink and Baltzer argued that the treaty pattern was also applied within individual smaller sections of Deuteronomy (e.g., 1:1-4:40; 28:69-30:20). Also significant elements of vocabulary are used as technical treaty terms (cf. Weinfeld, 1967, 254-255). Further, Frankena, arguing that part of Deut 28 shows literary dependence on the (Assyrian) Esarhaddon treaty, suggested that the treaty-covenant was formulated as a replacement of the vassal treaty with Assyria under Josiah. The tendency towards "pan-covenantalism" in which many significant phenomena, literary genres, and words of all periods are explained almost exclusively by the magic words treaty and covenant has been criticized by McCarthy, Gerstenberger, Fohrer and others. This critique assumes a polemical and often overstated form in Perlitt's thorough study which nevertheless demonstrates how ambiguous the evidence is for an influence of the treaty pattern on Israel's concept of covenant prior to the seventh century. Some argue that the treaty genre even in Deuteronomy is a theological and literary product influenced by foreign patterns but without any actualization in cultic ceremonies.

Lohfink also emphasizes Deut 5-11 as a literary production utilizing various ancient traditions for purposes of instruction (as does Weinfeld) . He equated Deut 5-11 with the postulated "basic stipulation" of the treaty pattern. What is new in this study is the effort to apply the techniques of literary criticism (the new stylistics) in conjunction with form criticism, without solving the relationship of these two approaches. Lohfink finds two new genres. The first is a recitation of history as a frame around the development of covenantal stipulations (the *Gebotsumrahmung*: 6:10-20) . The second links historical prologue and parenesis (the *Beweisführungen*: 8:2-6) . Though Lohfink argues that both develop from cultic application of the covenant form, we may instead have stylistic patterns developed by an author.

Like Lohfink's, Merendino's study of the Deuteronomic Code combines form critical, traditio-historical, and stylistic methodologies. Among the genres mentioned by Merendino are catechisms, apodictic laws, parenesis, war speeches, judgment speeches, and *bi'artâ* series. As legal sources he singles out 1) cultic laws, 2) *tô'ebâ* texts, 3) *bi'artâ* texts, 4) urban laws, 5) marriage laws, 6) humanitarian regulations, 7) independent apodictic series, and 8) individual liturgical texts. These various sources (often individually of complex origin) were combined to form the Deuteronomic Code. The final Deuteronomic redaction involved breaking up some existing series, a limited amount of new materials, the emphasis of parenesis, and the conscious literary structuring into two basic parts: c. 12-18 (community and Yahweh) and c. 19-25 (relationship to neighbor) . Merendino's work is systematic and impressive but often highly speculative. The elimination of material as late often seems arbitrary, and the breaking of verses into multiple parts is at times as extreme as were some excessive fragmentations of earlier source criticism. Various insufficiently supported assumptions occur: the short form is original, there is no original redundancy, the statement of the basic principle occurs at the earliest stage. Emphasis on rhythmic elements and chiasmus in reconstructing earlier stages tends to be self-fulfilling.

In summary, the treaty structure of Deut 5-28 accounts (in part) for the genre of the text, while the parenetic style points either towards preaching in the cult or usage in instruction. Unresolved is whether appropriation of the treaty genre is the work of the Deuteronomic circle or whether it rests on a long development in a covenantal cult. The prehistory and characteristics of the various proposed genres and traditions within the Deuteronomic Code remain to be more fully investigated. (For further bibliographical references on the Deuteronomic Code, see Merendino, *Das deuteronomische Gesetz.*)

There are two tendencies in recent research on the Holiness Code (Lev 17-26). Reventlow emphasizes the gradual and organic growth of the code in the covenant cult. The parenetical element, the formulation as a Yahweh speech, and the conclusion with blessings and curses demonstrate, according to Reventlow, that the Holiness Code is a covenant document. The collection utilizes many genres, such as priestly knowledge, tora, ritual, catalogues, apodictic law, and casuistic law. It has crystallized around two kernels: a decalogue emphasizing holiness in c. 19 and a section of priestly knowledge (*daat*) in c. 21. Yet, the covenant-treaty pattern is not obvious in the Holiness Code, and blessing-curse can alternatively be linked with the ancient Near Eastern law code framework rather than the treaty form.

Kilian's investigation of the Holiness Code is similar to Merendino's study of the Deuteronomic Code but with less attention both to stylistics and to the forms of the pre-existing units. His main thrust is to trace four developmental stages. 1) The older independent units, without specific Yahwistic links and hence noncovenantal. 2) Ur-H—c. 18-22, part of c. 24, and c. 25—collects, supplements, and comments (c. 586 BC). 3) H as we now have it except for c. 17 was composed as a constitution for the anticipated restored community in Palestine. 4) Incorporation into P, at which point also c. 17 was added. Similarly, both Feucht and Thiel distinguish three stages. Thiel also argues that the preaching style and affinity to Deuteronomy and the Deuteronomic history point to an exilic date rather than a setting in the covenant festival. We are left with the feeling that while Reventlow's conclusions are dubious, no one has yet gone far beyond him in applying form critical methodology to the study of the Holiness Code.

3. The Decalogue

W. Beyerlin, *Herkunft und Geschichte der ältesten Sinaitraditionen* (Tübingen: J. C. B. Mohr, 1961) = *Origins and History of the Oldest Sinaitic Traditions*, tr. by S. Rudman (Oxford: Basil Blackwell, 1965); H. Cazelles, "Les origines du décalogue," *EI* IX (1969) 14-19; R. Knierim, "Das erste Gebot," *ZAW* LXXVII (1965) 20-39; E. Nielsen, *Die Zehn Gebote* (AThD 8, Copenhagen: Munksgaard, 1965) = *The Ten Commandments in New Perspective*, tr. by D. J. Bourke (SBT II/7, London: SCM Press, 1968); A. Phillips, *Ancient Israel's Criminal Law: A New Approach to the Decalogue* (Oxford: Basil Blackwell, 1970); H. G. Reventlow, *Gebot und Predigt im Dekalog* (Gütersloh: Gerd Mohn, 1962); J. J. Stamm and M. Andrew, *The Ten Com-*

mandments in Recent Research (SBT II/2, London: SCM Press, 1967) ; W. Zimmerli, "Das zweite Gebot," in *Festschrift für Alfred Bertholet,* 550-563 = his *Gottes Offenbarung* (TB 19, Munich: Chr. Kaiser, 1963) 234-248.

Unfortunately we cannot discuss individual commandments on which significant form critical work has been done (e.g., Knierim, Zimmerli, and Reventlow) but must only outline some basic questions concerning the decalogue as a whole. 1) Relationship of the two versions (Ex 20:2-17; Deut 5:6-21). 2) Relationship to the so-called ritual decalogue of Ex 34 and to other "decalogue" series. 3) Literary context of both versions. 4) (Dubious) thesis of a uniform Urdecalogue. 5) Question of cultic life setting, which if affirmed might still be a late development. 6) Principle of the selection of the commandments. 7) Question of form: is there a decalogue type genre? The key characteristics are its series aspect (in common with some ancient Near Eastern series of ethical content, cf. Cazelles) , perhaps a particular sequence of content (religious, family, civil; cf. Schulz, *Das Todesrecht,* 67) , and the connection with the tablets and the number ten. Arguments that the decalogue is a covenant document in form (Beyerlin, Mendenhall) seem without basis, as the necessity to explain the absence of many elements of the treaty pattern demonstrates.

Certainly the basic tendency has been to regard the decalogue as old and as an original unity. Some arguments pointing however to a younger date and complex history are: 1) The longer apodictic series, especially of mixed content, is relatively late. 2) The series with different law genres is a later development. Both Reventlow and Fohrer utilize this criterion to distinguish several sources behind the decalogue. 3) The prohibitive genre generally has an object to the verb. 4) The prohibitive was originally more concrete than many of the decalogue commandments. 5) Deuteronomic language is extensive. 6) Specific laws point to the post-conquest period (e.g., Knierim on the first commandment) . Stylistic diversity indicates that either the formulation as a Yahweh speech is secondary or only the first several commandments are original. Of course, a characteristic which is a typologically secondary development may still be early in absolute dating, but taken together rather than in isolation these observations make a strong case for a post-conquest origin. Ironically, the same evidence which points to the complex origin of the decalogue is used to reconstruct proposed "Ur-decalogues." For example, Cazelles notes several double negatives (Ex 20:5,

16-17) and by eliminating the two positive commandments arrives at an original ten-member series. Nielsen and others secure a totally negative series simply by transforming the positive into negative commandments.

Phillips' interesting thesis is that the decalogue is Israel's criminal law, being formally the stipulations of the covenant made at Sinai (treaty) and only for this (noncivil) law was the death penalty exacted. The value of his book is limited because it ignores or dismisses without serious argumentation most form critical literature.

In conclusion, while the switch of attention from law series to specific law genres has been very fruitful, the form critical analysis of the genre (s) of a law series has yet to find any convincing solutions.

C. Cultic Law

J. Begrich, "Die priesterliche Tora," in *Werden und Wesen des Alten Testaments*, ed. by P. Volz (BZAW 66, Berlin: A. Töpelmann, 1936) 63-88 = his *Gesammelte Studien zum Alten Testament* (TB 21, Munich: Chr. Kaiser, 1964) 232-260; K. Koch, *Die Priesterschrift von Exodus 25 bis Leviticus 16* (FRLANT 71, Göttingen: Vandenhoeck & Ruprecht, 1959); R. Rendtorff, *Die Gesetze in der Priesterschrift* (FRLANT 62, Göttingen: Vandenhoeck & Ruprecht, 1953, 1963²); *idem, Studien zur Geschichte des Opfers im Alten Israel* (WMANT 24, Neukirchen: Neukirchener Verlag, 1967).

Tora: "Any fat of ox, or sheep, or goat, you shall not eat" (Lev 7:22). Priestly tora (Begrich) is instruction to the people, distinguishing principally between holy and profane. The most common subjects are cultic offerings and requirements for participation in the cult. Originally oral, it was legal in that it was authoritative and binding, though not technically derived from law. The basic form is a short, second person plural imperative or prohibitive statement understood to be spoken by Yahweh. A second style is the impersonal jussive formulation: "An abomination it will be to you" (Lev 11:11). A third style, the concessive, uses the imperfect or jussive and appears in both personal and impersonal forms: "the fat . . . may be put to any use" (Lev 7:24). A derived genre is "extended tora" (Koch), with additions from lists, declarative formulas, and apodictic series. Leviticus 11 is Koch's prime example, where in four sections there are similar schemata of superscription, demand to eat or not to eat, explanation, repetition of the demand, and in the case of a negative demand, a declarative formula.

Daat (*da'at*): "It shall be to the priest who sprinkles the

III

blood of the 'peace offering' " (Lev 7:14). Priestly daat (Begrich and Rendtorff) is directed to the priests and contains ritual procedures and the like. Especially the third person jussive or perfect consecutive is used. Rendtorff finds Lev 6-7 to be composed mainly of daat (cf. also Ex 12:43-49; Num 6:1-8). Koch's arguments denying the existence of a genre of daat are not convincing, but additional clarification of the relation of daat to ritual and to tora is needed.

Ritual (Rendtorff and Koch) is directed to the laity and fixes the steps by which the ritual is executed. These texts are composed of relatively short sentences, consisting of three of four clauses, using third person singular perfect consecutive verb forms (except at the beginning), and with normally three to twelve sentences in the series. Rendtorff's outline of Lev 1 and 3 is typical of a ritual: 1) bringing of offerings, 2) touching with the hand, 3) slaughtering, 4) sprinkling of blood, 5) other actions, 6) burning of the offering. Only the final element was done by the priest. Most of Lev 1-5 consists of rituals.

Finally, we recall that previously discussed law genres may be used for cultic content.

IV. PROCEDURAL LAW

A. Juridical Procedure

1) Secular Juridical Procedure

J. Begrich, *Studien zu Deuterojesaja* (BWANT 77, Stuttgart: W. Kohlhammer, 1938) = (TB 20, Munich: Chr. Kaiser, 1963); B. S. Childs, *Memory and Tradition in Israel* (SBT 37, London: SCM Press, 1962); W. M. Clark, "A Legal Background to the Yahwist's Use of 'Good and Evil' in Genesis 2-3," *JBL* LXXXVIII (1969) 266-278; A. Gamper, *Gott als Richter in Mesopotamien und im Alten Testament* (Innsbruck: Universitätsverlag Wagner, 1966); F. Horst, "Gerichtsverfassung in Israel," *RGG*[3] II 1427-1429; R. Knierim, "Exodus 18 und die Neuordnung der mosaischen Gerichtsbarkeit," *ZAW* LXXIII (1961) 147-171; *idem, Die Hauptbegriffe für Sünde im Alten Testament* (Gütersloh: Gerd Mohn, 1965); L. Köhler, "Die hebräische Rechtsgemeinde," in his *Der hebräische Mensch* (Tübingen: J. C. B. Mohr, 1953) 143-171 = "Justice in the Gate," in his *Hebrew Man*, tr. by P. R. Ackroyd (Nashville: Abingdon Press, 1956) 127-150; E. Kutsch, *Salbung als Rechtsakt im Alten Testament und im alten Orient* (BZAW 87, Berlin: A. Töpelmann, 1963); H. McKeating, "Justice and Truth in Israel's Legal Practice," *CQ* III (1970) 51-56; H. Richter, *Studien zu Hiob* (TA 11, Berlin: Evangelische Verlagsanstalt, 1959); J. Salmon, *Judicial Authority in Early Israel* (dissertation, Princeton Theological Seminary, 1968); I. Seeligmann, "Zur Terminologie für das Gerichtsverfahren im Wortschatz des biblischen Hebräisch," in *Hebräische Wortforschung* (VTS 16, Leiden: E. J. Brill, 1967) 251-278. (For further bibliography see Gamper and H. J. Boecker, *Redeformen des Rechtslebens* [1970[2]].)

Horst divides the different juridical spheres along gentilic (clan and family), political (tribe and city), and sacral lines. Juridical competence may be exercised by the family head, the military leader, the elders, certain amphictyonic officials, certain members of the priesthood, and the king and his officials. Although considerable controversy concerns the role of the king, administration of justice was predominantly a matter of local competence (see Köhler). There is a difference in procedure according to the type of case involved: a) Criminal, leading to an innocent or guilty pronouncement. b) Presentation and evaluation of claim and counter claim. c) "Notarizing" contracts.

There was much freedom in the detailed sequence of the trial. Begrich was among the first to study form critically certain speech patterns rooted in the juridical process, while H. Richter extended such analysis to the structure of the juridical process as a whole. The fundamental form critical study is Boecker's, upon which the following outline largely depends. Boecker follows Richter in distinguishing two parallel stages in the juridical process—interchanges of a formal nature which took place before the court was convened and interchanges which took place after convening. As the function of juridical procedure in the ancient Near East was to restore the harmony of the community, the process could break off at any point with or without a formal "decision." The roles in the process (accuser, accused, witness, judge) were fluid and often not sharply defined. There was no fixed office of prosecutor. Contrary to practice in the rest of the ancient Near East, written documents normally played only a minor role in ancient Israelite juridical practice.

In the pre-court stage, the first step is the accusation, which commonly is a question + a relative sentence indicating who did the act + an indication of what was done ("What is this thing + which you have done to us + that you have not called us . . .", Judg 8:1). Next is the response by the accused (1 Sam 26:18) or by a third party on his behalf (II Sam 20:32) : "What did I do?" If this response is deemed satisfactory, the procedure may end there (Jos 22:30). If the response is unsatisfactory, a call by accuser or accused convening the court follows (Gen 31:32, I Sam 26:15-16). The formal trial may contain several rounds of accusations and defenses and in some cases a formal acceptance of the judgment to prevent reactivation of the claim subsequently (Job 52:1-6). The indictment was addressed to the court, taking the form of a proposed judgment, a statement by a witness, or a report

III

of what had happened. Defense of the accused might be addressed directly to the court or to the accuser. The deed might be admitted but its illegality contested, or the deed might be denied and a counter accusation entered. The court may be called on to "credit to the defendant's account" (*zkr 1ᵉ*) his past deeds. At this stage there may occur a confession (commonly "I have sinned *ḥṭ'*," II Sam 19:21) or a proposed decision by any party (Jos 22:19). The formal decision may be positive or negative and if positive may be pronounced by the court or the opponent. There is either a general declaration (*ṣaddîq 'attâ*) in the second person or a specific statement in the third person which commonly says that a previously proposed sentence is not suitable (Jer 26:16). If the decision is negative, Boecker says there is only the third person specific sentence. But other evidence indicates that originally there was also a general, negative second person statement (Clark). A comprehensive examination of declarative formulas (Rendtorff, *Die Gesetze*, 74-76), is needed to help clarify this and other problems. In the case of two claims, there would be a recognition (*hikkîr*, I Kings 3:27). It still remained to assess the punishment, in the case of a capital crime, most often with the death declaration (*môt yûmat*).

2) Sacral Juridical Procedure

W. Beyerlin, *Die Rettung der Bedrängten in den Feindpsalmen* (FRLANT 99, Göttingen: Vandenhoeck & Ruprecht, 1970); L. Delekat, *Asylie und Schutzorakel am Zionheiligtum* (Leiden: E. J. Brill, 1967); R. Press, "Das Ordal im alten Israel," *ZAW* LI (1933) 121-140, 227-255; L. Rost, "Die Gerichtshoheit am Heiligtum," in *Archäologie und Altes Testament*, ed. by A. Kuschke and E. Kutsch (Tübingen: J. C. B. Mohr, 1970) 225-231; H. Schmidt, *Das Gebet der Angeklagten im Alten Testament* (BZAW 44, Giessen: A. Töpelmann, 1928). (See Schulz, *Das Todesrecht*, for additional bibliography.)

There is no agreement as to the existence or competence of a fully developed sacral juridical proceeding in Israel. 1) Oaths and divine decisions in a juridical context (Ex 22:6-12; Deut 21:1-8; Num 5; Judg 7) could take place within the normal juridical process. 2) The juridical function of the priest (Ex 18; Deut 17:8-13) may or may not imply a different juridical context or proceeding. 3) Schmidt thinks that I Kings 8:31-32 and a number of psalms reflect formal complaints lodged by falsely judged people. But this much contested genre analysis does not establish a separate sacral juridical process. Beyerlin has argued for the existence of a sacred legal institution associated with the temple. (On Schmidt and Beyerlin's suggestions, see below, p. 204.) Gamper's study of God as judge which concentrates on the prayer request "judge me" shows that such language does not support the existence of a normal cultic juridical procedure. 4) Other matters of relevance to the question are asylum and sin offerings. As for the latter, in Mari both sacral and secular punishments may result from the same (secular) juridical proceeding (cf. Marzal, "Mari Clauses in 'Casuistic' and 'Apodictic' Styles").

Basic questions are unanswered: Is it the type of offense, where it was committed, against whom, or by whom, which puts it into the proposed category of sacral procedure? Is it a matter of "appeal," of parallel jurisdictions with choice up to the parties, or of difficult cases? The most recent attempt to answer these questions is Schulz's analysis of Lev 18-20, which he claims is based on the protocol of such a sacral procedure containing three stages: 1) The trial, similar to the secular trial. 2) The recitation of prohibitives and the *môt yûmat* sentences. 3) The decision, consisting of five formulas: a) certification of the deed (e.g., "he has uncovered the nakedness of . . ."), b) qualification (e.g., "it is iniquity"), c) condemnation (e.g., "he has done folly"), d) guilt declaration (e.g., "he will bear his iniquity"), and e) death declaration (e.g., "he shall be cut off"), sometimes omitted. If this analysis is correct, it may reflect the sacralizing of all criminal juridical procedures. But Schulz's argument that the secular community did not have competence in capital cases (Jer 26 and I Kings 21) is very dubious. Lev 18-20 may represent a purely ideal literary construct without institutional realization.

B. Commercial Law

G. Tucker, *Contracts in the Old Testament: A Form-Critical Investigation* (dissertation, Yale University, 1963, cf. *DA* XXVII [1966-67] 530); *idem*, "Covenant Forms and Contract Forms," *VT* XV (1965) 487-503; *idem*, "Witnesses and 'Dates' in Israelite Contracts," *CBQ* XXVIII (1966) 42-45; R. Yaron, *Introduction to the Law of the Aramaic Papyri* (London: Oxford University Press, 1961).

Different schema for contracts of different areas, periods, and types (rent, lease, sale, adoption, marriage, etc.) in the ancient Near East are well known (see Haase, *Einführung in das Studium keilschriftlicher Rechtsquellen*; Yaron). In contrast, for Israel we lack sufficient data to do more than outline the basic common elements. Drawing principally on Tucker, we may distinguish two

III

128

stages relating to contracts: 1) Legal negotiations. Among related speech forms are opening summons, purchase requests, refusals, seller speeches, buyer speeches, haggling forms, and conclusions. 2) The actual contract, commonly oral, which is a witnessed agreement concluded before a court in order to prevent future disagreement. It consists of: a) the names of the parties, b) the "operative part" describing the transaction, c) specification of the property with name of the owner, d) attestation by witnesses but normally no oath, e) the date (*hayyôm*). Contracts for marriages and sale of slaves are similar. Marriage involves both betrothal (with payment of the bride price by the groom, at which point the contract becomes binding) and the marriage ceremony. Hiring, in contrast, was a private matter which usually did not take place before the court.

C. Additional Comments on Covenant and Treaty

G. Baena, "La terminología de la Alianza,"*EstBib* XXIX (1970) 1-54; P. Buis, "Les formulaires d'alliance," *VT* XVI (1966) 396-411; P. Calderone, *Dynastic Oracle and Suzerainty Treaty* (Manila: Ateneo University Publication, 1966); E. F. Campbell and G. E. Wright, "Tribal League Shrines in Amman and Shechem," *BA* XXXII (1969) 104-116; F. C. Fensham, "Father and Son as Terminology for Treaty and Covenant," in *Near Eastern Studies in Honor of W. F. Albright*, ed. by H. Goedicke (Baltimore: Johns Hopkins Press, 1971) 121-135; S. Herrmann, "Die Königsnovelle in Ägypten und in Israel," *WZKMUL* III (1953-54) 51-62; D. R. Hillers, *Covenant: The History of a Biblical Idea* (Baltimore: Johns Hopkins Press, 1969); E. Kutsch, "Der Begriff *berît* in vordeuteronomischer Zeit," in *Das ferne und nahe Worst*, ed. by F. Maass (BZAW 105, Berlin: A. Töpelmann, 1967) 133-143; *idem, "Sehen und Bestimmen*," in *Archäologie und Altes Testament*, 165-178; N. Lohfink, *Die Landverheissung als Eid* (SBS 28, Stuttgart: Katholisches Bibelwerk, 1967); D. J. McCarthy, *Old Testament Covenant: A Survey of Current Opinions* (Oxford: Basil Blackwell, 1972); M. Noth, *Das System der zwölf Stämme Israels* (BWANT IV/1, Stuttgart: W. Kohlhammer, 1930); H. Orlinsky, "The Tribal System of Israel and the Related Groups in the Period of the Judges," in *Studies and Essays in Honor of A. A. Neuman*, ed. by M. Ben-Horin, et al. (Leiden: E. J. Brill, 1962) 375-387; B. Rahtjen, "Philistine and Hebrew Amphictyonies," *JNES* XXIV (1965) 100-104; E. von Schuler, "Staatsverträge und Dokumente hethitischen Rechts," in *Neuere Hethiterforschung*, ed. by G. Walser (Wiesbaden: F. Steiner Verlag, 1964) 34-53; J. A. Soggin, "Akkadisch TAR *berîti* und hebräisch *krt bryt,*"*VT* XVIII (1968) 210-215; R. de Vaux, "Le roi d'Israël, vassal de Yahvé," *Mélanges E. Tisserant*, I (Rome: Biblioteca Apostolica Vaticana, 1964) 119-133; = his *Bible et Orient* (Paris: Éditions du Cerf, 1967) 287-301; = "The King of Israel, Vassal of Yahweh," in his *The Bible and the Ancient Near East*, tr. by J. McHugh (Garden City: Doubleday & Co., 1971) 152-166; *idem*, "La thèse de l'amphictyonie israélite," *HTR* LXIV (1970) 415-436; M. Weinfeld, "The Covenant of Grant in the Old Testament and in the Ancient Near East," *JAOS* XC (1970) 184-203; G. R. H. Wright, "Shechem and League Shrines," *VT* XXI (1971) 572-603. (For further bibliography, see McCarthy's work noted above.)

The basic treaty-covenant document has been studied by Mendenhall, Baltzer, and McCarthy and outlined above (see pp. 119-120). Formally, a covenant is a conditional self-curse with the statement of what is sworn (McCarthy; Tucker, "Covenant Forms"). In content, a covenant is essentially a mutual declaration of friendship (so Gerstenberger, "Covenant and Commandment"). As used in this section, covenant refers to the conjunction of these formal and content characteristics. It is necessary to distinguish between covenant document, ritual, and literary adaptations, and "mere" ideological construct. Baltzer gives a form critical analysis of renewal, transmission of office, and confirmation rituals. Buis outlines genres of "recit" (description of rites), "discourse of the mediator with citation of documents," and "predication" (the type of discourse common in Deuteronomy, which combines history, law, commentary, and blessing and curse). "Predication" is a purely literary adaptation.

The life setting of the covenant with Yahweh has usually been located in the institution of the sacral tribal league (amphictyony). Despite significant challenges to the existence of the Israelite amphictyony (Orlinsky, Rahtjen, Fohrer, and de Vaux), Noth's thesis remains the best explanation of certain data, such as the tribal lists, even if it requires modification (see Smend, *Yahweh War*; Campbell and Wright; G. R. H. Wright; and McCarthy, 61-65). The form of this covenant remains in doubt, whether between the tribes with Yahweh as guarantor or whether between Yahweh and Israel.

A related question is whether the Abraham and Davidic covenants are related to the treaty tradition. Some see the *'ēḏûṯ* given to the king at his coronation as the stipulations of a treaty (see de Vaux, 1964). However, if anointing was historically done by the people alone (Kutsch, *Salbung*), this does not support the existence of a culticly realized covenant between Yahweh and king. Calderone tries to show an ideological link of II Sam 7 with suzerainty treaties, but the genre links are more with the "royal novel" (Herrmann) and the royal oracles, as is also true for the Abraham covenant (the oracle structure of Gen 15: Lohfink). Weinfeld argues that the "land grant" covenant is the model of the Abraham and Davidic covenants, an interesting thesis requiring further investigation of related but distinct genres, such as treaties, instructions, royal grants, edicts, and the like (cf. von Schuler). This land-grant covenant (as in the *kudurru* inscriptions) is to be distinguished from the vassal covenant in its con-

III

cern for the rights of the recipient. Yet both types share certain common features. While the terminological and ideological parallels cited from many ancient Near Eastern texts are very impressive and valuable, the search for parallels seems to dominate and dictate the interpretation of the biblical texts. And despite the declared intent to compare two forms of covenant, no systematic form critical analysis of the texts or genres is attempted. Weinfeld is also unjustified in asserting that because influence from one area can be shown (e.g., forensic use of adoption terminology on the "son of God" concept) that this eliminates the possibility of the narrator or tradition also being influenced simultaneously by other areas.

We conclude with references to vocabulary. Kutsch argues strongly that *bᵉrît* means "obligation" and need not designate a covenant. An article by Soggin seems to suggest that the basic meaning of "cut a covenant" (*kārat bᵉrît*) is "to swear." Much other vocabulary has been linked to covenant including *yd'* (to know), *bḥr* (to choose), *šālôm* (wholeness), *ṭbt* (goodness), father-son, and *'hb* (to love.) However, as in the ancient Near East as a whole, most "covenantal" vocabulary derives from other usage. In each occurrence it is an open question whether a word which can have a technical treaty usage is so used in that text.

V. POLITICAL ADMINISTRATION AND PROTOCOLS

D. J. McCarthy, "An Installation Genre?" *JBL* XC (1971) 31-41; G. von Rad, "Das judäische Königsritual," *TLZ* LXXII (1947) 211-216 = his *Gesammelte Studien*, 205-213 = his *The Problem of the Hexateuch*, 222-231.

Two additional ceremonies will be mentioned here. The royal enthronement ritual, according to von Rad, had two stages: anointing in the sanctuary and enthronement in the palace. The sanctuary stage involved handing over the crown and the *'edût* (II Kings 11:12). Von Rad argues that the *'edût* is the Israelite parallel to the royal protocol of Egypt in which were written by the gods the king's (five) titles, his rights, and his duties. Following this there was the acclamation by the people and the procession to the palace, perhaps an oracle (Ps 2), and subsequent homage by the officials (I Kings 1:47). Functionally similar to the royal coronation is the installation genre. According to McCarthy, the basic structure (e.g., Deut 31:23) is: 1) an encouragement formula, 2) description of the task, and 3) promise of assistance. Often there is a double movement: appointment and installation.

VI. LEGAL TERMINOLOGY

R. Hentschke, *Satzung und Setzender. Ein Beitrag zur israelitischen Rechts-terminologie* (BWANT V/3, Stuttgart: W. Kohlhammer, 1963) ; A. Marzal, "The Provincial Governor at Mari: His Title and Appointment," *JNES* XXX (1971) 186-217; W. Richter, "Zu den 'Richtern Israels'," *ZAW* LXXVII (1965) 40-72. (See Liedke, *Gestalt und Bezeichnung alttestamentlicher Rechtssätze*, for additional bibliography.)

Methodologically, perhaps the most significant form critical study is Knierim's book on the words for "sin," some of which are closely linked to the legal sphere. Many other studies have been alluded to in preceding sections. Falk also has devoted attention to this area, without specific form critical orientation. Two additional items will be noted here. 1) Much discussion concerns whether *špṭ* in the OT refers only to judicial functions or whether it also includes "ruling." The latter position seems dominant at present (see Richter). 2) From the beginning of form critical study, efforts have been made to equate individual genres with specific words for law: *tôrâ, ḥōq, mišpāṭ, 'edût, miṣwâ, bᵉrît, dābār, derek,* and other words. The most extensive examination of this question is by Liedke. His methodology involves independently studying the genres (form critically) and the key substantive legal terms (according to classical philological methods). Then he attempts to demonstrate that a particular genre and a particular word share attributes which suggest that the word is a technical term for the genre. Liedke focuses on the authority behind the law or juridical process to which the genre and word relate. His effort to carry the syntactical analysis of the genres further than previously has been noted above. He concludes that *mišpaṭ* designates case law, often suggested but now given better support. The authority is that of the local community involving arbitration and a suggested rather than a binding judgment. *ḥōq/ḥuqqâ* has the basic meaning of "border, limit." Liedke thinks that *ḥōq* is a technical term for apodictic law (i.e., participle and relative formulations). In the legal sphere, both the genre and the word refer to the institution of a new order (boundary) by a binding authority rather than to the restoration of existing order, as in the case of the casuistic genre and words related to the root *špṭ*. *Ḥōq*, not referring originally to a speech act, is suited to express the impersonal nature of (Liedke's) apodictic genre. *Miṣwâ* is found to be the technical term for prohibitive/command, which is nonlegal. In contrast

III

to the impersonal nature of the apodictic genre, the command is direct address. This explains the use of the root *ṣwh*. Finally, pointing to the imperative as the clearest form of *tôrâ* and noting that such imperatives are found most often in wisdom exhortations (with the corresponding vetitive), Liedke suggests that the profane usage is original (rather than the priestly; cf. Begrich). It is from this profane usage that the prophetic imitations of *tôrâ* are derived.

This useful presentation thus produces a very neat correlation between four basic genres (only two of them said to be legal) and four words which designate the genres. Whether it is fully convincing is another matter. The argument for *tôrâ* and *miṣwâ* is intended more as a suggestion than a decisive proof. But even the evidence for his thesis concerning apodictic genre and the use of *ḥōq* is not conclusive. Liedke raises the question of whether one should expect any exact one-to-one correlation of genres and words and concludes that it would be remarkable if there were not a close congruence. But it is no more likely that division lines within related word (semantic) fields (e.g., substantive law terms) and within related genre fields will correspond exactly than that native kinship terminology will correspond precisely to actual kinship structures or that word and concept will precisely correlate. This one-to-one relationship of genres and terms, Liedke argues, goes back virtually to the beginning of Israel's history and involves little significant subsequent change. Etymology plays too large a role in his argument, and it is a very serious weakness that a study which combines form critical and philological analysis seems to be poorly if at all acquainted with recent developments in lexicographical methods within linguistics. Other general criticisms include: 1) The non-legal nature of the prohibitive is too quickly accepted. 2) The problem of the relationship between the political/administrative realm and the legal realm (crucial for Liedke's understanding of his apodictic genre) is not considered. 3) While much of Liedke's criticism of Schulz is valid, he would have done well to utilize a refinement similar to the distinctions suggested by Schulz (and cf. Marzal) of style, genre, and law concept. 4) The assumption that the oldest form is the purest and simplest is taken over uncritically at several points. Nevertheless this work is certainly the best effort to deal overall with the relationship between legal terminology and legal genres, especially if the areas of overlap are not pushed to the extremes of correspondence advocated by Liedke.

VII. LEGAL INFLUENCES IN NONLEGAL LITERATURE

Among matters to consider are: 1) The influence on legal material of nonlegal materials and genres. 2) The influence of legal materials and genres in nonlegal literature, including the use of legal genre to provide the structure for a nonlegal text. 3) The manifestation of similar concerns in two different areas (e.g., wisdom and legal) when direct dependence seems excluded. 4) The distinction of legal influence and "covenantal" influence. 5) The dating of a text by legal materials or genres contained in it. Do these represent the time of the written text or the time of the antecedent traditions?

A. Law in Wisdom and the Psalms

K. Koch, "Tempeleinlassliturgien und Dekaloge," in *Studien zur Theologie der alttestamentlichen Überlieferungen*, ed. by R. Rendtorff and K. Koch (Neukirchen: Neukirchener Verlag, 1961) 45-60; T. Leslow, "Die dreistufige Tora. Beobachtungen zu einer Form," *ZAW* LXXXII (1970) 263-280; J. Malfroy, "Sagesse et loi dans le Deutéronome. Etudes," *VT* XV (1965) 49-65; J. Tigay, "Psalms 7:5 and Ancient Near Eastern Treaties," *JBL* LXXXIX (1970) 178-186.

The "abomination" clause of certain laws finds its closest parallel in Proverbs. More significant is the similarity of apodictic law and wisdom admonitions in form, content, and life setting. The other context where we previously encountered a close link of law and wisdom was Weinfeld's thesis of the scribal setting of Deuteronomy. In addition, Malfroy points out close similarities in vocabulary ("obey," "hear," etc.) applied both to law and to wisdom instruction (cf. Landsberger, "Die babylonischen Termini für Gesetz und Recht"). Also the personal, direct style of address is similar in both.

In the Psalms, three genres will be mentioned. 1) Schmidt's questionable complaint genre, rooted in a sacral juridical process (e.g., Ps 107; 118). 2) Tigay (Ps 7) and others refer to "covenantal psalms." However, the discussions do not point to any distinct genre. 3) Koch suggests that the perfect statements in the middle section of the entrance liturgy genre (Ps 15; 24:3-5; Is 33:14-16) are a secondary appropriation from the decalogue.

III

Leslow however argues that these statements form a constituent part of a basic "instruction" genre which is used in but does not originate in the entrance liturgy.

B. Law and Prophets

R. Bach, "Gottes Recht und weltliches Recht in der Verkündigung des Propheten Amos," in *Festschrift Günter Dehn* (Neukirchen: Neukirchener Verlag, 1957) 23-34; W. Beyerlin, *Die Kulttraditionen Israels in der Verkündigung des Propheten Micha* (FRLANT 72, Göttingen: Vandenhoeck & Ruprecht, 1959) ; J. Boston, "The Wisdom Influence upon the Song of Moses," *JBL* LXXXVII (1968) 198-202; M. Boyle, "The Covenant Lawsuit of the Prophet Amos: iii 1-iv 12." *VT* XXI (1971) 338-363; W. Brueggeman, "Amos iv 4-13 and Israel's Covenant Worship," *VT* XV (1965) 1-15; E. Good, "Hosea 5:8-6:6: An Alternative to Alt," *JBL* LXXXV (1966) 273-286; J. Harvey, *Le plaidoyer prophétique contre Israël après le rupture de l'alliance* (Bruges: Desclée de Brouwer, 1967) ; H. Huffmon, "The Covenant Lawsuit and the Prophets," *JBL* LXXVIII (1959) 286-296; J. Jeremias, *Kultprophetie und Gerichtsverkündigung in der späten Königszeit Israels* (WMANT 35, Neukirchen: Neukirchener Verlag, 1970) ; H. -J. Kraus, *Die prophetische Verkündigung des Rechts in Israel* (BS 51, Zollikon: Evangelischer Verlag, 1957) ; J. Limburg, "The Root *ryb* and the Prophetic Lawsuit Speeches," *JBL* LXXXVIII (1969) 291-304; R. North, "Angel Prophet or Satan Prophet," *ZAW* (1970) 31-67; G. Ramsey, "Amos 4:12—A New Perspective," *JBL* LXXXIX (1970) 167-177; H. G. Reventlow, *Das Amt des Propheten bei Amos* (FRLANT 80, Göttingen: Vandenhoeck & Ruprecht, 1962) ; E. von Waldow, *Der traditionsgeschichtliche Hintergrund der prophetischen Gerichtsreden* (BZAW 85, Berlin: A. Töpelmann, 1963) ; W. Zimmerli, *Das Gesetz und die Propheten* (Göttingen: Vandenhoeck & Ruprecht, 1963) = *The Law and the Prophets*, tr. by R. E. Clements (Oxford: Basil Blackwell, 1965) .

At an earlier period the prophets were regarded as prior to the law. Now the question is rather whether the prophets invoke specific laws and argue forensically or whether they invoke common norms also manifested in law. The relationship of prophet and law leads directly to the question of the relationship of prophet and covenant. We may note three positions. 1) Covenant does not greatly influence the early classical prophets. (For a recent restatement of this position, see Perlitt, *Bundestheologie,* 1969.) 2) The prophets presuppose covenantal traditions even when they do not expressly refer to the covenant (Beyerlin on Micah) . 3) The prophet is the heir of an amphictyonic office involving prophetic proclamation of law (Kraus, Reventlow) .

For at least three prophetic genres a legal origin has been suggested. I) Schulz (*Das Todesrecht*) detects a "sacral-legal declaration word" genre (Ez 18; 14:1-11, 12-20; 33:1-20) , literarily derived from his proposed protocol of the sacral juridical process. II) Buis outlines five elements of a genre of proclamation of the new covenant (Jer 32:37-41), but this is more likely a popular motif than a genre. III) The extremely controversial "prophetic lawsuit" has been traced back to the legal sphere. 1) Origin: a) Boecker (*Redeformen*) argues that the genre is based on the secular juridical process. b) Huffmon argues that some but not all examples are covenant lawsuits. This position is developed impressively by Harvey, who tried to show that the lawsuit in form and ideology reflects ancient Near Eastern procedures which took place when a vassal broke a treaty. c) Von Waldow argues for the secular origin of the form but sees the influence of covenant ideology in its modification. Limburg supports the derivation from international treaty practices in an examination of the key term *rîb*, but his evidence would seem to argue better for diverse origins. The most often cited terminological evidence for the link of the prophetic lawsuit with treaty patterns is the invocation of heaven and earth (e.g., Deut 32:1; Is 1:2). But Boston has shown that the invocation is not constant in formulation or structural position, is neither limited to lawsuits nor necessary to them, and does not imply a single type of covenant. More generally, even when a link is granted between a prophetic lawsuit and covenant, it does not follow that the covenant model utilized must always be that of the international suzerainty treaty (cf. McCarthy [1972] 78-79). 2) Life setting: Is the prophetic lawsuit simply a rhetorical device, or is it rooted in actual covenant or cultic ceremonies? 3) The extent of the use of the prophetic lawsuit genre: Most early studies concentrated on a few texts (e.g., Mic 6:1-8; Is 1:2-3). Recently, there is a tendency to bring in more and more texts. Thus, for example, Brueggemann and Good make strong cases for relating Amos 4:4-13 and Hos 5:8-6:6 to ritual use of a covenant lawsuit. It should, however, be noted that the lawsuit model presupposes an accusation with punishment to follow, while some cited penitential rites presuppose existing misfortune. The variety of different—at least four—"covenantal" interpretations of the structure of Amos 4 suggests that with some ingenuity a covenantal explanation can be offered for the structure of almost any prophetic passage. Boyle provides an example of extreme "pan-covenantalism" when she derives the prophetic call genre and the structure of several prophetic books from the covenantal lawsuit pattern.

The issue of the prophetic lawsuit remains unresolved, and it appears that we should allow for diverse influences and developments rather than a single origin and application (cf. North).

III

136

C. Law and Narrative

R. O'Callahan, "Historical Parallels to Patriarchal Social Custom," *CBQ* VI (1944) 391-405; B. S. Childs, "The Birth of Moses," *JBL* LXXXIV (1965) 109-122; W. M. Clark, "The Flood and the Structure of the Pre-patriarchal History," *ZAW* LXXXIII (1971) 184-212; D. Daube, "Law in the Narratives," in his *Studies in Biblical Law* (London: Cambridge University Press, 1947) 1-73; *idem,* "Rechtsgedanken in den Erzählungen des Pentateuchs," in *Von Ugarit nach Qumran* (BZAW 77, Berlin: A. Töpelmann, 1958) 32-41; *idem, The Exodus Pattern in the Bible* (London: Faber & Faber, 1963); J. J. Finkelstein, "An Old Babylonian Herding Contract and Genesis 31:38f,"*JAOS* LXXXVIII (1968) 30-36; R. Frankena, "Some Remarks on the Semitic Background of Chapters XXIX-XXXI of the Book of Genesis," *OTS* XVII (1972) 53-64; D. Freedman, "A New Approach to the Nuzi Sistership Contract," *JANES* II (1970) 77-85; C. Gordon, "Biblical Customs and the Nuzu Tablets," *BA* III (1940) 1-12; M. Greenberg, "Another Look at Rachel's Theft of the Teraphim," *JBL* LXXXI (1962) 239-248; U. Kellermann, *Nehemia: Quellen Überlieferung und Geschichte* (BZAW 102, Berlin: A. Töpelmann, 1967); M. Lehmann, "Abraham's Purchase of Machpelah and Hittite Law," *BASOR* CXXIX (1953) 15-18; H. Petschow, "Die neubabylonische Zwiegesprächsurkunde und Genesis 23," *JCS* XIX (1965) 103-120; U. Simon, "The Poor Man's Ewe Lamb. An Example of a Juridical Parable," *Bib* XLVIII (1967) 207-242; E. Speiser, *Genesis* (AB 1, Garden City: Doubleday & Co., 1964); G. Tucker, "The Legal Background of Genesis 23," *JBL* LXXXV (1966) 77-84; J. Van Seters, "The Problem of Childlessness in Near Eastern Law and the Patriarchs of Israel," *JBL* LXXXVII (1968) 401-408; *idem,* "Jacob's Marriages and Ancient Near Eastern Customs: A Reexamination," *HTR* LXII (1970) 377-395.

Probably the closest to a specific legal narrative genre is the "juridical parable" analyzed by Simon in II Sam 11-12; I Kings 20:35-43; Is 5; and Jer 3:1-5. This is a realistic story about a law violation related to a person who has committed a similar crime. It is intended to evoke an unsuspecting self-condemnation. In his study of the Moses birth story, Childs demonstrates that in its structure this exposure saga reflects the content and structure of the contract form used for a wet nurse relationship. Similarly, Gen 3-4 (and II Sam 11-12) is structured according to the outline of a juridical proceeding (Clark). As in Ex 2, the legal structural pattern is imposed on the narrative rather than being intrinsic to the material. H. Richter (*Studien zu Hiob*) argues that legal influence dominates the vocabulary, the genres of individual units, and the sequence of the whole book of Job: the pre-court controversy (c. 4-14); the court controversy (c. 15-31); the divine judgment (c. 28-42:6). Finally, drawing on Schmidt's complaint genre, Kellermann argues that the genre of the "first person" source of Nehemia is a legal document calling to God for judgment along with proof of innocence and counter complaint against his enemies.

Comparisons made with some practices in ancient Near Eastern materials have led many to conclude that these customs are reflected in the patriarchal narratives and have been used to confirm a dating of the patriarchs in the first half of the second millennium (Gordon, O'Callahan, Speiser). The comparisons have often been based on isolated similarities and have ignored parallels from other periods. Without suggesting that all the parallels are invalid, we will look at efforts to refute three classic examples. 1) The theft of Laban's "gods" (teraphim; Gen 31) has been explained from Nuzi inheritance law. Greenberg, however, says that the adopted son does not need the gods for inheritance and that Laban could have disinherited Jacob for theft if he did have them. A closely related thesis is that Jacob's marriage was an *errebu* marriage in which the wife lives in her father's household and the husband is adopted by her father. Van Seters counters (1970) that a) the original proposal for *errebu* marriage (itself dubious) is not connected with adoption, b) Jacob's marriages are normal purchase marriages, and c) Neo-Assyrian purchase marriage provides a closer parallel. In an unrelated case which also concerns marriage contracts, Freedman makes very dubious Speiser's interpretation that the Abraham-Sarah (Isaac-Rebekah) relationship as brother and sister (Gen 12; 24) is an example of the Nuzi sistership contract and marriage. 2) The giving of a concubine by a barren wife to her husband to provide children (Sarah and Hagar, Gen 16) has also been related to Nuzi customs. Van Seters argues (1968) that the ancient Near Eastern texts are unique cases, that the slave was not the maid of the wife, and that closer parallels are found in a Neo-Babylonian text in which a barren wife must permit the husband to have a maid. 3) Lehmann argues that Genesis 23 shows Hittite influence in the desire to sell all the land (linked with feudal service) and the enumeration of the number of trees. Tucker counters that both of these factors apply also in Mesopotamia. A form critical analysis shows that the structure of the chapter parallels the dialogue-contract genre (Petschow, Tucker) which first appears in Neo-Babylonian times and is characterized by describing the negotiations leading to sale prior to switching over to an objective documentation of the agreement.

Because of the scope of material covered in this survey, no effort will be made to provide an overall summary. It has been impossible to mention many important works, especially those which treat the legal material without explicit attention to and/or familiarity with form critical methodology. Such works often contain significant form critical observations, especially in such an intrinsically institutionalized area as law. Without intending any slight to other areas, I conclude by mentioning that many writers have pointed out the extraordinary significance of legal materials, institutions, and concepts in the OT, and some have suggested a special genius among the Northwest Semites in the legal realm.

W. MALCOLM CLARK

Chapter Four

PROPHECY

If any student of the OT prophets is tempted to think that all of the major questions have been answered and that nothing, therefore, remains to be done, a few hours invested in studying the history and present status of form critical research on the prophetic literature should dispel any such illusion. Much has been accomplished, to be sure, but the task of analyzing, describing, and reporting the data pertinent to understanding the prophetic literature form critically is not even nearly complete. This chapter will be devoted to sketching some of the major advances, describing the major types that can be isolated in the prophetic corpus, and suggesting some directions future research in this area may need to take.

I. A BRIEF SURVEY OF FORM CRITICAL RESEARCH IN THE PROPHETS

R. Bach, *Die Aufforderung zur Flucht und zum Kampf im alttestamentliche Prophetenspruch* (WMANT 9, Neukirchen: Neukirchener Verlag, 1962) ; E. Balla, *Die Droh- und Scheltworte des Amos* (Leipzig: Alexander Edelmann, 1926) ; J. Begrich, "Das priesterliche Heilsorakel," *ZAW* LII (1934) 81-92 ═ his *Gesammelte Studien zum Alten Testament* (TB 21, Munich: Chr. Kaiser, 1964) 217-231; *idem, Studien zu Deuterojesaja* (BWANT IV/25, Stuttgart: W.

Kohlhammer, 1938) = (TB 20, Munich: Chr. Kaiser, 1963) ; A. Bentzen, *Introduction to the Old Testament*, 2 vols. (Copenhagen: G. E. C. Gad, 1948, 1952²) ; H.-J. Boecker, "Anklagereden und Verteidigungsreden im Alten Testament," *EvTh* XX (1960) 398-412; *idem, Redeformen des Rechtslebens im Alten Testament* (WMANT 14, Neukirchen: Neukirchener Verlag, 1964) ; M. J. Buss, *A Form-Critical Study of the Book of Hosea with Special Attention to Method* (dissertation, Yale University, 1958) ; A. Dillmann, *Handbuch der alttestamentliche Theologie* (Leipzig: S. Hirzel, 1895) ; B. Duhm, *Die Theologie der Propheten* (Bonn: Adolph Marcus, 1875) ; O. Eissfeldt, *Einleitung in das Alte Testament* (Tübingen: J. C. B. Mohr 1934. 1964³) = *The Old Testament: An Introduction*, tr. by P. R. Ackroyd (New York: Harper & Row, 1965) ; F. Ellermeier, *Prophetie in Mari und Israel* (TOA 1, Herzberg: Erwin Jungfer, 1968) ; E. Sellin-G. Fohrer, *Einleitung in das Alte Testament* (Heidelberg: Quelle & Meyer, 1965¹⁰) = *Introduction to the Old Testament*, tr. by D. Green (Nashville: Abingdon Press, 1968) ; B. Gemser, "The *rib*- or Controversy-Pattern in Hebrew Mentality," *VTS* III (1955) 120-137 = his *Adhuc Loquitur* (POS 7, Leiden: E. J. Brill, 1968) 116-137; H. Gressmann, *Die älteste Geschichtsschreibung und Prophetie Israels* (SAT II/1, Göttingen: Vandenhoeck & Ruprecht, 1910) ; *idem*, "Die literarische Analyse Deuterojesajas," *ZAW* XXXIV (1914) 254-297; *idem, Der Messias* (FRLANT 34, Göttingen: Vandenhoeck & Ruprecht, 1929) ; H. Gunkel, "Die israelitische Literatur," in *Die orientalischen Literaturen*, ed. by P. Hinneberg (KdG I/7, Leipzig: B. G. Teubner, 1906, 1925²) 53-112 = his *Die israelitische Literatur* (Darmstadt: Wissenschaftliche Buchgesellschaft, 1963) ; *idem*, "Jesaja 33; eine prophetische Liturgie," *ZAW* XLII (1924) 177-208; *idem, Die Propheten* (Göttingen: Vandenhoeck & Ruprecht, 1917) ; *idem*, "Einleitungen," in H. Schmidt, *Die grossen Propheten* (SAT II/2, Göttingen: Vandenhoeck & Ruprecht, 1923²) LX-LXX; *idem*, "Propheten II: Seit Amos," *RGG¹* IV 1866-1886 (= *RGG²* IV 1538-1554) = "The Israelite Prophecy from the Time of Amos," in *Twentieth Century Theology in the Making*, ed. by J. Pelikan, tr. by R. A. Wilson (New York: Harper & Row, 1969) 48-75; N. Habel, "The Form and Significance of the Call Narrative," *ZAW* LXXVII (1965) 297-323; J. Harvey, "Le 'rîb-Pattern,' réquisitoire prophétique sur la rupture de l'alliance," *Bib* XLIII (1962) 172-196; *idem, Le plaidoyer prophétique contre Israël après la rupture de l'alliance* (Bruges: Desclée de Brouwer, 1967) ; J. Hempel, *Die althebräische Literatur und ihr hellenistisch-jüdisches Nachleben* (Wildpark-Potsdam: Akademische Verlagsgesellschaft, 1934); *idem, Worte der Propheten* (Berlin: A. Töpelmann, 1949) ; F. Hesse, "Wurzelt die prophetische Gerichtsrede im israelitischen Kult?" *ZAW* LXV (1953) 45-53; D. Hillers, *Treaty-Curses and the Old Testament Prophets* (BibOr 16, Rome: Pontifical Biblical Institute, 1964) ; G. Hölscher, *Die Profeten* (Leipzig: J. C. Hinrichs, 1914) ; H. Huffmon, "The Covenant Lawsuit in the Prophets," *JBL* LXXVIII (1959) 285-295; W. Klatt, "Gunkels Beitrag zur Prophetenforschung," in his *Hermann Gunkel* (FRLANT 100, Göttingen: Vandenhoeck & Ruprecht, 1969) 192-218; K. Koch, *Was ist Formgeschichte?* (Neukirchen: Neukirchener Verlag, 1964, 1967²) = *The Growth of the Biblical Tradition: The Form-Critical Method*, tr. by S. Cupitt (New York: Charles Scribner's Sons, 1969) ; L. Köhler, "Der Botenspruch," in his *Kleine Lichter* (Zurich: Zwingli-Verlag, 1945) 13-17; *idem, Deuterojesaja (Jesaja 40-55) stilkritisch untersucht* (BZAW 37, Giessen: A. Töpelmann, 1923) ; J. Lindblom, *Die literarische Gattung der prophetischen Literatur* (UUA Theologi 1, Uppsala: A.-B. Lundequistska Bokhandeln, 1924) ; *idem, Prophecy in Ancient Israel* (Philadelphia: Muhlenberg Press, 1962) ; S. Mowinckel, *Zur Komposition des Buches Jeremia* (VKS II 1913 5, Kristiania: Jacob Dybwad, 1914) ; *idem*, "Stilformer og motiver i profeten Jeremias diktning," *Edda* XXVI (1926) 233-320; *idem, Prophecy and Tradition* (ANVAO) II/3, Oslo: Jacob Dybwad, 1946) ; R. North, "Angel-Prophet or Satan-Prophet," *ZAW* LXXXII (1970) 31-67; G. von Rad, *Theologie des Alten Testaments*, vol. II (Munich: Chr. Kaiser, 1960) = *Old Testament Theology*, vol. II, tr. by D. Stalker (New York: Harper & Brothers, 1965); R. Rendtorff, "Botenformel und Botenspruch," *ZAW* LXXIV (1962) 165-177; *idem*, "Zum Gebrauch der Formel *ne'um jahwe* in Jeremiabuch," *ZAW* LXVI (1954) 27-37; H. G. Reventlow, *Das Amt des Propheten bei Amos* (FRLANT 80, Göttingen: Vandenhoeck & Ruprecht, 1962); *idem*, "Gattung und Überlieferung in der 'Tempelrede Jeremias,' Jer 7 und 26," *ZAW* LXXXI (1969) 315-352; *idem*, *Liturgie und prophetisches Ich bei Jeremia* (Gütersloh: Gerd Mohn, 1963); *idem*, *Wächter über Israel: Ezechiel und seine Tradition* (BZAW 82, Berlin: A. Töpelmann, 1962); T. H. Robinson, "Higher Criticism and the Prophetic Literature," *ET* L (1938/39) 198-202; J. Ross, "The Prophet as Yahweh's Messenger," in *Israel's Prophetic Heritage*, ed. by B. W. Anderson and W. Harrelson (New York: Harper & Brothers, 1962) 98-107; H. Schmidt, *Die grossen Propheten* (SAT II/2, Göttingen: Vandenhoeck & Ruprecht, 1915, 1923²); W. Vatke, *Historisch-kritische Einleitung in das Alte Testament* (Bonn: Emil Strauss, 1886); E. von Waldow, *Der traditionsgeschichtliche Hintergrund der prophetischen Gerichtsreden* (BZAW 85, Berlin: A. Töpelmann, 1963); A. Weiser, *Einleitung in das Alte Testament* (Göttingen: Vandenhoeck & Ruprecht, 1948, 1957⁴) = *The Old Testament: Its Formation and Development*, tr. by D. M. Barton (New York: Association Press, 1961); C. Westermann, *Grundformen prophetischer Rede* (BEvTh 31, Munich: Chr. Kaiser, 1960) = *Basic Forms of Prophetic Speech*, tr. by H. C. White (Philadelphia: The Westminster Press, 1967); *idem*, *Das Buch Jesaja: Kapitel 40-66* (ATD 19, Göttingen: Vandenhoeck & Ruprecht, 1966) = *Isaiah 40-66* tr. by D. Stalker (Philadelphia: The Westminster Press, 1969); *idem*, "Das Heilswort bei Deuterojesaja," *EvTh* XXIV (1964) 355-373; *idem*, "Sprache und Struktur der Prophetie Deuterojesajas," in his *Forschung am Alten Testament* (TB 24, Munich: Chr. Kaiser, 1964) 92-170; *idem*, "Struktur und Geschichte der Klage im Alten Testament," *ZAW* LXVI (1954) 44-80 = his *Forschung am Alten Testament*, 266-305; *idem*, "The Way of the Promise through the Old Testament," in *The Old Testament and Christian Faith*, ed. by B. W. Anderson (New York: Harper & Row, 1963) 200-224; H. Wildberger, *Jahwewort und prophetische Rede bei Jeremia* (Zurich: Zwingli-Verlag, 1942); H. W. Wolff, "Der Aufruf zur Volksklage," *ZAW* LXXVI (1964) 48-56; *idem*, "Die Begründungen der prophetischen Heils- und Unheilssprüche," *ZAW* LII (1934) 1-22 = his *Gesammelte Studien zum Alten Testament* (TB 22, Munich: Chr. Kaiser, 1964) 9-35; *idem*, *Das Zitat im Prophetenspruch* (BEvTh 4, Munich: Chr. Kaiser, 1937) = his *Gesammelte Studien*, 36-129; E. Würthwein, "Amos-Studien," *ZAW* LXII (1949/50) 10-52 = his *Wort und Existenz: Studien zum Alten Testament* (Göttingen: Vandenhoeck & Ruprecht, 1970) 68-110; *idem*, "Der Ursprung der prophetischen Gerichtsrede," *ZTK* XLIX (1952) 1-16 = his *Wort und Existenz*, 111-126.

A discussion of form critical research must almost inevitably begin with the work of Hermann Gunkel, generally acknowledged pioneer of and inspiration for the discipline. It is not that Gunkel worked in isolation, nor that he was the first to recognize the problems. Indeed Duhm, Vatke, Dillmann, and others had already begun to point to some of the major concerns that were to attract Gunkel's attention (see Buss, 32-34). Rather Gunkel's dominant influence stems from the breadth of his interest and competence and his ability to capture the imagination of a generation of gifted students and colleagues. Gunkel was able to articulate his insights so as to draw upon prevailing consensus while at the same time breaking open whole new areas for consideration. His questions and suggestive comments provided stimulus for a fresh examination of the OT, an examination which was to offer new approaches to the study of the Hebrew prophets and prophetic literature.

With respect to the prophets, Gunkel's conclusions are presented in most detail in his introduction to H. Schmidt's *Die grossen Propheten*. The substance of his position had appeared earlier in "Die israelitische Literatur" and in "Propheten II: Seit Amos." Gunkel's *Die Propheten* was published in 1917, but it largely repeats what he had previously written. Unfortunately, he never produced a commentary on any prophetical book. It is thus impossible to see his methodological perspectives on the prophets at work in actual exegesis comparable to that in his books on Genesis and Psalms which reflects his work on narrative and psalm genres.

In his various writings on the prophets, Gunkel developed and furthered several theses (see Klatt and Westermann, *Basic Forms*, 23-31). He emphasized that the prophets must be seen as orators and not as writers. "We must try and imagine their sayings being uttered orally, and not as they now stand on paper, if we are to understand them" ("Israelite Prophecy," 61). Since the prophets were not originally writers, it is the spoken form which was the primary unit, a unit which may have little relationship to the present chapter and verse divisions in the text. The primary prophetic unit, according to Gunkel, is the short, separate saying concerning the future. It might take the form of a symbolic name, a play on words, or a brief oracle. It might be positive or negative, express weal or woe. Gunkel stressed the Yahweh enthusiasm or ecstasy of the prophets in which they experienced visions, heard sounds, and saw lights. These experiences were the occasions through which the deity often spoke and revealed himself, and they gave to the revealed word a secretive, mysterious quality which was often indefinite in reference. Thus "the short enigmatic words and combinations of words such as Jezreel, Lo-ammi, Emmanuel" and so forth "are examples of the very earliest prophetic style" ("Israelite Prophecy," 64-65). This primitive style, combined with the characteristic prophetic interest in the future, he saw exemplified in the oracles concerning foreign nations, which he considered to be one of if not the earliest form of prophetic address.

As time passed and the prophets had opportunity to reflect on their work and sayings, additions were made to the original oracles. This expansion of the sayings by the prophets reflects their development as preachers and teachers on one hand and as poets on the other. "They were not satisfied merely with foretelling the future, although this always remained their principal purpose; but they also began to give the ethical reason why what they prophesied had to come to pass" ("Israelite Prophecy," 74). The reproach (*Scheltrede*), for instance, was added to the primary word, the threat (*Drohrede*), to "explain" the reason for God's negative judgment. In elaborating this point, Gunkel wrote the following:

> Thus they added to their threats *reproaches*, in which they described Israel's wrongdoings (e.g., Isa. 1.2f.; Jer. 2.10-13) and used for preference the style of an accusation before a court (e.g., Isa. 3.13-15; Micah 6.1ff.). For the great prophets of doom, this revealing of sin formed one of the main parts of their preaching (Micah 3.8); there are whole prophetic books which consist essentially of these two categories, the threat and the reproach; an example is the book of Amos. Furthermore, it was an ancient prophetic practice to answer questions and give advice (Jer. 42.1ff.; Zech. 7.1ff.; Micah 6.6ff.); making use of this right, the prophets uttered *exhortations*, and so found an opportunity of developing their great religious and ethical ideas in a positive sense; such exhortations are characteristic of the style of Jeremiah (Jer. 7. 1-15; 11.1-8; 18.11; cf. also Amos 5.4f.; Isa. 1.10-17). On other occasions, they came into conflict with their opponents in angry *disputes*; sometimes the situation which gave rise to these disputes is described (Amos 7.10 ff.; Isa. 7; Jer. 28), and sometimes the words of their opponents were also recorded (Amos 5.14; Jer. 7.10; 28.9 ff. etc.; especially Haggai and Malachi); mostly the latter are left out, but whole passages in the prophets read like answers of the prophets to objections on the part of their audience, as it were a transcription of the prophet's part (e.g. Jer. 2.14 ff.). Many of the strangest turns of phrase in the prophets can only be understood when it is realized that they are drawn from such dialogues. Finally, prophecy became a form of *philosophy of religion*: the prophets proclaimed the law of God's rule (Jer. 18; Ezek. 18). To this end, they adopted the style of the priestly *torah*: in the doctrinal statements of Ezekiel the style of the legal ordinances is particularly evident (Ezek. 18). Again, in order to

express their ideas, they made use of *historical accounts* (Amos 4.6-12; Jer. 3.6 ff.), though of course they were not concerned with recounting facts, but in presenting a certain view of them. Ezekiel in particular contains extensive historical surveys of the whole past since the Exodus, by preference in the form of *allegory* (Ezek. 16; 20; 23). ["Israelite Prophecy," 74-75]

Reproaches, exhortations, disputation words, judicial speech (*Gerichtsrede*), historical review (*Geschichtsbetrachtung* or *Geschichtserzählung*), torah, and allegory represent secondary elaboration of the original short saying and are products of the prophets' didactic and reflective concerns (what Gunkel called their function as "preachers, teachers and thinkers"). The prophets were also poets, and in this capacity they drew upon the secular and religious lyrical traditions of Israel.

> Thus from secular literature, we find on occasions in their works a *sentry's song* (Isa. 21.11f.), *drinking songs* (Isa. 22. 13; 21.5, 56.12), and even a *song mocking a harlot* (Isa. 23. 16); they made particular use of the *funeral elegy*, which even before their time had been given a political significance (Isa. 14.4 ff.; Amos 5.1 f.; Ezek. 19; 28.11 ff.; 32). Besides these, there are a great number of imitations of forms used in worship; hymns, found particularly in the prophets of good fortune, and especially in Deutero-Isaiah (Isa. 42.10 ff.; 44.23; 40.22 ff; 42.5; 43.16 f.), *laments of the people*, either those which they now use as intercessions for the misfortunes of their people (e.g., Jer. 14.2ff., 19 ff.), or those which they present as uttered by the people, as prophecies of the future (Hosea 6.1 ff.; 14.4; Jer. 3.22 ff.), *hymns for a thanksgiving sacrifice* (Jer. 33.11), *pilgrimage songs* (Isa. 2.1ff.; Micah 4.1 ff.), *torahs for entry into the sanctuary* (Isa. 33.14 ff.), and finally even *individual laments*, made use of by Jeremiah (Jer. 15.15 ff.; 17.14 ff.; 20.7 ff.). They also imitated the forms of *liturgical worship* (Isa. 33.1ff.; Micah 7.7ff.) and by so doing often achieved their most telling effects. ["Israelite Prophecy," 73-74]

The prophets thus borrowed numerous and diverse forms as they reflected upon, elaborated, and communicated their message in attempts to win a hearing from their audience.

In discussing the prophetical books, Gunkel spoke of passages which are stories or narratives about the prophets and their deeds or events which happened to them. These "oracles" he divided into two separate groups: *"visions and verbal revelations,* what the prophets saw and what they heard, characterized by their opening words: 'Thus Yahweh showed me' and 'Thus Yahweh spoke to me' " ("Israelite Prophecy," 67). These accounts can be distinguished from the prophetic speeches proper. Gunkel did not assign as great a significance to the prophetic visions as to the verbal revelations or auditions since it was through the latter that the prophets had revealed to them the words of Yahweh which they then proclaimed to the people. As the result of the verbal revelation, "the prophet regards himself as the 'messenger' of Yahweh—a favourite and characteristic image from an early period—and just as a messenger reports the words of the master exactly as he heard them from him, so the prophet also has the right to speak in the first person in the name of Yahweh himself. 'Thus has Yahweh spoken,' his oracle begins . . ." ("Israelite Prophecy," 67-68). The original primary prophetic genre must have been the proclamation of the word received in the revelation, but Gunkel is never completely clear about its form. He did not proceed to draw the consequences from his insight that the prophets were messengers of Yahweh and introduced their oracles with the messenger formula.

Gunkel's analysis was perceptive and stimulating. To be sure, the master could not break entirely with his own age, and thus the genres are too much defined by content rather than form. The assumption that the "reproach" must reflect a secondary stage and be understood as an addition leaves much data unexplained. The suggestion that the earliest prophetic forms may have been oracles against foreign nations seems without support. Nonetheless, Gunkel's work initiated a reexamination of the prophetic literature. His agreement with the theory put forward by others (see Robinson, 198-199) that the short, single unit was primary in prophetic speech resulted in acceptance of this premise. The search for prophetic forms and the attempt to sketch the history of those forms were set in motion, and for many years Gunkel's work was to serve as the only proper starting point.

The extent of Gunkel's influence can be seen in the studies produced by a number of his contemporaries. In the commentary series *Die Schriften des Alten Testaments* and in the encyclopedia *Die Religion in Geschichte und Gegenwart* Gunkel's work as editor and contributor was complemented by the writings of numerous others stimulated by his approach. The accomplishments of Gressmann and Balla are particularly important, but Haller, Schmidt, and Volz made worthwhile contributions to examination of the prophetic literature from a form critical point of view. Hugo Gressmann's summary work is found in *Der Messias,* published in 1929. But as early as 1910 he had presented a clear, systematic description of prophetic genres, along the lines outlined by Gunkel, in his *Die älteste Geschichtsschreibung und Prophetie Israels*, prepared for the commentary series *Die Schriften des Alten Testaments* which he edited jointly with Gunkel. It is clear that Gressmann shared many of Gunkel's positions. The small, independent unit intended originally for oral delivery was primary. Oracles directed toward the future were assumed to be the earliest. The major types of prophetic material were the threat and the promise.

But Gressmann began to identify some of the forms a little more closely than had been done previously, and in the process he was to lay the groundwork for at least one significant revision in the understanding of prophetic forms. As Gressmann began a closer examination of the oracles against foreign nations, he found it necessary to distinguish between oracles against individual nations not actively hostile toward Israel (*Heidenorakel*) and those against nations whose armies were actively engaged in attack or threat of attack (*Völkerorakel*). Further, it became clear that the relationship between threat and promise was complicated at best. Gressmann attempted to argue that threat and promise originally formed a literary unity, the positive directed toward Israel and the negative toward the enemy, but his efforts fail for want of any clear example. While his claim that with Amos the threat was first separated from the promise and directed at Israel is interesting, little evidence supports the supposition. Rather, the data seem to indicate that both promise and threat could be directed to the prophet's people from the earliest times on record. Further, Gressmann's research pointed up how frequently the threat was accompanied by the reproach, a fact that raised some questions about the validity of Gunkel's assumption that the two were necessarily independent forms, with the reproach a secondary formulation.

The work of Emil Balla is particularly interesting for a number of reasons. In his several contributions to the second edition of *RGG* and in his earlier study in Amos, *Die Droh- und Scheltworte des Amos*, Balla showed the depth of Gunkel's influence. The distinction between threat and reproach was still assumed. The short unit was expected. The private experience of the prophet was still emphasized. However, Balla's work on Amos presented evidence which pointed in the same direction as some of Gressmann's work in *Der Messias*. First, the necessity of some distinction was recognized in properly describing two types of prophetic oracle. There was the threat (*Drohwort*), a direct word of divine judgment. But there was also a type of oracle of disaster (*Unheilsorakel*), which was more visionary and which was considered by Balla to be related to the ecstatic experience of the seers. Second, and even more significant, when Balla finished his study of Amos, he reached the conclusion that the units in Amos almost all consisted of a threat and an accompanying reason (*Begründung* or *Scheltwort*). "Pure" *Drohworte* and "pure" *Scheltworte*, unadulterated threats and reproaches, were almost completely lacking. Thus, again, the distinction made by Gunkel between threat and reproach was not supported by the text.

While the various explorations noted above were in progress, two other scholars not so closely related to Gunkel pursued research which pointed in a new and fruitful direction. Ludwig Köhler, in his work on Second Isaiah, *Deuterojesaja, stilkritisch untersucht*, and in a later summary entitled "Der Botenspruch" in his *Kleine Lichter*, reached the important conclusion that prophetic speech seems to have its background in the speech form of the messenger. While Second Isaiah used the form quite freely, the character of the prophet was best understood nonetheless in terms of the messenger. Johannes Lindblom in his *Die literarische Gattung der prophetischen Literatur* came to much the same conclusion almost despite himself. He approached the study from a much different angle, emphasizing the points of contact between the prophetic literature and the writings of medieval mystics. Only as he turned in his appendix to a detailed study of the phrase *kô 'āmar YHWH* did it become clear that this formula had its origin in the speech of the messenger and the proclamations committed to him.

Another outstanding student of Gunkel was Sigmund Mowinckel. He is best remembered for his work on the Psalter, particularly his suggestions concerning the nature of the cultus and the development of eschatology. But in addition to his study of the psalms, Mowinckel made numerous other contributions, among which are two significant form critical studies dealing with Jeremiah. The first, *Zur Komposition des Buches Jeremia*, records his attempt to classify the material in Jeremiah in terms of three main groups: poetic oracles (considered genuine); historical narratives influenced by legend; and prose, first person speeches clearly showing a relationship to the Deuteronomistic school. The second article, "Stilformer og motiver i profeten Jeremias diktning," presents an excellent description of the genres and style used by Jeremiah. The influence of this latter article has nowhere approached that of the first, primarily because of the language barrier.

In 1934 Johannes Hempel published a form critically oriented volume entitled *Die althebräische Literatur und ihr hellenistisch-jüdisches Nachleben*. Much in this work corresponds to Gunkel's original description of prophetic literature, but some very interesting alterations are to be noted. While accepting the basic notion of prophetic ecstasy developed by Hölscher in 1914 in his *Die Profeten*, Hempel argued that the ecstatic experience had to be translated into rational speech. Thus, the prophet was expected to add various comments concerning God, the people, and the situation. The short, rhythmic oracle which combined the reason for judgment directly with the word from God was considered the simplest form of prophetic speech, but in most instances, Hempel argued, the prophets developed larger units on the basis of their primary rationalizing (reasons were necessary to communicate the message) and their secondary personal reflection on the situation which led to warning, exhortation, etc. Even before Amos these more developed genres had appeared, so while the prophets do demonstrate an ever increasing freedom to "add" subjective comment, Hempel believed the origin of this practice to be quite early. In his scheme of classification he distinguished between *Epische Gattungen*, which included the biographical and autobiographical materials found in the prophetic corpus, and *Prädikative Sprüche*, predicative speeches, which were divided between the unconditional (*unbedingte*) types (*Drohwort, Heilswort, Scheltwort*) and the conditional (*bedingte*) forms (*Mahnung* —Exhortation, *Bussrede*—repentance speech, *bedingte Verheissung*—conditional promise). By separating the threat and reproach (*Drohwort* and *Scheltwort*) Hempel failed to build on his insight concerning the basic unity of the two found in the simplest oracles which contain reason and judgment side by side. But he did help better define what Gunkel had earlier tried to describe in terms of primary and secondary forms, for unconditional and conditional are much more helpful categories.

During the same year that Hempel's work appeared, Hans Walter Wolff wrote an article entitled "Die Begründung der prophetischen Heils- und Unheilssprüche." This was to be followed in 1937 by publication of a study of the use of quotations by the prophets, *Das Zitat im Prophetenspruch*. In the first article, Wolff attemped a very ambitious investigation of prophetic speech forms. He made a particularly helpful contribution in his careful analysis of the ways in which the reason (*Begründung*) is connected with the threat. The *Begründung*, Wolff noted, took the form usually of a declaratory sentence connected to the preceding threat by a connective like *lāḵēn* or *'al kēn*. Wolff in effect argued for the fundamental unity of threat and reason and discarded the category known as reproach (*Scheltwort*). As he understood prophetic speech, the threat was that part of the speech which the prophet delivered in his function as messenger, while the reason represented the prophet's reflection on the matter. But the main point that must be recognized is that *one* prophetic speech form is at issue: a word about the future with a reason. When Wolff turned to a consideration of the use of quotations by the prophets, the results of his first study were confirmed. It became clear that the quotation was usually made as part of the reason the prophet attached to his announcement of judgment. Further, Wolff showed that the use of the quotation originated as part of an accusation made by the prophet against the people. In this respect the prophetic use of quotation seemed to reflect legal procedure. Thus, Wolff decided that the more appropriate definition of the independent "reason" unit sometimes encountered was "accusation" and not "reproach."

The distinction made by both Hempel and Wolff between the words of the prophet and the divine word was further explored in a study of Jeremiah by Hans Wildberger, *Jahwewort und prophetische Rede bei Jeremia*. Wildberger described the relation of the prophet's word to the divine word as either explicative or adversative. This classification seems somewhat simplistic, and it appears that Wildberger could have profited from a consideration of Mowinckel's study of Jeremiah. But Wildberger did make a contribution to form critical research by his careful study of the introductory formulas encountered in Jeremiah. There are four basic groups, each associated with a particular type of material in Jeremiah (after some emendation and adjustment); autobiographical material introduced by *wayᵉhî dᵉḇar YHWH 'ēlay* ("the word of the Lord came to me"); biographical narratives developed from the autobiographical with *wayᵉhî dᵉḇar YHWH 'el yirmᵉyāhû* ("the word of the Lord came to Jeremiah"); private words of Yahweh to the prophet signaled by *wayyō'mer YHWH 'ēlay* ("the Lord said to me"); and finally, the formula *kô 'āmar YHWH* ("thus says the Lord") which introduced divine words addressed by the prophet to the public. On the basis of this study Wildberger further concluded that a complete account of a revelation to the prophet could be expected to begin with either of the first two formulas, then to move to a word of commissioning to the prophet which was followed by the messenger formula *kô 'āmar YHWH*, and finally to proceed to the messenger's speech (the divine word) with *ne'um YHWH* (oracle of Yahweh) perhaps in the middle and at the conclusion of the announcement.

In 1960 Claus Westermann brought one particular line of development in prophetic research to a logical conclusion with the publication of *Grundformen prophetischer Rede*. Westermann had already presented a careful study of the lament in 1954, "Struktur und Geschichte der Klage im Alten Testament," and followed his work on the prophetic speech forms with a study of the psalms, *Das Loben Gottes in den Psalmen*, in 1961. Along with numerous other articles, he also produced a significant study of Second Isaiah, which appeared in 1966.

The significance of Westermann's *Grundformen prophetischer Rede* is found in the way he summarized and correlated the results of previous studies. After a careful review of prior research, he turned to a consideration of the types of material actually found in the prophetic books and the possible background for these types. He concluded that the prophets were best understood as messengers and that their speech forms were essentially patterned after the messenger speech. To back up his contention Westermann carefully compared accounts which reported the sending of messengers in the bible and in the Mari letters. Out of all of this came the conclusion that the prophets used two basic forms: first the "Judgment-speech to the Individual" and second, the "Judgment-speech against Israel," which was an expansion of the first. The simplest form of the "Judgment-speech to the Individual" consisted of a summons to hear, an accusation, an introduction to the announcement of judgment with "therefore" and the messenger formula "Thus says the Lord," and finally the announcement of judgment. In the "Judgment-speech against Israel" the form was expanded by developing both the accusation and the announcement of judgment. Nonetheless, the form was essentially the same. Westermann concluded his study with a brief review of speech forms borrowed by the prophets from other spheres of Israel's life such as law, funeral practices, and priestly instructions.

While Westermann's work has by no means settled all the

IV

issues, it has served the very worthwhile function of providing a specific, well-demonstrated description of two very frequent prophetic types as a basis for the continuing discussion. His plea for specific examples and for clarification of the terminology used in form critical discussions has also affected the course of scholarly debate.

Westermann's description of prophetic speech as *Botenspruch*, messenger speech, has found both support and objection. James Ross devoted an article, "The Prophet as Yahweh's Messenger," to exploring this possibility, and, while not drawing directly on Westermann, he reached the conclusion that such a definition was certainly fitting. In his article on the form and significance of the call narratives, Habel developed this theme and sought to demonstrate the existence of a call *Gattung* common to the several "call" narratives found in the prophetic literature.

The strongest objections to Westermann's position have been raised by Rolf Rendtorff, Friedrich Ellermeier, and Robert North. In his article "Botenformel und Botenspruch," Rendtorff admitted that the messenger form of address had greatly influenced prophetic speech, but his study raised serious questions concerning the validity of relating the messenger form in any simplistic manner to prophetic patterns of address and of using it as the exclusive clue for interpreting prophetic genres. Ellermeier, in his study of Mari prophecy, has challenged Westermann's use of the Mari texts in his arguments supporting the claim that the judgment speech formulated as a messenger address was the basic form of prophetic address. In addition to a section in his *Basic Forms of Prophetic Speech* (115-128), Westermann has written an article comparing Mari and Israelite prophecy ("Die Mari-Briefe und die Prophetie in Israel," in his *Forschung am Alten Testament*, 171-188). Ellermeier (187-217) rightly contends that the messenger formula and messenger speech are not dominant in the prophetic texts from Mari, especially in those published most recently (after Westermann wrote; see *ANET*, 623-625 and W. L. Moran, "New Evidence from Mari on the History of Prophecy," *Bib* L [1969] 15-56). In addition, he claims that the word of judgment appears in some of the Mari texts, but that the appearance of other forms—exhortations, warnings, salvation oracles, etc.—makes it impossible to argue for the exclusive priority of the judgment speech. North has recently stressed the complexity of the messenger function in ancient Israel in so far as the prophets are concerned. The messenger or "runner" function of the prophet has been combined with priestly and legal functions, and this complexity is reflected in the speech genres. North warns against reducing "disparate phenomena to a single unproved origin," even though he appreciates the insights which can come from such an attempt.

The search for the *Sitz im Leben* of prophetic speech has led in directions other than the commissioning and function of the messenger. Robert Bach's study of the "call to battle" and the "call to flight," which occur most frequently in the book of Jeremiah, points to the use of these genres and to the existence of a prophetic function within the context of warfare. These two genres were originally, according to Bach, employed within the "holy war" of the period of the judges. They were then taken over early in the period of the monarchy by the prophets, who played important roles in warfare, functioning as the "spiritual successors of the pre-monarchial charismatic leaders. (Association of the prophets and prophetic genres with warfare was suggested in the article by Rendtorff noted above.)

H. G. Reventlow, in a number of works, has associated the prophetic office with the ritual of the covenantal cult. According to him, as well as other scholars (see North, 44-49, 64-66; and see above, chapter three, section VII.B. for additional literature and discussion), the primary faith of Israelite life was given expression in a covenant festival in which the law and covenant were proclaimed along with blessings and curses. For Reventlow, the prophetic office was anchored in the ritual of covenant renewal; the prophet was the successor to the covenant mediator of the pre-monarchial tribal amphictyony. The prophetic forms and their background could not be divorced from the rituals of the covenant people.

A somewhat similar conclusion was reached by Eberhard von Waldow in his study on the traditional and historical background of the prophetic speeches of judgment. Two divergent lines of inquiry have developed in regard to these speeches. Joachim Begrich, in his *Studien zu Deuterojesaja*, related these forms to legal traditions. Various passages in Second Isaiah seemed best understood in terms of *Gattungen* drawn from the legal courts. Hans-Jochen Boecker, in an article entitled "Anklagereden und Verteidigungsreden im Alten Testament," and in a later, more extensive volume on the speech forms of the legal community sought to describe and to distinguish between the various forms of speech appropriate before, during, and at the conclusion of a trial (see above, pp. 126-127). Boecker considered the "secular" sential and nonessential elements. Essential elements of the form position very much in keeping with Begrich and Gunkel before him. On the other hand, Ernst Würthwein, in his article on the origin of the prophetic judgment speech, argued that the *Sitz im Leben* for the prophetic judicial speech was cultic. He saw these speeches as reflections of types used in the cultus and related them to the appearance of God as Judge. Psalms 50, 75, 76, 96, and 98 portray Yahweh in judgment, and Würthwein argued that Israel encountered Yahweh as judge within the cult. The proclamation of judgment against the chosen, covenant people within the cult was the antecedent and source of the prophetic preaching of judgment. Würthwein's cultic origin theory has stimulated considerable debate. A recent study by Jörg Jeremias on cultic prophecy and the preaching of judgment (*Kultprophetie und Gerichtsverkündigung in der späten Königszeit Israels* [WMANT 35, Neukirchen: Neukirchener Verlag, 1970] does argue for prophetic preaching of judgment within the cult, especially in late pre-exilic times. However, Jeremias concludes that such preaching was never directed against Israel as a whole but only against groups of evildoers within the community. In a direct response to Würthwein, Franz Hesse has related the prophetic judgment speech to the cult, but he believed the original background to be the proclamation of judgment on foreign nations rather than against Israel. Against this background von Waldow, in the work referred to above, tried to suggest that the "secular" legal tradition had provided significant influence on prophetic speech, but that the covenant tradition and cult were such that the prophets could use the defined legal forms to express the recognized reality of God as both accuser and judge at the same time and be clearly understood by their hearers, although such a situation would not have been appropriate in an ordinary "secular" trial.

In conjunction with the above discussion, significant contributions by other scholars should be noted. Berend Gemser, Herbert Huffmon, and Julien Harvey have sought to define the prophetic lawsuit form more carefully and to consider its implications. Gemser studied the so-called *rîb*, or what he designated the "controversy pattern" in Hebrew thought. The *rîb* or lawsuit he found to be characteristic of prophetic preaching. He was, however, more interested in the controversy mentality than in the form of the lawsuit per se. The theme of a controversy between

IV
—

God and his people expressed in terminology of a legal character he declared to be "typically prophetic and genuinely Israelite-prophetic" (133). Huffmon distinguished between two types of *rib* or lawsuit, each with a different Near Eastern background and content. One type is to be associated with the heavenly council or tribunal and makes reference to the earthly and heavenly forces but not to the covenant. The other type, "especially if it has an appeal to the natural elements, the covenant witness, and a historical prologue, is an indictment of Israel for breach of covenant" (295). Thus the covenant lawsuit, according to Huffmon, has its background in the treaty form of ancient Near Eastern international relations. Harvey has made the most extensive study of the lawsuit form and has sought to show the closest relationship with international treaties. He has attempted to draw parallels between prophetic lawsuit passages and the formal prosecution of violators of international treaties. If the covenant faith were given expression in the cult, then one could assume a covenant and cultic setting for the covenant lawsuit, a proposition reasonably close to Würthwein's. Harvey also distinguishes between a *rib* of warning and one of condemnation. (A judicious summary of the literature on the prophetic *rib* is to be found in North, "Angel-Prophet or Satan-Prophet.") The curses found in ancient international treaties have been studied in relation to the judgment speeches of the prophets by Delbert Hillers. No definite relationship was established, but it was recognized that the traditional maledictions used in the treaties might have had some influence on the prophets.

A different sort of contribution to form critical research has been made by several writers of "critical introductions" and "theologies" of the OT. Since 1948 the English speaking world has had the benefit of Aage Bentzen's *Introduction to the Old Testament*, with its brief but helpful description of a number of prophetic literary forms. In 1961 Artur Weiser's German work was translated with the title *The Old Testament: Its Formation and Development*. Of even greater assistance was the appearance in English in 1965 of Otto Eissfeldt's massive work *The Old Testament: An Introduction*. Then in 1968 Georg Fohrer, the author of numerous form critical studies, saw his OT introduction translated into English. All of these deal with and contribute to form critical research. In 1965, the English translation of the second volume of Gerhard von Rad's *Old Testament Theology* was published. This outstanding work, devoted in large part to

IV

the prophets, reflects the form critical research of the author and that of many others on whom he drew. These various volumes met a great need. They have now been joined by the work of Klaus Koch, published in English translation in 1969 under the title *The Growth of the Biblical Tradition: The Form-Critical Method*. Naturally, it is not devoted exclusively to the study of prophetic material, but it does have one section on the prophetic corpus, and an index to various *Gattungen* which have been isolated and described.

Form critical research continues. To discuss all of it is beyond the scope of this brief review, but the many references included in the bibilography to this and the following section give some indication of the areas of interest and the problems being considered. A great deal has been accomplished, but the task is nowhere near completion.

II. THE BASIC TYPES OF PROPHETIC SPEECH

F. Baumgärtel, "Die formel *ne'um jahwe*," *ZAW* LXXIII (1961) 277-290; *idem*, "Zu den Gottesnamen in den Büchern Jeremia und Ezechiel," in *Verbannung und Heimkehr*, ed. by A. Kuschke (Tübingen: J. C. B. Mohr, 1961) 1-30; W. Baumgartner, *Die Klagegedichte des Jeremia* (BZAW 32, Giessen: A. Töpelmann, 1917); *idem*, "Joel 1 und 2," in *Beiträge zur alttestamentliche Wissenschaft*, ed. by K. Marti (BZAW 34, Giessen: A. Töpelmann, 1920) 10-19; K. H. Bernhardt, *Die gattungsgeschichtliche Forschung am Alten Testament als exegetische Methode* (Berlin: Evangelische Verlagsanstalt, 1959) ; J. M. Berridge, *Prophet, People, and the Word of Yahweh: An Examination of Form and Content in the Proclamation of the Prophet Jeremiah* (BST 4, Zurich: EVZ-Verlag, 1970) ; H.-J. Boecker, "Bemerkungen zur formgeschichtlichen Terminologie des Buches Maleachi," *ZAW* LXXVIII (1966) 78-80; N. Bratsiotis, "Der Monolog im Alten Testament," *ZAW* LXXIII (1961) 30-70; J. Bright, "The Prophetic Reminiscence: Its Place and Function in the Book of Jeremiah," in *Biblical Essays, 1966* (Pretoria: OTWSA, 1966) 11-30; K. Budde, "Das hebräische Klagelied," *ZAW* II (1882) 1-52; *idem*, "Ein althebräisches Klagelied," *ZAW* III (1883) 299-306; M. J. Buss, *The Prophetic Word of Hosea* (BZAW 111, Berlin: A. Töpelmann, 1969) ; R. J. Clifford, "The Use of HÔY in the Prophets," *CBQ* XXVIII (1966) 458-464; J. L. Crenshaw, "*YHWH Ṣeba'ôt Šemô*: A Form-Critical Analysis," *ZAW* LXXXI (1969) 156-175; G. Fohrer, "Die Gattung der Berichte über symbolische Handlungen der Propheten," *ZAW* LXIV (1952) 101-120 = his *Studien zur alttestamentlichen Prophetie (1949-1965)* (BZAW 99, Berlin: A. Töpelmann, 1967) 92-112; *idem*, "Micha 1," in *Das ferne und nahe Wort*, ed. by F. Maass (BZAW 105, Berlin: A. Töpelmann, 1967) 65-80; *idem*, "Prophetie und Magie," *ZAW* LXXVIII (1966) 25-47 = his *Studien*, 265-293; *idem*, *Die symbolischen Handlungen der Propheten* (ATANT 25, Zurich: Zwingli-Verlag, 1953); E. Gerstenberger, "The Woe-Oracles of the Prophets," *JBL* LXXXI (1962) 249-263; *idem*, "Jeremiah's Complaints. Observations on Jeremiah 15:10-21," *JBL* LXXXII (1963) 393-408; F. Goldbaum, "Two Hebrew Quasi-Verbs *lkn* and *'kn*," *JNES* XXIII (1964) 132-135; D. E. Gowan, "Habakkuk and Wisdom,"*Perspective* IX

(1968) 157-166; *idem,* "Progress and Confusion: On a New Introduction to the
Old Testament," *JR* XLIX (1969) 268-275; A. H. J. Gunneweg, "Ordinationsformular oder Berufungsbericht in Jeremia 1," in *Glaube, Geist, Geschichte,*
ed. by G. Müller and W. Zeller (Leiden: E. J. Brill, 1967) 91-98; W. L. Holla-
day, "Isa iii 10-11: An Archaic Wisdom Passage," *VT* XVIII (1968) 481-487;
idem, "The Recovery of Poetic Passages in Jeremiah," *JBL* LXXXV (1966)
401-435; F. Horst, "Die Visionsschilderungen der alttestamentlichen Prophet-
en," *EvTh* XX (1960) 193-205; P. Humbert, "Die Herausforderungsformel
'hinnenî êlékâ'," *ZAW* LI (1933) 101-108; H. Jahnow, *Das hebräische Leichenlied im Rahmen der Völkerdichtung* (BZAW 36, Giessen: A. Töpelmann,
1923); M. Kessler, "Form-Critical Suggestions on Jer 36," *CBQ* XXVIII (1966)
389-401; *idem,* "Jeremiah Chapters 26-45 Reconsidered," *JNES* XXVII (1968)
81-88; R. Kilian, "Die prophetischen Berufungsberichte," in *Theologie im
Wandel* (TTR 1, Freiburg: Erich Wewel, 1967) 356-376; H. Kosmala, "Form
and Structure of Isaiah 58," *ASTI* V (1967) 69-81; J. Limburg, "The Root
ryb and the Prophetic Lawsuit Speeches," *JBL* LXXXVIII (1969) 291-304; I.
von Loewenclau, "Zur Auslegung von Jesaja 1, 2-3," *EvTh* XXVI (1966) 294-
308; W. Lofthouse, " 'Thus Hath Jahveh Said'," *AJSL* XL (1923-24) 231-251;
B. O. Long, "Two Question and Answer Schemata in the Prophets," *JBL* XC
(1971) 129-139; P. Matheney, "Interpretation of Hebrew Prophetic Symbolic
Act," *Encounter* XXIX (1968) 256-267; R. Melugin, "Deutero-Isaiah and
Form Criticism,"*VT* XXI (1971) 326-337; J. Muilenburg, "Baruch the Scribe,"
in *Proclamation and Presence,* ed. by J. I. Durham and J. R. Porter (London:
SCM Press, 1970) 215-238; *idem,* "The Book of Isaiah, Chapters 40-66," *IB* V
(1956) 381-773; *idem,* "Form Criticism and Beyond," *JBL* LXXXVIII (1969)
1-18; *idem,* "The Linguistic Usages of the Particle *ki* in the Old Testament,"
HUCA XX (1961) 135-160; E. W. Nicholson, *Preaching to the Exiles: A
Study of the Prose Tradition in the Book of Jeremiah* (Oxford: Basil Blackwell, 1970); E. Nielsen, "Deuterojesaja; Erwägungen zur Formkritik, Tradi-
tions- und Redaktionsgeschichte," *VT* XX (1970) 190-205; E. Pfeiffer, "Die
Disputationsworte im Buche Maleachi," *EvTh* XIX (1959) 546-568; K. von
Rabenau, "Die Form des Rätsels im Buche Hesekiel," *WZMLU* VII (1957-58)
1055-1057; T. Raitt, "The Prophetic Summons to Repentance," *ZAW* LXXXIII
(1971) 30-49; B. Reicke, "Liturgical Traditions in Micah 7," *HTR* LX (1967)
349-367; W. Richter, *Die sogenannten vorprophetischen Berufungsberichte*
(FRLANT 101, Göttingen: Vandenhoeck & Ruprecht, 1970); C. Rietzschel,
*Das Problem der Urrolle: Ein Beitrag zur Redaktionsgeschichte des Jeremia-
buches* (Gütersloh: Gerd Mohn, 1966); A. Rofé, "The Classification of the
Prophetical Stories," *JBL* LXXXIX (1970) 427-440; R. B. Y. Scott, "The Literary Structure of Isaiah's Oracles," in *Studies in Old Testament Prophecy,* ed.
by H. H. Rowley (Edinburgh: T. and T. Clark, 1950) 175-186; M. Sister,
"Die Typen der prophetischen Visionen in der Bibel," *MGWJ* LXXVIII
(1934) 399-430; M. Tsevat, "The Neo-Assyrian and Neo-Babylonian Vassal
Oaths and the Prophet Ezekiel," *JBL* LXXVIII (1959) 199-204; G. Wanke,
" *'ôy* und *hôy,*" *ZAW* LXXVIII (1966) 215-218; *idem, Untersuchungen zur
sogenannten Baruchschrift* (BZAW 122, Berlin: Walter de Gruyter & Co.,
1971); J. G. Williams, "The Alas-Oracles of the Eighth Century Prophets,"
HUCA XXXVIII (1967) 75-91; G. E. Wright, "The Lawsuit of God: A Form-
Critical Study of Deuteronomy 32," in *Israel's Prophetic Heritage,* eds., B. W.
Anderson and W. Harrelson (New York: Harper and Brothers, 1962) 26-67;
W. Zimmerli, *Ezechiel* (BK 13, Neukirchen: Neukirchener Verlag, 1956-1969);
idem, "The Special Form- and Traditio-Historical Character of Ezekiel's
Prophecy," *VT* XV (1965) 515-527; *idem,* "Das Wort des göttlichen Selbster-
weises (Erweiswort), eine prophetische Gattung," in *Mélanges Bibliques ré-
digés en l'honneur de André Robert* (TICP 4, Paris: Bloud et Gay, 1957) 154-
164 = his *Gottes Offenbarung* (TB 19, Munich: Chr. Kaiser, 1963) 120-132.

When Gunkel first began the classification of prophetic speech forms, the most obvious units in the books of the "writing" prophets were the so-called "threats" and "reproaches." As we noted above, Gunkel considered the threatening word delivered by the prophet, the *Drohrede*, to be primary, and the reproach, invective, or diatribe, the *Scheltrede*, to be secondary and the result of the prophet's reflection on the situation. Thus, the most frequently encountered material in the prophetic books was divided into these two types. The works of Wolff (1934) and Westermann (1960, 1967) have sharply criticized this analysis of the prophetic speech forms. In his introduction (347-358) Fohrer tends to preserve more of Gunkel's terminology than does Westermann and to argue that the reproach is only in part a secondary type. (For a discussion of the terminological question and a comparison of Fohrer and Westermann, see Gowan, 1969, 271-273.)

It is now generally recognized that Gunkel erred in separating the diatribe or reproach from the threat, for these two are actually parts of one type of prophetic speech, the *prophecy of disaster*. This can be seen clearly through examination of the basic structure of the prophecy of disaster in one of the narratives about the prophets in Samuel or Kings. It is not so clear if one tries to begin with the prophetic books themselves, as Gunkel did, because these books are basically collections of the prophetic speeches with many formulas omitted to avoid repetition and with an emphasis on preserving the words about the future, namely the "threats" (Koch, 210-211). Once the basic pattern is recognized, then the propetic books can be studied with great benefit.

In II Kings 1:3-4, 6, 15-16 there is recorded the prophetic word of Elijah the Tishbite concerning Ahaziah the king, and in Jer 28:12-16 two of Jeremiah's speeches to Hananiah are preserved. A comparison of these texts reveals the basic structure of the prophecy of disaster. The unit frequently begins with some introductory word. This may be in the form of a commissioning of the prophet for the task (Westermann, *Basic Forms*, 142) as in II Kings 1:3, "Arise, go up . . . and say." In addition or by itself there may appear an appeal for attention (Koch, 205) as in Jer 28:15, "Listen, Hananiah . . ." The appeal for attention is encountered much more frequently after the time of Amos.

Next comes the first major section of the prophecy of disaster, the "indication of the situation" (Koch, 192, 211). Westermann rightly objected to calling this section a "diatribe" or a "reproach" and argued for either the term "reason" or "accusation"

(Westermann, *Basic Forms*, 68-69) as this part is integral to the whole and not a separable unit. However, Koch's more neutral "indication of the situation" seems quite adequate and appropriate as a description of the function of this portion of the prophecy. The point of this section is a statement of the situation making clear the problem or problems requiring remedy. The section may begin with an indignant question, as in II Kings 1:3, or with a brief statement, as in Jer 28:13, 15. Or again, the more formal *ya'an 'ªšer* ("because," "in as much") may open the section, as in II Kings 1:16.

The second major division of the prophecy of disaster is the "prediction of disaster." Frequently *lāḵēn* ("therefore") connects the "prediction of disaster" with the preceding section. Also, the formula *kô 'āmar YHWH* ("thus says Yahweh") regularly stands at the beginning of this section, though in later prophetic books it may stand before the "indication of the situation" as well. This section comprises what was formerly called the "threat." Westermann challenged the appropriateness of this term and suggested "announcement of judgment" or "announcement of ill" (Westermann, *Basic Forms*, 65-67). Again, however, Koch's term "prediction of disaster" (Koch, 193) seems to underline the future aspect of the announcement and its disastrous nature and avoids giving the impression that a legal decision necessarily lies in the background of the form. The "prediction of disaster" is usually expressed in a brief, negative sentence using the imperfect form of the verb as in II Kings 1:4. But it can also be articulated by an initial participial clause, the subject of which is the intervention of God by which the present evil situation will be altered, followed by a sentence which describes the effect of God's intervention, as in Jer 28:16.

The final section of the prophecy of disaster is termed by Koch the "concluding characterization" (Koch, 193-194). This short section usually begins with *kî* and describes either the sender of the prophecy or those to whom it is sent, as in II Kings 1:4. Gunkel called this the "motive clause," but "concluding characterization" is more appropriate.

The basic structure of the prophecy of disaster as described above is fairly fixed when the prophecy is addressed to an individual. When the type is employed with reference to a group, the prophet's people or a foreign nation, the form is less rigid. Indeed, it is this flexibility which causes some to question whether in fact the "indication of situation" (the "reproach," "diatribe," "in-

IV

160

vective," "reason") is an inseparable part of a larger form. Fohrer maintains that it is proper to describe some invectives as autonomous elements (Fohrer, *Introduction*, 353-355). Nevertheless, Westermann's explanation that the dislocation and expansion of units result from the gradual loosening of the basic structure seems adequate to account for the data encountered (Westermann, *Basic Forms*, 181-189).

According to Westermann (*Basic Forms*, 169-175), the changes in form that are seen in the prophecy of disaster when directed to a group mainly consist of expansions of the "indication of situation" and in the "prediction of disaster." The former usually begins with a general description and then is expanded or developed by being made more concrete. The "prediction of disaster" more frequently occurs in the form of an announcement of God's intended intervention and is expanded by a description of the results of this intervention. The use of the full phrase "therefore, thus says Yahweh" is less regular. Sometimes only the "therefore" is found; sometimes the "thus says Yahweh" is found preceding the "indication of the situation." Further, sometimes the elements of the basic structure are inverted, with the "prediction of disaster" being followed by the description of the situation which prompts the divine word. Despite all of these variations, it still seems best to understand the various units against the background of the basic structure outlined above rather than in terms of independent types.

The extended description of the prophecy of disaster has been necessary, both because so much of the prophetic material is related to this speech form and because general agreement about the full structure is only beginning to emerge. Particularly is the nomenclature yet debated. Koch's terminology has been accepted as the best presently available, but the discussion is certainly not finished. Neither has the question of the *Sitz im Leben* been settled. Westermann, building on the suggestions of Lindblom and Köhler, decided that the prophet was best understood as a messenger speaking in forms appropriate to a messenger, a decision supported by a comparison of messenger speeches found in the Mari texts (Westermann, *Basic Forms*, 98-128). This view, as noted above (p. 153), has not gone unchallenged. However, even if the prophet did use the speech form of a messenger, where did he deliver his message? Sometimes the prophecy of disaster was delivered in the context of the cult, but other times it was not. Certainly there were prophets who functioned in relation to the cult, but was that essential or accidental? While there is a growing conviction that most of the prophets certainly drew upon cultic traditions and possibly functioned in the context of the Israelite cult, many questions are yet undecided, and no definition of the *Sitz im Leben* for the prophecy of disaster has yet won general agreement.

A second major type of prophetic speech is the *prophecy of salvation*. Its structure, according to Koch (213-214), is essentially the same as that of the prophecy of disaster. There are three sections: "indication of the situation"; "prediction of salvation" or "promise"; and "concluding characterization." "Indication of the situation" may be preceded by an "appeal for attention" ("hear . . ."). The phrase *ya'an 'ašer* ("because," "in as much") may introduce the section. Substance of the section may consist of a description of the way God has already acted to alter the present situation, or there may be an exhortation to seek Yahweh's deliverance. In the prophecy of salvation "indication of the situation" is not as fixed as in the prophecy of disaster. The "prediction of salvation" is expressed usually in a negative sentence employing the imperfect form of the verb or by a participial clause beginning with "behold, I." Transition between the two sections is made by using "therefore," and the "concluding characterization" usually refers to the one who stands behind the promise and will bring about deliverance. The phrase "thus says Yahweh" occurs before the "indication of the situation" and the "prediction of salvation" or before only one of the two parts. The prophecy of salvation could be addressed to an individual or a group.

The *Sitz im Leben* for the prophecy of salvation is as uncertain as that for the prophecy of disaster, which it is so much like in structure. There are not too many samples of this form, but a consideration of Jer 28:2-4, 32:14-15, 32:36-41, 34:4-5, 35:18-19, I Kings 17:14 and II Kings 3:16-19 does make clear that the setting for such prophetic speech was quite varied. Before a king, to a widow, to a fellow prophet—numerous settings for the prophecy of salvation. This prophecy is frequently associated with the "official" prophets or so-called "professional" prophets and considered less authentic, but the examples cited above do not give such a simple picture. The similarity in structure of the prophecies of salvation and disaster suggests that a *Sitz* common to both should be sought. The notion that these speeches are messenger speeches is certainly attractive, but the future emphasis common to both

IV

prompts one to think of cultic situations such as the pronouncing of a benediction or curse or the giving of an answer to an oracle as the possible original *Sitz im Leben* of these forms.

It is appropriate to turn at this point to two other prophetic forms which also announce salvation.. The first, and more clearly defined, is the *oracle of salvation*. Begrich described what he termed the *priesterliche Heilsorakel* as the word of assurance which the priest might give in answer to the petition of the individual in the lament ceremony (Begrich, "Das priesterliche Heilsorakel"). In his study of Second Isaiah Begrich pointed out numerous passages which seemed to follow the basic form of the "priestly oracle of salvation." There was a promise of divine intervention on behalf of those in need, a statement of the results of God's intervention, and a declaration of God's purpose in choosing to intervene. Thus, Begrich concluded that the writer of Second Isaiah had "borrowed" a speech form at home in the cultus and used it to declare his message of God's imminent salvation. Since Begrich, Westermann has also studied the use of this form by Second Isaiah (Westermann, "Das Heilswort bei Deuterojesaja").

The oracle of salvation can be found in passages like Is 41:8-13, 41:14-16, 43:1-4, 43:5-7, and 44:1-5. In Is 41:8-13, for instance, the oracle begins with a statement of God's past dealings with Israel (8-9), moves to the promise of intervention, introduced by the formula "fear not" which is typical of the form (10), proceeds to a description of the results of God's act (11-12) and concludes with an explanation of why God chose to act (13). The original *Sitz im Leben* does seem to be the ceremony of individual lament with its hoped for oracle of assurance or promise. That the prophet could use this cultic form to communicate with his people is easy to understand, but whether he had to do so in the setting of the cultus is not at all certain.

The *proclamation of salvation* is a form related to the oracle of salvation but clearly distinct from it. Both do speak of God's gracious turn toward his people, but the proclamation of salvation is future oriented whereas the oracle of salvation is concerned more with the present. The formula "fear not" does not appear in the proclamation of salvation as it does in the oracle. Further, there is usually allusion to the lament ceremony or a quote from the lament which the proclamation of salvation intends to answer. In Second Isaiah, where the form has been primarily studied, the proclamation of salvation is found frequently in combination with other forms (Westermann, *Isaiah 40-66*, 13-14, 79).

Examples of the proclamation of salvation are found in Is 41: 17-20, 42:14-17, 43:16-21, and 49:7-12. The structure essentially consists of a quote from or allusion to the people's lament, proclamation of salvation proper, which includes the declaration of God's turning toward Israel and his intention to intervene, and finally a statement of God's purpose. Westermann believes that the differences noted above between the proclamation of salvation and the oracle of salvation arise from the difference in the original *Sitz im Leben* of each, the oracle being related to the ceremony of individual lament and announced by a priest, while the proclamation was part of the community lament service and was proclaimed by a prophet (Westermann, *Isaiah 40-66*, 79).

It becomes clear as the various prophetic speech forms are considered that it is difficult to separate the "independent" from the "borrowed" despite Gunkel's assumption that it could be done. We have already examined several types that seem to have a *Sitz im Leben* which, if not foreign to the prophets, were certainly not exclusive to them. There are, however, speech forms which are used less frequently by the prophets which can be considered "secondary," in the sense that they are more appropriate to some other sphere of Israel's life than that normally associated with the prophets.

The *woe-oracle* or the *alas-oracle* is one such "secondary" form found in the prophetic books. Westermann has isolated this particular type and described its basic structure (*Basic Forms*, 190-194). Clifford, Gerstenberger, Wanke, and Williams have defined the form more fully and sought its original life setting from which the prophets borrowed the form. Primary examples of the woe-oracle are found in Am 5:18-20, 6:1-7; Is 5:8-10, 11-14, 18-19, 20, 21, 22-24, 10:1-3, 28:1-4, 29:1-4, 15, 30:1-3, 31:1-4; Mic 2:1-4; with other examples found in Habbakuk, Jeremiah, Ezekiel, and Zechariah (a survey of the occurrences is given by Clifford).

The structure is marked first of all by the cry *hôy*, the interjection generally translated "woe" or "alas." The opening interjection is then followed by a participle, or in some cases by some other substantive, which is descriptive of those who are the subject of the oracle. A second participial clause and explanatory sentence using a finite verb follows, specifying the offense. Announcement of divine judgment usually comes at the conclusion of the oracle, or at times it may be placed after a series of short

IV

woe-oracles (Williams, 83). For the most part, the third person singular or plural is used, but occasionally the form is modified by use of the second person (Gerstenberger, 255).

Outside of Jeremiah and Ezekiel, the formula "therefore, thus says Yahweh" is missing from the woe-oracle. Westermann took this as evidence that the woe-oracle was not originally understood as messenger speech (*Basic Forms*, 192). He posited the curse as the form from which the woe-oracle developed since the curse, like the prophetic woe, declared the future intervention of Yahweh against the offender. In addition, he suggested the possibility that the *woe-oracle* had once functioned as a feature in salvation prophecy, with the woe being directed against Israel's enemies (*Basic Forms*, 194-198). Gerstenberger, however, has argued that the curse was more formal and belonged to a more official setting that the woe. Rather than the cult or some other formal situation, the woe-oracle, according to him, could be best understood as an offspring of wisdom reflecting the thinking and teaching form of the wise man. The woe was the negative counterpart to the "blessing" or "bliss" saying of the wise (159-262). Gerstenberger's conclusions have been challenged by others. The absence of the use of *hôy* in the wisdom traditions in the OT weakens Gerstenberger's position (so Clifford). While agreeing with Gerstenberger that the curse was not the starting point from which to understand the woe-oracle, Clifford, Wanke, and Williams stress the association of the characteristic exclamation *hôy* with the funerary ritual of mourning and lamentation. Thus we find agreement concerning the form of the woe-oracle, but the definition of the original *Sitz im Leben* is yet unsettled.

Drawn from the legal sphere of Israel's life are the *trial speeches* (*Gerichtsreden*) or judicial speeches. Begrich, in his work on Second Isaiah noted above, described a number of these speeches in Isaiah and elsewhere. Others have continued the examination. The structure has basically three parts: the summons, the trial (which includes speeches by plaintiff and defendant and an examination of the witnesses), and the sentencing (Westermann, "Sprache und Struktur der Prophetie Deuterojesajas," 135-144). This form can be used either to express Yahweh's opposition to the gods of the nations or to portray Yahweh's relationship with his own people. Examples of the former are found in Is 41:1-5, 21-29; 43:8-15 and 44:6-8. Is 42:18-25; 43:22-28 and 50:1-3 are examples where the judicial proceeding involves Yahweh and Israel. In each example not all elements of the basic form are to be found, but the various parts of the trial procedure provide the background against which to understand the material encountered in these passages.

While there has been agreement that there is a genre properly designated as "trial speech" or "judicial speech," the quest for the *Sitz im Leben* has led to different conclusions. As was noted in the review of scholarship earlier in this chapter, Würthwein sought the *Sitz* in the cultus and thereby challenged Begrich's view that everyday legal custom was the basic *Sitz* for the trial speech. Since then Boecker and Westermann have argued for Begrich's view, and von Waldow has taken a position in between, emphasizing the place of the covenant in Israel's life as affecting both legal practice and worship. It is at this point that the work of Harvey should be discussed a little more fully than was done earlier, for he has tried to define the *Sitz im Leben* in terms of international treaty customs of the period.

On the basis of passages such as Is 1, Mic 6, and Jer 2, and in comparison with extrabiblical materials gathered from the ancient Near East, Harvey argues that there was a literary form that could be defined more precisely than the general trial speech. The structure of this form, the *rib*, had five parts: an introduction in which a call for a hearing was made and in which the heavens and the earth were frequently addressed; the questioning of witnesses and statement of the accusation; an address by the prosecutor before the court, in which Yahweh's gracious acts were compared with Israel's rebelliousness; a reference to the vanity of cultic efforts at compensation; and finally a declaration of guilt and the threat of total destruction. Two versions of the *rib* were distinguished by Harvey on the basis of the final element of the form. If an announcement of guilt and a threat of destruction are found, then the unit is the *rib* of condemnation, but if instead the fifth section consists of a warning and a call for a change in conduct, then it is a *rib* of warning. The *rib* is patterned in either instance essentially after the internationally used treaty form and assumes a covenant as the basis for the relationship between Yahweh and his people. For this reason, Huffmon has designated the *rib* as the "covenant lawsuit."

In his study of the *rib*, based on Deut 32, G. Ernest Wright combines the concepts of the international treaty with those of the "heavenly council" and designates the *rib* as the "heavenly lawsuit." The heavenly assembly functions only as witness and counsel; it is the suzerain Yahweh (an analogy with the Hittite overlord) who acts as judge, plaintiff, and jury. The legal basis for the lawsuit of God rests on Mosaic covenant form with its parallels in Hittite suzerainty treaties. Thus Wright agrees with Harvey and Huffmon in seeing the international treaty pattern as the background for the prophetic *rib*. Wright distinguishes five elements in the heavenly or covenant lawsuit form: a call to the witnesses to give ear to the proceedings; introductory statement of the case at issue by the Divine Judge and Prosecutor or by his earthly official; recital of the benevolent acts of the Suzerain; indictment; and sentence.

Was there an actual ceremony in which a rebellious vassal was "placed on trial"? Limburg has attempted to answer this question affirmatively and supports his case by appealing to the Jephthah story (Judg 10:17-12:6) and the Sefire inscriptions. Harvey argues for the existence of some formal prosecution of violators of international treaties, which he sees reflected in royal correspondence and the *Tukulti-Ninurta Epic*. One OT passage does suggest such a formal prosecution. After Zedekiah rebelled against Nebuchadnezzar and was captured, he was carried before the Baylonian king who "spoke to him the judgments" (Jer 39:5; cf. II Kings 25:6). This passage obviously refers to the passing of sentence in terms of the Judean king's vassal treaty with Nebuchadnezzar. The prophet Ezekiel condemned Zedekiah for this disloyalty to the treaty (Ez 17:11-21; 21:23-29; 29:14-16; see Tsevat). In the prophet's speech in 17:11-21, there are a statement of the case, an indictment, and sentence, all elements which one can imagine as part of Nebuchadnezzar's actions against Zedekiah. In the sixth century, there was a correlation between international treaty, covenant infidelity, and prophetic accusation, at least in the preaching of Ezekiel. Such a situation however does not suggest that the origin of the *rib* is to be sought solely or primarily in the arena of international relations.

Was the *rib* form of address an established genre in the liturgical life of Israel? This question has been noted above. However, at this point something should be said about Wright's discussion of lawsuit and liturgy. While arguing from different presuppositions and approaches than Würthwein, Wright reaches, although rather hesitatingly, somewhat similar conclusions. He suggests that "at one time in North Israel the covenant-renewal celebration was revised and turned into a penitential service by the use of the *rib* motif" (59). Such a use is reflected in both Deuteronomy and the prophets. Wright warns "that none of the extant materials dealing with the subject was composed for liturgical purposes. The most that can be said is that liturgical practice is *reflected* in the Old Testament literature, or that the original forms of celebration have given form to present compositions" (53) .

Another speech type that has some relationship with the trial speech is the *disputation speech*. It is difficult to describe a clear pattern for the disputation speech (Westermann, "Sprache und Struktur," 125) , but its essence is the answering of implied or expressed charges made against God by his people or against the prophet. The disputation speech occurs frequently in Deutero-Isaiah, where it has been studied by Westermann ("Sprache und Struktur," 124-134) and in Malachi (see Pfeiffer). Examples are found elsewhere in Mic 2:6-11, Is 28:23-29; Jer 2:23-25, 29-30, 34-35, 3:1-5, 8:8-9. This speech form is found frequently mixed with other forms. While recognizing the affinities that the disputation has with the trial speech, Westermann has noted the fact that the "charges" answered are usually much like the complaints found in the laments. The disputation may have emerged as a prophetic answer to the laments and complaints of the people (Westermann, *Isaiah 40-66*, 18-19) .

Many older scholars often spoke of prophetic admonitions or calls to repentance (Lindblom, *Die literarische Gattung*, 98; Hempel, *Die althebräische Literatur*, 66) . Contemporary research has tended to ignore or to deny the existence of such prophetic admonitions. The influential work of Hans Walter Wolff ("Das Thema 'Umkehr' in der alttestamentlichen Prophetie," *ZTK* XLVIII [1951] 129-148 = his *Gesammelte Studien*, 130-150) has contributed to this condition. He argued against the existence of any independent admonition speech form and suggested that the repentance motif appears only as a subordinate theme in the prophecies of disaster and salvation. The general form critical studies by Koch and Westermann contain no discussion of calls to repentance. Fohrer, in his *Introduction*, devotes one paragraph to the matter but does affirm their existence as independent forms and designates them "exhortations and warnings," whose purpose was to "call upon the hearer to turn from the path of sin and commit himself to a new way of life based on obedience and submission to God" (355) .

A recent study by Thomas M. Raitt provides a reconsideration of the prophetic admonition or call to repentance. He terms this form the prophetic *summons to repentance*. Twenty nine distinct

IV

168

examples are isolated, with a preponderance in Jeremiah. The structure of the summons consists of an appeal (with messenger formula, vocative, and admonition) and the motivation (with promise, accusation, and threat). Not all of the sub-elements in the structure occur in every instance. Amos 5:4-5, for example, offers the following structure: messenger formula ("thus says Yahweh to the house of Israel"), admonition ("seek me"), promise ("and live"), accusation ("but do not seek Bethel, and do not enter Gilgal"), and threat ("for Gilgal shall surely go into exile, and Bethel shall come to nought"). While agreeing with Wolff that the repentance motif often occurs in association with a prophecy of disaster, Raitt distinguishes five uses of the summons to repentance in the OT: 1) as independent literary units (Am 5:4-5, 6-7, 14-15; Jer 3:12-13, 22, 4:1-2, 3-4); 2) as oracles within narrative frameworks which explain their function (II Kings 17:13; II Chron 30:6-9; Jer 18:11b, 25:5-6, 35:15b; Ez 14:6-11, 18:30-32; Jon 3:7-9; Zech 1:2-6); 3) as distinct and dominant elements within larger linguistic units (Is 1:19-20, 55:6-7 ; Joel 2:12-13); 4) as distinct but subordinate elements within larger linguistic units (Jer 3:14a, 4:14, 7:3-7, 15:19, 22:3-5, 26:13, 31:21-22; Mal 3:7; Zeph 2:1-3; Neh 1:8-9); and 5) as subordinate elements fading into larger structures (Josh 23:11-12; Hos 10:12, 12:6; Is 31:6; Jer 38:20-23). Raitt sees the origin of the prophetic summons to repentance not in the wisdom admonition but in the challenge to the people associated with the covenant renewal ritual.

There are many other secondary forms which one finds in the prophetic corpus (see Gunkel's statements, above, pp. 145-146). Occasionally a *drinking song* or *love song* or *dirge* was employed. From the customs of war came the *calls to battle* and the *retreat order*. From the cultus came the *hymn*, the *lament*, and the *liturgies*. The priestly torah with its combination of reproof and instruction prompted the development of *prophetic torah* along the same line. All of these, and many more, were forms which the prophets used to express their message. Since these genres have their basic *Sitz im Leben* in other spheres of Israel's life and many of them will be discussed elsewhere in this book, we will not consider each of them separately as we have done with the more frequently used speech forms.

Thus far we have examined the literary types used to shape the words of the prophets. But there are two other kinds of material found in the prophetic books which warrant attention. In the period preceding the era of the "writing" prophets and in the major prophetic books there are accounts preserved about the actions of the prophets told in what are generally called biographical and/or autobiographical styles (see above, p. 146). Emphasis is on what the prophet did and the response that he received, or upon his own reception of God's word and his determination to act on the basis of that word. It is to these third and first person accounts that we now shall turn.

One of the "autobiographical" types of material found in the prophetic literature is the *vision report*. It is autobiographical in so far as it usually relates the occasion of the prophet's reception of the divine word, the "private oracle" as Koch terms it (*The Growth*, 219). But generally the emphasis is on the word and not on the prophet. The style of the vision report is autobiographical in that the first person is used to describe the vision. Characteristic of the vision report is the technical term "I saw" placed near the beginning and sometimes repeated. The vision may be termed a *ḥāzôn* or a *mar'eh*, as opposed to a *ḥᵃlôm*, a dream. Not infrequently an audition is linked with the vision.

Sister has studied the structure of the vision and demonstrated the basic similarity of form in a number of different contexts. The typical structure includes an introduction with some form of *r'h* ("to see") followed by *hinnē*, the description of the scene or event envisioned, and a concluding explanation of the significance of the vision, if it is not self-evident, by means of a question and answer dialogue with or a direct word from the divine agent. Horst has drawn several distinctions between different types of vision reports, primarily on the basis of content. There is the "presence vision" (*Anwesenheitsvisionen*), which recounts the prophet's vision as he stands before God. The "event vision" (*Geschehnisvisionen*) centers on an event envisioned by the prophet, such as the fall of Nineveh. And finally the "word play vision" (*Wortassonanzvisionen*) involves a play on similar sounds, such as the vision in Amos 8:1-3 of the basket of summer fruit and the play on the word "end." The structure of the report then varies slightly depending upon the content and type of the vision involved.

A more specialized form of vision report is used by the prophets to relate their "calls." Generally this form is known as the *call narrative*, but the term "call" has been challenged as inappropriate as a technical form critical term. Such passages as Is 6, Jer 1, Ez 1-2 and others supply the primary examples. Until rather re-

IV

cently call narratives were considered highly personal and auto-biographical, but with clear elaboration of their form and stylized language has come the opinion that they well may have been intended for public, formal occasions. The autobiographical character has been severely criticized and the formal character stressed most adamantly by Reventlow in his book *Liturgie und prophetisches Ich bei Jeremia* (see especially 68).

In his commentary on Ezekiel, Walther Zimmerli offered a detailed study of the call narratives (16-21), dividing them into two classifications. In one, the call reports a very personal encounter between God and the prophet, in which the "called" individual could express reluctance and even opposition to the call but was appeased with a sign or word of assurance. The call of Jeremiah represents such a form. In the second type, emphasis is placed on the divine council or the enthroned deity, the prophet experiencing the deity in a vision of the transcendent. The calls of Isaiah and Ezekiel fit the second pattern. The call of Micaiah (I Kings 22:19-22), Zimmerli sees as a prototype of the second classification.

Norman Habel has attempted to discern a common pattern in all the call narratives of the OT. He has outlined a six-element structure which seeks to accommodate all the narratives. The form consists of divine confrontation, introductory word, commission, objection, reassurance, and sign. As the possible *Sitz im Leben* for this form, Habel suggests the ceremony where a messenger or ambassador publicly presented his credentials (see Gen 24:34-48).

Recently, Wolfgang Richter has studied the preprophetical call narratives associated with Saul, Moses, and Gideon. In these, he detects what he designates a "call schema," containing five elements: indication of distress, commission, objection, assurance of assistance, and sign (see especially 136-142). The passages investigated are not termed call narratives but are seen as prose texts which have been greatly influenced by the call schema. Elements of this schema are to be seen in the call narratives of the classical prophets, but the process which produced the prophetic call narratives is not identical with the process which produced the call narratives of Israelite heroes.

Until recently, the call narratives of the prophets were seen either as accounts of the prophets' personal experiences or as public prophetic proclamations used to establish the prophets' credentials as divine messengers. Origin of the form would, in these terms, be either the personal experience of the prophet or his public preaching. This view has been challenged in a radical way by Reventlow. He argues that the situation in which the call narrative was employed was a public one and not simply the account of a private experience. Further, he considers it likely that such a form was used in the ordination of a prophet. As he defined it, the full form had nine elements: Yahweh's epiphany, a lament or complaint, introduction to an oracle of salvation, the oracle of salvation (with "fear not"), commissioning or sending of the prophet (with use of the verb *šlḥ*), the prophet's response, stating unworthiness, restatement of Yahweh's call, a sign, and a word explaining the sign (*Liturgie*, 70-75). His idea of the form as an ordination *Gattung* reflecting an actual ceremony which took place within the cult has been disputed and has not found very wide acceptance. Gunneweg, while prepared to admit that the outer form might have been used in an ordination service, nevertheless contended that the private, inner experience of the prophet was very much at stake and that the proper way to understand the call narrative was to consider it first as the report of a prophet's call, a form then used for ordination ("Ordinationsformular oder Berufungsbericht," 97-98). The tension between these two different approaches to reading the prophetic material is as yet unresolved.

In discussing the vision report and the call narrative there has been mention of a sign occasionally accompanying the vision. This leads to another type of "autobiographical" material, namely the *report of the symbolic* act. Frequently prophets received instructions in visions and by other means to perform some action as symbol of God's intentions toward his people. A few examples include Hos 1 and 3; Is 7:3; 8:1-4; 20:1-6; Jer 13:1-11; 16:1-4, 5-7, 8-9; and 32:1-15. Fohrer outlined the basic form in terms of essential and nonessential elements. Essential elements of the form are: an order to perform a symbolic act, the report that the act was performed, and a statement of the meaning of the act. Sometimes other points were added: statements to eyewitnesses who were present, calls for Yahweh's assurance that the symbolized action would be realized, and expression of the relationship between symbol and reality (Fohrer, "Die Gattung der Berichte über symbolische Handlungen der Propheten"). The original *Sitz* for such prophetic acts was probably the practice of magic (Fohrer, "Die Gattung," 110 and "Prophetie und Magie," 32-35).

The so-called "autobiographical" materials considered above

IV

did pass along some details concerning the person of the prophet and his "history," but it is questionable whether that was the original intention. In certain prophetical stories, however, "biographical" information was intentionally gathered and shared among the prophet's followers, though not in the "objective" style of the modern historian. These stories have been commonly referred to as *prophetic legends*. The term "legend" creates problems in this regard since many of these prophetic stories do not conform to the traditional and historical use of the term, which describes an edifying and pious story relating the virtuous life, miracles, and fate of holy men intended to be read, at least in the medieval church, on special days and to be emulated in the lives of the faithful. The genre is of course not limited to Christianity. Judaism developed a similar class of stories (Rofé, 429-430). (For a discussion of the term and legend as a genre, see above, p. 78; and A. Jolles, *Einfache Formen* [Tübingen: Max Niemeyer, 1958², 23-61]).

The prophetical stories have been notoriously difficult to characterize form critically, although differences among them are rather obvious. Rofé has attempted a classification primarily on the basis of content. His work is limited to a consideration of the prophetic stories in Kings, and here primarily to the Elisha cycle. He distinguishes three types of legends. 1) Simple Legenda. This can be seen in II Kings 2:19-22, 23-24; 4:1-7, 38-41, 42-44; 6:1-7; 13:20-21. In each case, there is a description of the facts which constitute the need for a miracle, a statement of the despair or wonder, and culmination in a miracle which produces a satisfactory solution. Character of the prophet, background and personality of the protagonists, and large plot setting are not developed. The miracle occurs without any significant historico-theological meaning and is generally unrelated to any ethical categories. It reveals the prophet's mastering of the forces of nature. Rofé sees in these stories the basic categories of "holy" and "profane." "The holy man performs miracles for the benefit of the profane; they, in return, are expected to respond with respect and veneration" (432). These tales had a popular origin, were transmitted orally in a form more lengthy than is now recorded, and were skillfully condensed when written down. 2) Literary Elaboration of the Legenda. This class, represented by such stories as the tale of the Shunammite (II Kings 4:8-37), are longer, display an entire plot with full development of the circumstances, and manifest personality sketches in which the characters transcend the circumstances. 3) *Vita*. Some of the prophetic stories possess a definite biographical drive and seek to describe the beginning and end of a holy man's career. Such a story Rofé sees in the account of Elijah's ascension (II Kings 2:1-18). Although he limits his study to these three forms, Rofé argues that it would be possible to classify other prophetic stories as biography, historiography, didactic legenda, parable, and martyrology.

Prophetic legends function in various ways. They portray the prophet as bearer of a divine power, as bearer of a divine word, and as the instrument through whom Yahweh worked his will. Only occasionally, and then often secondarily, do they set out to provide something of the "history" of the prophet; nonetheless, they do often supply some biographical information (Koch, 201). Stories like those in I Kings 11:29-39; 13:1-32; 18:1-46; II Kings 18:17-19:37; and Jer 28, to mention only a few, clearly are intended to preserve memorable words and deeds of the prophets.

The prophetic legend is marked by several features which help set it apart from other literary forms. Usually introductory and concluding remarks are kept to a minimum. A long story such as that in II Kings 1:1-17 can be opened and closed with but one brief sentence. The story is developed primarily by recounting the speeches of the divine and human characters involved. Style is full and repetitive. In the earliest stages of development of the prophetic legend, there are few details concerning places, names (even of the prophet himself at times) and so forth, a contrast to the saga. By the time of Jeremiah, however, details begin to appear in the accounts in greater number. The prophetic legend was created by followers and admirers of the prophet and thus was always an account about, rather than by, the prophet. Since the primary use of the prophetic legend was within the circle of prophets and their followers, themes such as obedience to God's word and fearlessness of the righteous prophet are emphasized. And of course, as mentioned above, the continuing theme of many of the prophetic legends is the vitality and effectiveness of God's word (Koch, 184-187).

The final form to be considered is the *prophetic biography*. This genre has been discussed in greatest detail with regard to Jeremiah, where such chapters as 26-28 and 36-45 have been considered biographical and related in various ways to Jeremiah's scribe Baruch, to whom the prophet dictated his early oracles (Jer 36:1-4; and see the recent work by Rietzschel). Much of the

IV

174

narrative material in Jeremiah has been historically attributed to Baruch as his biography of the prophet (see Wanke, 1971). Whether or not this material is biographical in intent or Baruch's has in recent scholarship become an open question. Muilenburg, in his article "Baruch the Scribe," attributes to Baruch the authorship of practically all of this material and the editing of most of the book of Jeremiah. The narrative material he considers historical and biographical, and thus reliable for use in reconstruction of the "historical Jeremiah." (For a recent attempt to utilize even the "lamentations of Jeremiah" as historical reflections and biographically useful, see the work of Berridge.) Many scholars ascribe the prose sermons of Jeremiah and the narratives, at least in their present form, to the preaching interest of the exilic community meeting in worship assemblies not unlike the later synagogues (so Nicholson, 134-135, and Rietzschel, 21-24). Nicholson assigns much of the prose material to the "deuteronomistic school," while Muilenburg sees the so-called "deuteronomic additions" as reflections of "conventional scribal compositions" (237). Koch relates this biographical form to the prophetic legends (so Wanke, 151-153) and suggests that what we have here in fact is a new literary form created by connecting a number of prophetic legends back to back. The purpose, however, is not to describe the life of the prophet so much as to relate the outcome of his warnings and promises and the personal fate of one committed to declare God's word (Koch, 203-204).

III. CONCLUDING REMARKS

It should be obvious that a great deal has been accomplished in the isolation and description of prophetic forms of speech. We have only considered the *Gattungen* that have been generally acknowledged and are fairly well-defined. But much remains to be done, and some suggestions concerning future work are in order.

One need which the above review has reemphasized is that of uniform terminology. If there is to be an agreed upon vocabulary, two things seem necessary. First, past efforts of scholars should not be neglected. Westermann set a good example by trying to go back and reclaim some terminology that had been forgotten. This effort might not always be worthwhile, but to begin each new study as if nothing had gone before is self-defeating. Confusion in the technical language used in form criticism is partly the result of a failure to digest earlier studies.

Second, there must be a more consistent attempt to describe literary genres in terms of function rather than content. For instance, when the term "call" is used to designate the narratives found in Is 6 and Jer 1, immediately a whole set of theological presuppositions is brought into the picture. Is the intent of these passages to "call" the prophet; that is, are they primarily private diary entries? Or do they serve another function in that they report the basis on which a prophet feels compelled to speak? The name given the genre should describe as accurately as possible the function of the literary type.

This immediately leads to another area where continuing research is necessary. Repeatedly we noted above that agreement was lacking concerning the proper *Sitz im Leben* of particular forms. The difficulty of deciding this kind of question is obvious, but that does not diminish the need. The ever-increasing number of extrabiblical materials certainly offers a source for parallels which will help in the interpretation of biblical forms. What has already been learned concerning custom in the legal, social, and cultic spheres of life, for instance, has helped settle some questions. Definition of the prophet as messenger, while probably overstated by Westermann, did receive some confirmation from the Mari texts. The question of whether there were "cultic" prophets, the cause of a great stir little more than a decade ago, now seems clearly settled. This does not mean that every prophetic form has its *Sitz* in the cult, but a sharp division between prophet and priest is no longer assumed. Still the definition of the *Sitz im Leben* remains a pressing problem in the study of prophetic speech forms.

Finally, James Muilenburg has placed a challenge before form critics in general, and has demonstrated his concern in particular in the study of Second Isaiah. In his article entitled "Form Criticism and Beyond," Muilenburg calls for no less attention to form criticism but for something in addition. His primary concern is to remind critics that the manner in which a prophet used a form is finally the most important point, and this can in part be determined by careful examination of the way the prophet articulated his message, a discipline Muilenburg terms "rhetorical criticism." In his study of Second Isaiah, Muilenburg shows numerous places where the prophet combined forms or altered them in a dramatic manner. This emphasis is not foreign to form criticism and can provide the reminder that the critic must begin and eventually conclude his study with the material that has been preserved. He may try to trace the development of a form or a particular text, but his final obligation is to the text as it has come to him. Form criticism is an essential tool, but it is but one of several which should be employed in a study of the prophets.

W. EUGENE MARCH

Chapter Five

PSALMS

I. HISTORY OF RESEARCH AND DEVELOPMENT OF METHOD

1. Hermann Gunkel and Sigmund Mowinckel: Parents of Form Critical Work

D. R. Ap-Thomas, "An Appreciation of Sigmund Mowinckel's Contribution to Biblical Studies," *JBL* LXXXV (1966) 315-325; H. Gunkel, *Die Psalmen* (HKAT II/2, Göttingen: Vandenhoeck & Ruprecht, 1926⁴); H. Gunkel and J. Begrich, *Einleitung in die Psalmen* (HKAT, suppl., Göttingen:Vandenhoeck & Ruprecht, 1933); F. Heiler, *Das Gebet. Eine religionsgeschichtliche und religionspsychologische Untersuchung* (Munich: E. Reinhardt Verlag, 1923⁵) = *Prayer, A Study in the History and Psychology of Religion*, ed. and tr. by S. McComb (London: Oxford University Press, 1932); A. R. Johnson, "The Psalms," in H. H. Rowley, ed., *The Old Testament and Modern Study* (London: Oxford University Press, 1951) 162-209; A. S. Kapelrud, "Die skandinavische Einleitungswissenschaft zu den Psalmen," *VuF* XI (1966) 62-93; W. Klatt, *Hermann Gunkel* (FRLANT 100, Göttingen: Vandenhoeck & Ruprecht, 1969); S. Mowinckel, *Psalmenstudien I-IV* (SNVAO, Kristiania: Jacob Dybwad, 1921-1924); *idem, Offersang og sangoffer* (Oslo: H. Aschehoug & Co., 1951) = *The Psalms in Israel's Worship*, 2 vols., tr. by D. R. Ap-Thomas (Nashville: Abingdon Press, 1962).

Modern psalm exegesis until some fifty years ago traveled in the wake of scholars like Heinrich Ewald, W. M. L. de Wette and

Julius Wellhausen in Germany, Abraham Kuenen in the Netherlands, S. R. Driver in Great Britain, Adolphe Lods in France, Frants Buhl in Denmark, and G. F. Moore in the United States, all of whom were outstanding literary critics. This meant that in prevailing academic fashion most OT exegetes would look upon the Psalter even as a product of literary art. Each psalm was considered first and foremost the written proclamation of a poet. Focal points of interest, consequently, were, in the first place, the author's historical situation, the events and the environment to which he reacted in his poem, and secondly, his inner feelings, the psychological and religious condition he presumably lived in. Thus OT scholars between 1800 and 1920 mainly dedicated themselves to uncovering in each psalm traces of the history of Israel; and they were eager to learn how the psalmists had put their personal experiences of national affairs into words and poetic structures. Of course this "literary," "historical," and "psychological" preoccupation (as all our exegetical endeavors always are) was prompted by presuppositions virulent in that period. History and psyche were of burning interest to nineteenth-century thinkers, philosophers and theologians alike, since F. W. Hegel had so masterfully described the rolling movements of human progress and the spirit propelling them. Small wonder, then, that essays and commentaries on the Psalter would, as a rule, concentrate on the personal and historical features in each poem and on literary techniques used. Notable examples are the expositions of T. K. Cheyne, C. A. Briggs, R. Kittel, and B. Duhm. Their commentaries on the psalms still can be used with profit, if their limitations are kept in mind. No doubt, nineteenth-century exegetes tended to take their own way of producing written work as the overall matrix for literary activity. (Later generations will discover, probably, the same affinity between culture and exegesis in our present time.)

Close to the turn of the century some basic attitudes started to change. Cause and effect, people felt, were not the only categories in comprehending history; emphasis on literary and poetic forms alone would not suffice to reveal the meaning of ancient documents. A new romantic movement rediscovered "mystery" and "unpredictability" as constitutive factors of reality. So it happened that in Germany a number of angry young men gathered in opposition against the prevailing Wellhausen school with its literary approach to the documents. Albert Eichhorn, Wilhelm Wrede, Wilhelm Bousset, and Ernst Troeltsch became their lead-

V

ers, and by the turn of the century they were known as the *"religionsgeschichtliche Schule."* Hugo Gressmann, a close friend of Gunkel's and an important member of that movement, bluntly described the feelings of the group: "We are fed up with being treated with literary criticism only " (Klatt, 74) . The point was: The new school demanded—on top of literary criticism, or better, preceding it—a comprehensive analysis of history, culture, and religion. The rebels could not content themselves with reconstructions of conceptual systems or historical surface structures. They were searching for the very soul of the ancient writers, and, what is even more important, they took into account both general cultural and religious backgrounds and all those social factors which influence the growth of oral traditions.

Hermann Gunkel (1862-1932) became a member and a leading figure of this "religious-historical" circle, and since the new school of thought was suspect by the church and state authorities he had to fight for recognition and promotion almost to the end of his life. Gunkel indeed took a different avenue also to psalm exegesis. "Religion" and "History" were his watchwords; he aimed at retelling the story of Israel's faith in the context of the ancient Near East. OT poetry and prose no longer were considered a product of literary activity, the work of authors, redactors, and publishers, but the fruit of long processes of transmission. Group life and institutionalized customs were considered instrumental in bringing about the variety of "literary" forms preserved in the OT. Writing down the old traditions was only a final step, usually signalizing the end of a period in which a text was used naturally. The composition of written literature, according to Gunkel, was in most cases indicative of the fact that some learned author had cut the umbilical cord of a particular genre severing its connection to its source of life. To reduce a living text to writing in ancient times was artificial, even decadent. Gunkel wanted to portray the history of Israel's literature from the dawn of its existence in popular sayings, songs, and narrations through its period of living use to its final disintegration and codification.

How did this "religious and historical" breakthrough affect psalm interpretation in particular? Gunkel, referring back to old and new romanticists (e.g. R. Lowth, J. G. Herder, G. Wünsch) , located ancient poetry in popular activities, in various feasts and gatherings. More specifically, the majority of psalms for him clearly reflect cultic happenings: the exuberant joy or the deadly dejection of the community or individual who felt in close alliance with their God, Yahweh. There were plenty of references in the psalms, Gunkel felt, to cultic music, to processions and ritual acts, to temple and divine throne to support this genealogy. The language of the songs, furthermore, showed marks of communal and cultic use. It was repetitious and full of religious imagery. Some psalms even betrayed the activities of choirs and temple personnel as part of a worship service (cf. Pss 24; 48; 136; I Chron 16). Gunkel, especially after an exchange of arguments with Sigmund Mowinckel, was fully convinced that the temple cult was the ultimate source for most of Israel's psalms (cf. H. Gunkel and J. Begrich, *Einleitung*, 175-180).

By what technique did Gunkel establish his far-reaching conclusions? Several qualities had to come together in one man to insure any results in form critical psalm exegesis: a keen observation of linguistic patterns; a new evaluation of the formulaic character of the poems; a vivid sympathy with their "authors"; and a deep sensitivity to ancient life situations. Gunkel was able to apply his talents to the work. Because of our remoteness from the ancient scene, grammatical and syntactical analysis had to take precedence. But the listing and description of recurring phrases immediately went hand in hand with a depiction of form elements and genres and their function in real-life settings. All these different steps of investigation belong close together. The written documents were the material with which he began, but the vision of specific cult situations was always in focus whenever Gunkel worked on the psalms. There were, in short, five major psalm genres and settings for Gunkel: festive hymns, communal complaints, individual complaints, royal psalms, and thanksgiving songs—each connected with their respective worship services. Discovery of the existence and usage of the types prior to the beginning of their so-called "literary history," their generic description, and their cultic foundation were most important impulses for subsequent research.

Gunkel's way of looking at the psalms soon gained some reputation among younger scholars. His most eminent and most independent pupil in this field became Sigmund Mowinckel (1884-1965). The young Norwegian had studied with two prominent Danish teachers, V. Grønbech and J. Pedersen, before he met Gunkel and became intrigued by the new method. Grønbech and Pedersen both had emphasized the mysterious faculties of the soul, individual and communal, as creative powers of religion. Thus Mowinckel's background prepared him to add a new dimension to Gunkel's work and to move even more resolutely into the new direction of psalm research.

As early as 1921 Mowinckel's first volume of *Psalmenstudien* appeared, to be followed by five more weighty essays on topics in the same area. Together with his later comprehensive survey *Offersang og sangoffer* and numerous articles, these books constitute the most challenging ventures in the newer psalm research. Mowinckel's basic ideas may be summarized as follows:

1) Form critical analysis and generic classification of the psalms as inaugurated by Gunkel are sound methods.

2) Many hymns, royal psalms, and even complaint songs can be understood only within the framework of a comprehensive Israelite festival celebrated in the fall, at the beginning of the New Year.

3) Psalms with a more individualistic outlook (e.g. psalms of sickness) are to be connected with more private services in the temple.

4) The remaining psalms are stamped by reflection, by instructional rather than cultic use and may be attributed to learned psalmographers and wise men who possibly were involved in composing and collecting liturgical texts.

It was his emphasis on specific cultic situations and his distinct conception of the ancient mentality which made Mowinckel's work such a valuable contribution to psalm research. Sometimes his approach is labeled "cult-historical" in contradistinction to Gunkel's method. But there is no real need to separate the two aspects of modern psalm exegesis that distinctly. They belong together in that Gunkel worked from literary documents towards the institutions, while Mowinckel concentrated his attention on cultic and sociological problems. Both men, as it were, called the tunes of today's psalm interpretation. The main problem still seems to be how well scholarship—even after fifty years of form critical investigation of the psalms—can cope with the double challenge brought forth by the parents of modern psalm interpretation.

2. Formal Analysis: From Begrich to Westermann and Beyond

E. Balla, *Das Ich der Psalmen* (FRLANT 16, Göttingen: Vandenhoeck & Ruprecht, 1912) ; Chr. Barth, *Einführung in die Psalmen* (BS 32, Neukirchen: Neukirchener Verlag, 1961) = *Introduction to the Psalms*, tr. by R. A. Wilson (New York: Charles Scribner's Sons, 1966); W. Baumgartner, *Die Klagegedichte des Jeremia* (BZAW 32, Giessen: A. Töpelmann, 1917); D. J. A. Clines, "Psalm Research since 1955," *TyndB* XVIII (1967) 103-126, XX (1969) 105-125; P. Drijvers, *Over de Psalmen* (Utrecht: Uitgeverij Het Spectrum, 1956, 1964⁵) = *The Psalms: Their Structure and Meaning* (New York: Herder and Herder, 1965); H. Jahnow, *Das hebräische Leichenlied im Rahmen der Völkerdichtung* (BZAW 36, Giessen: A. Töpelmann, 1923); A. S. Kapelrud, "Scandinavian Research in the Psalms after Mowinckel," *ASTI* IV (1965) 74-90; H.-J. Kraus, *Psalmen*, 2 vols. (BK XV, Neukirchen: Neukirchener Verlag, 1960); E. A. Leslie, *The Psalms* (Nashville: Abingdon Press, 1949); L. Sabourin, *The Psalms: Their Origin and Meaning*, 2 vols. (Staten Island: Alba House, 1969); H. Schmidt, *Die Psalmen* (HAT I/15, Tübingen: J. C. B. Mohr, 1934); W. Staerk, *Lyrik* (SAT III/1, Göttingen: Vandenhoeck & Ruprecht, 1911, 1920²); J. J. Stamm, "Ein Vierteljahrhundert Psalmenforschung," *ThR* XXIII (1955) 1-68; C. Westermann, *Das Loben Gottes in der Psalmen* (Göttingen: Vandenhoeck & Ruprecht, 1961²) = *The Praise of God in the Psalms*, tr. by K. R. Crim (Richmond: John Knox Press, 1965); *idem, Der Psalter* (Stuttgart: Calwer Verlag, 1967²).

We shall now look at the first step of form critical exegesis of the psalms and try to sketch the development from Gunkel to our present time. In Germany, no doubt, this aspect of analyzing and defining formal elements retained a certain predominance, which does not mean, of course, that German scholars altogether neglected the social backgrounds and cultic settings of the psalms (see below section 4).

Gunkel, who in his own way was a sociable man with many friends (cf. W. Baumgartner, "Zum 100. Geburtstag von Hermann Gunkel," *VTS* IX [1963] 1-18), influenced some of his colleagues with his methods. R. Kittel, for instance, at least took note of the program, and W. Staerk as early as 1911 tried to arrange his whole psalm exegesis according to Gunkel's principles. More important, however, were Gunkel's pupils. Among those who received firsthand instruction in form critical analysis were scholars like Hans Schmidt, Emil Balla, Walter Baumgartner, Joachim Begrich, Hedwig Jahnow, all of whom later contributed pioneering studies in the area of Hebrew poetry. But first generation form criticism in the Psalter came to an abrupt end as a result of the second World War. J. Begrich, for example, was killed in action; H. Schmidt in 1945 lost his chair at Halle University on account of his former political leniency, while W. Baumgartner had withdrawn to Basel before the Nazis took power. Thus there was a long break in German psalm research, and when the studies were renewed after the war theological presuppositions had drastically changed. Karl Barth's theology of the "Word of God" had captured the minds of those who tried to resist the devastating political dictatorship. The "Word" was set apart from any other

V

religious phenomenon, it (or HE, as many theologians preferred to say) had become a genre all by itself, incomparable and incompatible with anything else. Most of all it was G. von Rad who influenced psalm investigation in this direction. In addition to his lectures at Göttingen and Heidelberg Universities, several of his publications made significant contributions to form critical research on the psalms (for bibliographical data, see below, section 4). Other scholars with somewhat differing outlook who flourished in the fifties were C. Westermann, A. Weiser (cf. section 4) and F. Horst. H.-J. Kraus, theologically speaking, although not in terms of age, firmly belongs to this older group. In the next decade, another shift in psalm research becomes discernible. The Barthian school of thought loses ground, and younger form critics take over, scholars like K. Koch, E. Kutsch, H. Gese, D. Michel, L. Delekat, W. Beyerlin, G. Wanke, and F. Crüsemann. Thus form critical work on the psalms after Gunkel can be roughly divided into three periods which are characterized by their own theological principles. A real problem is to understand how form critical method survived the basic shifts that occurred between 1920 and 1970 (cf. Klatt, 13).

The first decade of psalm research after Gunkel (roughly 1930-1940) was filled with enthusiastic work along the trail the master had blazed. Begrich and Schmidt were prototypes of faithful pupils. They worked independently and sometimes insisted on details not to Gunkel's liking (cf. Gunkel-Begrich, *Einleitung*, 195), but they completely shared all the fundamental persuasions of their master. Begrich, for instance, finished the important *Einleitung* in such a way that there is hardly any break between his own contribution and Gunkel's. Schmidt, among other things, edited a two-volume "Festschrift" for Gunkel's sixtieth birthday and completed a full commentary on the psalms along his master's lines. Form critical method, therefore, as applied by these early "practitioners" in the main was identical with that of Gunkel. It was he who had laid down the three necessary requirements (cf. Gunkel-Begrich, *Einleitung*, 22-23): first, to classify the psalms by their respective life situations; second, to recognize that psalms of the same genre are governed by "a common treasure of thoughts and moods"; and third, to analyze the linguistic and poetic structures of each psalm, because this "form" of the literary text is a reflection of life conditions, thoughts, and moods.

Now, it is important to note that when Gunkel and his first

pupils are talking about the "outward form" of a poem, they do not aim at a philologic explanation but an aesthetic description of phraseology, structure, and genre. Take the hymnic language for an example. Early form critics would carefully note the use of imperatives, the vocabulary, verbal tenses, number of nouns and the like, and then delineate the function and impact of such language in the context of a presupposed life situation. They noted the. change of speaker or addressee in many psalms and the shift from dejection to exuberance in some complaints as well as a good number of more formal observations. These were all understood to reveal underlying sentiments and religious feelings. Linguistic surface structures emphatically are not exploited for the sake of their theological contents or concepts, but because they are outpourings of religious beings. And these sentiments are basically common to all peoples; in the particular case of the OT they are tied to ancient—more specifically, to ancient Near Eastern—group life, and to those religious feelings which were dominant in the respective cultural groups. Thus Gunkel and his first generation offspring could freely draw on ancient Near Eastern analogies in form and content. Israel, in their opinion, had reached a higher level of religion, but she still used the outward structures common to all in order to communicate her deeper insights and experiences. Linguistic forms, especially in the psalms, have to be placed back into full-blooded religious life according to Gunkel and his pupils, and form critical analysis in their opinion was doing just that.

After the second World War the scene had changed. Linguistic surface structures no longer were searched for their human sentiments by Protestant theologians but rather for revelations of the divine will. Of course there are certain difficulties in regarding prayers such as the psalms as the direct word of God. But they certainly may be taken as responses to God's will and action. Consequently von Rad, in his famous *Theology of the OT*, puts the psalms in juxtaposition to salvation history. And form critical method used along this line now is applied to quite different ends, namely to clarify the message of Yahweh to his people and secondly, to determine the role of the believer vis-à-vis this absolutely unique God. Westermann's book *The Praise of God in the Psalms* is quite a typical example. Surface structures are to be investigated because of their underlying word events. "It is therefore not the fact of the oracle as such that created this

V

special type of Psalms of petition, but the word which in these oracles came from God. . . ." (*Praise,* 65-70) .

Sometimes one cannot help feeling that outright trinitarian structures are visualized behind the texts (cf. Westermann, *ZAW* LXVI [1954] 47: the "threefold subject of complaint") . In consequence, real life situations seem to be sacrificed in favor of those mysterious "basic modes of that which occurs when man turns to God with words" (Westermann, *Praise,* 153) . Words and structures, form elements, and genres become indicators of divine "occurrences." Formal analysis remains a tool of exegesis, but the theological perspective is a new one. There are some brilliant studies in ancient Near Eastern comparative materials, notably Chr. Barth's *Die Errettung vom Tode in den individuellen Klage- und Dankliedern des Alten Testaments* (Zollikon: Evangelischer Verlag, 1947) . But as a rule comparisons are kept to a minimum in this period, and they sometimes look rather strained. Small wonder, because God's activity in this world supposedly was confined to Israel's history, and from this perspective all formal and structural affinities to Israel's neighbors must pose a problem. H.-J. Kraus' commentary on the psalms and Chr. Barth's introduction to the psalms are good examples of form critical work governed by a theology of the "Word of God."

In the sixties a new consciousness gradually came to the fore in Protestant Germany while form criticism as a method in psalm research was catching on also among Roman Catholic exegetes (cf. e.g. F. Nötscher, *Die Psalmen* [Echterbibel IV, Würzburg: Echter-Verlag, 1947]; A. Deissler, *Die Psalmen,* 3 vols. [Düsseldorf: Patmos-Verlag, 1963-1965]) . The influence of Karl Barth's theology has since been receding. The old problems of general religious history and development again are debated, and psalm research has been slowly drawn into this discussion. Among younger scholars there is an increasing feeling that the results of the preceding decade have to be rechecked. There is pressure to go back to Gunkel, to study again the individual genres of the psalms and their life settings (see below, sections 6-9) and to avoid hasty and general conclusions in regard to theological purpose and meaning. Gunkel's genre classifications are subject to minor changes and relabeling. In general they still stand, or at least they can serve as a point of departure. The same holds true for form critical method. Strangely enough the same techniques of observation and classification, the same theories of language, of oral transmission, of genre growth and decay are still in vogue, although some skepticism seems to be seeping in and the goals of research again are shifting. Today's exegetes care less about the pious soul or the "Word of God" behind the psalm texts. Apparently they are rediscovering the importance of sociological settings, even though the older schemes and methods are still lingering on. If it is religiosity upon which attention is focused, it will be group religiosity rather than Gunkel's aesthetic and individualistic piety. And if the group itself is looked for, it will be some cultic gathering in Israel which may be illuminated by analogies from other cultures.

3. Near Eastern Ritual and the Biblical Psalms

J. Aistleitner, *Die mythologischen und kultischen Texte aus Ras Schamra* (BH 8, Budapest: Akademiai Kiadó, 1959); A. Bentzen, *Messias—Moses redivivus—Menschensohn* (ATANT 17, Zurich: Zwingli-Verlag, 1948) = *King and Messiah* (London: Lutterworth Press, 1955; 2nd ed., Oxford: Basil Blackwell, 1970); K. H. Bernhardt, *Das Problem der altorientalischen Königsideologie im Alten Testament* (VTS 8, Leiden: E. J. Brill, 1961); G. R. Driver, "The Psalms in the Light of Babylonian Research," in D. C. Simpson, ed., *The Psalmists* (London: Oxford University Press, 1926) 109-175; idem, *Canaanite Myths and Legends* (OTS 3, Edinburgh: T. and T. Clark, 1956); C. M. Edsman, "Zum sakralen Königtum in der Forschung der letzten hundert Jahre," *NumenS* IV (1959) 3-17; M. Eliade, *Le Mythe de l'éternel retour* (Paris: Librairie Gallimard, 1949) = *The Myth of the Eternal Return* tr. by W. R. Trask (New York: Pantheon Books, 1954) = *Cosmos and History* (New York: Harper Torchbooks, 1959); I. Engnell, *Studies in Divine Kingship in the Ancient Near East* (Uppsala: Almqvist & Wiksell, 1943; 2nd ed., Oxford: Basil Blackwell, 1967); H. Frankfort, *Kingship and the Gods* (Chicago: University of Chicago Press, 1948); T. H. Gaster, *Thespis: Ritual, Myth, and Drama in the Ancient Near East* (New York: Henry Schuman, 1950; 2nd ed., Garden City: Doubleday & Co., 1961); S. H. Hooke, ed., *Myth and Ritual* (London: Oxford University Press, 1933); idem, *The Labyrinth* (London: Oxford University Press, 1935); idem, *Myth, Ritual, and Kingship* (London: Oxford University Press, 1958); A. R. Johnson, "Divine Kingship and the Old Testament," *ET* LXII (1950/51) 36-42; idem, *Sacral Kingship in Ancient Israel* (Cardiff: University of Wales Press, 1955, 1967²); S. Mowinckel, *Psalmenstudien, II* (SNVAO II/1921/6, Kristiania: Jacob Dybwad, 1922); idem, *Han som kommer* (Copenhagen: G. E. C. Gad, 1951) = *He That Cometh*, tr. by G. W. Anderson (Nashville: Abingdon Press, 1956); M. Noth, "Gott, König, Volk im Alten Testament," *ZTK* XLVII (1950) 157-191 = his *Gesammelte Studien zum Alten Testament* (TB 6, Munich: Chr. Kaiser, 1957) 188-229 = *The Laws in the Pentateuch and Other Essays*, tr. by D. R. Ap-Thomas (Edinburgh: Oliver & Boyd, 1966) 145-178; H. Schmidt, *Die Thronfahrt Jahves am Fest der Jahreswende im alten Israel* (SGV 122, Tübingen: J. C. B. Mohr, 1927); P. Volz, *Das Neujahrsfest Jahwes* (Tübingen: J. C. B. Mohr, 1912); G. Widengren, *Sakrales Königtum im Alten Testament und im Judentum* (Stuttgart: W. Kohlhammer, 1955); J. T. Willis, "I. Engnell's Contribution to Old Testament Scholarship," *TZ* XXVI (1970) 385-394.

The nineteenth century had witnessed a tremendous rise in

ethnological and anthropological studies (cf. E. E. Evans-Pritchard, *Social Anthropology* [New York: Free Press, 1966²] especially 21-42). Since early romanticism and the pioneering work of the Grimm brothers, as well as that of J. G. Herder, there had been a steady increase in scholarly dedication to the study of folk tales, folk customs, and folk beliefs. Primitive man became the subject of investigation. Illumination of the lowest stages of human development promised to shed light also on the destinies of present-day generations. (Cf. two titles which were the fruit of nineteenth-century research: F. Boas, *The Mind of Primitive Man* [New York: The Macmillan Company, 1911]; L. Lévy-Bruhl, *Les fonctions mentales dans les sociétés inférieurs* [Paris: F. Alcan, 1910].) In the course of such studies, quite naturally, theories emerged about the origin and nature of religious thinking. In contradistinction to earlier views the explanation of "religion" now included not only the psychic conditions of the individual but the life of the group or nation in which religious ideas were actually practiced. The sociological basis of all religious thinking came to be emphasized; rituals and customs, patterns of behavior, and structures of society were more and more taken into account. To mention but three outstanding scholars who paved the way to fuller investigations of religious rites and ceremonies: Sir E. B. Tylor (1832-1917; cf. his *Primitive Culture* [New York: Henry Holt and Company, 1871]); Sir J. G. Frazer (1854-1941; cf. his famous multivolume work *The Golden Bough* [New York: The Macmillan Company, 1911-1915]); E. Durkheim (1858-1917; cf. his *Les formes elementaries de la vie religieuse* [Paris: F. Alcan, 1912] = *The Elementary Forms of the Religious Life*, tr. by J. W. Swain [New York: The Macmillan Company, 1915]).

It is first against this background and second in the context of contemporaneous archaeological discoveries in the ancient Near East that the ritualistic approach to psalm research has to be seen. As the mounds of Mesopotamia were opened and innumerable tablets, temple ruins and religious artifacts found, it became clear that the Sumerians and Akkadians had been great liturgists (cf. H. Zimmern, *Beiträge zur Kenntnis der babylonischen Religion* [Leipzig: J. C. Hinrichs, 1901]; *ANET*, 325-401; 573-586). What could be more logical than looking for connections to and affinities with the mythological and cultic world of the Hebrews? Soon, indeed, and partly in opposition to narrow-minded orthodox Christian militants, pan-Babylonian ideas sprang up. Some scholars, especially A. Jeremias and H. Winckler, with verve promoted the thesis that Mesopotamian cult and culture had permeated those of all the other peoples of the ancient Near East and had perhaps extended their influence beyond this area. Israel, they held, also had copied the ritual patterns of the Babylonians; the OT was but a dim reflection of the light emanating from the vast literatures of the Mesopotamian civilizations.

Thus we find the ritualistic interpretation of the psalms does emerge from a different direction. But we also have to realize some converging lines in ethnological and form critical research. Form critics starting out from a purely literary point of view had discovered the importance of social relationships and ceremonial practices. Were ethnologists—at least those working in the OT field—ready to concede the merits of form critical analysis?

P. Volz and S. Mowinckel were the first to draw special attention to the central affair in the Babylonian festive calendar, namely the New Year Festival. The evil powers of the past year had to be defeated and the good fortunes, fertility, and happiness of the coming year had to be procured annually in twelve days of celebrations and ceremonies. The king and the priesthood of the capital were the main actors in the dramatic performances; the populace took part in mourning and feasting and accompanied the processions of the god Marduk. For, in fact, the New Year Festival at Babylon was the feast of Marduk. The suffering, death, and resurrection of this deity were reenacted during those crucial days at the beginning of each new year. The elaborate ritual has come down to us (cf. F. Thureau-Dangin, *Rituels acadiens* [Paris: Leroux, 1921]) as well as the mythological background of the event, contained in *Enuma Elis*, the poem of the chaos battle and world creation (cf. W. G. Lambert and S. B. Parker, *Enuma Elis* [London: Oxford University Press, 1966]). Main elements of the feast, then, were the death and resurrection of the deity according to seasonal archetypes, the fixing of destinies for the new year, the performance of the sacred marriage, the enthronement of the victorious god on his olympic seat, and the acclamation of the subordinate deities.

P. Volz and S. Mowinckel took up the results of Near Eastern studies in cultic matters and looked for traces of similar rituals and festivals in ancient Israel. Even if the OT should yield only fragmentary glimpses of a ceremony comparable to the Babylonian New Year, the two scholars (independently of each other) felt encouraged by much later evidence such as Mishnaic texts

V

(cf. e.g. the rites described in tractate *sukkah*). Late Jewish rituals could help to fill in details of that ancient Israelite festival, the outlines of which could be found in the OT itself. And there were quite formidable hints in the bible, especially in the book of Psalms, which would suggest some big cultic event also at the beginning of the Hebrew New Year. The autumn celebration (the feast of tabernacles, cf. Ex 34:22; Lev 23:34-44) in early times may have had that particular purpose. A good number of psalms could be interpreted—in the light of Babylonian motifs—as reflecting the ceremonials of a New Year celebration. Thus Mowinckel forcefully pointed out that those songs acclaiming Yahweh's enthronement (cf. "Yahweh has become king!" in Pss 47; 93; 96; 97; 99) fell in line with the Babylonian idea of reinstating the victorious Marduk. And there were other traits in the book of Psalms: the procession of the ark (cf. Ps 132), the taming of chaos powers (cf. Ps 77), the creation of heaven and earth (cf. Ps 104), the revitalization of the parched fields by rain (cf. Ps 65), and the charge of the Davidic king with divine and liturgical responsibilities (cf. Pss 2; 45; 110).

At first sight the methodology implied in all this is purely ethnological: a comparison of motifs, ideas, and individual ritualistic practices. But Mowinckel at least had recognized the value of form critical analysis. His studies in the psalms demonstrate that he was able and willing to employ the "literary" tools furnished by Gunkel. Analysis of the structure of a given text and subsequent working back towards its intention and life setting were imperative for Mowinckel.

In the decades to come this integration of methods was not always mastered by the scholars of the "cult-functional" schools. By and large those who stressed the common ritualistic pattern in the ancient Near East tended to come to rash and generalized conclusions, while their more formalistic opponents (notably M. Noth and K. H. Bernhardt) sometimes were in danger of overemphasizing literary structures and what they thought could be deduced from them.

The ritualistic approach to the psalms was boosted by the discoveries at the site of ancient Ugarit. Excavations started in 1928 and soon brought forth, together with invaluable other documents, the well-known mythological texts which gave rise to a whole new branch of studies and decisively influenced OT research. Scholars like C. H. Gordon, G. R. Driver, and J. Aistleitner gained well-deserved merit in editing and interpreting this material. Its cultic origin and use soon had become apparent. Here was Baal, the deity of fertility, waging battle against Mot, the power of death. We read about Baal's death and resurrection, of concomitant weeping and rejoicing on earth. Baal is made king over the whole universe; banquets and exuberant joy among his fellow deities mark his victory. These and many more details fit the scheme of a New Year festival according to the Babylonian pattern. One has to imagine that the myths were enacted by king, priestesses, and priests and adorned by various ritual activities, like processions, sacrifices, meals, prayers, recitations and the like. British and Scandinavian OT scholars were quick to point out the affinities of the Ugaritic myths to the Babylonian ritual on the one hand and the OT practices on the other hand. The works of S. H. Hooke, A. R. Johnson, A. Bentzen, I. Engnell, G. Widengren and others bear witness to the virtuosity with which the Babylonian and Canaanite patterns were applied to the OT. The direct consequence for the studies of the OT psalms are that virtually all the genres and even most of the individual texts are assigned to the New Year Festival. And since the king was the central figure in the life-creating drama he was supposed to have been the recitor of most of the psalms.

This is precisely the point where the form critics like to launch their most severe attacks against "patternism." Aside from the many problems surrounding the "comparability of cultures" or their "uniformity," the specific question in our case may be: Is it possible to visualize a king in Israel or Judah who as a divine representative restaged the tale of a dying and revitalized Yahweh? Certainly, the ancient (and nomadic!) Israelite traditions did not embrace such seasonal myths. Certainly, the Hebrews were hesitant to copy the institution of kingship once they had settled among the Canaanites. But eventually they did, and we may be sure that some elements in the ancient Near Eastern kingship ideology and royal ritual as well as the belief in the renewal of the year came in at the very same time. The psalms and other OT texts do show that Israel was touched by these foreign influences, although it is very hard to estimate how deeply they penetrated or whether they came to dominate the cultic life of the people of Yahweh.

4. Covenant Theology and the Psalms

A. Arens, *Die Psalmen im Gottesdienst des alten Bundes* (Trier: Paulinus Verlag, 1961) ; A. Deissler, *Die Psalmen*, 3 vols. (Düsseldorf: Patmos Verlag, 1963-

65) ; F. C. Fensham, "Psalm 21—A Covenant Song?" *ZAW* LXXVII (1965) 193-205; K. Koch, "Tempeleinlassliturgien und Dekaloge," in R. Rendtorff, ed., *Studien zur Theologie der alttestamentlichen Überlieferungen* (Neukirchen: Neukirchener Verlag, 1961) 45-60; G. E. Mendenhall, "Ancient Oriental and Biblical Law," *BA* XVII (1954) 26-46 and "Covenant Forms in Israelite Tradition," *BA* 1954 50-76 = *The Biblical Archaeologist Reader, III,* ed. by E. F. Campbell and D. N. Freedman (Garden City: Doubleday & Co., 1970) 3-53; E. Nielsen, *Shechem: A Traditio-Historical Investigation* (Copenhagen: G. E. C. Gad, 1955); Q. Quell, *Das kultische Problem der Psalmen* (Berlin: Kohlhammer-Verlag, 1926) ; G. von Rad, *Das formgeschichtliche Problem des Hexateuch* (BWANT IV/26, Stuttgart: W. Kohlhammer, 1938) = his *Gesammelte Studien* (TB 6, Munich: Chr. Kaiser, 1958) 9-86 = *The Problem of the Hexateuch and Other Essays* (New York: McGraw-Hill, 1966) 1-78; *idem,* "Das judäische Königsritual," *TLZ* LXXII (1947) 211-216 = *Gesammelte Studien,* 205-213 = *The Problem,* 222-231, " 'Gerechtigkeit' und 'Leben' in der Kultsprache der Psalmen," in *Festschrift für Alfred Bertholet* (Tübingen: J. C. B. Mohr, 1950) 418-437 = *Gesammelte Studien,* 225-247 = *The Problem,* 243-266; *idem,* "Israel vor Jahwe (Die Antwort Israels) ," in his *Theologie des Alten Testaments,* vol. I (Munich: Chr. Kaiser, 1957) 352-415 = *Old Testament Theology,* vol. I, tr. by D. M. G. Stalker (New York: Harper & Brothers, 1962) 355-418; A. Weiser, *Die Psalmen* (ATD 14/15, Göttingen: Vandenhoeck & Ruprecht, 1950, 1959⁵) = *The Psalms,* tr. by H. Hartwell (Philadelphia: The Westminster Press, 1962) ; *idem,* "Die Darstellung der Theophanie in den Psalmen und im Festkult," in *Festschrift für Alfred Bertholet,* 513-531.

The decisive role theological thinking played even in form critical psalm research has already been referred to in section 2. It is fascinating to study this problem in more detail and in doing so provide a sequel to the discussion of feasts in OT scholarship. The discovery of ancient Near Eastern ceremonialism in fact did influence even those form critics who worked on the basis of a "pure theology of the Word of God." The result was a peculiar understanding of those ancient Israelite customs which were considered the life setting of the OT psalms.

Between 1933 and 1939 Walther Eichrodt published his three-volume *Theologie des Alten Testaments*. The author then was Professor of OT Scriptures at Basel University and a colleague of Karl Barth. In what we may call a remarkable synchronization of events, Eichrodt pointed out that the covenant between Yahweh and Israel—a unique institution in the ancient world—was the focal point for all theological thinking in the OT (cf. Karl Barth, *Church Dogmatics* e.g. §§ 41; 57). Consequently he proceeded to explain systematically all OT life and literature from this perspective. When G. von Rad established the existence of the *Fest der Bundeserneuerung* ("the feast of covenant renewal") of the Hebrew tribal amphictyony as the backgound of the hexateuchal traditions, Eichrodt's ideas seemed to be reinforced. Later G. E. Mendenhall, K. Baltzer, and others gave form critical assistance to this prevailing taste in OT interpretation cherished at least in Germany and the United States. They tried to demonstrate that an overall ancient Near Eastern treaty scheme had been adopted by the Israelites in order to express their belief in a covenantal relationship to Yahweh. As a result, "covenant" really became the master key for some circles of OT exegetes; covenantal interpretations sprang up like a torrent; and there was hardly any text in the OT which could escape being incorporated into the fashionable scheme. The specter lasted until D. J. McCarthy analyzed more soberly the pros and cons of the treaty form (see his *Treaty and Covenant* [AnBib 21, Rome: Pontifical Biblical Institute, 1963]), and L. Perlitt finally proved that covenant theology in the OT is basically the result of the critical developments of the sixth and seventh centuries (see his *Bundestheologie im Alten Testament* [WMANT 36, Neukirchen: Neukirchener Verlag, 1969]).

The surge of "covenantalism" had to affect form critical psalm research as well. One typical example is presented by A. Weiser and his interpretation of the OT Psalter. There are several observations and presuppositions which led him to assume that the fall festival in Israel was centered around the renewal of the covenant. First of all he finds evidence within the psalms themselves: Yahweh's self-revelation looms large in some of the liturgical texts (see the description of a theophany in Pss 18; 50; 81; etc., as well as the critical assessment of this pivotal point by J. Jeremias, *Theophanie* [WMANT 10, Neukirchen: Neukirchener Verlag, 1965]). Secondly, other features fall in line with and are subordinate to this central act of revelation: the proclamation of apodictic, divine commandments (cf. Ps 81; E. Gerstenberger, "Covenant and Commandment," *JBL* LXXXIV [1965] 38-51); the enumeration of saving acts in history (cf. Ps 78); the celebration of Yahweh's creative power and royal rule (cf. Pss 47; 104); the universal judgment over peoples and nations (cf. Pss 68; 82; 99); the enthronement of the Judaean king (cf. Pss 2; 45), and many more. For Weiser, all these motifs perfectly fit the covenant ideology. He argues that the cultic tradition of Yahweh's covenant festival had a distinctive character of its own which dominated all the essential thoughts in the book of Psalms (*The Psalms*, 23-35). Thirdly, Weiser freely draws upon every bit of information in the historical and legal books of the OT which might pertain to the autumnal covenant festival. Thus he hopes

V

to convince the reader that the comprehensive celebration at the end of the year really was designed by the ancient Israelites to reestablish their formal alliance with Yahweh rather than renewing the potencies of nature.

· Small wonder, then, that according to Weiser virtually all the genres of OT psalmody should be attributed to the covenant festival; at least they should be seen in close proximity to the ideology of the covenant. That means that those form elements and genres which cannot originally be tied to covenantal customs and ceremonies have been adapted to it at a larger stage. They, too, need to be interpreted in the light of Israel's covenant faith.

Festive hymns of all sorts raise small difficulties for Weiser. If they praise Yahweh's deeds in history, Yahweh's victories over the enemy, or Yahweh's chastisement of Israel they automatically are earmarked for the covenant liturgy. In case they are prayers for rain and fertility (cf. Ps 65) or adoration of sky and sun (cf. Ps 19A) or reminiscent of chaos battle and other nature mythology (cf. Pss 29; 77) these hymns have been drawn in from a pagan environment and incorporated into the covenantal (and genuinely Israelite) framework. Likewise all the hymns concerning "kingship," be it heavenly or earthly, are basically of foreign provenance but fully adapted to covenant ideology. Complaint psalms and thanksgiving songs too can easily be claimed for the covenant festival as long as they are communal in character. Israel—suffering under the punishment of a "jealous" covenant partner whenever breaking away from him—would turn to her God at the fall festival or on special days of mourning and confess her sins or complain about injustice done to her in order to be restored to a good standing within the covenant relationship (cf. Pss 44; 106). Communal thanksgivings according to Weiser come close to hymns in style and character (cf. Pss 67; 124; 129).

The individual complaint poses much more serious problems, however. Weiser recognizes that in these prayers a real individual is pouring out his sorrows before Yahweh (cf. Ps 102:1), and there is no doubt in his mind that the earlier collective interpretation held by the elder R. Smend and others is not tenable. How then can individual prayers be connected to anything as comprehensive as the covenant ceremony of all Israelite tribes? Weiser in the main has a twofold answer. The individual Israelite is part and parcel of the covenant community; he cannot possibly exist

V

on his own and thus *per definitionem* can approach his God only by way of the communal cult. Weiser uses I Sam 1, Hannah's distress and prayer, as one strong argument in this context. The covenant community on the other hand is highly interested to see its covenant God also help the individual member. This mutual interdependence of individual and community Weiser takes as a warrant for the idea that communal and individual worship are tied together in the very same way. Within some individual prayers he indeed discovers communal traits, and quite a number of motifs and terms in such songs prove to be identical with their communal variety (cf. *The Psalms*, 66-72).

Finally there are the so-called wisdom poems, notorious especially among German form critics for their "natural theology," their black and white clichés of the pious and the wicked man, their legalism, their speculative theodicy, and their total lack of interest in matters of cult or salvation history. For Weiser all these features do not pose insurmountable obstacles. He simply believes that the covenant cult in Israel also made use of wisdom forms and topics in order to illuminate genuine covenant structures by wisdom elements (cf. *The Psalms*, 88-89).

There should be some concluding and critical comments at this point on what has been said so far about the development of form critical psalm research.

a) From the very outset form critical work on the OT psalms got entangled with other methods of research, that is with other interests, aspects, and presuppositions, with value judgments and theological assumptions. And in fact nobody should expect it to be otherwise; there is no way of avoiding a merger of methods. The reason is quite apparent. Form critical analysis *has* to search for life situations which in themselves are satisfactory explanations for the origin and growth of a given genre. Settings like these, however, cannot be grasped by mere analyses of linguistic structures; they call for appropriate application of sociological, anthropological, historical, and even theological methods. This is why Gunkel and Mowinckel would not limit form critical work to stupefying vivisection of literary remains but included all possible avenues which might lead back towards a fuller understanding of the pertinent life situations. Naturally, the path backwards into the shadows of history is long and arduous and there are many places where direct and precise information is lacking so that mere speculation can intervene.

V

Basically, however, form critical method in its wider sense as visualized by Gunkel and Mowinckel is a sound one to serve psalm research now and in the future. All the evidence gathered until now furthermore points to the fact that cultic performances of some kind have been background and fertile soil for most of the OT psalms.

b) Scandinavian and British ceremonialists and continental covenantalists as pictured above are both correct in pursuing form critical work on the psalms towards possible fountainheads for the different genres. Again, they are both perfectly correct in singling out cultic activities as the life settings for the psalms. But they are overzealous in postulating, each group according to its own upbringing and mentality; only one point of origin for a great variety of psalm types. Perhaps they both miss their point because they employ too many general truths and hypotheses, combining them freely, instead of looking for empirical and full-blooded details. A seasonal feast probably cannot be reconstructed by means of motifs and ideas supposedly inherent in the rituals but by assembling data about the real performances. Since such data are lacking in the OT the ceremonialists and covenantalists fill in the gaps with their preconceived ideas of what could have happened at the grand autumnal festival in Israel. And their feast, be it called New Year/Enthronement Festival or Covenant Renewal Festival, at times looks like a specter or a bag of bubbles.

c) Maybe there is a way to be more realistic in portraying ancient life situations in general and those cultic ceremonies in particular which gave birth to our OT psalms. We can possibly find much needed information outside the OT. Of course many sources, especially in the ancient Near East, have been tapped already. What is meant here is this: More data about rites and feasts, songs and liturgies, taken from Israel's neighbors as well as from other times and cultures could give us a better idea of what was feasible in the field of cultic activities. In other words, the vast information about cult and ritual which is at our disposal as the product of scores of anthropological and historical investigations should be used by OT scholars to narrow down the number of choices we have for depicting or reconstructing the cultic affairs of ancient Israel. To give but one example, by way of careful comparison with other cultures one could perhaps establish that worship services catering to the needs of individuals (even though they are considered members of a religious group) need not be tied to a communal cult pertaining to the affairs of tribe, nation, or community at large the way our "ceremonialists" or "covenantalists" would like to make us believe.

II. CLASSIFICATION OF PSALMS: THE GENRES

5. Complaints and Thanksgivings

G. W. Ahlström, *Psalm 89: Eine Liturgie aus dem Ritual des leidenden Königs* (Lund: CWK Gleerups, 1959) ; G. W. Anderson, "Enemies and Evildoers in the Book of Psalms," *BJRL* XLVIII (1965) 16-29; Chr. Barth, *Die Errettung vom Tode in den individuellen Klage- und Dankliedern des Alten Testaments* (Zollikon: Evangelischer Verlag, 1947) ; W. Beyerlin, *Die Rettung der Bedrängten in den Feindpsalmen der Einzelnen auf institutionelle Zusammenhänge untersucht* (FRLANT 99, Göttingen: Vandenhoeck & Ruprecht, 1970) ; H. Birkeland, *The Evildoers in the Book of Psalms* (ANVAO II/2, Oslo: Jacob Dybwad, 1955) ; R. L. Caplice, "Namburbi Texts in the British Museum," *Or* XXXIV (1965) 105-131, XXXVI (1967) 1-38, 273-298, XXXIX (1970) 1-32, XL (1971) 133-183; *idem*, "Participants in the Namburbi-Rituals," *CBQ* XXIX (1967) 346-352; G. R. Castellino, *Le lamentazioni individuali e gli inni in Babilonia e in Israele* (Turin: S. E. I., 1939) ; E. R. Dalglish, *Psalm Fifty-One* (Leiden: E. J. Brill, 1962) ; L. Delekat, *Asylie und Schutzorakel an Zionheiligtum* (Leiden: E. J. Brill, 1967) ; E. Gerstenberger, *Die bittende Mensch. Bittritual und Klagelied des Einzelnen im Alten Testament* (Habilitationsschrift, Heidelberg, 1970) ; W. W. Hallo, "Individual Prayer in Sumerian," *JAOS* LXXXVIII (1968) 71-89; J. Krecher, *Sumerische Kultlyrik* (Wiesbaden: Otto Harrassowitz, 1966) ; S. Mowinckel, *Psalmenstudien I: Awän und die individuellen Klagepsalmen* (SNVAO II/4, Kristiania: Jacob Dybwad, 1921) ; K. Ritter, "Magical Expert and Physician in Babylonian Medicine," *AS* XVI (1965) 299-321; H. Schmidt, *Das Gebet der Angeklagten im Alten Testament* (BZAW 49, Giessen: A. Töpelmann, 1929) ; C. Westermann, *Das Loben Gottes in den Psalmen* (Göttingen: Vandenhoeck & Ruprecht, 1961²) = *The Praise of God in the Psalms*, tr. by K. R. Krim (Richmond: John Knox Press, 1965) ; *idem*, "Struktur und Geschichte der Klage im Alten Testament," *ZAW* LXVI (1954) 44-80 = his *Forschung am Alten Testament* (TB 24, Munich: Chr. Kaiser, 1964) 266-305; J. W. Wevers, "A Study in the Form-Criticism of Individual Complaint Psalms," *VT* VI (1956) 80-96; G. Widengren, *The Accadian and Hebrew Psalms of Lamentation as Religious Documents* (Stockholm: Bokförlags Aktiebolaget Thule, 1937) ; H. W. Wolff, "Der Aufruf zur Volksklage," *ZAW* LXXVI (1964) 48-65.

Gunkel's fourfold design of complaint psalms and thanksgiving songs still is fundamental to all discussions of the matter today. He distinguished between individual and communal complaints, provoked by personal or collective danger and distress and performed in appropriate worship services at the temple. Correspondence of genres seems to be very reasonable and in agreement with what we know about ancient (and modern for that matter) cultic practices. Unfortunately our OT source material is not so unambiguous that we can take things·for granted.

A strange phenomenon, to begin with, is the fact that in the

V

extant body of material we realize a great preponderance of individual prayers. There are in the OT Psalter about fifty complaint psalms of the private type and nearly twenty thanksgiving songs to go with them according to Gunkel's count. Communal complaints, although clearly attested in terms of structure and life setting by quite a number of OT passages, comprise less than ten specimens in the book of Psalms, and communal thanksgivings pretty much merge with the hymnic genre (cf. Gunkel-Begrich, *Einleitung*, 314-323; F. Crüsemann, *Hymnus*, 202-206, see below section 6). Looking, then, at the four genres at hand it is certainly impressive to see the large number of psalms destined to serve the needs of individuals. Most form critics so far have been overly fascinated by the communal or national aspects of Israel's faith. Following Gunkel they dealt with hymns and congregational songs in the first place and attribute to this order of things quite a bit of theological significance. A better starting point is individual prayers and their settings.

Of course this view can be maintained only after an express refutation of that contrary opinion which seeks to eliminate all "private" psalms from the OT scene. Mainly, the Scandinavian and British scholars referred to above as "ceremonialists" hold that all complaints and thanksgivings which on the surface use the personal "I" were originally national psalms sung by the king. He, representing the corporate personality, the soul of his people, would stand up before Yahweh in national services, probably at the New Year celebrations. Only later on, after the kingdom had vanished in Israel, so this opinion goes, did such psalms become "democratized" and handed over to "everyman" for "private" use. Birkeland went to the extreme in defending this view, and Mowinckel in his later years followed his pupil rather closely (cf. Mowinckel, *The Psalms*, I, 225-246).

Granted, there is a whole cluster of presuppositions and observations which make up the fabric of this collective scheme. Nevertheless it may be sufficient to point to a few cardinal errors in order to establish the legitimacy of dealing with individual prayers in the OT psalter. For example, the "enemy" in OT complaint songs by no means can be construed as a national foe in the majority of cases. The "king" cannot simply be taken out of royal psalms like Pss 20, 45, or 110 and transplanted into all the other texts. Most important, worship services for individuals in the OT are unquestionable. Also there is positive evidence from many other cultures that the official and national cult quite often goes side by side with the more "private" rites (*rites de passage,* etc.) without too much interference or interdependence.

A) . Individual Complaints and Thanksgivings

Form critics of differing schools of thought show significant agreement regarding the structure and formal elements of the psalms to be discussed here. According to Gunkel individual complaints may roughly display the following outline and setup (we have to keep in mind, however, that there is no fixed order to these texts and that each element may be more or less elaborate within one poem or at times altogether missing) :

1) Invocation (usually including an appellation to Yahweh and initial plea) cf. Pss 6:2, 26:1, 38:2.
2) Complaints (description of suffering, reproachful questions, etc.) cf. Pss 22:1-9, 13-19, 38:1-9, 11-15, 18, 20-21, 69:2b-5, 8-13, 20-22.
3) Plea or petition for help (usually imperatives: "help, save me, wake up, have mercy," etc.) cf. Pss 3:8, 26:11, 57:2, 86:2.
4) Condemnation of enemies or imprecation against wrong doers; cf. Pss 35:1-8, 69:23-29, 109:6-20.
5) Affirmation of confidence (Gunkel considered this part as the outstanding example of a more general category of elements, namely the "motives for Yahweh's intervention"; cf. Gunkel-Begrich, *Einleitung,* 231-232. But the general label is hardly of any use, for, in fact, all the form elements thus brought together can be aligned with either plea or complaint), cf. Pss 13:6, 22:10-11, 31:2-6; 142:6.
6) Confession of sins or assertion of innocence; cf. Pss 26:4-6, 51:5-7.
7) Acknowledgment of divine response; vow or pledge: cf. Pss 6:10, 7:18, 56:13, 109:30.
8) Hymnic elements, blessings; cf. Pss 5:5-7, 31:20-25, 69:33-37.

Reading through Gunkel's and Begrich's treatment of the matter (cf. Gunkel-Begrich, *Einleitung,* 212-250) , one cannot help but be amazed at the immense variety of forms, the proliferation of formulaic expressions (cf. R. C. Culley, *Oral Formulaic Language in the Biblical Psalms* [Toronto: Toronto University Press, 1967]) , and syntactical structures. It is equally astonishing to see Gunkel's mind at work bringing about a plausible and comprehensible order without pressing the material into rigid patterns. Gunkel was never a formalist; he always paid due tribute to life

V

conditions. In fact he was bent on recovering the *Sitz im Leben* in as vivid and colorful details as possible. So up to this day there is little reason to take issue with his formal analysis of the individual complaints. Only minor questions may be raised. Is it really necessary to distinguish between "wish" and "plea" the way he does on the strength of different Hebrew grammatical forms (imperative versus jussive) ? (See Gunkel-Begrich, *Einleitung*, 218-229.) "These wishes contain all the motifs we already found in the request forms" (*op. cit.*, 224). Both forms furthermore can serve the same end within the complaint structure. So, why keep them segregated that strictly? Or another question already raised above: Should we retain the general category of "motives for Yahweh's intervention" which seems so vague and elusive? While such minor corrections without doubt are necessary, Gunkel's analysis of the individual complaint must still stand basically uncontested. Scholars as different as G. Widengren, H.-J. Kraus (*Psalmen*, I, XLV-XLVI), S. Mowinckel (*The Psalms*, II, 9-11), C. Westermann (*ZAW* LXVI [1954] 48 = TB 24, 270), L. Sabourin (*Psalms*, II, 1-4), A. Deissler (*Psalmen*, I, 16-18), J. W. Wevers, and many others are almost unanimous in following Gunkel's lead in so far as structural observations are concerned.

The same holds true in a small degree for the individual thanksgiving songs. Gunkel's analysis here has come under more critical scrutiny (cf. C. Westermann, *Praise*; F. Mand, *ZAW* LXX [1958] 185-199; W. Beyerlin, *ZAW* LXXIX [1967] 208-224; and especially F. Crüsemann, 210-284) and has been sharpened and modified to a certain extent. Nevertheless, his basic insights still hold true.

Gunkel quite correctly pointed out: "It is this genre in particular which we are able to locate with complete certainty in its original setting, the worship service" (Gunkel-Begrich, *Einleitung*, 265). There are clear records in the OT showing Israelites who bring their offerings after being heard and helped by God. Before or during presentation of the offering, they recited their thanksgiving prayer (cf. I Sam 1:24-2:10). There is such an intricate connection between thanksgiving and preceding complaint ceremonies that occasionally it seems thanks are offered immediately after the complaint has been "filed" and Yahweh's favorable answer received. The connecting link in this situation between the complaint and the thanksgiving is the *Heilsorakel*, the salvation oracle (cf. J. Begrich, "Das priesterliche Heilsorakel," *ZAW* LII [1934] 81-92 = his *Gesammelte Studien zum Alten Testa-*

ment [TB 21, Munich: Chr. Kaiser, 1964] 217-231), and Ps 22:23-32 is a telling example which should also warn us not to draw the dividing line between thanksgiving song and hymn too sharply (cf. also Ps 92 and Crüsemann's work which attempts to clarify the matter).

The following are the structural elements of the personal thanksgiving song as Gunkel visualized them:

1) Call to sing, give thanks, etc. (directed either to the supplicant's own self or to the participants in the ritual; akin to the hymnic introduction); cf. Pss 30:2, 107:1, 118:1-4.

2) Account of trouble and salvation (narration to the worshipping community, usually talks of the great danger to which the supplicant was about to succumb and of Yahweh's merciful help); cf. Pss 18:5-20, 30:3-4, 9-12, 40:3-4.

3) Praise of Yahweh the savior; cf. Pss 18:2-4, 47-49, 40:6, 118:28.

4) Announcement of sacrifice; cf. Pss 66:13-15, Jonah 2:10.

5) Blessings upon participants; cf. Pss 40:5, 118:8-9, 26.

6) Hymnic elements (general praises of Yahweh) cf. Pss 30:5-6, 138:2, 4-6.

For this basic structure, reference must be made first of all to Gunkel-Begrich, *Einleitung*, 267-274. For modifications of this scheme one has to turn to C. Westermann. Presupposing that "the 'categories' of the Psalms are not first of all literary or cultic in nature" but "basic modes of that which occurs when man turns to God with words," or "basic occurrences" (*The Praise*, 153), he resolutely merges personal hymns and personal thanksgivings (as well as the corresponding communal genres) into one new type (18), and with equal resolution divides it again into two new categories, namely, the declarative and the descriptive psalms of praise (102-142). Crüsemann on the other hand refutes Westermann's efforts and postulates two original types of thanksgivings distinguished by their usage of "thou" and "he" styles respectively when addressing Yahweh (cf. *Hymnus*, 225-267). Those differences supposedly reflect two stages in the thanksgiving ceremony, the address of the worshipping community *before* the sacrifice (the "he" style) and the address to Yahweh when the sacrifice is offered (the "thou" style). In spite of these and other contributions Gunkel's structural arrangement of the thanksgiving song of the individual may still serve as the starting point for our discussion.

While the structural problems of individual complaints and

thanksgivings are not too severe, a heated debate has been going on since the days of Gunkel as to the proper occasions and life settings to be attributed to these prayers. What precisely were the cultic ceremonies in which these texts were performed? Who were the performers and participants? Several theories have been advanced, of which the two main types will be sketched here. They both of course refer initially to the complaint psalm.

We have to leave Gunkel behind at this point, for in his opinion the extant texts already are far removed from their original cultic situation. The complaint psalms in the OT, he assumed, had been composed by a later, more "spiritual" and less "cultic" generation ("Spiritualization" ever since has been a catchword among continental form critics, possibly because of their subconscious distrust of all cultic affairs, cf. G. von Rad, *Theologie des AT¹*, I, 400-405 = *Old Testament Theology*, I, 402-408; H. J. Hermisson, *Sprache und Ritus im altisraelitischen Kult* [WMANT 19, Neukirchen: Neukirchener Verlag, 1965].) But there are scholars who have overcome their aversion to the cult. Insofar as they believe in personal OT prayers and rites they agree that the individual complaints were answering deadly perils against personal life and well-being such as sickness, slander, persecution, and misfortune. Most experts favor one or the other of these as the cause for the individual prayer.

Mowinckel was the first to publish a detailed situational analysis of the personal complaint. For the most part he considered these prayers as psalms of sickness (cf. *Psalmenstudien I*). Although he later restated his case (cf. *The Psalms*, I, 225-246; II, 1-25), hazards to physical or mental health remain for him predominant motivations for personal prayer. Among those hazards, less known to modern man, are evil deeds performed by word of mouth, by secret or open curse and slanderous talk. All of these in ancient times were held to be contributory causes of sickness and misfortune. Mowinckel in particular singled out the phrase *pōᵃlê 'āwen*, evildoers (cf. Pss 6:9, 59:3, 8, 64:3-7) and their machinations. Sickness could be inflicted by sorcerers, and the only way to counteract their evil deeds was by supplication to Yahweh (for excellent comparative material from a far-away culture, cf. R. Fortune, *Sorcerers of Dobu* [New York: E. P. Dutton, 1932]). Complaint psalms of the individual, then, are integral liturgical parts of a ritual performed at the request of people suffering from severe ills, especially in cases where an evil spell had been diagnosed as the root of the trouble. Thanksgiving songs which were enjoined when a sick person had been healed belong to the ritual of the thanksgiving sacrificial service. Mowinckel's view has much to commend it and in fact has been taken into account by most exegetes with more or less enthusiasm as far as the sorcery part is concerned.

H. Schmidt discovered another location for individual complaints, which he tended to overstress at times. There are psalms which can rightly be called "protestations of innocence" (cf. Pss 7, 17, 26). Supported by chance references in the OT, like I Kings 8:30-32, Schmidt concluded that persons indicted, imprisoned, or sentenced subjected themselves to some kind of ordeal (cf. Num 5:11-31) and were given a chance to appeal to Yahweh in prayer. Mesmerized by his idea, he found numerous vestiges of judicial procedures. According to him, even the psalms of sickness might have carried this additional feature; the sick person being shunned and even accused for his alleged contact with evil deeds or powers.

L. Delekat and W. Beyerlin each in his own way carry the judicial aspects of the individual complaints some steps further. Delekat considers most texts of this genre to be mural inscriptions scribbled on the temple wall by people who sought refuge in the sanctuary (cf. Deut 19:1-13). Complaints and thanksgivings added later even tell him exactly how the refugee subsequently fared. He held his "sleep of incubation" in the temple, received oracles, experienced dreams, had to undergo ordeals, and was finally hired and put under contract as a temple worker. Beyerlin is more elusive and general in his descriptions. He talks about an institution attached to the temple which promulgated and enforced divine jurisdiction in special cases. The complaints of the individual partly are to be understood as appeals to this *kultische Gottesgerichtsinstitution*, a divine court of justice at the temple.

The "judicial" approach to the complaints of the individual also has something to recommend it. After being rid of some hypothetical exaggerations, especially those of Delekat, one cannot help but admit that "protestations of innocence" may have been used in worship services or ordeal ceremonies which were considered as appeals to Yahweh the supreme judge. What kind of "institution" really acted as recipient of the plea or took action to implement a divine sentence is hard to tell. Possibly there was no one but a priest leading a given complaint ceremony, and all the judicial terms were nothing but profane imagery adapted to a religious rite. And yet, the judicial aspect should not be neglected;

V

it deserves notice along with the "medical" type which Mowinckel inaugurated. Most scholars actually regard both explanations as legitimate, and there are numerous variations and nuances to each of them as well as various combinations and exegetical operations on every single text (cf. H.-J. Kraus, A. Deissler, A. Weiser, E. A. Leslie, L. Sabourin, Chr. Barth, J. W. Wevers, et al.).

B. Royal Complaints and Thanksgivings

A few remarks concerning royal complaints and thanksgivings may be in order at this point because we do not want to classify the royal psalms as an altogether new and separate genre. Gunkel and Begrich did (cf. *Einleitung*, 140-171), and most commentators and exegetes accept their view (cf. bibliographical references above in section 3 and K. R. Crim, *The Royal Psalms*). Gunkel himself, however, knew quite well that the royal psalms are no homogeneous group but songs of different origin and function which happen to be used with royal festivities (*Einleitung*, 146-147). Therefore royal complaints and thanksgivings should be placed in between individual and communal prayers of that type. The court had adapted such psalms for its own needs to be used in royal worship services. We may say that all the extant psalms which are clearly designed to be spoken by or for the king and which can best be explained against the background of a ritual petition or thanksgiving to Yahweh may be claimed as royal complaints, petitions, or thanksgivings. This interpretation, of course, is in direct contrast to that which rates all royal ceremonies as first and much older than "private" rites. For Israel we may safely assume, however, that popular use of complaint and thanksgiving prayers has a longer tradition and that the masters of ceremony at the northern and southern court drew from this tradition.

In the area of complaint, petition, and thanksgiving we find a few good examples: Pss 18, 20, 21, 72, 89, 101, 132, 144. Careful analysis of each text would reveal that a great number of structural elements, formulaic expressions and motifs from "popular" counterparts have gone into the royal psalms of petition and thanksgiving (cf. most of all the commentaries by Gunkel, Schmidt, Leslie, Weiser, Kraus, Sabourin, et al.). On the other hand the influence of imperial court tradition of the ancient Near East can be detected. Yahweh's theophany (cf. Ps 18) certainly was not to be expected to honor some plain Israelite; supplication for the king and thanksgiving for him (cf. Pss 20; 21), with due reverence for the anointed, are reminiscent of oriental court etiquette; references to the king's enthronement (cf. Ps 89; 101) reflect ritual features of this important event, as well as the divine promise to the new king (Ps 89:20-38) and the royal oath (Ps 101). The presence of hymnic elements also may point to the exuberance and national dimension of court festivities. Still, the royal psalms should be seen in conjunction with their "popular" counterparts.

C. Communal Complaints and Thanksgivings

Communal complaints in their structure and setting are comparable to individual prayers of the same sort, the basic difference being that now "all kinds of community distress: war, captivity, plague, drought, famine . . ." (Gunkel-Begrich, *Einleitung*, 118) are prompting religious activities. A day of fasting is called (cf. Judg 20:26-28, 21:2-3; Jer. 14:2; Neh 9:1), sacrifices are prepared, and communal complaints are sung by choirs, priests, or all the congregation, perhaps in a repetitious ceremony which may have included many rites of which we no longer have knowledge. The contents of the communal prayer we know from the individual complaint: An invocation, a complaint, plea, or petition, an affirmation of confidence, a confession of guilt or protestation of innocence, and hymnic elements. The main formal distinction between the two genres is the fact that collective complaints usually speak in the first person plural, and quite often the national calamity is clearly referred to (cf. Pss 44, 74). This is not to deny that there may be communal complaints in the "I" form (cf. Mowinckel, *The Psalms*, I, 225-246). Because the situation of danger, threat, and fear is so much alike whether one person or a whole community is affected, there is a good chance that elements and motifs of the individual and communal liturgies may have been interchanged or mutually influenced. Indeed we witness the same sort of wandering of texts in our hymnbooks and church services. Individual expressions of faith are used by a whole congregation, and communal poems may be read or sung by one person who includes himself in the "we" form of the text. In spite of all affinities between OT complaints, be it individual or collective, it should be taken for granted that the "I" psalms are basically personal in character and reflect services for an individual. Because communal complaints "are recognizable partly by the use of 'we,'

V

206

partly by the occasion which produced them" (Mowinckel, *The Psalms*, I, 194), scholars in large measure agree as to the concrete texts which are to be so named: Pss 44; 58; 60; 74; 79; 80; 83. Even so, a more substantial group of psalms remains under debate (cf. Sabourin, *Psalms*, II, 141-143).

About congregational thanksgivings there is no need to say very much more. Since it is perfectly clear that there were in Israel public fasting days with complaint services, there is no reason whatsoever to doubt that public thanksgiving days were also observed. It is especially awkward to argue from a dogmatic viewpoint as follows: Israel continuously praised her Lord; the eternal praise was interrupted by complaint days only in time of grave danger; there was no need to celebrate special thanksgivings, as it was entirely sufficient to resume the normal praise after the crisis had been overcome (thus, in all seriousness, Crüsemann, *Hymnus*, 204-206, following von Rad and Westermann). We may safely assume that special thanksgiving days were held in Israel in the ordinary course of events. It is an entirely different problem whether or not these special days "gave birth" to a separate genre of psalms. Judging from the evidence preserved in the OT Psalter we indeed may be pessimistic. Only Pss 66:8-12, 67, 124, 129 have a chance to qualify as national thanksgiving songs. But the OT, we must remember, preserves only a tiny selection of all the songs actually used in the long history of Israel. And, furthermore, hymns proper could very well take the place and function of a thanksgiving song in a day of feasting and joy over Yahweh's help.

6. Hymns of Praise

W. F. Albright, "A Catalogue of Early Hebrew Lyric Poems (Ps 68) ," *HUCA* XXIII (1950/51) 1-39; J. Blenkinsopp, "Ballad Style and Psalm Style in the Song of Deborah," *Bib* XLII (1961) 61-76; F. Crüsemann, *Studien zur Formgeschichte von Hymnus und Danklied in Israel* (WMANT 32, Neukirchen: Neukirchener Verlag, 1969) ; A. Deissler, "Zur Datierung und Situierung der 'kosmischen' Hymnen Pss 8; 19; 29," *Festschrift H. Junker (Lex tua veritas)*, ed. by H. Gross and F. Mussner (Trier: Paulinus-Verlag, 1961) 47-58; T. E. Fretheim, "Psalm 132: A Form-Critical Study," *JBL* LXXXVI (1967) 289-300; T. H. Gaster, "Psalm 45," *JBL* LXXIV (1955) 239-251; H. L. Ginsberg, "A Phoenician Hymn in the Psalter," *Atti del XIX. Congresso Internazionale degli Orientalisti Roma-1935* (Rome: G. Bardi, 1938) 472-476; J. Gray, "The Kingship of God in the Prophets and Psalms," *VT* XI (1961) 1-29; K. Koch, "Denn seine Güte währet ewiglich," *EvTh* XXI (1961) 531-544; H.-J. Kraus, *Die Königsherrschaft Gottes im Alten Testament* (BHT 13, Tübingen: J. C. B. Mohr, 1951) ; L. Krinetzki, "Zur Poetik und Exegese von Psalm 48," *BZ* IV (1960) 70-97; E. Lipinski, *La royauté de Yahwé dans la poésie et le culte de l'ancien Israël* (Brussel: Koninklijke Academie, 1965) ; *idem*, *Le Poème royal du Psaume LXXXIX, 1-5. 20-38* (CRB 6, Paris: J. Gabalda, 1967) ; J. Morgen-

stern, "The Cultic Setting of the Enthronement Psalms," *HUCA* XXV (1964)
1-42 ; S. Mowinckel, *Der achtundsechzigste Psalm* (ANVAO II/1, Oslo: Jacob
Dybwad, 1953) ; J. Patterson, *Praises of Israel* (New York: Charles Scribner's
Sons, 1950) ; H. G. Reventlow, "Der Psalm 8," *Poetica I* (1967) 304-332; H. H.
Rowley, "The Text and Structure of Psalm 2," *JTS* XLII (1941) 143-154;
N. H. Snaith, *Hymns of the Temple* (London: SCM Press, 1951) ; W. S.
Towner, " 'Blessed be YHWH' and 'Blessed art thou, YHWH': The Modula-
tion of a Biblical Formula," *CBQ* XXX (1968) 386-399.

A hymn, in our understanding, is a "song of praise to God"
(Merriam-Webster), and not only the name but also the contents
of this definition have come down to us in the stream of Greco-
Christian tradition. We think of melodious presentations, of
solemn and joyful crowds, of colorful clergy, festive congrega-
tions, lofty domes. Not many of the traits customary to us may
hold true when we discuss Israelite hymnody. What is even more
troublesome in form critical research is the fact that the term
"hymn" from the very beginning proved too general and too
vague and, on top of this, too heavily freighted with emotional
values. "The basic moods of these poems are enthusiasm, adoration, reverence, praise and laudation . . ." (Gunkel-Begrich, *Einleitung*, 68) . "The core of the hymn of praise is the consciousness
of the poet and congregation that they are standing face to face
with the Lord himself . . . and worshipping him with praise and
adoration" (Mowinckel, *The Psalms*, I, 81) .

A common stock of phrases and moods alone is not sufficient to
delineate a genre (this is Gunkel's own insight, cf. Gunkel-
Begrich, *Einleitung*, 22-23) . Westermann's futile search for some
"basic occurrence" beyond cultic affairs (cf. above, p. 187) only
proves that thus far the first condition of form critical investigation, namely to locate a recurring event which can be considered
the fountainhead of a literary genre, has not been fulfilled. For
the "hymn" does not imply any specific event of praise; it rather
encompasses a very wide range of possible occasions—weddings
and dedications, victories in battle, harvest times and seasonal
feasts, as well as spontaneous gatherings after a plague or drought
had come to an end. Therefore, form critics all along have been
wrestling with the "hymn" and the appropriate life situations.

Unfortunately, precise knowledge about the different festive occasions in Israel is hard to attain. Furthermore, we may be sure
that during the centuries feasts and their liturgies underwent substantial changes and that those texts which survived the process of
transmission to be incorporated into the OT had possibly migrated through a number of life settings (this is the grain of

V

truth in Beyerlin's attempt to redefine the concept of literary genre: cf. *Rettung*, 154-158).

In spite of all the difficulties at hand we should try to subdivide the general category of "hymn of praise" according to the specific situations to which each owes its existence instead of dealing with one broad group only. We keep in mind that indeed there is a certain common mood to all the hymns and that we may consider the following three-part structure as a kind of basic pattern which seems to fit most of the hymns preserved:

1) Call to praise (usually understood as an exhortation by a choir leader or the like to a group or the whole of the congregation)
2) Account of Yahweh's deeds or qualities (the body of the hymn may feature various styles and formulaic expressions) and
3) Conclusion (renewed call to praise; blessings; petitions; or other forms).

Again, this general structural analysis already suggested by Gunkel, has been widely adopted as valid (cf. Gunkel-Begrich, *Einleitung*, 38-58; Mowinckel, *The Psalms*, I, 81-89; Kraus, *Psalmen*, XLI-XLII; Sabourin, *Psalms*, 1, 181, etc.). If we take it as a working scheme and in addition ask for possible settings we may get a clearer picture of Israel's hymns.

A. Victory Songs

Cultic activities of any human group tend to be determined by seasonal needs. The OT festival calendars (cf. Ex 23:14-17, 34:22-23; Lev 23; Deut 16:1-7) make it perfectly clear that Israel was no exception to the general rule. Yahweh's people in Canaan adopted quite naturally the local seasonal cultic patterns and probably merged them with their own tradition. The fixed cycle of yearly events, however, does not extinguish spontaneous religious activities.

In the OT we find some beautiful examples of such spontaneous praise in the victory songs performed after a battle had been won. Ex 15:21 (cf. the short phrases in Judg 16:23-24) ; Judg 5:2-31 and Ps 68 are specimens of this type of hymn. What Crüsemann considers the most basic form of all genuinely Israelite hymn singing is located in this situation (*Hymnus*, 34).

> Sing to the Lord!
> Yea, he rose high!
> Horse and rider he threw into the sea! (Ex 15:21)

Two out of our three hymnic elements are present—the call to sing and the account of Yahweh's deeds (Hebrew *ki*, according to Crüsemann, does not introduce a mere appendix to the exhortation but as a deictic particle starts off the communal refrain). This is all there is to a hymn: In endless repetition, accompanied by drums and dancing (cf. Ex 15:20; Judg 11:34) and with terrific noise, the Israelites may have celebrated their small and big victories.

Of course, virtually all of this spontaneous poetry has been lost. There was nobody to take notes in ancient times. If some examples were preserved, the reason must be that they by some chance got into the stream of recurring events. Judges 5 for instance probably became part of the historical tradition put to memory; Ps 68, with its "spontaneous" verses 12-15, was drawn into the liturgy of some regular festival (cf. Ps 68:25-26) but may at some time have commemorated an historical event. The same may be true for Ex 15:21 in relation to Ex 15:1-19; and even Pss 118:15-16, 78:65-66, 18:33-49 may go back to some spontaneous lines composed and sung after victorious battles (thus Westermann, *BHHW*, III, 1790-1791). The other way around also may hold some truth: There is absolutely no reason to exclude the possibility that Israelite warriors (and their women-folk) in the course of victory celebrations did sing older hymns, even taken out of different contexts. (Soccer fans on the continent sometimes behave that way.)

We can think of more occasions in which spontaneous hymnic poetry was used to praise Yahweh: When the harvest was reaped in the fields or vineyards; when a caravan successfully returned home, etc. But we do not have sufficient information about such customs. The only other situation we can speak of with some certainty is the public thanksgiving ceremony in general (cf. above section 5 C). If there were festivities to celebrate deliverance from some evil, spontaneous hymns certainly may have been used. But again, poems historically unique and specific to the event are easily lost from tradition; fixed formulations expressing gratitude and adoration will usually suffice in such "emergencies."

B. Pilgrim Songs and Processional Hymns

Some hymns, it is quite obvious, were not sung by a congregation standing in a sanctuary but rather by people on the move. Whether performed during the pilgrimage to Jerusalem to attend

V

one of the major festivals or for some more private occasion, or during a procession around the holy city or the temple grounds, these hymns should be considered separately according to their specific life situation. We have to keep in mind, however, that again the borderline between different kinds of hymns may be uncertain and that the songs could be used across genre classification.

One of the earlier collections within the Psalter (Pss 120-134) preserves, in the psalm superscriptions, the memory of those "ascents" to Jerusalem (cf. C. C. Keet, *A Study of the Psalms of Ascent* [London: Mitre Press, 1969], a learned philological and historical treatise with little reference to form criticism; the superscriptions are discussed on pages 1-17). At least one of these psalms (Ps 122) is a true pilgrim song, as is Ps 84 (cf. Gunkel-Begrich, *Einleitung*, 309-311; H.-J. Kraus, *Psalmen*, II, 581-587; 838-842). Judging from just two examples little can be said about the specific structure of these psalms. However, within them the "moods" of the pilgrims are quite clear: They long for the holy city and the presence of Yahweh; they dwell on their strenuous journey and the joy of arriving at their destination. A direct formal outcome of these sentiments may be seen in their predilection for blessings and benedictions (cf. Pss 84:5-6, 122:6-9), the praise of city and temple (cf. Pss 84:2, 11; 122:3), and the description of personal longings (cf. Pss 84:3, 122:1). There are numerous other psalms which allude to such pilgrimages or betray the same sentiments (e.g. Pss 87, 121, 126; Is 2:3), so that the life setting "pilgrimage" should be recognized as the formative factor for a category of hymns.

Closely connected with either pilgrimage or local procession were the entrance liturgies in Pss 15 and 24. Arriving groups would ritually inquire about the conditions of being admitted into the sanctuary (cf. S. Mowinckel, *Le Décalogue* [Paris: L. Alcan, 1927]; K. Koch, "Tempeleinlassliturgien und Dekaloge"; L. Delekat, *Asylie*, chapter III/2). Finally, processions also played a great role in the ancient Israelite cult (cf. II Sam 6), and a good number of psalms belonging to different genres refer to them (e.g. Pss 42:5, 55:15, 118:19-20). Pss 48, 68 and 132 may be named as possible examples of processional hymns (cf. W. O. E. Oesterley, *The Sacred Dance* [London: Cambridge University Press, 1923]; A. Alt, "Die Wallfahrt von Sichem nach Bethel," *In piam memoriam Alexander von Bulmerincq* [Riga: Ernst Plates, 1938] = *Kleine Schriften zur Geschichte des Volkes Israel* I [Munich: C. H. Beck, 1953] 79-88; S. Mowinckel, *The Psalms,* I, 169-182).

Pilgrimages and processions, religious communities on the move, of course are tied to those cultic affairs proper which are happening at the sanctuary. They deserve, however, to be recognized as special settings for a distinct category of hymns. We can easily imagine that psalms first composed for one particular pageant became adapted to other occasions and even incorporated into the liturgy of the festival itself (cf. the Zion hymns, below section E).

C. Hymns of the Festival Cycle

We possess some knowledge of Israel's main yearly festivals, namely those three seasonal assemblies which very probably had been taken over from the Canaanites (cf. R. de Vaux, *Les institutions de l'Ancien Testament,* II [Paris: Cerf, 1960] 383-413 = *Ancient Israel: Its Life and Institutions,* tr. by J. McHugh [New York: McGraw-Hill, 1961] 484-506). Precise historical developments and liturgical details of these celebrations are unknown. All we can be reasonably sure of is that the seasonal pattern of feasts set the stage for most of the hymns preserved in the OT Psalter. And a second point is even more important: The oldest cultic calendars found in the OT (cf. Ex 23:14-17; H.-J. Kraus, *Gottesdienst in Israel* [Munich: Chr. Kaiser, 1962²] 40-88 = *Worship in Israel,* tr. by G. Buswell [Richmond: John Knox Press, 1966] 26-76) already betray the complex traditions which were combined in Israel's cult. We discover traits of agricultural as well as of nomadic ways of life; the intertwining of motifs is particularly apparent in the Passover-Mazzot tradition (cf. E. Kutsch, "Erwägungen zur Geschichte der Passahfeier und des Massotfestes," *ZTK* LV [1958] 1-35).

We cannot possibly discuss the difficult problem of whether or not it is legitimate to distinguish in OT scholarship between a religious mentality which was mythical in character and bent on preserving or revitalizing all "natural" powers and Israel's faith which kept in touch with the historic acts of Yahweh. Let it be sufficient here to note that both aspects reflect fundamental human needs and that both are integral parts of OT hymnic tradition. We use this distinction only because it is impossible any more to attribute the individual texts of the hymns to this or that one of the three Israelite festivals.

V

After settling in Canaan one of the main concerns of the Israelite farming communities had to be rain and fertility of the fields. Pss 65 and 67 are thanksgiving hymns after bountiful harvests; they may have belonged to either of the old ingathering festivals (cf. E. Kutsch, *op. cit.*). Which hymns were intoned when the sowing season started we do not know. Maybe Ps 126:5 is a quotation from this kind of opening hymn. The god Yahweh who proved his creative powers by providing a good year for the farmers was of course the same god who once "had made heaven and earth" (cf. Pss 8, 19A, 33, 104, 136:1-9). Creation "once upon a time" is reexperienced in nature's growth and crops. Mowinckel's idea therefore that creation was dramatically reenacted at some point in the festive cycle (he prefers the New Year celebrations) is quite plausible. Yahweh had become for Israel a God who also gave "grain, wine and oil" (Hos 2:10). He was responsible for the fertility of the fields and herds. The agricultural festivals celebrated his powers; the hymns sung praised him as a fertility deity. Small wonder that numerous features and formulations used in neighboring cults were adopted by Israel to glorify Yahweh. Egyptian, Babylonian, and Canaanite influences have been increasingly discovered in Israelite hymns of this type. Most ancient Near Eastern cults knew one deity which procured growth and fertility, which commanded the winds and weathers, which defeated the primeval chaotic powers, etc. Israel's indebtedness to the older traditions of her neighbors has always been admitted by all form critics, and it has been corroborated by outstanding Ugaritic scholars (cf. G. R. Driver, C. H. Gordon, J. Aistleitner, M. Pope, M. Dahood, et al.; cf. e.g. the discussion of Ps 29 by Ginsberg, and in the commentaries).

The fact of "foreign" influence on Israel's hymnody does not entitle us to draw a line between forms or genres which have been contaminated and those which remain totally Israelite. Crüsemann, for example, in his painstaking analyses wants to separate hymns of imperative provenience, participle style, and direct address forms (cf. *Hymnus* 135-152, especially 153: "Hymnic participles . . . . in general describe such divine acts as are materializing in creation and natural events."), restricting the concerns for fertility to one kind only. Distinctions of this sort are dogmatic in character; they are not tenable because they are not provable. Concerning the forms used in the "nature" hymns we have to stay with the observation of Gunkel and Mowinckel, namely that the songs in their praising parts use a variety of expressions side by side in the very same function, and that each "composition itself is very far from following any set pattern or schedule" (S. Mowinckel, *The Psalms*, I, 88).

Yahweh was Israel's God; his faculties and qualities were praised at the major festivals. The praise centered on Yahweh's providing fertility and produce, but also to him who revealed himself in terrifying phenomena, in lightning, storm, fire, and clouds and who commanded the forces of war and pestilence. Yahweh's deeds only happened in relation to his people; that is why the hymns tell of his saving acts in history (cf. Pss 66:1-12; 77, 78, 105, 114, 115, 126, 135, 136). From other parts of the OT it is known that the seasonal cycle, if it did not feature such motifs from the beginning, later attracted historical reminiscences. We can recognize in the "historical" psalms the counterparts to the "nature" hymns. They both have their original setting in the great Israelite festivals which determined the yearly cultic activities of the people. All efforts to introduce basic differences between these types of hymns are of little avail. This is true for Mowinckel's distinction between hymns celebrating general and others praising special deeds of Yahweh (cf. Mowinckel, *The Psalms*, I, 85) as well as for Westermann's artificial operation to gain "declarative" and "descriptive" psalms of praise (cf. C. Westermann, *The Praise*, 31: descriptive praise "praises God for a specific deed").

D. Yahweh Kingship Hymns and Royal Psalms

Few psalms have received more attention among biblical scholars and prompted greater changes in psalm research than the small group of "enthronement" hymns—Pss 47, 93, 96-99 (see above, section 3). They form a distinct and separate group in the Psalter in that their structure, imagery, and motifs are very much alike. They all center around Yahweh's enthronement as the universal king over all the nations. (Cf. the one central phrase: *jahweh malak*, "Yahweh has become king," Pss 93:1; 97:1 and the very description of his ascension in Ps 47:6. In spite of D. Michel, "Studien zu den sogenannten Thronbesteigungspsalmen" *VT* VI [1956] 40-68, these passages speak of a real enthronement; they are not merely describing an eternal state of affairs.) Because of their characteristic features we are simply compelled to concede that these psalms had a special life setting; a festival which Mowinckel and the "patternists" claim was intimately linked with

V
214

the New Year's celebrations. We are uncertain as to the date of this festival of Yahweh's assuming regal authority over the whole world, but a festive occasion of this sort must have existed in Israel. Babylonian parallels indeed point to the New Year's celebration; Ugaritic mythology seems to strengthen the argument. We leave the dating open and just state that the Yahweh kingship psalms are sufficient evidence for an Israelite festival which praised Yahweh's taking power over the nations and which probably was tied to the seasonal cycle of cultic activities. If the day of "enthronement" was part of some other agricultural cultic event, it certainly has brought forth this particular genre of hymns we mentioned above. The best summaries of all the problems involved are found in S. Mowinckel, *The Psalms*, I, 106-192 and A. R. Johnson, *Sacral Kingship* (cf. above section 3). For some corrective points of view one should consult K. H. Bernhardt, *Königsideologie* (cf. above section 3) and W. Schmidt, *Königtum Gottes in Ugarit und Israel* (BZAW 80, Berlin: A Töpelmann, 1961).

The main form elements of the psalms of Yahweh's kingship are (and this pattern fits perfectly the general hymnic structure having been adapted to the singular event in minor details):

1) Exhortation to praise, directed to the nations and nature; c. Pss. 47:2, 7; 96:1-3, 7-9; 98:4-8.

2) Praise of Yahweh as the new world ruler (including: praise of his strength, Pss 47:3, 99:4; glory, Ps 96:6; justice, Ps 97:6; victory, Ps 47:4; epiphany, Ps 97:2-5; former deeds for Israel, Ps 99:6-7; accepted acts of salvation, Ps 97:7, etc.).

The hymns belonging to this type truly show cosmic dimensions, and this must reflect the outlook and content of the festivities behind the text. It is perfectly clear that Israel learned to praise Yahweh in this way from her neighbors, but, as Mowinckel has adroitly pointed out, the changes which the ancient Near Eastern kingship ideology underwent in Israel are equally remarkable. No trace is left, for instance, of the mythical story of a dying and resurrected deity within our psalms (cf. Mowinckel, *The Psalms*, I, 136-140).

The so-called "royal psalms" pertaining to a human ruler, for the most part the Davidic king in Jerusalem, are only loosely connected with the hymns celebrating Yahweh's kingship. For, as was pointed out above p. 205, we may safely assume (even under the protest of quite a number of eminent scholars) that the needs of the royal court in terms of liturgical items and texts were met partly by using popular prototypes and partly by drawing from neighboring oriental court etiquette. The former way may hold true for complaint psalms and thanksgiving in particular, while the latter may have been followed for ceremonial enthronizations and the like. This is the point where we might find some connection with the Yahweh kingship hymns: Taking office certainly was no mean affair for an heir to David's throne (cf. Pss 2, 110, 89, 101). He was the "son of God" (II Sam 7:14; Ps 2:7); he may have taken the place of Yahweh in ritual drama, as the "patternists" strongly suggest, or he may have celebrated his own coronation in conjunction with the New Year festival of Yahweh either yearly or at the beginning of his reign. In any case, some of the glory of Yahweh's own enthronement seems to reflect on that of his anointed, and the coronation hymns bear witness to this. That the wedding song Ps 45 should be indicative of a sacred marriage, according to Babylonian ritual, is hard to believe; we would prefer rather to interpret it as a piece out of a real wedding ceremony. (For a different interpretation of the royal psalms as reflections of a festival of the "election of Zion and of David" and a subsequent understanding of the Yahweh kingship developing from a celebration of Yahweh's eternal kingship with only the ark moving into city and temple, see H.-J. Kraus, *Die Königsherrschaft Gottes im Alten Testament*.)

E. Zion Songs

When discussing the pilgrim songs (above, section 6 B) we touched upon hymns which hailed the holy city as Yahweh's sacred dwelling place. A small group of texts, viz, Pss. 46, 48, 76 have been set apart by virtually all form critics from all the other psalms referring to Zion (cf. Gunkel-Begrich, *Einleitung*, 80-82; S. Mowinckel, *The Psalms*, I, 90; L. Sabourin, *Psalms*, I, 230-243). Although various scholars would add to the three poems mentioned one or more related songs (e.g. Pss 84, 87, 122, 132, etc.) we will restrict ourselves to the examples which are most characteristic and recognized by all experts in the field.

The formal structure of Pss 46, 48, and 76 betrays just one conspicuous deviation from the hymn structure in general: a proper introit ("exhortation to praise") is missing (Gunkel). This may be accidental, because the texts do have an occasional address to the congregation (cf. Pss 46:9; 76:12). The body of the

V

hymn celebrates Yahweh, Israel's powerful God, who has taken his abode on Mount Zion which is likened to a mythical sacred mountain (cf. Ps 48:3). Zion and Jerusalem thus become the invincible fortress of Yahweh and his people. The praise of Yahweh is expressed in various ways: as an affirmation of confidence (Ps 46:2-8), in direct-address form (Ps 76:8: "But, thou, terrible art thou! . . ."), as well as in third person formulations (Ps 48:2: "Great is the Lord and greatly to be praised"). What makes these psalms so extraordinary, therefore, is not their formal structure but their content. They all speak of a kind of primeval attack upon the holy city, of Yahweh fighting back against the evil powers and securing victory (cf. G. von Rad, *Theologie des Alten Testaments*, II [Munich: Chrs. Kaiser, 1960] 166-179 = *Old Testament Theology*, II, tr. by D. M. G. Stalker [New York: Harper & Row, 1965] 155-169). This fact, together with some signs of special rites to be performed in connection with the hymn singing (e.g. Ps 48:13-14), has sparked the idea that there must have been some peculiar festive occasion celebrated in the Zion songs.

It is the life setting which again is most important in determining a genre of psalms. Unfortunately we do not know about any regular Zion festival outside of these psalms. Speculations which find some support in archaic texts such as Gen 14:18 (Melchizedek of Salem! cf. Ps 110:4) assume that the sacred traditions of Jerusalem were taken over by the Israelites when David took possession of this Canaanite city. One essential part of the pre-Israelite cult then would have been a Zion festival centering around an ancient belief in a sacred mountain and the god's eternal presence. In the light of these theories, G. Wanke's suggestion that the Zion songs are exilic or postexilic in origin would seem rather improbable (cf. G. Wanke, *Die Zionstheologie der Korachiten* [BZAW 97, Berlin: A Töpelmann, 1966]). For an extensive discussion of the Jerusalem cultic traditions, see H. Schmid, "Jahwe und die Kulttraditionen von Jerusalem," *ZAW* LXVII (1955) 168-197.

Even if we take into consideration a possible Zion festival which, however, cannot now be located in the seasonal cycle of cultic festivities, the problem of how to interpret the Zion hymns has still not been solved. It is reasonably clear that Israelite beliefs have merged with Canaanite traditions. But the very intention of the psalms remains an enigma. Historical interpretations of attacking nations (Krinetzki), the cult dramatic understanding

(Mowinckel), and an eschatological view (Gunkel) are in dissonance. Mowinckel still seems to have opened up the most likely avenue to grasp the meaning of these hymns.

Hymn singing, we may conclude, in Israel as well as among most other people, belongs to communal cultic festivals. This does not preclude the possibility that congregational hymns could also be used in rites which served the needs of individual persons. But, on the whole, we are dealing with collective praises of Yahweh, when trying to understand OT hymns. While the formal structure of all the hymns is plain enough, and while the moods of joy, exuberance, and adoration are to be met in all types of hymns, the real distinctions can be made only when we get some notion of the original setting of a given psalm or, better, group of psalms. We need to know more about Israel's feasts in order to be more confident of the life situations of the hymns.

7. Didactic or Wisdom Psalms

A. Deissler, *Psalm 119 (118) und seine Theologie* (Munich: Karl Zink, 1955) ; W. G. Lambert, *Babylonian Wisdom Literature* (London: Oxford University Press, 1960) ; S. Mowinckel, "Psalms and Wisdom," *VTS* III (1955) 204-224; R. E. Murphy, "A Consideration of the Classification 'Wisdom Psalms'," *VTS* IX (1963) 156-157; *idem,* "The Interpretation of Old Testament Wisdom Literature," *Inter* XXIII (1969) 289-301; G. von Rad, *Weisheit in Israel* (Neukirchen: Neukirchener Verlag, 1970) ; H. Reinelt, *Die altorientalische und biblische Weisheit und ihr Einfluss auf den Psalter* (dissertation, Freiburg, 1966) ; H. Ringgren, "Einige Bemerkungen zum LXXIII. Psalm," *VT* III (1953) 265-272; P. W. Skehan, "Borrowings from the Psalms in the Book of Wisdom," *CBQ* X (1948) 384-397; E. Würthwein, "Erwägungen zu Psalm 73," *Festschrift für Alfred Bertholet* (Tübingen: J. C. B. Mohr, 1950) 532-549 = his *Wort und Existenz: Studien zum Alten Testament* (Göttingen: Vandenhoeck & Ruprecht, 1970) 161-178.

Since it has come to be a fundamental belief among form critics and cult historians that the vast majority of the psalms reflect ceremonial activities, "a problem arises when we find in the Psalter some poems which do not seem to have been composed for cultic use" (Mowinckel, "Psalms and Wisdom," 205). The influence of the "sages" on some of the extant psalms cannot possibly be overlooked, however, and since "wisdom" in OT scholarly terminology is tantamount to acultic or even anti-cultic attitudes, form critics really are in some trouble. How could these bastard compositions sneak into a collection of liturgical and strictly cultic songs? Even worse, how could they exert influence on otherwise clean-cut cultic poems?

In the first place, we have to ask ourselves in what way wisdom

V

218

influence on the psalms can be established, and second we should raise the question of setting in regard to wisdom poems preserved in the Psalter.

There are, in fact, enough criteria to tell with some degree of certainty which psalms have grown out of that wide (and still fairly unknown) realm of the "wise man" (cf. H. J. Hermisson, *Studien zur israelitischen Spruchweisheit* [WMANT 28, Neukirchen: Neukirchener Verlag, 1968] and E. Gerstenberger, "Zur alttestamentlichen Weisheit," *VuF* XIV [1969] 28-44). Firstly, formulaic expressions and form elements quite common in wisdom writings reappear in some psalms (cf. Gunkel-Begrich, *Einleitung*, 389-390). The mode of addressing people sometimes is directly gleaned from instruction (cf. Pss 34:12; 49:2-5; 78:1-2); there are typical makarisms ("Lucky the man who . . .," cf. Pss 1:1; 112:5); sentences structured as numerical sayings (Ps 62:12); proverbial sayings which seem almost to be quoted from Proverbs (Ps 37:16—Prov 15:16, Ps 37:21); and exhortations so common in wisdom literature (cf. Ps 34:14-15; 37:1-8). Larger literary devices out of the treasury of the sages are the acrostic arrangement of a poem (in the psalms the alphabet is used as the artistic guideline, cf. Pss 25, 34, 37, 119) and the so-called anthological style whereby sayings are strung together by certain catchwords (cf. Pss 33, 119).

Second we find outspoken didactic interests and intentions, sometimes in the introduction of a poem (cf. Pss 49, 78) or in its whole tone and structure (cf. Pss 1, 19, 34, 119). Instruction in fact can be surmised to be the driving force behind most of the wisdom poems. Whether or not this instruction is flowing out of (royal) schools or coming from more or less professional sages is an open question. It seems most probable that guidance concerning the right or wrong life was primarily communicated within families and clans. However that may be, didactic overtones and undertones in most of the wisdom psalms are obvious.

There is a third point to be made. The topics and motifs of the psalms concerned are those also present in other wisdom literature. The problem of good and evil men and their respective fates is inherent in Pss 1, 9-10, 14, 119 for example; the vexing question of why a righteous person has to suffer comes to the fore in Pss 37, 49, 73. Reverence for a God-given and already written *torah* (cf. Pss 1, 19B, 119) may point towards theological circles as to authorship and into late postexilic times when the scrolls of Moses already were considered holy scriptures.

The wisdom psalms, in short, are substantially molded by a characteristic language, the reflective mood and didactic intention, and the imagery, topics, and motifs of Israel's sages, whoever they were. Language, structure, and themes of complaints, thanksgivings, and hymns on the other hand are conspicuously absent. Full recognition of these facts is certainly a merit of form critical research.

Again, the problem which remains is one concerning the life setting of these psalms. Since the wisdom genre in the Psalter was form critically assessed (cf. especially Gunkel-Begrich, *Einleitung*, 381-397; Mowinckel, *The Psalms*, II, 104-125 and "Psalms and Wisdom"), the wise man in Israel was visualized as the counterpart of an ancient Greek philosopher or a self-sufficient nineteenth-century German idealist—an Immanuel Kant walking around Königsberg. That is to say, the concept of a sage was quite academic and abstract; there was little sociological flesh and blood to it. The sage and his wisdom, in Gunkel's mind, were private and personalistic, uncultic, and ahistoric; humanistic and cosmopolitan in nature. And this view is *communis opinio*, up to our own time encompassing even G. von Rad and J. Hermisson. Wisdom is depicted as aloof from religious practice and attributable to rather "spiritual" schools, court circles, and wise individuals.

There may be something wrong with this picture which we project into Israel's life. Gunkel was the first to feel this way. When contemplating Ps 91 as a possible wisdom poem, he remarks: "It is remarkable that in vss. 14-16 a divine oracle was added to the wisdom poem. . . . This would indicate that the poem was performed in a worship service" (Gunkel-Begrich, *Einleitung*, 394). Mowinckel barely airs the thought that "learned psalmographers" could have anything to do with the cult. R. E. Murphy has asked the decisive question: ". . . is there any good reason to rule out cultic use and cultic life setting" for the wisdom psalms? (*VTS* IX, 161). Indeed, this question must be raised even if a positive answer cannot be easily found. If Mowinckel's assertion is correct: "The psalmists have learnt from the learned men and the learned men have learnt from the psalmists . . ." (*VTS* III, 208), and if Murphy's suggestion that wisdom influence penetrated deeply into other psalm genres should prove right (". . . the psalmists found wisdom themes useful and . . . exploited the wisdom style as an apt mode of expression" 167), then we could postulate a much closer connection

V

between the genres and their authors than has hitherto been assumed.

A striking Babylonian parallel to the biblical material may point in the right direction. The poem known under the title "The Babylonian Theodicy" (Lambert, 63-91; ANET, 601-604) is an acrostic one, and the author gives his name and profession: "I, Saggilkinam-ubbib, the incantation priest, am adorant of the god and the king" (Lambert, 63). The professional performer of ritual prayers for individual and community (cf. Caplice, *op. cit.*, above section 5) certainly did not compose such a poem for his private edification. The number of copies found in Babylonia and Assyria alone would witness to a widespread use, probably in cultic rites. Thus we may seriously ask whether the authors of Israelite wisdom psalms could not be found among those priests who were responsible for complaint and thanksgiving ceremonies. Of course this is a mere hypothesis which might draw some of the wisdom psalms over into the group of cultic poems.

III. WHITHER PSALM RESEARCH

After more than half a century of form critical studies on the psalms, an evaluation of achieved ends and further goals should go into greater detail than is possible here. The brief sketch of some main trends in scholarly thinking given above demonstrates one thing: Form critical work on the psalms has not yet come to an end but rather stands at a new beginning. There is no real "beyond" to form critical psalm exegesis. The method itself certainly has changed through the decades because those unavoidable ideological presuppositions and outlooks have also changed. Gunkel's basic idea that the psalms for the most part have grown out of cultic activities and that their linguistic and sentimental structure is indicative of their liturgical background is still as valid as ever. And while formal analysis in many instances has reached a final stage, the exploration of settings is still very much a task of the future. Of course, in the past decades some important books have been published concerning the institutional life of ancient Israel, studies which would have been impossible without form critical work also in the area of OT psalms (e.g. R. de Vaux, *Ancient Israel: Its Life and Institutions*; H.-J. Kraus, *Worship in Ancient Israel*; H. H. Rowley, *Worship in Ancient Israel* [Philadelphia: Fortress Press, 1967]). A wealth of information concerning cultic practices has been collected, but still there are too many questions open. They can be answered only by further resolute research along form critical lines; all the other modes of investigation naturally tie in with this approach.

Form critical work on the psalms means that an all inclusive method has to be applied on the basis of those principles established by Gunkel and Mowinckel. The fact that queries from other than literary and formal standpoints have to join "form" critical investigation has been touched upon occasionally but not sufficiently stressed. It will gain more importance in future research. For example: Modes of investigation which do not start out from "form" analysis in the strict sense can still promote in a high degree recognition of both formal structures and settings. Philological and lexical studies will help to illuminate dark passages which so far cannot be classified according to genre characteristics; statistical (even computerized) counts of vocabulary will help to circumscribe more exactly specific layers of language and usages typical for fixed life situations (so far these efforts often are based on literary units of the OT which in reality are very "unoriginal" conglomerates of various genres); stylistic and literary investigations, particularly in the field of comparative literature, will enhance our understanding of analogies and peculiarities in the OT psalms; ancient Near Eastern scholarship in general and form critical exploitation of cuneiform materials, as well as archaeological discoveries in particular, will increasingly shed light on all matters relevant to OT psalm exegesis (the special role of Ugaritic studies has been mentioned earlier).

Most important of all, however, and already pointed out above, is the fact that the social sciences of our day have given and will further supply invaluable insights into the nature of rites, feasts, and cultic activities which will help us to understand better Israel's ceremonial ways. Anthropological field studies, for instance, can tell us how rites function in a given, living society, what roles officials and participants play in ritual activities, etc. Won by direct observation of life performances, this knowledge will enable us by careful comparison and inference to arrive at a better estimation of Israel's analogous activities.

Thus, form critical research on the psalms, much more so than Gunkel or Mowinckel could know, today has to be augmented by probes into life settings. If the latter become sufficiently clear for each main genre, analyses of formal structures again can move out of some formalistic impasses and become oriented to-

V
———

wards living reality once more. This is to reemphasize the fact that formal analysis alone cannot possibly be sufficient in form critical research. The term "form" critical has been misleading in this regard in that it signalized only one (for Gunkel, the most natural) starting point of investigation. Although the term "form" critical does not say anything about Gunkel's real intention in its original meaning, it always included the "cult functional" aspects as propagated by Mowinckel. Formal analysis, then, gives us clues as to which direction to look for the appropriate life situation. Formal analysis can be a corrective if a life setting has been postulated for a given text and the OT scholar needs to check the validity of his hypothesis. Only if life settings can be reconstructed with sufficient clarity and plausibility is formal analysis worth the effort.

Another string of thoughts seems to follow from this intimate connection between formal structures and life settings. We must not look upon life situations in a rigid, schematic fashion. A setting for a literary genre is no slot machine which produces standardized items without end. Life always, even in recurring situations governed by custom and ritual, allows for a certain latitude of verbal expression. Certainly, there are guidelines which cannot be overruled without risking serious misunderstandings. But even very formalized situations and genres show a certain flexibility, a variety of accepted formulas and expressions which can be used to fulfill a particular communicative function. This flexibility implies a slow and gradual change going on always in all "settings" and their ritualistic paraphernalia, a shift which even in ancient times makes itself felt over long periods.

Another observation is also true: Verbal expressions and texts born in one particular life situation by accident or on purpose may be used in quite different situations and there sink their roots. In other words, all texts and words transmitted in human groups are themselves alive in the sense that they are prone to migrate from one original setting into other settings, and it may be difficult or impossible in each individual case to pinpoint the different stations of a given psalm.

The result is simply this: Form critical psalm research is still extremely young and promises to be a very exciting pursuit in the decades to come.

ERHARD GERSTENBERGER

Chapter Six

WISDOM

W. Baumgartner, "The Wisdom Literature," in *The Old Testament and Modern Study*, ed. by H. H. Rowley (London: Oxford University Press, 1951) 210-237; S. H. Blank, "Wisdom," *IDB* IV 852-861; J. L. Crenshaw, "Method in Determining Wisdom Influence upon 'Historical' Literature," *JBL* LXXXVIII (1969) 129-142; J. Fichtner, *Die altorientalische Weisheit in ihrer israelitisch-jüdischen Ausprägung* (BZAW 62, Giessen: A. Töpelmann, 1933); *idem*, *Gottes Weisheit*, (ATh II/3, Stuttgart: Calwer Verlag, 1965); E. Sellin-G. Fohrer, *Einleitung in das Alte Testament* (Heidelberg: Quelle & Meyer, 1965[10]) 331-373 = *Introduction to the Old Testament*, tr. by D. Green (Nashville: Abingdon Press, 1965) 304-341; E. Gerstenberger, "Zur alttestamentlichen Weisheit," *VuF* XIV (1969) 28-44; W. A. Irwin, "The Wisdom Literature," *IB* I (1952) 212-219; C. B. Kayatz, *Einführung in die alttestamentliche Weisheit* (BS 55, Neukirchen: Neukirchener Verlag, 1969); W. Lambert, *Babylonian Wisdom Literature* (London: Oxford University Press, 1960); *Les Sagesses du Proche-Orient ancien* (Paris: Presses Universitaires de France. 1963); W. McKane, *Prophets and Wise Men* (SBT 44, London: SCM Press, 1965); J. L. McKenzie, "Reflections on Wisdom," *JBL* LXXXVI (1967) 1-9; R. Murphy, "Form Criticism and Wisdom Literature," *CBQ* XXXI (1969) 475-483; *idem*, "The Interpretation of Old Testament Wisdom Literature," *Inter* XXIII (1969) 289-301; M. Noth and D. W. Thomas, eds., *Wisdom in Israel and in the Ancient Near East* (VTS III, Leiden: E. J. Brill, 1960); H. D. Preuss, "Erwägungen zum theologischen Ort alttestamentlicher Weisheits-literatur," *EvTh* XXX (1970) 393-417; G. von Rad, *Weisheit in Israel* (Neukirchen: Neukirchener Verlag, 1970); O. S. Rankin, *Israel's Wisdom Literature* (Edinburgh: T. & T. Clark, 1936); H. H. Schmid, *Gerechtigkeit als Weltordnung* (BHT 40, Tübingen: J. C. B. Mohr, 1968); *idem*, "Hauptprobleme der altorientalischen und alttestamentlichen Weisheitsliteratur,"

STU XXXV (1965) 68-74; *idem, Wesen und Geschichte der Weisheit* (BZAW 101, Berlin: A. Töpelmann, 1966) ; R. B. Y. Scott, "The Study of the Wisdom Literature," *Inter* XXIV (1970) 20-45; *idem, The Way of Wisdom in the Old Testament* (New York: The Macmillan Company, 1971) ; P. Skehan, *Studies in Israelite Poetry and Wisdom* (CBQMS 1, 1971) ; W. Zimmerli, "Zur Struktur der alttestamentlichen Weisheit," *ZAW* LI (1933) 177-204.

I. INTRODUCTION

Form critical investigation of wisdom literature advances only to the degree that it gives adequate answers to the following questions: (1) what is the scope of the literature? (2) what are the literary forms making up this body of literature? (3) what precise setting in life did these forms occupy? (4) what function did they perform in the life of ancient Israel? The significance of the definitional question cannot be overestimated, for solutions to the other three questions will be greatly affected by this decision. For example, if one assumes that historiography is by its very nature a product of the sages, then the literary genres which would demand attention would be wholly different from what is usually the case in studies of wisdom literature. Our primary task, then, is to determine at the outset what is to be the basis for all that follows.

The question of the assessment of Israelite literature in terms of wisdom thought can be answered, as is to be expected, from two extremes and several mediating positions. At one extreme is the critic who seeks to define wisdom literature as broadly as possible, specifically as nonrevelatory speech. Accordingly, anything that does not fall under the category of divine speech is fair game for the interpreter of wisdom literature. This means that all historiography is the product of the wise man, who by use of reason attempts to make sense of the course of human events (cf. McKenzie). When the nonrevelatory argument is coupled with the psychological one, namely that wisdom thinking is anthropocentric in the sense of laying bare the deepest feelings and aspirations of man, much of the OT suddenly falls within the category of wisdom (cf. von Rad). I have reference to the Primeval History (Gen 1-11), the Joseph Narrative (Gen 37-50), the Succession Narrative (II Sam 9-20, I Kings 1-2), and Esther. Furthermore, once a didactic tendency is recognized as clear evidence that a sage has been at work, additional literature enters the discussion, especially Tobit, Judith, I Esdras 3-4, and Ahiqar. Even a humanitarian concern has been viewed as evidence of wisdom origin; thus, Deuteronomy is seen as the legal expression of the sages (cf. M. Weinfeld, "The Origin of the Humanism in Deuteronomy," *JBL* LXXX [1961] 241-247). Still others have used a concatenation of factors as proof that various literary works are wisdom in orientation (Amos, Hab 3, Deut 32, Ex 34, and specific texts in Is, Jer, and Hos). The kinship of wisdom thinking and apocalyptic has led some to the view that Daniel is wisdom literature, particularly since the hero of the book that bears his name is a wise man. Finally, reflection on the problem of innocent suffering has been used as a basis for inclusion of a number of psalms in the wisdom corpus.

At the other end of the spectrum is the interpreter who chooses to define wisdom literature as narrowly as possible so as to retain the distinctiveness of that body of texts. Accordingly, the minimal literary works are emphasized, specifically Job, Qoheleth, Proverbs, Sirach, and Wisdom of Solomon. I shall adopt this position for the following discussion, inasmuch as there is general agreement that the above-mentioned are, to a degree at least, normative for wisdom thought.

On the basis of this literature it can be stated that wisdom literature is of four kinds: (1) juridical, (2) nature, (3) practical, and (4) theological. Distinction must be made between wisdom literature, wisdom tradition, and wisdom thinking. Similarly, there exist (1) family/clan wisdom, the goal of which is the mastering of life, the stance hortatory and the style proverbial; (2) court wisdom, with the goal of education for a select group, the stance secular, and method didactic; and (3) scribal wisdom, with the aim of providing education for everyone, a stance that is dogmatico-religious, and a dialogico-admonitory method. It would be a mistake to assume that these differences in style are chronological, although they correspond roughly to the three stages through which the wisdom movement passed.

Wisdom literature has its origins in the family, and from the period of the clan ethos derive many of the proverbs whose purpose was to equip one for the mastery of life regardless of circumstance. To this period belong also the onomastica, in rudimentary form, or lists of character traits and experiences of nature. From the family ethos arose the terms for teacher and student (father/son), as well as the emphasis upon domestic illustrations for emulation or shunning. With the emergence of court wisdom, in the Solomonic era perhaps, came a decisive shift in the interests of the sage, who now found himself in the employ of the state and commissioned to see to its welfare. An elite group, these counsellors were soon at odds with representatives of the prophetic movement and more and more apart from the common man and his concerns. Religious interests increasingly come under the wings of the wisdom movement, possibly at the impetus of Hezekiah, but certainly in the person of Sirach and the unknown author of Wisdom of Solomon (Fichtner). Similarly, the religious quest for meaning in the midst of the suffering of the innocent elicits from the fringes of wisdom thought the poetic masterpieces Job and Qoheleth. The diversity of literature and its concomitant emphases would lead one to expect a multiplicity of literary forms, and one is not disappointed in such anticipation.

Delineation of literary genres, while still in its infancy, has made considerable progress. Job has posed the most difficult problem, and some scholars have been willing to consider the book *sui generis*. Others have seen the poetry as a variant of the philosophical dialogue, a *Streitgespräch*, a Paradigm of the Answered Lament, or a Lawsuit. The dominant characteristic of Qoheleth, the confession, is recognized as a *Gattung* of Egyptian wisdom literature, while most of the final chapter is clearly an allegory (12:1-8; cf. Prov 9:1-6, 13-18). The book of Proverbs is composed of sentences (aphorisms) and admonitions, while the riddle may be hidden behind certain numerical proverbs. Additional categories present in one (or all) of these books are the hymn, which appears frequently in Sirach and Wisdom of Solomon, the prayer (likewise dominant in these two late works), didactic poetry and narrative (for lack of a better term), and lists. Apparently, no particular form is limited to one period of the wisdom movement or to any type of wise man. On the contrary, the forms are in use at every period in the history of the movement and in all facets of wisdom thinking.

Little precision is possible in specifying settings within which each literary genre functioned, that is, beyond the general category of didactic. Still this function is capable of a number of locales, including the home, school (cf. H.-J. Hermisson, *Studien zur israelitischen Spruchweisheit* [WMANT 28, Neukirchen: Neukirchener Verlag, 1968] 192: "Israelite wisdom has its center, its locus of origin, and its nurture in the Israelite school"), court and possibly the temple (if the Mesopotamian parallel of a temple school has any importance for Israel, and if the hymns and prayers in Sirach may be in any way normative). But even these settings provide little clarity, for there is room for diversity within each. The school, for example, may have served totally different purposes, perhaps simultaneously, depending on whether the welfare of the state or of the individual was uppermost. The latter aim would be religious in distinction from the purely secular emphases of the counsellor to the king (if such extreme secularity ever existed, as McKane thinks).

Finally, there is evidence of multi-verse structuring of various proverbs, as well as acrostic and categorizing sequence of larger paragraphs. This means that the individual sentence or admonition exists within a context that is didactic, hence has received a new *Sitz*. It may be, too, that the total book is the product of intentional arrangement, so that one must speak of a unit larger than verse or paragraph. I have reference to Skehan's hypothesis about Wisdom's House as the conscious architectonic construct of the final editor of Proverbs, as well as to the book of Job.

After these preliminary remarks about the scope of wisdom and the genres, both as to form and function, I now turn to an analysis of the forms within wisdom literature. Eight categories will be discussed: proverb, riddle, fable and allegory, hymn and prayer, *Streitgespräch* or dialogue, confession, lists, didactic poetry and narrative.

II. THE FORMS

A. Proverb (*māšāl*)

A. Barucq, *Le Livre des Proverbes* (SB, Paris: J. Gabalda & Co., 1964) ; A. Bea, "Der Zahlenspruch im Hebräischen und Ugaritischen," *Bib* XXI (1940) 196-198; G. Boström, *Proverbiastudien. Die Weisheit und das fremde Weib in Spr. 1-9* (LUA NF I xxx 3, Lund: C. W. K. Gleerup, 1935) ; O. Eissfeldt, *Der Maschal im Alten Testament* (BZAW 24, Giessen: Töpelmann, 1913) ; E. Gerstenberger, *Wesen und Herkunft des sogenannten "apodiktischen Rechts" im Alten Testament* (WMANT 20, Neukirchen: Neukirchener Verlag, 1965) ; A. H. Godbey, "The Hebrew *Masal*," *AJSL* XXXIX (1922/3) 89-108; A. S. Herbert, "The 'Parable' (*Masal*) in the Old Testament," *SJT* VII (1954) 180-196; H.-J. Hermisson, *Studien zur israelitischen Spruchweisheit* (WMANT 28, Neukirchen: Neukirchener Verlag, 1968) ; A. R. Johnson, "*Masal*," *VTS* III (1955) 162-169; C. Kayatz, *Studien zu Proverbien 1-9* (WMANT 22, Neukirchen: Neukirchener Verlag, 1966) ; W. McKane, *Proverbs* (Philadelphia: The Westminster Press, 1970) ; W. Richter, *Recht und Ethos: Versuch einer Ortung des weisheitlichen Mahnspruches* (SANT 15, Munich: Kösel-Verlag, 1966) ; H. Ringgren, *Word and Wisdom* (Lund: H. Ohlssons, 1947) ; W. M. W. Roth, *Numerical Sayings in the Old Testament* (VTS 13, Leiden: E. J. Brill, 1965) ; idem, "The Numerical Sequence X/X+1 in the Old Testament," *VT* XII (1962) 300-311; G. Sauer, *Die Spruche Agurs* (BWANT IV/4, Stuttgart: W. Kohlhammer, 1963) ; R. B. Y. Scott, *Proverbs, Ecclesiastes* (AB 18, Garden City: Doubleday & Company, 1965) ; U. Skladny, *Die ältesten Spruchsammlungen in Israel* (Göttingen: Vandenhoeck & Ruprecht, 1962) ; W. B. Stevenson, "A Mnemonic Use of Numbers in Proverbs and Ben Sira," *TGUOS* IX (1938/9) 26-38; W. A. van der Weiden, *Le Livre des Proverbes* (BibOr 23,

Rome: Biblical Institute Press, 1970) ; R. N. Whybray, *Wisdom in Proverbs* (SBT 45, London: SCM Press, 1965) ; H. W. Wolff, *Amos' geistige Heimat* (WMANT 18, Neukirchen: Neukirchener Verlag, 1964) 24-29; A. Wünsche, "Die Zahlenspruche in Talmud und Midrasch," *ZDMG* LXV (1911) 57-100.

"One must possess discernment in order to grasp its meaning, and emotion to feel the beauty of its expression" (J. G. Herder, *Spruch und Bild insonderheit bei den Morgenländern*, ed by B. Suphan, 16 [1887] 9-10, quoted by G. von Rad, 49). The precise sense of *māšāl* is not known, although "similitude" and "ruling word" appear to cover the broad spectrum of usage. Both meanings are possible etymologically; the former focuses on the sense of likeness, representativeness, hence similitude (Eissfeldt, Godbey), while the latter takes its departure from the root meaning "to rule, have dominion, reign," thus a word spoken by a ruler or a word bearing special power (Boström). Hylmö's definition of *māšāl* as "a winged word, outliving the fleeting moment" (see A. Bentzen, *Introduction to the Old Testament*, I [Copenhagen: G. E. C. Gad, 1948] 168) is an interesting variant that has found a recent champion in W. McKane (22-33), for whom the timeless, paradigmatic character of the proverb is decisive. Accordingly McKane translates *māšāl* by "paradigm, model, exemplar" and judges a saying on the basis of its universal character.

Such diversity of meaning derives from the fact that *māšāl* not only refers to similitudes (Ez 16:44; Gen 10:9; I Sam 10:11), but also to popular sayings (Jer 23:28; 31:29; I Sam 24:13; Is 32:6; I Kings 20:11), literary aphorisms (Prov 10:1-22:16, 25-29; Qoh 9:17-10:20), taunt songs (Is 14:4; Mic 2:4; Hab 2:6-8; Ez 12:22-23; 18:2-3), bywords (Deut 28:37; I Kings 9:7; Jer 24:9; Ez 14:8), allegories (Ez 17:1-10; 20:45-49; 24:3-14), and discourses (Num 23:7, 18; 24:3-24; Job 27:1; 29:1; Ps 49:4; 78:2).

A further complication is the multiplicity of forms of *mᵉšālîm* in the book of Proverbs. At least five types are discernible, namely sentence (*Spruch* or *Aussage*), instruction, exhortation or admonition (*Mahnrede, Mahnwort, Mahnspruch, Rat*), numerical (*Zahlenspruch*), comparison or excluding, to use H. H. Schmid's descriptive term, and antithetic proverb. Biblical proverbial patterns are likewise disparate and in their variety are at one with nonbiblical parallels. Scott's delineation of both isolates seven patterns: (1) identity, equivalence, invariable association; (2) nonidentity, contrast, paradox; (3) similarity, analogy, type; (4) contrary to right order, futile, absurd; (5) classification and clarification; (6) value, relative value or priority, proportion or de-

gree; (7) consequences of human character and behavior (5-7).
The basic unit of gnomic apperception is the saying, either
proverb or aphorism. The simplest form of *Sprichwort* is the
popular proverb, a number of which have been preserved in the
narrative literature of the OT. While most of these brief
Volkspruche are in prose, on occasion they are clothed in metrical
garb (Jer 31:29; Ez 18:2, "The fathers have eaten sour grapes,
and the children's teeth are set on edge") and make use of con-
sonantal and vocalic assonance (Prov 11:2; 13:3). Studies of popular proverbs have singled out such passages as Gen 10:9 ("Like
Nimrod a mighty hunter before the Lord"), I Sam 10:12 ("Is
Saul also among the prophets?" cf: 19:24), II Sam 5:8 ("The
blind and the lame shall not come into the house"), I Kings
20:11 ("Let not him that girds on his armor boast himself as he
that puts it off"), Prov 10:6, 11 ("The mouth of the wicked conceals violence" to which should be compared I Sam 24:13 "Out of
the wicked comes forth wickedness"), Jer 13:23 ("Can the Ethiopi-
an change his skin, or the leopard his spots?"), 23:28 ("What has
straw in common with wheat?"), Ez 16:44 ("Like mother, like
daughter"; cf. Hos 4:9, Sir 10:2), as well as the above-mentioned
poetic popular proverbs (Eissfeldt; Scott, XXVI-XXIX). By nature
secular and nondidactic, these popular proverbs were occasionally
enlisted in the service of morality and consequently assumed a
religious tenor.

The proverb is bilinear and registers a conclusion based on
experience; as such it must be self-confirming, commending itself
to empirical validation or to disconfirmation. Since the saying is
a result of the collective experience of mankind, it has a retro-
spective character, and because of its nature as an observation
of how things are, it lacks the imperative. Hence any didactic intent is secondary to the proverb, and the style is succinct, epi-
grammatic, and highly metaphorical. However, even the literary
proverb may be set within a didactic context, as in the case of
the folk proverb. This pedagogic function of the aphorism was
abetted by the addition of motivation clauses, which led to a
disintegration of the form of the proverb, as well as by the attach-
ing of consequences of conduct. Certain stylistic features give
evidence of serious reflection in the service of teaching, for
example the parallels of comparison (parabolic parallelism) that
express evaluative judgments ("as . . . so," "better is . . . than"),
and the frequent use of paranomasia, assonance, alliteration,
puns, listing, repetition, synonymy, rhyme (Fohrer, *Introduc-*

tion, 313). In synonymous parallelism the second line emphasizes the moral of the first, whereas in synthetic parallelism it frequently resolves the image. In a didactic setting the interrogative form, particularly rhetorical questions, comes into prominence.

The relative chronology of the popular and literary proverbs, that is, the development of the unilinear and bilinear proverb, has been the subject of much discussion. Eissfeldt's study of the *māšāl* led him to the conclusion that the popular proverb was anterior to the literary proverb, which was the result of artistic refinement. Similarly J. Schmidt contended that the proverb developed from a brief one-line popular saying to a poetic, two-line *Kunstspruch*, and ultimately, on analogy with the development of multi-verses, into larger units by the addition of motivation clauses and reasons for conduct, attached syntactically to the original proverb by dependent clauses (*Studien zur Stilistik der alttestamentlichen Spruchliteratur*, ATA 13/1, Münster: Aschendorffsche Verlagsbuchhandlung, 1936). This assumption of a development from the simpler form to the more complex came to serve as an axiom of form criticism, so that the date of proverb collections was determined largely on the basis of complexity of sayings contained therein, despite the possibility that the short saying may be fragmentary, a corruption of an original two-line proverb. This procedure has come under attack from several quarters recently, both on literary and sociological grounds.

In every instance comparison with Egyptian wisdom literature has forced a reexamination of the assumption of development from simple to complex sentence structure. R. N. Whybray based his analysis of Prov 1-9 on the Egyptian instruction genre and called into question the lateness of these chapters. In dating them early Whybray took up a major conclusion of U. Skladny, who emphasized the architectonic nature of the collection of biblical proverbs and claimed to have discovered four major sections with thematic coherence: (1) 10-15, contrast between righteousness and wickedness; (2) 16:1-22:16, Yahweh and the king; (3) 25-27, nature and agriculture; (4) 28-29, the king, or potential rulers. Kayatz examined Prov 1-9 in terms of a formal analysis of the instruction genre in Egypt, concluding that the prototype of the personification of wisdom may be the divine speeches in Egyptian wisdom literature. A thoroughgoing analysis of the instruction genre has been undertaken by McKane, who argues for two types of proverb: (1) Instruction, Prov 1-9; 22:17-24:22; 31:1-9; and (2) Sentence, Prov 10:1-22:16; 24:23-34; 25-29.

The very existence of folk proverbs (with rare exceptions) has been challenged by H.-J. Hermisson, who submits Eissfeldt's conclusions to exhaustive analysis, both as to the definition of proverb and criteria employed for distinguishing a folk proverb from a literary proverb. But Hermisson goes further than the mere rejection of form critical arguments based on a temporal priority of the simplest form; rather he postulates a fundamentally different community that is responsible for creating and collecting biblical proverbs. In this regard he gives confirmation to Bentzen's observation that the popular proverb could not be the origin of wisdom poetry, which was *literature by scholars for scholars* (so Hylmö; see Bentzen, *Introduction* I, 168, 173) and encourages the view that folk proverbs and artistic sayings existed simultaneously as is the case in extrabiblical literature.

The presuppositions of the community that expressed its observations about reality in succinct proverbs are difficult to ascertain, although much can be known (see especially von Rad, *Weisheit in Israel*, and Kayatz, *Einführung in die alttestamentliche Weisheit*). A distinction between *Erfahrungsweisheit* (the wisdom of experience) and *theologische Weisheit* (theological wisdom) is essential, the former embracing both clan and court wisdom. The proverb is an elementary quest for order, comparisons, and contrasts, as well as numerical speech serving to assure the Israelite of regularity and dependability in the universe. The concerns of the clan were encapsulated in proverbs, specifically the contrast between rich and poor, good and bad, hate and love, wisdom and folly. By means of comparative speech, direct admonition, questions, riddles, and numerical speech as the concept of retribution was promulgated, and Yahweh's role as guarantor of order was emphasized.

Inasmuch as all knowledge leads to self-knowledge, experiential and nature wisdom were recognized as complementary rather than contradictory. Since the order of the universe was fundamental, there was no room for the heroic individual, yet both Proverbs and Sirach have examples of ethical radicalization. The wise man is the just man, and the fool is the practical atheist, not the ignorant. This implies the necessity for obedience, since the word is empty unless it is given a hearing. In the process of listening, however, the word is submitted to new personal and communal experience, is subjected to occasional disconfirmation. Out of this struggle between the claims of the past and the reality of the present, ambiguity emerges, and the riddle of the world changes, resulting in contradictory statements. Such ambiquity forces upon the community an awareness of the limits of human wisdom; these limitations were also the result of the Israelite view of God, who always retained sovereign freedom to dispose of man's best-laid plans. (See H. Brunner, "Der freie Wille Gottes in der ägyptischen Weisheitstexten," *Les Sagesses du Proche-Orient ancien*, 103-120, for the Egyptian scene; W. Zimmerli, "Ort und Grenze der Weisheit in Rahmen der alttestamentliche Theologie," *ibid.*, 121-138 = his *Gottes Offenbarung* [TB 19, Munich: Chr. Kaiser, 1963] 300-315 = "The Place and Limit of the Wisdom in the Framework of Old Testament Theology," *SJT* XXVIII [1964] 146-158, and H. Gese, *Lehre und Wirklichkeit in der alten Weisheit* [Tübingen: J. C. B. Mohr, 1958] 45-50 for the Israelite.) The mystery of God was, nevertheless, a source of comfort, a basis for joy, and all creation was thought to sing his praises. Hence there was no possibility for a tragic view of life, and the ancient Israelite was remarkably at home in the world, which was God's great secret, worthy of trust and punishing false trust.

Court wisdom focused on the king and his responsibilities, both as guarantor of justice and as one whose throne is established on righteousness, an Egyptian concept (H. Brunner, "Gerechtigkeit als Fundament des Throns," *VT* VIII [1958] 426-428; H. Schmid, *Gerechtigkeit als Weltordnung*, 23). Other prominent themes were the education of potential rulers and court personnel, the limitations of wisdom, and the fear of the Lord. Here one finds a commingling of urban and agricultural concerns, particularly those of the wealthy plantation owner (R. Gordis, "The Social Background of Wisdom Literature," *HUCA* XVIII [1943/4] 77-118). The humanization of man is evident in the concern for the welfare of the poor, the art of eloquence and cultivation of the proper silence, warnings about the wiles of the adulteress and the deleterious effect of excessive drinking, together with the enumeration of obstacles to the mastery of the tongue (cf. Prov 23:29-35, which may originally have been a riddle).

Theologische Weisheit, on the other hand, consists of long poems of theological reflection on the relation of Yahweh to wisdom and creation. The personification of wisdom is the means of maintaining an intimate relationship between the creator and the created order where revelation is not assumed; such hypostatization, if the term is applicable (von Rad would deny its

VI

appropriateness except for Wisdom of Solomon; see *Weisheit in Israel,* 193) , may have emerged into prominence as a response to the problem of theodicy (see B. L. Mack, "Wisdom Myth and Mytho-logy," *Inter* XXIV [1970] 46-60). The influence of prophetic speech, however, is felt in the manner of Dame Wisdom's call to obedience, although she goes beyond the prophetic oracle by inviting men to *come to her* for life.

It has been said that the proverb is self-validating, that it cannot appeal to any authority other than that of human experience (Zimmerli, "Zur Struktur der alttestamentlichen Weisheit"). This understanding of *'eṣâ* as advice devoid of compelling authority came to be normative until recently, when syntactical, thematic, and contextual arguments were mustered against it (see J. L. Crenshaw, " *'eṣâ* and *dābār*: The Problem of Authority/ Certitude in Wisdom and Prophetic Literature," in *Prophetic Conflict, Its Effect Upon Israelite Religion* [BZAW 124, Berlin: Walter de Gruyter, 1971] 116-123) .

The didactic character of the proverb is heightened in the admonition, which seeks to inculcate a desired behavior pattern and right thinking. To accomplish this end the admonition makes use of motive clauses, positive commands, and grounds for conduct. The whole weight of tradition undergirds the exhortation and warning, for the *Mahnrede* purports to embody the findings of generations of experience. Furthermore, the authority of the instructor, either as father, clan leader, counsellor, scribe or teacher in a school, stands behind every word. But an even greater authority is assumed, namely that of the creator and sustainer of order. Since God is the ultimate source of all justice, the fear of the Lord is indeed the beginning of wisdom. Given the authoritative character of the admonition, one can understand the wise man's contempt for the fool, the man too stubborn to act on what everyone knew to be right.

The admonition may also be negative. This phenomenon has been the subject of much discussion recently, particularly as to the *Sitz* indicated by the form of negative employed. W. Richter views the negative admonitions as the product of *Gruppenethos* in schools responsible for the education of public officials, hence associated with the royal court and probably the temple. For him the distinction between a vetitive and prohibitive is fundamental. The vetitive uses the jussive with *'al* and is a negation of the imperative, usually with a motive clause. It seldom occurs in legal codes. On the other hand, the prohibitive uses the negative particle *lō'* with the imperfect; it appears mostly in legal corpora. The life setting of both is said to be the *Gruppenethos* of the school (Richter, *Recht und Ethos*).

A different understanding of the prohibition is offered by E. Gerstenberger, for whom the occurrence of *'al* in legal codes without any diminution of seriousness constitutes a refutation of Richter's thesis. Gerstenberger attempts to locate the prohibitions in the *Sippenethos* (clan ethos), which is for him a milieu in which law and wisdom coincide.

The absence of any correspondence in wisdom literature between form and setting renders a decision between these theses virtually impossible; a further complication is the fact that the prehistory of the legal admonition is the everyday intercourse of human activity. In addition, there is in court wisdom an intermingling of agricultural imagery and other concerns of the *Sippenethos* with the more office-oriented interests of the *Gruppenethos*. It is thus not possible to limit agricultural metaphors to folk wisdom, royal to court wisdom; accordingly, the precise origin of any passage is open to question. As a criticism of Richter's contention that the two forms of negative admonitions, vetitive and prohibitive, constitute distinct *Gattungen*, R. Murphy's stricture that only one basic form is present here, namely negative admonition, appears to be justified ("Form Criticism and Wisdom Literature," 481).

The numerical proverb moves one step further in the direction of didacticism; despite its probable origin in connection with the riddle, the *Zahlenspruch* gives the impression of a mnemonic device in schools. It is at home, however, in the earliest stage of wisdom and represents an elementary need of man seeking order. Fohrer has surmised that its origin is Canaanite, appealing to RŠ 51 iii 17-21 (*Introduction*, 312); in any case G. Sauer emphasizes the kinship between the numerical proverbs and Ugaritic literature (70-112). The favorite scheme is three/four, although one/two (Job 33:14-15; cf. Ps 62:12; Sir 50:25-26), two/three (Job 13:20-22; Sir 26:28), six/seven (Prov 6:16-19; Job 5:19-22, cf. "Dispute between the Tamarisk and the Date Palm," *ANET*, 592-593), and nine/ten (Sir 25:7-11) are also attested (perhaps even four/five in Prov 30:24-28, if Sauer is correct [103-104]). In some instances, only one fact is mentioned, despite the formula calling for three/four; this is particularly striking in the prophetic use of the stylistic device (Am 1:3-2:8), where the expression appears to represent the totality of offenses, that is, stands for compre-

hensiveness. In still other passages the demand for parallelism,
if that is the actual explanation for the formula, does not neces-
sitate an ascending scale, but is content with an elaboration of
the things making up the number (Prov 30:7-9, 24-28; Sir 25:1-2).
The usual form, however, is x/x plus one, with emphasis being
placed on the larger number as if the answer to a "riddle" (Prov
6:16-19; 30:15b-16, 18-19, 21-23, 29-31; Sir 25:7-11; 26:5-6, 28).
As Torczyner perceived, Prov 30:18-19 may originally have existed
in question, that is, riddle form: "What three or four things move
without leaving any trace?" ("The Riddle in the Bible," *HUCA*
I [1924] 125-149, see 135-136). Another variant is a moralistic
addition to the last-mentioned component, which amounts to an
admission that further clarification of the reason for including it
within such a nexus of relationships was necessary (Sir 26:5-6,
28). This appendage calls attention to the fact that the emphasis
in numerical proverbs is most often to be found on the final element, the previous ones merely serving to heighten the wonder
or disgust over the point at issue.

Each of these variants may be illustrated from Proverbs or
Sirach, there being no numerical proverbs in Qoh (11:2?) or
Wisdom of Solomon. First, the simple number without any
heightening: "Two things I ask of thee; do not withold them
from me before I die. Put fraud and lying far from me; give me
neither poverty nor wealth, provide me only with the food I
need. If I have too much, I shall deny thee and say, 'Who is the
Lord?' If I am reduced to poverty, I shall steal and blacken the
name of my God" (Prov 30:7-9 NEB; cf. Job 13:20-27). Again:
"There are three sights which warm my heart and are beautiful
in the eyes of the Lord and men: concord among brothers, friendship among neighbors, and a man and wife who are inseparable.
There are three kinds of men who arouse my hatred, who disgust
me by their manner of life: a poor man who boasts, a rich man
who lies, and an old fool who commits adultery" (Sir 25:1-2
NEB). In this example there is the additional stylistic device of
contrast, to be discussed below. The usual form occurs often in
Prov 30, but also in 6:16-19, where one reads: "Six things the
Lord hates, seven things are detestable to him: a proud eye, a
false tongue, hands that shed innocent blood, a heart that forges
thoughts of mischief, and feet that run swiftly to do evil, a false
witness telling a pack of lies, and one who stirs up quarrels between brothers" (NEB). Here the attempt was made to use parts
of the body as illustrative of evil conduct, although the author

was unable to maintain the analogy throughout. Possibly Prov 6:12-15 was also a numerical proverb, as K. Budde suggested (*Geschichte der althebräischen Literatur* [Leipzig: C. F. Amelang, 1906] 301). The third type is evidence of the use of the numerical proverb in religious instruction. "Two things grieve my heart, and a third excites my anger: a soldier in distress through poverty, wise men treated with contempt, and a man deserting right conduct for wrong—the Lord will bring him to the scaffold" (Sir 26:28 NEB). The frequent use of numerical proverbs to refer to sexuality, both its wonder (Prov 30:18-19) and the *Angst* of a bad marriage, may further attest to the kinship of this form with the riddle, in which sexual themes abound. In this regard Sir 26:5-6 is instructive: "Three things there are that alarm me, and a fourth I am afraid to face: the scandal of the town, the gathering of a mob, and calumny—all harder to bear than death; but it is heartache and grief when a wife is jealous of a rival, and everyone alike feels the lash of her tongue" (NEB). While it is impossible to trace the history of the form, the numerical proverb changed drastically from the time of Prov 30:18-19 to Sirach's use in 25:7-11, which stands apart both in style and content (use of the interrogative, the *'ašrê* formula, the comparative, and the religious motif of the fear of Yahweh as the most excellent gift), as von Rad has observed (*Weisheit in Israel*, 55).

Less debate has taken place over the form or function of the comparison and antithetic proverb. The comparative aphorism occurs frequently in wisdom literature, its purpose being to single out certain kinds of character or conduct as superior to others. Its origin was in clan wisdom, but the comparison was also a favorite of later sages. In Proverbs the majority of occurrences are in the oldest collections: 12:9; 15:16-17; 16:8, 16, 19; 17:1; 19:1; 21:9, 19; 25:24; 27:10c; 28:6; cf. 17:12; 21:3; 22:1. The didactic intent is given religious overtones in 15:16-17:

"Better is a little with the fear of the Lord than great treasure and trouble with it. Better is a dinner of herbs where love is than a fatted ox and hatred with it."

Domestic problems gave rise to the following comparison, which appears twice in Proverbs:

"It is better to live in a corner of the housetop than in a house shared with a contentious woman."

(21:9; 25:24; cf. Sir 25:16) A variant is found in Prov 21:19.

"It is better to live in a desert land than with a contentious and fretful woman."

The comparison is used frequently in Qoh, where it calls attention to the limits of human wisdom. Here one finds a poem with the comparison as its motivating force (7:1-12), as well as excluding sayings that sum up Qoheleth's despair (2:24; 3:22; 9:16). But the more common form of the comparison also appears (4:6, 9, 13; 5:5; 6:9; 9:4). It is used in Wisd of Sol 4:1, where the Greek attitude to progeny has made an impact ("Better than this is childlessness with virtue, for in the memory of virtue is immortality, because it is known both by God and by men"). To this may be compared Sir 16:3 ("Do not trust in their survival and do not rely on their multitude; for one is better than a thousand, and to die childless is better than to have ungodly children"). "Better" sayings abound in Sirach (11:3; 19:24; 20:2, 18, 25, 31; 25:16; 30:14-17; 41:15; 42:14, for example). The last, a clear expression of misogyny ("Better is the wickedness of a man than a woman who does good; and it is a woman who brings shame and disgrace") witnesses to the emerging speculation about woman's role in man's fall (cf. II Esdras, II Enoch).

Antithetical proverbs make up the gist of the collection in Prov 10-15. Their purpose is to expose folly at its worst by contrasting it sharply with its opposite. Their subject matter ranges from parental guidance to the control of the tongue and takes up anything worthy of discussion (false balances, laziness, gossip, anxiety, hope deferred, sacrifice of the wicked, and so forth). These proverbs are found throughout wisdom literature and require no documentation. Even Qoh makes use of the antithetic maxim to describe the orientation of a fool in contrast to that of a wise man ("A wise man's heart inclines him toward the right, but a fool's heart toward the left" 10:2).

B. Riddle (*ḥîdâ*)

T. Andrae, "Rätsel," *RGG*² IV 1685; S. H. Blank, "Riddle," *IDB* IV 78-79; O. Eissfeldt, "Die Rätsel in Jud 14," *ZAW* XXX (1910) 132-135; H. Gunkel, "Dictung, profane, im Alten Testament," *RGG*² I 56; M. Hain, *Rätsel* (Stuttgart: J. B. Metzler, 1966); H. Hepding, "Zwei biblische Rätsel," *Humaniora, Archer Taylor Festschrift* (Locust Valley: J. J. Augustin, 1960) 270-276; V. E. Hull and A. Taylor, *A Collection of Welsh Riddles* (Berkeley: University of California Press, 1942); J. Jacobs, "Riddle," *JE* X (1905) 408-409; A. Jolles, *Einfache Formen* (Halle: Max Niemeyer, 1956²); H.-P. Müller, "Der Begriff 'Rätsel' im Alten Testament," *VT* XX (1970) 465-489; J. R. Porter, "Samson's Riddle: Judges XIV, 18," *JTS* XIII (1962) 106-109; L. Röhrich, "Rätsel," *RGG*³ V 767; S. Schechter, "The Riddles of Solomon in Rabbinic Literature,"

Folklore I (1890) 349-358; A. Taylor, *A Bibliography of Riddles* (FFC 126, Helsinki: Academia scientarum fennica, 1939); *idem, The Literary Riddle Before 1600* (Berkeley: University of California Press, 1948); H. Torczyner (Tur Sinai), "The Riddle in the Bible," *HUCA* I (1924) 125-149; A. Wünsche, *Die Rätselweisheit bei den Hebräern mit Hinblick auf andere alte Völker* (Leipzig: Otto Schulze, 1883).

"Whoever wishes to understand the world discovers it as a riddle." (W. Porzig, "Das Rätsel im Rigveda. Ein Beitrag zum Kapital 'Sondersprache'," *Germanica* (Sievers Festschrift) 1925, 660.) Porzig's striking observation is fully in accord with that of Wünsche, for whom the entire universe and human nature itself are alive with riddles (7). In such a context the riddle functions as a paradox that is paradigmatic of the paradox of reality, and the propounder of riddles, namely the wise man, takes as his elementary function the formulating of analogies descriptive of the structure of reality. Hence there is a close relationship between riddle and myth, described aptly by A. Jolles as follows: "Myth is an answer in which a question is presupposed; riddle is a question that conceals an answer" (106). Jolles goes on to point out decisive differences in regard to the polarities of freedom and bondage, activity and passivity, and to establish a connection between riddle and divination, a thesis championed subsequently by E. Peuckert (*Deutsches Volkstum in Märchen und Sage* [Berlin: W. de Gruyter & Co., 1938]). Since every riddle is a judgment situation in which the ambiguities of the riddle stand between the one who seeks to conceal and him who strives to unveil the secret "watchword," a measure of *Angst* is generated. Whenever the questioner is divine, an element of the demonic surfaces; such a contest necessarily assumes grave proportions, becomes a struggle for life, against death. Fundamentally, all riddles are *Halsrätsel*—a matter of life or death—if Jolles is to be trusted (110), although riddles come to function in festive occasions once the burden of mythology and divination eases. Since knowledge of another is power over him, the riddle functions as a defensive mechanism; the contest therefore becomes one to establish worthiness, or, in other words, it determines the one who possesses magical power rather than the superior intelligence of the contestants (so Tor Andrae). Although missing from the Old Testament, the *Halsrätel* is not far removed from the *Streitgespräch*, hence makes itself felt both in wisdom and prophetic literature.

Basic to the riddle is the ambiguity of language; it can only operate where words bear meanings that are common knowledge and at the same time conceal special connotations for an exclusive group. This movement from *Gemeinsprache* to *Sondersprache* is essential to the riddle; for example, in the expressions "foot of the mountain" or "lamp of the body" the words "foot" and "lamp" are used in a special, symbolic sense. Once such ambiguity is possible, riddles can be formulated by use of ambivalent language stated interrogatively: "What has a foot but cannot walk?" Inasmuch as there is ambiguity in the symbolism of the riddle, there is often no final, sole solution, for the answer can itself be a riddle, hence ambiguous. Besides the use of metaphor and cipher, other stylistic features of the riddle are paranomasia, onomatopoeia, description, personification, narrative debate, and the like. Nor is the riddle necessarily poetic; on the contrary, it varies from popular prose to strict parallelism and strophic formulation (Röhrich). Such stylistic devices as those mentioned above originally served as mnemonic aids and without a doubt point to a didactic setting for the artistic riddle. But the life setting of the riddle was diverse, ranging from initiation ceremonies to courtship and marriage, as well as the political contests between kings and their courtiers, ritual questions in catechetical form, banquets (as, for example, in Plutarch's "The Feast of the Seven Wise Men" and the Epistle of Aristeas, 187-300), children at play, and in the schools (Hain, 1).

Strictly speaking, the riddle is rare in the OT, occurring in pure form only in Judg 14:10-18. A number of passages suggest, however, that the riddle was far more prominent in ancient Israel than the scarcity of examples would lead one to believe. In Num 12:8 there is a tradition that Yahweh spoke with Moses "mouth to mouth, clearly, and not in dark speech" ($b^e\d{h}i\d{d}\bar{o}\d{t}$). Furthermore, this statement implies that normal oracular utterance was in riddle form, an exception being made in Moses' case. In Prov 1:6 there is a practical equation between $\d{h}id\hat{a}$ and $m\bar{a}\check{s}\bar{a}l$, and this parallelism is by no means unique (cf. Ps 78:2; Wisd of Sol 8:8; Sir 39:3, and with $m^e li\d{s}\hat{a}$, Hab 2:6; Sir 47:17). Besides this linguistic evidence for the important role of the riddle in ancient Israel, there is the "historical" tradition of Solomon's mastery of the art of riddle solving (I Kings 10:1-5 and II Chron 9:1-4), a tradition elaborated upon in Josephus (*Antiquities* VIII, 5, 3, par. 141-149), who mentions a riddle contest between Solomon and envoys sent by Hiram, king of Tyre. While the Solomonic tradition cannot be accepted at face value, Alt's thesis about this king's sponsorship of sages whose task was to gather onomastica (*Naturweisheit*) has merit (see his "Die Weisheit Salomos," *TLZ* LXXVI (1951) 139-144 = his *Kleine Schriften zur Geschichte des Volkes Israel II* [Munich: C. H. Beck, 1953] 90-99).

The presence of only one riddle in the OT, despite impressive evidence for the popularity of the form, suggests that we may be able to discover additional riddles now in disintegrated form. Such attempts have been made as early as Herder, who believed that riddles lurked behind the numerical proverbs in Prov 30:15-33, and Gunkel, who claimed the same for Prov 6:16-19, Sir 25:7-11, as well as for Prov 30:15-31. So far the search for riddles has been limited to numerical sayings, which are generally thought to be derived from or integrally related to the riddle. Recently, however, Müller has mustered strong arguments against the putative bond between riddle and numerical proverb. These have to do with the attitude toward paradox, nature of the solution, and specificity of the answer. Whereas the riddle is concerned to call attention to the paradox of reality, the numerical proverb displays little interest in the paradox as such, but rather seeks to identify it in various situations. Again, he who gives a riddle knows its solution; by way of contrast, the numerical proverb expresses the astonishment of *discovery*. While for the riddle many answers are possible, the numerical proverb is capable of only one solution. In any case, it may be possible to identify still other broken riddles by means of a careful investigation of figures of speech, particularly sexual imagery, in the OT (what Wünsche has referred to by the rabbinic phrase *lᵉšôn ḥoḵmâ*). As a start I would suggest the following passages as possible bearers of disintegrated riddles: Prov 23:29-35; 23:27; 16:15; 20:27; 25:2-3; 27:20; 5:1-6; 5:15-23; 6:23-24.

The riddle in Judg 14:10-18 appears to antedate its context; its appropriateness for a wedding celebration, however, tempers the intrusive nature. As H. Gressmann perceived, the answers to the two riddles ("Out of the eater came something to eat. Out of the strong came something sweet" and "What is stronger than a lion," 14:14,18) may be "vomit" and "love" respectively (Gressmann, *Die Anfänge Israels*, [SAT I/2, 1922] 243; see also Blank, 79). The first alludes to the aftermath of a round of debauchery during the wedding festivities, when even the strong man is unable to retain the unaccustomed delicacies, while the other refers to the power of love (cf. Cant 8:6, *kî-'azzâ ḵammāwet 'ahᵃḇâ*), a theme taken up at length in the contest between the court pages recorded in I Esd 3:1-4:47. Even the final response of Samson may echo a standard riddle ("If you had not plowed with my heifer, you would not have found out my riddle," or in riddle form, "What is plowed, but not with oxen?"). As is well known, the wife is frequently likened to a field, cultivated or uncultivated depending upon whether it is positive or a curse of barrenness, and sexual intercourse is thought of in terms of "plowing." ("As for me, my vulva is a . . . hillock—for me, I, the maid, who will be its plower? My vulva is . . . wet ground for me, I, the queen, who will station there the ox? Lady, the king will plow it for you, Dumuzi, the king, will plow it for you. 'Plow my vulva, my sweetheart?'" *ANET*, 643.) Only one of the riddles is in interrogative form, while the other (s) is narration. The poetic form of the riddles belies their popular origin; each is composed of 3 plus 3 meter, while the letter "m" begins four words in the first and five in the second (it begins one and terminates two in the "third," while "l" and "h" introduce two words each). Within the first stand four cipher words—'okēl signifies the lion, i.e., the bridegroom; ma'ᵃkāl represents honey, i.e., the sperm; while 'az and māṯôq are indicators for the quality of love. As has already been pointed out, 'eglâ is a symbol for the bride. The technical term for solving a riddle appears to be ngd in the hiphil, as Müller has recognized (465, 477, 481). The malicious character of the riddle, here on the human level, stands out with unforgettable pathos, even though permeated with a touch of humor ("You only hate me, you do not love me. . . ."; "And Samson's wife was given to his companion, who had been his best man" 14:16, 20).

The close relationship between riddle and divination, together with the fact that oracular utterance had an enigmatic character, raises a question about the narrow definition of riddle functioning above. Müller's thoroughgoing analysis of riddle in the OT operates on the broadest possible basis; he distinguishes four types: (1) the popular riddle, namely Judg 14:10-18; (2) the symbolic dream and enigmatic oracle, as found in Gen 37:40-41; Dan 2, 4 (the dream); Dan 5; Ez 17:1-10; Dan 12:7-10 ("The dream unveils a special *reality* which the peculiar *language* unfolds in the dream narrative for the first time" [475-476]); (3) royal contests, alluded to in I Kings 10, the intention of which is to drain the opponent of all strength (it is said of the Queen of Sheba: wᵉlō'-hāyâ ḇāh 'ōḏ rûaḥ, 10:5), and in Dan 8:23; and (4) court-school wisdom. While one can agree with Müller that the symbolic dream and enigmatic oracle concern themselves with the "peculiar speech of a transcendental world," it seems better to consider these passages under the *Gattungen* of dream and oracle, while at the same time being conscious of the considerable interpenetration of the three genres. The riddle is related to the simile/parable on the one hand and allegory on the other. Accordingly Wünsche treated Ez 17:1-10 as a symbolic riddle, following the lead of the text, which designates the oracle as a *ḥîḏâ*. The line of demarcation between this passage and allegory, Qoh 12:1-7, for example, is virtually nonexistent, so that one hesitates to classify it as a riddle, even though it makes use of ciphers. It must be admitted, however, that a comparable "riddle" is found in *Bereshit Rabba* 67, according to which Judah the Patriarch gives political advice to envoys of Marcus Aurelius by uprooting mature plants in his garden and replacing them with younger ones. In light of the loose use of *ḥîḏâ* in the OT, some diversity in interpretation is to be expected; regardless of whether one operates with a narrow definition, or a broad one, any discussion of riddle inevitably moves into the area of mantic oracle, symbolic dream, and allegory (see H.-P. Müller, "Magisch-Mantische Weisheit und die Gestalt Daniels," *UF* I [1969] 79-94).

A note on postbiblical riddles is in order, particularly since they make extensive use of the bible. In rabbinic literature there is considerable speculation about the nature of the riddles put to Solomon by the Queen of Sheba. The subjects of these riddles placed in the mouth of the royal visitor include, among others, pregnancy and nursing, the unique relationship between Lot's daughters and their father and sons, male and female characteristics, antimony (used for cosmetic purposes), flax and naphtha. There is also an account of a riddle contest between the children of Jerusalem and men of Athens, where the answer is obtained from a rabbi familiar with Jewish practice in regard to circumcision and with the number of months required for pregnancy, nursing, and weaning. The reply of the children indicates the relevance of this riddle to our discussion: "If you had not plowed with my heifer, you would not have found out my riddle" (*Echa Rabbati* 1:1). Finally, the contest literature gave rise to catechetical texts, both in Jewish and Christian settings; worthy of mention are the Pesach haggadah where the refrain " *'eḥāḏ mî yôḏēaʿ* " is used to lead up to the number thirteen ("One, who knows it? One, I know it. One is our Lord in heaven and earth. Two, who knows it? Two, I know it. Two are the covenants of the law. One is . . . Thirteen are the qualities of divine compassion. . . .") and the "Jocha Monachorum," which makes use of the Adam/Eve, Noah, Lot, and Jonah narratives for catechetical purposes.

C. Fable and Allegory

H. Gressmann, *Israels Spruchweisheit in Zusammenhang der Weltliteratur* (KA 6, Berlin: K. Curtis, 1925); H. Gunkel, *Das Märchen im Alten Testament* (Tübingen: J. C. B. Mohr, 1921); W. Lambert, *Babylonian Wisdom Literature*, 150-212; K. Mueli, "Herkunft und Wesen der Fabel" *SAVK* L (1954) 65-93; R. J. Williams, "The Fable in the Ancient Near East," in *A Stubborn Faith*, ed. by E. C. Hobbs (Dallas: Southern Methodist University Press, 1956) 3-26; A. Wünsche, *Die Pflanzenfabel in der Weltliteratur* (Leipzig: Akademischer Verlag für Kunst und Wissenschaft, 1905).

Closely kin to the riddle are the fable and allegory, both of which make use of metaphors or ciphers. Ancient Near Eastern fables abound, particularly in Mesopotamian wisdom literature (cf. "Dispute between the Tamarisk and the Date Palm," *ANET*, 592-593), in sharp contrast to the Israelite wisdom corpus. It is possible that the reference in I Kings 4:32-34 to Solomon's three thousand proverbs and one thousand and five songs, the content of which was "trees, from the cedar that is in Lebanon to the hyssop that grows out of the wall" and "also of beasts, and of birds, and of reptiles, and of fish," should be taken to mean that the son of David was remembered as a master of coining fables. If that is the case, the absence of fables in the collection of wisdom texts that survived is difficult to comprehend; however, the same difficulty adheres to the alternative explanation of this passage in terms of lists or onomastica, for this genre is likewise scantily represented in the final collection of Israelite wisdom. Little weight can be given to the argument that Solomon must have learned fables from Nathan, in whose charge he was placed by David, for Nathan's well-known indictment of the king is actually a parable and appears to antedate its context (II Sam 12:1-4). Despite the inapplicability of some of the elements of the story to the relationship among David, Bathsheba, and Uriah, the parable has been placed within a didactic setting rather successfully. The same may be said of the Jotham fable (Judg 9:8-15) and of the fable in truncated form preserved in II Kings 14:9 ("A thistle on Lebanon sent to a cedar on Lebanon, saying, 'Give your daughter to my son for a wife'; and a wild beast of Lebanon passed by and trampled down the thistle").

The fable is characterized by "dramatis personae" which are

animals or plants; hence, it bears an element of the comic. However, it is often used to underscore the horror of a situation, even when half comical (Num 22:21-35; Gen 3; 37:5-11; 41). Originally the fable was amoral, but it soon came to function in didactic contexts; it is particularly useful for an ability to call attention to the obvious, which because of its everyday character is often overlooked. Essentially, however, the fable was at home in political settings, and found ready acceptance by those with appreciation for the satirical. In time it disintegrated into pure allegory, particularly in prophetic hands (Ez 17:1-10; 19:1-14; von Rad, *Weisheit in Israel*, 65: "Here the form of the fable is completely dismantled by the prophet for his purposes").

Two allegories have been preserved in wisdom literature, namely Prov 5:15-23 and Qoh 12:1-6. Each of these texts may originally have been a riddle; nevertheless, the present form is that of an admonition with an allegorical key. In Prov 5:15-23 the metaphorical significance of "cistern" is explained, so that none can read the text without recognizing the allusion to one's wife. Furthermore, the common reference to woman as a fountain from which man drinks becomes an occasion for warning against foul water, specifically, the loose woman. The text reads as follows: "Drink water from your own cistern, flowing water from your own well. Should your springs be scattered abroad, streams of water in the streets? Let them be for yourself alone, and not for strangers with you. Let your fountain be blessed, and rejoice in the wife of your youth, a lovely hind, a graceful doe. . . ."

The allegory of Qoh 12:1-6 takes up the metaphor of a wife as a fountain or cistern (cf. *ANET*, 642), and juxtaposes it against an exquisite description of old age. The allusion to *bôreʾekâ* is a *double entendre*; by this means the author recalls both the positive and negative assessment of reality in the preceding pages of his work, namely "the wife whom you love" and the grim reaper, death (on this unusual form, *bôreʾekâ*, see P. Humbert, "Emploi et portée du verbe bara [créer] dans l'Ancien Testament," *TZ* III [1947] 402, where it is argued that the root is *bārāʾ*, to split). The passage is susceptible to two interpretations, intentionally so: before crippling old age sets in, enjoy the woman whom you love, but at the same time keep in mind that the ancient sentence stands—"you shall die" (cf. Sir 14:17). Although some of the metaphors are difficult, the following appear to be self-evident: the keepers of the house are the arms, the strong men are the legs, the grinders are the teeth, those that look

VI

through the windows are the eyes, the doors on the street are the ears, the daughters of song is the voice, the almond tree is the gray hair, the grasshopper is the creaking bone or sluggish movement, the snapped silver cord, broken golden bowl, shattered pitcher and broken wheel are death.

D. Hymn and Prayer

W. Baumgartner, "Die literarischen Gattungen in der Weisheit des Jesus Sirach," *ZAW* XXXIV (1914) 161-198; F. Crüsemann, *Studien zur Formgeschichte von Hymnus und Danklied in Israel* (WMANT 32, Neukirchen: Neukirchener Verlag, 1969) ; H. L. Jansen, *Die Spätjüdische Psalmendichtung. Ihr Entstehungskreis und ihr "Sitz im Leben"* (SNVOA II/3, Oslo: Jacob Dybwad, 1937) ; J. K. Kuntz, "Considerations of Form and Intention in the Canonical Wisdom Psalms with Special Reference to Psalm 34" (privately circulated, 1970); B. L. Mack, "Wisdom Myth and Mytho-logy," *Inter* XXIV (1970) 46-60; S. Mowinckel, "Psalms and Wisdom," in *Wisdom in Israel and in the Ancient Near East*, 205-224; *idem*, "The Learned Psalmography" in his *The Psalms in Israel's Worship*, II, tr. by D. R. Ap-Thomas (Nashville: Abingdon Press, 1962) 104-125; P. A. Munch, "Die jüdischen 'Weisheitspsalmen' und ihr Platz im Leben," *AO* XV (1937) 112-140; R. Murphy, "A Consideration of the Classification 'Wisdom Psalms'," *VTS* IX (1962) 156-167; H. Ringgren, *Word and Wisdom* (Lund: H. Ohlssons, 1947) ; G. von Rad, *Weisheit in Israel*, 189-228.

Baumgartner's distinction between a sage, whose task was to describe things exactly as they are, and a poet, for whom hyperbole is an indispensable tool, suggests that one should expect little, if any hymnic material in wisdom literature (193-194, 198). Nevertheless, this observation did not blind him to the presence of hymns and hymnic themes within Sirach, namely 42:15-43:33; 39:12-35; 24:1-22; 1:1-10; 10:14-18; 16:18-19; 16:26-17:24; 17:29-30; 18:1-7; 23:19-20 and 44-50 (a "profanen Hymnus" since it praises men rather than God). Baumgartner also identified a *Danklied* or Thanksgiving song (51:1-12) and three *Klagelieder* or Lamentations (51:10-11; 33:1-13a; 36:16b-22), as well as themes belonging to the lament (14:17-19; 17:27; 18:8-10; 22:27-23:6).

In this regard Sirach is typical, for hymns and hymnic motifs appear in Job (5:9-16; 9:5-12; 12:13-25; 26:5-14; 28), Proverbs (8), and Wisdom of Solomon (11:21-12:22). However, the presence of hymns in wisdom texts does not make them wisdom genres, as Murphy has noted (160-161). Rather these texts are hymns, thanksgiving songs, and laments and are to be compared with similar passages from nonwisdom literature. Most of these wisdom texts make use of the participial style and frequently praise God as creator and redeemer, even when including rhetorical questions and concluding warnings. Likewise, the thanksgiving song is made up of introduction, a reference to the deliverance, a description of the plight from which rescue was a deliverance, a plea, vow, and confession of confidence. The lament, too, bears the customary invocation, request and vow, so that there is no justification for speaking of wisdom genres.

The case is different with a series of hymns dealing with the relationship between Yahweh and creation, each of which praises Wisdom as the point of contact between the two (Prov 1:20-33; 8; Job 28; Sir 24:1-22; Wisd of Sol 6:12-20; 7:22-8:21). The Egyptian background for these hymns is virtually certain, as has recently been perceived (cf. Kayatz, *Einführung in die alttestamentliche Weisheit*, 70-78), but the accuracy of the term "hypostasis" is subject to question for all texts except Wisd of Sol (von Rad, 193, 200). In Job 28, which is probably an addition to the book, man's amazing success at extracting precious metals from the deep recesses of the earth is contrasted with his miserable failure at laying hold of wisdom, whose price is far above that of the ores. Even Abaddon and Death have only heard a rumor of wisdom, and man's efforts at finding her are futile. Yet God knows her place and has searched her out. The text closes with an identification of wisdom with the fear of the Lord (*yir'at 'adōnai*).

In Prov 1:20-33 wisdom stands in the busy streets and cries aloud in the style of a prophetic indictment; even the language is that of the divine oracle in prophecy: the hand stretched out in invitation, the summons that was spurned, the threat that they will seek her but not be able to find her, and the rather harsh description of the results of a refusal to hear. Chapter 8 again takes up the motif of wisdom calling beside the gates; this time she describes her wares and defends their high value, particularly for ruling officials. But wisdom also identifies herself as the first of God's acts, hence as one who existed before the creation of the universe (cf. H. Grapow, "Die Welt vor der Schöpfung," *ZÄS* LXVII [1931] 34-38; the Egyptian background for this series of metaphors is incontrovertible). Despite the danger to Yahwism created by the presence of a female deity alongside God, wisdom is characterized as his daily delight and master workman (or little child; for a discussion of the meaning of the difficult *'āmōn*, see R. B. Y. Scott, "Wisdom in Creation: The *'āmōn of Proverbs* viii 30," *VT* X [1960] 213-223).

The identification of wisdom and torah is the hidden theme of Sir 24:1-22, explicitly stated by Sirach in 24:23. In this text wisdom's source is said to be the mouth of the Most High, an epithet preferred by Sirach, and her availability in some measure to all mankind is proclaimed. However, the creator commanded her to make a dwelling in Israel, at Zion; having taken root there, she is likened to trees and plants of the land and invites all to eat and drink from her with promise that one taste or sip will create greater thirst or hunger. An appendix to the hymn concludes with a reference to the mystery inherent within wisdom, which makes mastery of her an impossibility .

Augustine's comment that Wisdom of Solomon stinks of Greek rhetoric is particularly apropos to 6:12-20, 7:22-8:21 (note the *sorites* in 6:17-20, as well as the list of attributes in 7:22-23). Here the easy access to wisdom is highlighted, in contrast to earlier texts. She is called the breath of the power of God, "a pure emanation of the glory of the Almighty," who in every generation passes into holy souls, and who orders all things well. Striking is the statement that she teaches the four cardinal virtues: self-control, prudence, justice, courage.

These hymns are distinctive both in subject matter and form, so that one may legitimately refer to them as a wisdom genre, the praise of wisdom. Their style is strongly influenced by Egyptian wisdom and Israelite prophetic texts, as well as Greek rhetoric. The occasion for borrowing an Egyptian concept (*Maat*) may have been a crisis of confidence, so that the function of the idea of personified wisdom was to soften the problem of theodicy, although one gets the impression that these texts are less polemical than would be the case if this thesis of Mack's were accurate. In any case, the hypostatization of wisdom serves as a means of relating God to his universe in a nonrevelatory wisdom tradition and addresses itself to the problem of authority (see J. C. Rylaarsdam, *Revelation in Jewish Wisdom Literature* [Chicago: University of Chicago Press, 1946] and J. Marböck, *Weisheit im Wandel* [BBB 37, Bonn: Peter Hanstein Verlag, 1971]).

Certain stylistic and thematic characteristics distinguish a small group of psalms, to which has been given the title "wisdom psalms," from the rest of the Psalter (see above, chapter five, section II/7). Unfortunately there is little agreement as to which psalms belong to this category; indeed, its very existence has been denied by Engnell. Most critics, however, would find themselves somewhere between the position of Bentzen, for whom only 1, 112, 127 are *de rigueur* wisdom psalms, and that of Castellino, who views 1, 9-10, 12, 14-15, 17, 36-37, 49, 52, 73, 91, 94, 112, 119, 127-

128, 139 from this perspective. Two of the more prominent psalms interpreters, Gunkel and Mowinckel, reject the title "wisdom psalms" but not their existence; to these psalms Gunkel gives the name *Weisheitsdichtung* but insists that no *Gattung* is involved, while Mowinckel writes (somewhat derogatively on stylistic grounds) of "Learned Psalmography," the purposes of which are to praise the deity and to instruct the youth. Likewise Munch discerns a dual purpose *within the cult* for these psalms, which are to him *school texts*, namely devotional and instructional. The school setting for the wisdom psalms is also defended by Jansen, although he does not feel confident of any ability to describe the setting precisely. Murphy's delineation of wisdom psalms, based on careful methodological considerations, gives prominence to 1, 32, 34, 37, 49, 112, 128 but recognizes wisdom influence elsewhere, for example, in 25:8-10, 12-14; 31:24-25; 39:5-7; 40:5-6; 62:9-11; 92:7-9; 94:8-15.

Stylistic features that have been decisive in identifying wisdom psalms are: *'ašrê* formulas, numerical sayings, "better" sayings, an address of a teacher to a "son," alphabetic structure, simple comparisons and admonitions, and rhetorical questions. Thematic considerations are: a contrast between the *rāšā'* and the *ṣaddîq*, the two ways, preoccupation with the problem of retribution, practical advice about conduct, fear of the Lord, and special wisdom vocabulary, such as *māšāl, bînâ, ḥîdâ*, and *ḥokmâ*. While Murphy discerns the significance of life setting as a criterion for distinguishing wisdom psalms, in the end he has to admit that by and large the *Sitz* eludes scholarly research, although he thinks the didactic character of the testimony points to the cult, quoting with approval Mand's claim that "Aus dem Beter ist ein Lehrer geworden" ("The worshiper has become a teacher") (167).

Even with the use of such criteria, however, identification of wisdom psalms is no simple matter. The presence of any one of these characteristics is not sufficient to classify a psalm; a good example is Ps 111, which employs the wisdom motto, "The fear of the Lord is the beginning of wisdom" but is still not a wisdom psalm. Rather, it is only as several of these traits appear that the psalm assumes the "tone" of wisdom. Particular care has to be taken lest a concern for retribution lead one astray into a hasty conclusion that wisdom is at work here (cf. von Rad, 171); the same may be said of *'ašrê* formulas and the idea of the fear of the Lord, both of which occur frequently in the Psalter.

Inasmuch as the list of wisdom psalms in Murphy's definitive article has much to commend it, I shall use it as the point of departure for discussion. The use of the figure of a flourishing tree to describe a sage in Egyptian wisdom literature strengthens the argument for the inclusion of Ps 1 in the wisdom group (but see 52:8 and 92:14). As for 32, Murphy rightly notes that the crucial factor is a matter of emphasis but opts for a *sapiential structure* as decisive. This decision, while admittedly subjective, may be an accurate assessment of the situation, although I would be more inclined to view the psalm under Murphy's second category of wisdom influence. Accordingly, I would find wisdom influence only in verses 8-9. In any case, the mood of the entire psalm does not strike me as sapiential. The use of the style of Dame Wisdom in Ps 49 is not conclusive proof of a wisdom origin, for Prov 6 is imitative of *prophetic preaching*; one could just as readily argue for prophetic influence here. Nevertheless, other factors such as vocabulary, theme, and the use of a summary appraisal give some force to the contention that a wisdom psalm is under consideration. Ps 128 is less certain; its form is that of a benediction, and the putative wisdom traits are precisely the ones that are least reliable, namely the oft-used *'ašrê* formulas and the idea of the fear of the Lord.

Murphy's intriguing suggestion that Book One of the Psalter (1-41) has been subjected to redaction at the hands of the sages merits closer scrutiny. A strong case can be made for the inclusion of Pss 19, 33, and 39 in the wisdom category. In 19 one finds instruction, special language of wisdom, creation theology, fear of the Lord, and comparatives ("more than" . . . "sweeter than"), none of which is exclusively wisdom thought but the whole of which permits a suspicion of sapiential impact. Ps 33 mentions counsel, fear of the Lord, divine plans, *creation of all men alike*, salvation by means other than weapons, and makes use of the *'ašrê* formula. Furthermore, Ps 39 gives the impression of schooling at the feet of Qoh; the description of life as phantom existence, as a puff of wind, and the emphasis on the vanity of wealth since man *cannot know* who will inherit it echo many of the themes of the skeptical genius who saw life as "vanity of vanities."

Other psalms outside Book One also give the impression of wisdom influence, especially 94:8-11 and 127. The first draws on a hymn that is apparently a product of the sages used to attack those who deny the justice of God (cf. Ps 10). The accusation of divine blindness is found frequently in wisdom literature, though not exclusively there. In any case, I would suggest a possible origin of this hymn in wisdom, particularly in its emphasis upon the all-seeing eye of the Judge of all mankind (cf. 33:13-15; 34: 15). Again, the theme and language of Ps 127 is that of Qoh, Prov and Sir. This includes the idea of the vanity of human effort, as well as the corrective from the more optimistic strain of wisdom that Yahweh is the guarantee of all that is good, and the image of sons as arrows in a quiver, which Sirach takes over for a different image, though still sexual. A word should also be said about Ps 104, particularly verses 13-18, which are strikingly similar to onomastica both in Egypt and in Israel. A wisdom milieu for the Egyptian Hymn to the Sun (*ANET*, 369-371), the ultimate source for Ps 104, is highly likely.

A word of caution needs to be registered, however, lest the problematic character of the above arguments be overlooked and excessive confidence in our ability to identify influence, whether sapiential, prophetic, or priestly, be spawned. The evidence does, nevertheless, permit one to conclude that the closest parallels to the above-mentioned "wisdom psalms" are found in sapiential literature.

While one cannot speak of a fixed *Gattung* of wisdom prayer, it is possible to distinguish common language and themes (von Rad, 70). The wisdom psalms and prayer are closely related, as has been pointed out above. Evidently the wise men coined prayers for instruction in schools, but in any case they are pure prayer rather than didactic instruction; in post-canonical wisdom literature the didactic element prevails, as in Ps of Sol 15 (von Rad, 70). Normally the prayer is expressed in hymnic form, as Tob 13:1 illustrates clearly.

From Sirach the following prayers deserve mention: 22:27-23:6, 36:1-17, and 51:1-12, while Wisd of Sol 9:1-18 is a distinct prayer and 11:21-12:27 is in broken prayer form. In Sir 22:27-23:6 there are two indirect requests (22:27; 23:2) and an additional two direct requests preceded by the vocative address ("O Lord, Father and Ruler of my life," "O Lord, Father and God of my life"). The prayer is for protection, as well as for deliverance from gluttony and lust. Chapter 36:1-17 is a lament familiar from the Psalter, while 51:1-12 is a typical thanksgiving song. The influence of the well-known Solomonic prayer in I Kings 8 is discernible in Wisd of Sol 9, even though alien concepts appear (man's reasoning is worthless since "a perishable body weighs down the soul, and this earthly tent burdens the thoughtful mind," vs. 14-18).

Von Rad has called attention to the *Gerichtsdoxologie* (judgment doxology) (Ps 49, 73, 139) as a special prayer form in wisdom texts; he recognizes, however, the original sacral-legal context for these passages (71, 263-266). The similarity of these texts to the prose prayers of narrative cultic texts (Dan 9, Ezra 9, Neh 9, I Kings 8, Jer 32) demands that caution be used in treating them as special wisdom prayers (see my discussion in "*YHWH Ṣebā'ôt Šᵉmô*: A Form-Critical Analysis," *ZAW* LXXXI [1969] 171-174).

It is difficult to determine the precise setting of these prayers within Sirach and Wisdom of Solomon. One can surmise that the wise man came to recognize a need to instruct the student in prayer and made use of the Psalter as a model. A didactic setting, then, is probable, although little more can be said.

E. *Streitgespräch* or Dialogue

J. L. Crenshaw, "Popular Questioning of the Justice of God in Ancient Israel," *ZAW LXXXII* (1970) 380-395; H. Gese, *Lehre und Wirklichkeit in der alten Weisheit* (Tübingen: J. C. B. Mohr, 1958) 51-78; J. Gray, "The Book of Job in the Context of Near Eastern Literature," *ZAW* LXXXII (1970) 251-269; W. Lambert, *Babylonian Wisdom Literature*, 21-117; H. Richter, "Erwägungen zum Hiobproblem," *EvTh* XVIII (1958) 302-324; *idem, Studien zu Hiob. Der Aufbau des Hiobbuches, dargestellt an den Gattungen des Rechtsleben* (AT II/11, Stuttgart: Calwer Verlag, 1959); N. Snaith, *The Book of Job* (SBT II/11, London: SCM Press, 1968); J. J. Stamm, "Die Theodizee in Babylon und Israel," *JEOL* IX (1944) 99-107; von Rad, *Weisheit in Israel*, 267-291; C. Westermann, *Der Aufbau des Buches Hiob* (BHT 23, Tübingen: J. C. B. Mohr, 1956); J. G. Williams, " 'You Have Not Spoken Truth of Me': Mystery and Irony in Job," *ZAW* LXXXIII (1971) 231-254; R. J. Williams, "Theodicy in the Ancient Near East," *CJT* II (1956) 14-26.

At the outset it should be stated that Job is *sui generis,* so that what is written below is an attempt to discern the components that make up this masterpiece. No single genre can explain all the facets of the book, and several have certainly contributed to it. There are traces of the *rîb* (lawsuit) within Job, and much of the book can be successfully illuminated from this perspective (Stamm, 104). The speeches of Job often make use of the language of litigation, Job accusing God of a breach of contract. Legal terminology, therefore, is at home in the accusations, and there is a full-fledged oath of innocence (ch. 31) that has its closest parallels in the negative confession within Babylonian literature. Furthermore, the intimate relationship between law and wisdom, particularly during the period of the *Sippenethos* (clan ethos), strengthens the thesis that Job is a covenant lawsuit (Gerstenberger, *Wesen und Herkunft des sogenannten "apodiktischen*

Rechts," and "Covenant and Commandment," *JBL* LXXXIV [1965] 38-51; and see above, p. 126). According to this view of Job as a secular lawsuit chapters 4-14 comprise a preliminary attempt at reconciliation; 15-31, a formal legal effort at reconciling Job and his friends; 32-37, Elihu's appeal of the case; 38-41, God's judgment in the form of a secular lawsuit between God and Job, resulting in Job's withdrawal of the accusation (Richter).

Others interpret the book of Job as a lament, either dramatized or a paradigm of an answered lament (so Westermann and Gese). The components of the lament (see above, p. 200) are: (1) the lament proper, (2) complaint, and (3) an indictment of the enemies. There can be no question about the similarity of the laments and sections of Job; however, the narrative framework and the character of the poetic dialogue suggest another answer to the form of the book.

The closest parallels to Job are the disputations within Egyptian and especially Babylonian literature. These controversy dialogues are composed of a mythological introduction, a debate between two friends, and a divine resolution of the issue (see Lambert, 150-212). Job makes use of the form of the *Streitgespräch*, although influenced by its function within prophetic literature as self-vindication. Whereas the Mesopotamian disputations are calm treatises on the relative worth of things, animals, or professions, Job employs the *Streitgespräch* as a weapon of warfare, his own vindication being at stake. The key to Job, according to this interpretation, is 13:16 ("This will be my salvation, that a godless man will not come before him"). The mythological introduction and legendary conclusion (the prose prologue and epilogue) are probably of popular origin and antedate the dispute, which utilizes three formal traditions (wisdom disputational material, legal terminology associated with the lawsuit, and cultic laments).

Von Rad has objected to viewing Job as a *Streitgespräch* on the grounds that the *dialogue* is between friends with God present from the beginning as a third party (270-272). He rejects the understanding of Job as a biography of the soul and emphasizes the difference between the main character and his friends as theological: they stress *the order* of the universe, whereas Job is concerned about the *relationship* between him and God. The new feature of the book, from this perspective, is the recognition that God is Job's *personal enemy*, that the wrath of God singles out one individual who according to the prologue was God's glory

VI

and pride (Herder). The single issue of Job, von Rad argues, is *Yahweh pro me*. Nevertheless, he is obliged to admit that the dissent between Job and his friends was greater at the end than in the beginning, so that his refusal to recognize the intensity of strife, the basis for rejecting the *Streitgespräch* as descriptive of the book, carries little weight. The same must be said of his claim that the dogma of retribution is more accurately a dogma of interpreters, indeed, that the impact of Job and Qoheleth was minimal. For however much truth there is in his charge that the dogma has been overemphasized, the fact is that a cause-effect theory was operative and precipitated a crisis in ancient Israel comparable to the failure of dogma to accord with reality in Egypt and Babylon (Schmid, *Wesen und Geschichte der Weisheit*, 74-78; Crenshaw, *Prophetic Conflict*, 23-38, 103-109 and "Popular Questioning of the Justice of God in Ancient Israel").

A variant of the *Streitgespräch*, namely the "Imagined Speech," appears in Wisd of Sol 2:1-20 and 5:3-13. Here again the similarity to prophetic texts is noteworthy. In each case the musings of wicked men are brought to light, together with the warning that such reasoning leads to destruction. The subject of the imagined speech is usually the contradiction between promise and fulfillment, expectation and reality, as intensified by the transitoriness of life. In 2:1-20 the pessimism of Qoheleth has left its mark, the similarity of language being rather noticeable (chance, fleetingness, finality of death, man's portion). "Come, therefore, let us enjoy the good things that exist, and make use of the creation to the full as in youth" (v. 6) reads like a restatement of Qoh 12:1; 9:7. However, the mild "hedonism" of Qoh has given way to violence in search of pleasure regardless of the cost, as well as to malicious persecution of the devout man. The error of this evil way is confessed in 5:3-13, this time utilizing an older proverb or perhaps a riddle (Prov 30:18-19). Here the serpent on the rock has been replaced by an arrow, and the climactic way of a man with a maiden has been omitted. Furthermore, this passage interprets the original in terms of movement without leaving a trace (cf. the gloss in Prov 30:20; note the imagined speech!), which does not appear to be the intent of the proverb in its earliest form (Murphy, "The Interpretation of Old Testament Wisdom Literature," 295-297, emphasizes *derek* in these verses and suggests that the impossibility of recovering a trace of movement is the original point of the proverb).

The "imagined speech" is found frequently in Proverbs, for

example, in 1:11-14, 22-33; 3:28; 5:12-14; 7:14-20; 8:4-36; 9:4a-6, 16a-17; 20:9, 14a, 22a, 25a; 22:13; 23:7b, 35; 24:12a, 24a, 29; 25:7; 26:13, 19b; 28:24b; 30:9b, 20c; 31:29. It functions both as stimulus for correct thinking (31:29) and as a critique of false reasoning (30:20), which it holds up to ridicule. Often the malicious words prompt a strong admonition or even a pronouncement of judgment upon those who so think (cf. 1:19, "Such are the ways of all who get gain by violence; it takes away the life of its possessors"; see also 7:21-27; 24:12, 24). On occasion the whole imagined speech is given over to a castigation of those who stubbornly stick to their own way (1:22-33).

F. Confession (Autobiographical Narrative)

R. Gordis, *Koheleth—The Man and His World* (New York: Schocken Books, 1951); G. von Rad, *Weisheit in Israel*; R. N. Whybray, *The Succession Narrative* (SBT II/9, London: SCM Press, 1968).

Wisdom's rootedness in experience led to a confessional style in which the aged sage gave his pupils the advantages of his varied experience. When the wise man was at the same time a king the authority of such retrospection was increased, as in the Instruction for Merikare (*ANET*, 414-418) and the Instruction of Amenemhet (*ANET*, 418-419), as well as the fiction of Solomonic authorship of Qoheleth. The Egyptian origin of the autobiographical style is generally acknowledged. In the Egyptian context not only kings and prominent officials left their confessions for the benefit of progeny, however, for the tomb inscriptions describe the experiences of ordinary individuals and laud their examplary lives (Whybray, 74). It is possible that the form of the cultic thanksgiving song (see above, pp. 202) has influenced the confession in Israel, although such affinity is not necessarily an indication of direct borrowing (Whybray, 74, appeals to Pss 18; 34; 40:9-10). The formula for the autobiographical narrative is generally *rā'iti . . . wā'erē'* ("I saw . . . and I have seen"), together with the verb *'ābar* ("pass by"), while the moral of the story usually is spelled out at the end. What is not certain, however, is the extent of this genre; should it include observations about other persons' experiences? Despite the positive response to this question by Whybray (75), I have chosen to limit this discussion to first person confessions, treating the third person narratives under the category of didactic poetry and narrative.

From Proverbs two examples of autobiographical narrative are instructive: 4:3-9; 24:30-34. The first of these appears to be

VI

modeled on Egyptian prototypes; in any case it includes the Egyptian motif of a garland to be placed around the wise man's neck (Kayatz, *Einführung in die alttestamentliche Weisheit*, 47). In Prov 24:30-34 the observation (vs. 30-31) prompts reflection (v. 32), the result of which is a moral lesson (vs. 33-34). To this may be compared Ps 37:25, 35-36, a wisdom psalm. In verse 25 there appears what I have elsewhere called "the creed of the blind man" ("I have been young, and now am old; yet I have not seen the righteous forsaken or his children begging bread"; see "Popular Questioning of the Justice of God in Ancient Israel," 395). The other verses (35-36) make use of *rā'îtî* and *'ābar*, together with the customary *wᵉhinnê* ("and behold").

The confession is used in Qoh 1:12-2:26 with great impact; here the affinity with the royal *Bekenntnis* (confession) of Egypt is undeniable. Emphasis is placed on the fact that the author has been "king over Israel in Jerusalem" (v. 12). Here again *rā'îtî* (v. 14) points to the ground of Qoheleth's conclusions: he has applied his mind to all that is done and has seen with his own eyes everything under the sun, thus arriving at the conclusion that all is vanity and a striving after wind. Qoh has tried every possible avenue to purpose in life, in each instance despairing of any meaning. Wisdom (note *yāda'tî* ["I know"] rather than *rā'îtî* ["I saw"] in v. 17), pleasure (*'ad '°šer-'er'eh* v. 3), madness and folly (*wᵉyāda'tî*, v. 14), despair, all lead to the same conclusion and force upon Qoheleth a hatred of life, the opposite of everything wisdom literature stands for (Zimmerli, "Zur Struktur der alttestamentlichen Weisheit," 201). The same style occurs in Qoh 3:10; 4:8; 5:18; 8:9-9:1; 9:11, 13, 16; 10:5, 7 (Gordis, 109, 385).

Sir 33:16-18 makes use of confessional language to invite people to the *bēt midraš* ("the house of instruction"), the author comparing himself to the last watchman and grape gleaner who has excelled despite the obstacles to knowledge. Sirach cannot resist the temptation to call attention to his altruism: "Consider that I have not labored for myself alone, but for all who seek instruction," v. 17). Similarly, 51:13-22 employs autobiographical narrative, although set within a thanksgiving song, which has colored the language considerably, and is again followed by an invitation to the house of learning (51:23-30). In this passage emphasis is placed on wisdom as the answer to fervent prayer, and the heartfelt gratitude to God for answering the request for knowledge. The transition to devotional confession is complete in Wisd of Sol 7-9, where the great patron of wisdom praises God for the gift of understanding. Here, however, the confession alternates with prayer and lists, and praise of wisdom has, indeed, disintegrated.

The two invitations to the school in Sirach suggest a probable *Sitz* for the confession; the autobiographical narrative serves as a certificate of credentials for the head of a school. Whether such a setting can be posited for the origin of the form is impossible to determine, but the principle that prompted these accounts is the value of recording for posterity the lessons learned from life itself by one who is trained to reflect on experience and to sift its teachings for the benefit of those less gifted.

G. Lists (Onomastica)

A. Alt, "Syrien und Palästina im Onomastikon des Amenemope," *STU* XX (1950) 58-71 = his *Kleine Schriften des Volkes Israel*, I (Munich: C. H. Beck, 1953) 231-245; H. Richter, "Die Naturweisheit des Alten Testaments in Buche Hiob," *ZAW* LXX (1958) 1-20; G. von Rad, "Hiob xxxviii und die altägyptische Weisheit," *Wisdom in Israel and in the Ancient Near East*, 293-301 = his *Gesammelte Studien zum Alten Testament* (TB 8, Munich: Chr. Kaiser, 1958) 262-271 = his *The Problem of the Hexateuch and Other Essays*, tr. by E. W. T. Dicken (New York: McGraw-Hill, 1966) 281-291.

The presence of onomastica or lists (*Naturweisheit*) in Egypt and Mesopotamia suggests that Israelite wisdom literature may have comparable material. The epoch making study of Job 38 and Egyptian wisdom by von Rad recognized this fact and attempted to comprehend the unusual juxtaposition of onomastica and rhetorical questions addressed to Job.

While it might be argued that anyone wishing to enumerate the marvels of nature would have just so many phenomena to work with—hence the remarkable similarity between Amenemope (*ANET*, 421-425), Sir 43, Ps 148, The Song of the Three Hebrews, and Job 38 could be accidental—it seems more plausible to follow von Rad in postulating geographical, cosmological, and meteorological "catechisms" within the repertoire of the sages of Israel. That being the case, a number of passages in Job, Sirach and Wisdom of Solomon become more comprehensible: Job 28; 36:27-37:13; 38:4-39:30; 40:15-41:34; Sir 43; Wisd of Sol 7:17-20, 22-23; 14:25-26 (cf. II Esd 7:39-42; Ps 104; and Gen 1; 10). In Wisd of Sol 7:17-20 the author alludes to the entire curriculum of the wise man:

> For it is he who gave me unerring knowledge of what exists,
> to know the structure of the world and the activity of the
> elements; the beginning and end and middle times, the al-

ternations of the solstices and the changes of the seasons, the cycles of the year and the constellations of the stars, the natures of animals and the tempers of wild beasts, the powers of spirits and the reasonings of men, the varieties of plants and the virtues of roots. . . .

There is reference in this passage to philosophy, cosmology, chronology, astronomy, zoology, demonology, botany, and medicine. The other examples from this author consist of a list of virtues and vices, the Greek style of which is quite pronounced.

Sir 43, like Wisd of Sol 7:17-20, uses the *Naturweisheit* for the glory of God; the majestic hymn describes the wonders of nature as those especially fashioned to assure the prosperity of the righteous and to make certain the downfall of the wicked. Sirach's response to the burning problem of theodicy grows out of the dilemma forced upon him by rigid adherence to the dogma of retribution and tenacious refusal to opt for Hellenism's easy way out (the belief in immortality). However, Job and Qoheleth had made their point, forcing Sirach into a two-fold retreat, namely into psychology (the wicked man has excessive nightmares) and metaphysics (nature itself fights for the good man and against the sinner).

Another passage from Sirach may be viewed from the perspective of onomastica, namely 38:24-39:11 (although "character portrayal" has been suggested as a better description of this text). Here the wise man describes various trades, as in the Egyptian "The Instruction of Duauf" (*ANET*, 432-434), and contrasts the leisurely life of the sage. However, Sirach has a genuine appreciation for the farmer, craftsman, smith, and potter: "Without them a city cannot be established, and men can neither sojourn nor live there . . . But they keep stable the fabric of the world, and their prayer is in the practice of their trade" (38:32, 34). Nevertheless, the emphasis is placed upon the attributes of a wise man, who "devotes himself to the study of the law of the Most High," seeks out the wisdom of all the ancients, concerns himself with prophecies, preserves the discourse of notable men, penetrates the subtleties of parables, searches out the hidden meaning of proverbs, and is at home with the obscurities of parables (39:1-3).

H. Didactic Poetry and Narrative

B. Childs, *Isaiah and the Assyrian Crisis* (SBT II/3, London: SCM Press, 1967); J. L. Crenshaw, "A Liturgy of Wasted Opportunity (Am. 4:6-12; Isa. 9:7-10:4; 5:25-29)," *Sem* 1 (1970) 27-37; von Rad, *Weisheit in Israel*; W. Whedbee,

Isaiah and Wisdom (Nashville: Abingdon Press, 1970); and R. N. Whybray, *The Succession Narrative.*

In his form critical study of *Isaiah and the Assyrian Crisis* Childs came across a literary form to which he gave the name Summary-Appraisal and which he attributed to the wisdom tradition. Specimens of this genre are said to occur in Is 14:26-27, 17: 14b, and 28:29, the function of which is to summarize an oracle and evaluate it. The character of the statement as summary necessitates its appearing at the end of an oracle, and each time a demonstrative pronoun or similar word establishes a reference and serves as an indication of an independent appraisal. The summary appraisal is differentiated from concluding hortatory sentences, confessions, divine judgment or popular word, and is not connected syntactically in a causal relationship to a main oracle, but serves an independent role. Childs is unable to discover close parallels in other prophets (despite Is 54:17; Jer 13:25; Is 47:14-15); the didactic flavor and analogies from nature provide for him the clue, namely wisdom. The reflective tone supports such an identification, as does the vocabulary, Childs argues. Accordingly he finds close parallels in Prov 1:19 (cf. 6:29), Ps 49:13 [14], Job 5:27; 8:13; 18:21; 20:29; 27:13, Qoh 4:8 and *passim*, and Sir 43: 27. In spite of his belief that the summary appraisal form is probably employed in the wisdom literature of the ancient Near East in general, Childs is obliged to write that "a close parallel in the extra-biblical material to the summary-appraisal form does not appear" (129-136, especially 136).

The arguments of Childs have been accepted, with some reservation, by Whedbee, who adds Sir 16:23 and 39:27, while rejecting Is 17:14b as doubtful inasmuch as it uses the first person plural and bears the marks of cultic interests (76-79). Von Rad, on the other hand, is not entirely convinced that the form appears only in summary or concluding position; accordingly he adds to Childs' list two texts with the formula in the middle (Job 8:13 and Wisd of Sol 2:9) and one, perhaps two, at the beginning (Job 27:13; Jer 13:25; *Weisheit in Israel*, 58).

While Childs has illuminated a form that occurs in wisdom literature, he has not, in my opinion, demonstrated that it is a *wisdom form*. On the contrary, the evidence points to its use both in prophetic and wisdom texts, the differences between Is 54:17; 47:14-15 and Jer 13:25, on the one hand and Is 14:26-27; 17:14b; and 28:29, on the other, being less decisive than Childs thinks. When one recognizes the didactic character of legal and cultic texts, indeed of some prophetic ones, as well as the reflection upon nature's lessons for mankind, which also appears in texts other than wisdom, it becomes hazardous to argue for a wisdom origin of the summary-appraisal, particularly in view of the absence of ancient Near Eastern parallels. The summary-appraisal is nonetheless present in wisdom literature, and Childs has gone a long way in elucidating its form and function.

Another form of didactic poetry is the *Auseinandersetzungsliteratur* or problem poetry (Pss 37; 49; 73; 139), Egyptian parallels of which are well known (E. Otto, *Der Vorwurf an Gott: Zur Entstehgeschichte der ägyptische Auseinandersetzungsliteratur* [Hildesheim: Gerstenberg, 1951]). This literature concerns itself with the fate of the wicked in light of their apparent prosperity, urging the just man to bide his time and trust in Yahweh's ability to enforce ultimate justice. Often the theme of the all-seeing eye of God is appealed to in contexts dealing with the fate of the wicked (37:13, 18; cf. 73:11, which questions God's vision; 139:1-18). It is even said that God knows man before he is born and writes down the life span allotted to each creature.

> I praise thee, for thou art fearful and wonderful. Wonderful are thy works! Thou knowest me right well; My frame was not hidden from thee, when I was being made in secret, intricately wrought in the depths of the earth. Thy eyes beheld my unformed substance; in thy book were written, every one of them, the days that were formed for me, when as yet there was none of them (Ps 139:14-16).

Related to the autobiographical narrative (confession) discussed above is the didactic narrative (Prov 7:6-23). In this instance the narrator describes a typical happening, giving the minutest details and livening the account with superb dialogue. The event is a common seduction scene, which the narrator had viewed from his window, and which the adulterous wife whose husband had gone on a long journey played with perfection. The metaphors descriptive of the obedient compliance of the foolish young man are intended to suggest that his conduct is animalic.

> With much seductive speech she persuades him; with her smooth talk she compels him. All at once he follows her, as an ox goes to the slaughter, or as a stag is caught fast till an arrow pierces its entrails; as a bird rushes into a snare; he does not know that it will cost him his life (Prov 7:21-23).

The didactic narrative was not the exclusive domain of the wise men, for it is found throughout the OT (the Joseph narrative, the succession narrative, Esther, Dan 1:3-6; Tobit, Judith). All attempts to trace each of these to wisdom circles must be judged a failure, if the term wisdom literature is to have any meaning at all (cf. my "Method in Determining Wisdom Influence upon 'Historical' Literature").

Another type of didactic narrative is the historical summary (or historical retrospect); Sir 44-50 and Wisd of Sol 10-19 fall into this category. The former is a "hymn" in praise of famous men and, indirectly, of God who poured out his spirit upon each. Cultic interests surface in the selection of heroes of the faith; there can be no question but that Sirach's heart throbs at the mention of Aaron, David the founder of the Jerusalem cult, Josiah, Hezekiah, and Simon the high priest. The entire second part of Wisd of Sol is devoted to illustrating God's control of historical events to encourage virtue and to punish the wicked, in this instance, the Egyptians. This material has the characteristics of a midrash (but see J. Reese, *Hellenistic Influence on the Book of Wisdom* [AnBib 41, Rome: Pontifical Biblical Institute, 1970]), the exodus event providing the source for the imaginative interpretation of divine causality. The transition from historical summary to prayer and again to historical summary points to the close relationship between prayer and what I have termed negative historical retrospect ("A Liturgy of Wasted Opportunity [Am. 4:6-12; Is 9:7-10:4; 5:25-29]"). The function of these prayers in cultic contexts is beyond question; what is still unclear is their role in didactic settings, although it is likely that prayers were an occasion for viewing the history of Israel from the perspective of the moral lessons to be gained therefrom.

This survey of eight types of wisdom literature is suggestive rather than exhaustive; other examples for some of the genres could be given, particularly prayer (in Job), allegory (within the description of Dame Wisdom and Madam Folly), and narrative (cf. Hermisson, *Studien zur israelitischen Spruchweisheit*, 183-186). In time it is hoped that further precision can be given each form, but before such clarity will be possible, a number of unresolved issues must be faced squarely.

III. UNRESOLVED ISSUES

A desideratum of form critical study of wisdom literature is a standardization of vocabulary, which hopefully will be addressed in the Interpreter's Handbook of Old Testament Form Criticism

VI

(see Murphy, "Form Criticism and Wisdom Literature"). The problem is complicated by the difficulty of finding precise English equivalents for German genre terminology and by the variety of terms in use among German scholars. To give a single example, there are at least six words for admonition in use currently (*Mahnwort, Mahnspruch, Mahnrede, Mahnung, Warnung, Rat*).

Far more formidable is the problem of definition: what is meant by wisdom (*ḥokmâ*)? The scope of wisdom literature, tradition, and thinking is not merely an Israelite phenomenon, for nonbiblical ancient Near Eastern literature must also be taken into consideration, particularly since wisdom literature has been reckoned an "alien body" within the Israelite canon (cf. the highly questionable position of H. D. Preuss, "Erwägungen zum theologischen Ort alttestamentlicher Weisheitsliteratur," 393-417, particularly 412-417). But how does one discern influence, either of one wisdom tradition upon another or of prophetic and priestly traditions upon the sage? Some progress has been made in this regard, but much more needs to be done (cf. my "Method in Determining Wisdom Influence upon 'Historical' Literature").

Arriving at an operable definition of wisdom is difficult because of the diversity of witness within the wisdom tradition. In view of this remarkable variety of forms and of sociological-theological settings, the composition of a literary history of the genres is virtually impossible. So long as the date of the literary complexes eludes scholarly pursuit, and the precise form of each genre cannot be discerned, real confidence in the results of form critical analysis will be wanting. To illustrate, how does one distinguish the original form of the "better sayings"? Is it *ṭôb . . . mē/mî, kî ṭôb . . . mē*, or (in the negative) *'ēn ṭôb . . . b* (Qoh 2:24; 3:12; contrast 3:22)? Does not this variety reflect the author's desire to express himself by means of the total linguistic stock available to him (cf. the suggestive remarks of Hermisson in *Studien zur israelitischen Spruchweisheit*, 137-186)? Any attempt, therefore, to date these passages in terms of the form, given our limited knowledge, would be to miss the mark. Nor is the issue any less complicated when one does research in sociological and theological development, for differences of viewpoint and of sophistication may have existed alongside one another in every generation. Certainly a rigid evolutionary scheme of progress must be rejected, even in regard to the religionization of wisdom.

So far very little attention has been devoted to the discovery of the larger structure of wisdom literature, that is, to the intention of the final editor. Of course the recognition of stylistic features that led to larger complexes is a step in this direction, for example, the initial "b" in Prov 11: 9-12; *lēḇ* and *ṭôḇ* in 15:13-17, the acrostic in Prov 31:10-31, and numerical sayings. But what of architectonic expression now in veiled form? Despite some reserve as to the methodology employed by P. Skehan, I am inclined to applaud his asking of a significant question. The same may be said about the so-called "new criticism" or structural analysis, which carries its own set of presuppositions, sometimes unawares. Furthermore, what of the relation of wisdom literature and the cult, a crucial issue when one considers Job 31, as well as the *tô'ēḇâ* and *'ašrê* sayings (cf. W. Jansen, *"'AŠRÊ in the Old Testament,"* *HTR* LVIII [1965] 215-226 and W. Zimmerli, "The Place and Limit of the Wisdom," 153-154) ?

Finally, who will take up Muilenburg's challenge to move beyond form criticism to rhetorical criticism? What is the function of refrain (cf. Song of Songs), rhetorical question (R. N. Whybray, *The Heavenly Counselor in Isaiah xl 13-14* [SOTSMS 1, London: Cambridge University Press, 1971] 19-26), quotation, imagined speech, and so forth in wisdom literature? These and other questions like them will be given appropriate answers only by scholars who know the tradition but refuse to be enslaved by it.

JAMES L. CRENSHAW

AUTHOR INDEX

Aarne, A., 31, 37
Abbott, L., 39, 43
Abelard, 16
Ackermann, J., 52, 55
Ahlström, G. W., 198
Ahlwardt, W., 4, 6
Aistleitner, J., 188, 191, 213
Alain de Lille, 16
Albert, E., 4, 8
Albright, W. F., 52, 56, 58, 63, 94, 207
Alonso-Schökel, L., 24, 29, 39, 41, 51, 88, 90, 92
Alt, A., 79, 94, 103, 105, 107, 108, 115, 211, 241, 258
Ambrose, 14
Anderson, B. W., 58, 59, 143, 158
Anderson, G. W., 198
Andrae, T., 239, 240
Andrew, M., 122
Ankum, J., 116
Ap-Thomas, D. R., 179
Apuleius, 10
Aquinas, 16, 41
Arens, A., 192
Aristeas, 241
Aristotle, 2, 6-9, 15, 26, 50, 92
Arnheim, R., 31, 33
Arnold, M., 39, 41
Athanasius, 13
Auerbach, E., 10, 15, 24, 27, 116
Augusti, J. C. W., 29
Augustine, 14-16, 249

Bach, R., 102, 103, 135, 141, 154
Baena, G., 129
Baentsch, B., 52
Baldermann, I., 52, 55, 56
Baldwin, E., 45
Balla, E., 141, 147, 148-149, 183, 184

Baltzer, K., 118, 119, 120, 130, 193
Barkun, M., 102
Barnard, F., 24, 27
Barner, W., 17, 21
Baroway, I., 10, 13, 17, 20
Barth, C., 183, 187, 205
Barth, K., 184, 185, 193, 198
Barucq, A., 99, 229
Basil, 13
Bastian, A., 31, 35
Baumgärtel, F., 157
Baumgartner, W., 69, 73, 157, 183, 184, 225, 247
Bea, A., 229
Bede, 16
Begrich, J., 39, 124, 125, 126, 133, 141, 154-155, 163, 165, 166, 179, 184, 185, 199, 200, 201, 202, 205, 206, 208, 209, 211, 216, 219, 220
Ben-Amos, D., 1, 37
Ben-Horin, M., 129
Bentzen, A., 79, 81, 85-86, 88, 93, 119, 142, 156, 188, 192, 230, 232, 249
Bernhardt, K. H., 157, 188, 191, 215
Bernheim, E., 31, 34
Berridge, J. M., 157, 175
Bethe, E., 52, 69, 70
Bewer, J. A., 79, 80
Beyer, C., 39, 52
Beyerlin, W., 118, 119, 122, 123, 127, 135, 185, 198, 201, 204, 209
Bickermann, E., 24, 27
Birkeland, H., 198, 199
Blackwell, A., 22
Blank, S. H., 225, 239, 242
Blass, F., 4
Blenkinsopp, J., 207
Boas, F., 189
Böckmann, P., 52, 55

BIBLICAL REFERENCES INDEX

OLD TESTAMENT

SUBJECT INDEX